THE ARAB REVOLTS

Public Cultures of the Middle East and North Africa

Paul Silverstein, Susan Slyomovics, and Ted Swedenburg, editors

Published in association with
Middle East Research and Information Project (MERIP)

THE ARAB REVOLTS

DISPATCHES ON MILITANT DEMOCRACY IN THE MIDDLE EAST

Edited by David McMurray and Amanda Ufheil-Somers

Indiana University Press
Bloomington and Indianapolis

This book is a publication of

Indiana University Press
601 North Morton Street
Bloomington, Indiana 47404-3797 USA

iupress.indiana.edu

Telephone orders   800-842-6796
Fax orders   812-855-7931

⊖ The paper used in this publication meets the minimum requirements of the American National Standard for Information Sciences—Permanence of Paper for Printed Library Materials, ANSI Z39.48-1992.

Manufactured in the United States of America

Cataloging information is available from the Library of Congress.

ISBN 978-0-253-00968-5 (cloth)
ISBN 978-0-253-00975-3 (pbk.)
ISBN 978-0-253-00978-4 (eb)

1 2 3 4 5 18 17 16 15 14 13

Contents

Acknowledgments

We would like to thank Ted Swedenburg and Paul Silverstein for getting this project up and running, and Chris Toensing, editor of *Middle East Report*, for his essential input throughout the process. Rebecca Tolen, our sponsoring editor at Indiana University Press, provided valuable guidance in shaping this study. Thank you to Karen Mills, Executive Secretary, and Susan Shaw, Interim Director, both in the School of Language, Culture and Society at Oregon State University, for providing much-needed funds for the completion of the book.

Most importantly, this project would not exist without the generosity and enthusiasm of the contributing authors. Thank you.

THE ARAB REVOLTS

INTRODUCTION

DAVID MCMURRAY AND AMANDA UFHEIL-SOMERS

On December 17, 2010 Mohamed Bouazizi set himself on fire in Sidi Bouzid, Tunisia, to protest the humiliation and loss of income visited upon him by the Tunisian police. What Bouazizi experienced was a routine act of petty harassment, the kind of indignity suffered daily by thousands of inhabitants across North Africa and the Middle East. But this time they didn't take it lying down. Spontaneous outbursts of popular support and action by the Tunisian trade union movement turned the tragic event into an insurrection that brought down the government of President Zine El Abidine Ben Ali on January 14.

Within days of the fall of Ben Ali's regime in Tunisia, Egyptian protesters were filling public spaces in Cairo, Port Said, Alexandria and smaller cities, energized by the news and images pouring in from Tunis. Wildcat strikes, massive protests and occupations of public space brought down the regine of Husni Mubarak on February 11.

News of events in Tunisia reverberated as far away as Sanaa, Yemen where it helped launch protests in January calling for the removal from power of President 'Ali 'Abdallah Salih. Youth kept the movement going. They were eventually joined by oppositional political parties. The regime responded violently to the protests using live ammunition and large amounts of tear gas against demonstrators; fifty unarmed demonstrators were killed in Sanaa on one day in March 2011. This hardened the demands of the protesters and alienated a good share of the Yemeni public. Salih managed to hold onto power for another year but—after narrowly surviving an assassination attempt in June 2011—eventually reached an agreement to resign from the presidency and retire to New York, which he did in January 2012.

By February 14, 2011 the events in North Africa had emboldened large segments of the Shi'i majority in Bahrain who organized mass protests and the occupation of Pearl Square in the capital of Manama. The protesters demanded the implementation of political reforms by the Sunni monarchy that would guarantee political representation and rights to the majority, ending discrimination against the Shi'a. In the early morning of February 17, soldiers using live ammunition raided the encampment, killing four. The protests swelled in the aftermath of the attack, as pro-government demonstrations were launched in response. On March 14 the Bahraini king declared a national emergency and invited Saudi troops to enter the country and crush the protest movement. A year later, the movement remained in a state of limbo over a year later with pro-government and anti-government forces refusing to talk while state security and anti-government protesters engaged in periodic street battles.

March 2011 also saw the beginnings of insurrection in Syria, inspired by the revolts of Tunisia and Egypt. Unlike Egypt, Bahrain and Tunisia, in Syria an opposition did not rapidly coalesce and engage large sections of the country in revolt. Instead, resistance built up over months. When a group of young teenagers in the town of Daraa were arrested and tortured on March 15 for spray painting anti-regime slogans on school walls, residents took to the streets to protest the security forces' overreaction. This event rippled throughout the country, leading to larger protests met with greater violence and repression until much of Syria had been pulled into a spiral of violence that has continued for over a year with no end in sight.

The 2011 eruptions of popular discontent in Tunisia, Egypt, Yemen, Bahrain, and Syria represent local manifestations of a regional mass movement for democracy, freedom and human dignity. In a region ruled by varying forms of authoritarianism since the end of European colonialism, the insurrectionary spark from Tunisia ignited a fiery mix of anger and hope that had been heretofore suppressed. Aided by newer forms of transnational communication and cultural exchange like Al Jazeera and satellite television, people across the Arab world saw the problems of corrupt, anti-democratic government and growing poverty multiplied across the region. A shared sense of suffering—a perhaps unexpected corollary of pan-Arabism—united people across national boundaries and strengthened the idea of "the people" (*sha'b*) as distinct from the state. Thus the slogans and demands expressed in different vernaculars reflect the same core ideas. Citizens are battling to reform and restructure national institutions and to introduce levels of political participation and social justice unknown to them previously. They want to be free of brutalization, they want accountability for those wielding power, and they want to be respected citizens of nations legitimately governed. They want jobs, decent wages, public services, and other basic economic and human rights.

Yet the revolts were also shaped by particular histories and social contexts. The countries differ in their forms of government, socio-economic elites as well as socio-economic stresses, political party histories, legacies of labor organization, levels of civil society engagement, and the structure of their internal security apparatuses. These factors also guided how each regime reacted to the onset of local revolts. The extent to which outside forces became involved, in conjunction with the sometimes shifting loyalty of internal and external allies of the respective regimes as they battled resistance also played an important part in giving each uprising its unique character and trajectory.

The collection of essays gathered here were originally published in *Middle East Report*, an independent quarterly magazine providing in-depth analysis of the region's political economy since 1971. The articles in this volume offer what *Middle East Report* does best: "meso-level" analysis of the causes and consequences of current events, something between the "big picture" supplied by journalistic reporting and the granular detail found in scholarship whose main audience consists of other specialists.

Each section is arranged in a present-past-present structure. Rather than providing a teleological search for origins, this form of organization sets the stage and attempts to unearth conditions that made the revolts possible and launched each nation on its own course. The articles, grouped by country, thus start in the thick of the uprisings, then take the analysis back over the last two decades to shed light on some of the historical developments that have shaped the specificity of each national context before returning again to the present to comment on current conditions.

Though there can be no singular narrative of uprisings that occurred in such different national contexts, the articles in this volume do highlight some shared underlying conditions that laid the groundwork for the insurrections. Relatively stagnant economic systems made worse by the 2008 financial crisis and recent rises in food prices, combined with relatively high unemployment—especially among educated youth—poorly managed public services, and rampant corruption created systems of entrenched and pervasive social inequality. Metastasizing security apparatuses inserted themselves into ever more aspects of daily life and impinged upon higher levels of the social spectrum. Though some countries saw a lessening of election fraud that allowed opposition parties into parliaments, constitutional acrobatics were institutionalizing the rule of autocrats and their family members. The increasingly organized opposition to declining living conditions and political freedoms, however, provided people with experiences and strategies that proved essential for the 2011 uprisings.

Yet the whole of the pre-revolt situation is more than the sum of its parts: Authoritarian practices combined with economic inequality in ways that rendered the state—as arbiter of both political activity and socioeconomic well-being—utterly alien to most citizens. The region faced a comprehensive crisis of governance.

The Socio-Economic Crisis in the Region

The official economic record of the Middle East and North Africa is mixed. The states that have been rocked by democratic uprisings have seen an overall rise in living standards over the last forty years. It is undeniable that most people are living longer and healthier lives, with more access to formal education than their parents and grandparents. At the same time, rising unemployment and increasing poverty over the last twenty years have sharpened the divides between elites—often ensconced in glittering gated communities—and the rest, the middle and working classes and the peasantry who live in increasingly crowded and underserved cities and towns. Despite varying degrees of economic socialization across the five states, the better social and economic future promised by post-independence governments seemed to materialize only for the well-connected.

The region has been dramatically—though unevenly—transformed by the privatization and globalization of national economies under the influence of the International Monetary Fund, the World Bank and other advocates of neoliberal policies. Though nominally socialist regimes across the region had begun turning away from statist economic polices in the late 1960s, most Arab states did not begin implementing neoliberal reforms in earnest until the 1980s when the fall in global oil prices precipitated a regional economic slump. For states seeking international loans, monies were conditioned upon shifting economic activity toward export-oriented agriculture, manufacturing, and services as well as selling state-owned corporations to private investors—the standard recipe for structural adjustment. Dismantling the institutions of state-driven development necessarily threatened the professed populism of many of these regimes: Raising the standard of living of people long held down by the colonial yoke was understood to be the first priority of the new regimes. But privatization of industry and agriculture, and the shift to service-based economies, combined with reduced price supports on necessities, rendered life increasingly precarious for urban and rural workers as well as the middle class. Such programs often served parallel regime interests by rewarding political allies with privileged access to formerly public assets and new markets. Even for governments that were not pressured into structural adjustment by supranational bodies (like Bahrain and Syria), privatization was often a means of personal enrichment sold as good liberal economics. In some cases, "privatization" was merely a reorganization of ownership such that certain sectors of the regime remained in control.

An accelerant of declining socioeconomic conditions, and handmaiden to privatization programs, has been the steady erosion in government spending on public welfare. Such public services as did emerge during the early decades of post-independence state building have gradually been allowed to rot on the vine. Structural adjustment requires the reduction of state spending as an end in itself, though as some states (Egypt and Tunisia) became increasingly indebted to foreign lenders, cutting public investments in education, health care and pensions also freed more capital for debt servicing. Fluctuations in the price of oil put budgetary pressures on all of the states under consideration, whose economies are intricately linked to oil through either direct export, taxation, the remittances of migrant laborers working in more oil-rich countries (namely Saudi Arabia) or a combination of all these factors. In Syria, the economic stagnation wrought by inflexible central planning has also burdened the state's finances, even though its external debt has remained very low. Bahrain has not seen as dramatic a shift away from public spending—indeed, the monarchy has consistently boosted public sector salaries or distributed household bonuses to mitigate political unrest—though deficits over the past several years have slowed the growth of social spending.

The benefits of these twin processes redounded primarily to the core of each regime—the president's extended family and high-ranking members of the ruling party or government—and in some cases to a larger stratum of elites. In the nominally republican regimes, the role of the president's family became increasingly prominent during the period of structural adjustment as key industries were sold to or controlled by members of the ruling family. In Egypt, Mubarak's son Gamal became the official face of restructuring through his leadership of various National Democratic Party and government organs responsible for economic liberalization, not to mention his social clique of wealthy financiers with links to US companies.[1] In Tunisia, the near-exclusive control the extended families of Ben Ali and his wife, Leila Trabelsi, exercised over all sectors of the economy alienated larger and larger segments of the middle class. The Asad family's multi-generational rule in Syria inspired the term *jumlukiyya*, coined by Egyptian intellectual Saad Edin Ibrahim to describe the masking of monarchy (*malakiyya*) with the trappings of republicanism (*jumhuriyya*). Despite the more blatant republico-monarchism of the Asads, they were more careful about distributing the benefits of their rule among various competing classes of merchants and industrialists. Yemen's north-south axis of power, further calcified after the failed 1994 rebellion against the newly unified government, enriched northern elites through the sale of southern land and oil infrastructure to regime backers. As a constitutional monarchy, Bahrain's laws institutionalize the Al Khalifa's control over all aspects of governance, including the semi-opaque management of Bahrain's national wealth. Yet the family has also distributed some of the spoils to the island's Sunni minority through access to government contracts and public sector jobs.

The upward flow of public wealth into private coffers has spawned both conspicuous and hidden forms of inequality. Official salaries of government ministers and state employees masked supplementary income streams from kickbacks, investments and petty bribery. Indeed, measuring income inequality has proven difficult because of dysfunctional or non-existent systems of taxation. (These regulatory gaps are seen by some observers, like the conservative Heritage Foundation, as a measure of economic freedom and therefore a boon for foreign investment.) Statistics on unemployment and poverty were often similarly skewed in state-sponsored reports. Consumption inequality was easier to observe. Access to quality housing has diminished, with improvised, substandard housing going up in and around major cities, while the wealthy increasingly sequester themselves in gated communities. The demand for more meat and dairy products by affluent consumers has stratified eating patterns, diverting state resources from grain and legume production. The shift toward consuming meat and wheat, while boosting the overall caloric intake across the region, has led to more obesity and diabetes among the wealthy and growing malnutrition among the poor.

Increasing Investment in Security and Surveillance

The rise of neoliberal economic strategies coupled with the general decline across the region of command economies, fewer pro-peasant and pro-worker policies, and deteriorating public services did not alone ignite the Arab uprisings. As those elements of the socioeconomic compact began to wither away, coercive apparatuses became increasingly important for regime survival. Expressions of political frustration were met with ever-harsher methods of surveillance and oppression. The agents of coercion were often distributed across a complex of different government branches, such as the ministries of interior and defense, the military, intelligence services, and the presidential office, so that the regime inserted itself into people's lives in multiple ways. Shakedowns or spying by the local police, visits from the *mukhabarat* (intelligence services), encounters with riot police or *baltagiyya* (mercenary thugs)—these activities enforced domestic tranquility through fear, intimidation, arbitrary arrest, torture and sometimes public displays of violence.

Yet broad networks of coercion also became a liability for several of the regimes when the momentum of popular protests rendered the status quo untenable. In both Tunisia and Egypt, the military refused to fire live ammunition on protesters and broke publicly with the regimes. The motivation for these moves was different in each case: The power of the military in Tunisia has been tightly controlled since Habib Bourguiba's presidency, with the effect of maintaining the institution's professionalism, while the independent political and economic interests of the Egyptian military were best preserved by cutting ties with Mubarak and forcing him to relinquish power. But these moments reveal the varying interests on which these authoritarian governments relied. Indeed, Ben Ali had used employment in the police force as a kind of economic stimulus as the effects of structural adjustment and regime cronyism devastated the country's middle and working classes. Yet low pay and other grievances failed to secure the allegiance of most workaday police officers, many of whom joined in the protests within the first few weeks. Within Salih's regime, internal fragmentation and rivalry led to high-profile defections from the government and the army in the first two months of protests. The Asad regime, in contrast, kept a firm hold over the intelligence and security services as well as the military leadership; the allegiance and discipline of mid- and low-level military officers, many of whom are conscripts, must be actively maintained through force and fear. In Bahrain, the internal police and the military are entirely Sunni—Shi'a are effectively barred from these sectors—and a significant percentage are naturalized citizens from Pakistan, Syria and Jordan whose livelihoods are directly reliant on the monarchy's sectarian beneficence.

Following the attacks of September 11, 2001, the US-led war on terror provided funding and political cover to regimes looking for more resources to suppress internal dissent. Ben Ali and Mubarak had long emphasized the threat of domestic and international Islamist groups to justify crackdowns on political freedoms and state violence. After 2011, the United States provided materiel (light and heavy weaponry, tear gas) and training (investigation, interrogation, counterterrorism) to expand regime campaigns against armed and peaceful opposition alike. In Yemen, the US has also engaged in years of drone warfare with a Yemeni intelligence apparatus whose loose definition of Al Qaeda includes many domestic opponents of the Salih regime. The Baathist Asad regime has also violently suppressed Islamist politics in Syria, killing thousands in Hama in 1982 to put down a Muslim Brotherhood-led uprising. The Asads have been able to present their secularist regime as a bulwark against religious and sectarian politics to a populace that fears the instability of neighboring Iraq. Though Syria was an early ally in the war on terror and a key site in the CIA's global torture network, the country's political links to Hizballah and Iran, as well as its opposition to the invasion of Iraq, have kept it on the US government's "state sponsors of terrorism" list. The strategic importance of Bahrain for US foreign policy objectives—the Fifth Fleet based in Manama ensures the free flow of oil in the Persian Gulf and maintains US military dominance over the region—has become even more entrenched since the invasions of Afghanistan and Iraq. Even as the Bahraini military and security police continue to harass and kill protesters, Congress approved $53 million in arms sales to the monarchy in May 2012 to "maintain its external defense capabilities."

As the security networks grew and the targets of repression multiplied, state violence became visible to wider swaths of the population. State police in Tunisia turned to harassing women with headscarves, gathering intelligence on mosque activities and worshippers, and occasionally rounding up youth and holding them merely on the suspicion that they were involved in "terrorist activities."[2] In addition to the proliferation of military checkpoints across southern Yemen, climbing body counts from the Yemeni government's war on the Houthi rebels in the northwest and from US drone strikes in Shabwa, Abyan and Hadramawt provinces broadened discontent with Salih's government. Though Egypt's emergency law had codified police impunity for three decades, in the last few years of the Mubarak regime, incidents of arbitrary arrest and torture became so common and well-documented that the regime stopped denying that torture occurred.[3] Growing discontent with the police state was catalyzed in June 2010 when Alexandria police officers dragged a young man named Khalid Sa'id out of an internet cafe and beat him to death in public during a petty drug arrest. (Subsequent reports alleged that Sa'id possessed a video showing evidence of police corruption; though discounted by those close to him, this story helped fuel public outrage.)[4] The murder inspired a "We Are All Khalid Sa'id" Facebook page and protest movement that staged demonstrations over the summer and fall of 2010 against police brutality and human rights abuses. This organization became a major promoter of the demonstrations on January 25, 2011. Harassment of regime critics has always been quite public in Bahrain; when the ruling Al Khalifa family dissolved parliament in 1975, it detained or deported most members of the political opposition. Pro-democracy uprisings in the mid-1990s were violently suppressed by the army and torture was a common tactic of the security services during times of political turmoil.[5] State violence in Syria has been similarly spectacular. Hafiz al-Asad's suppression of the Muslim Brotherhood and other critics between 1979 and 1982 killed over five thousand people[6] (not counting the twenty thousand killed in the shelling of Hama). Syrian *mukhabarat* forces are well-known for nighttime arrests, torture and detaining family members of wanted persons as hostages. That there is virtually no immunity from this kind of violence was an important factor in Bashar's resilience against the protests and armed uprising.[7]

Civil Society and Political Participation

The shadow cast over daily life by state security services was compounded by the ever-tightening grip of regimes over the organs of civil society and the political process. In the countries that did hold elections, uncontested polls, voter intimidation and outright fraud were rife. Constitutions were amended to allow aging presidents to run again. Under light pressure from international funders and allies, many states instituted sham reforms to make rigged elections appear legitimate: licensing opposition parties, loosening restrictions on political literature and "winning" reelection by lower margins. While the international community praised these pantomimes of democratization, voters either went through the motions or stayed home.

Parliamentary elections were similarly engineered to allow only marginal representation for a "loyal" opposition. Legislative bodies acted either as rubber stamps or scapegoats for the executive, as the occasion required. In the case of Bahrain's lower parliamentary house, the toothless body's gerrymandered districts heavily favor the Sunni minority. Ruling parties also functioned as the primary outlet of social and political activity, and as gateways to positions of influence. Membership in Tunisia's Rassemblement Constitutionnel Démocratique (RCD) was practically a requirement for public service, from municipal workers to university administrators, and conferred extra perks like business permits and university scholarships.[8] In Syria, the Arab Socialist Baath Party's dominance is codified in the constitution, and the handful of other socialist and communist parties that hold seats in the legislature are little more than fronts for the Baath Party. Egypt's National Democratic Party, in contrast, served as a patronage network rather than an ideological organization. Party membership was more important for strongmen of the hinterlands and ambitious entrepreneurs than for civil servants or average Egyptians. Yemen's political landscape, like Egypt's, is somewhat more diverse and membership in the dominant General People's Congress is less useful outside of politics.

Regimes also gradually coopted, shut down or severely restricted independent civil society groups, often under the guise of rooting out "foreign agents." In Tunisia, most independent organizations working on human rights and women's issues were absorbed by the state and transformed into committees headed by RCD appointees. Civil society under successive Asad regimes has been suppressed for decades. Syrian NGOs are barred from political activity and most officially recognized organizations perform charitable and (since legal openings in 2005) development work rather than advocacy.[9] NGOs in Egypt, Bahrain and Yemen operate with more independence from the state, though strict registration rules and near total bans on foreign funding keep groups in Egypt and Yemen reliant on state largesse. The Egyptian government still has the power to dissolve and seize the assets of groups it deems non-compliant, and a bill proposed by the newly-elected legislature in April 2012 would essentially transform NGOs into appendages of the state and classify their employees as civil servants.[10] Yemeni groups that criticize the government or its policies are often silenced through "cloning," whereby the state registers a pro-government organization with the same name. In Bahrain, the Al Khalifa have also used travel restrictions, arrests and torture to stall the activities of human rights organizations whom they accuse of working with foreign conspirators to overthrow the government. Most of Bahrain's five hundred civil associations are related to professions, faith or sports (and according to a leaked cable, most groups on the rolls are "essentially defunct").[11]

One area of civil society whose prominence grew over the last decade is that of private charities and health organizations. Rising rates of poverty and a decline in the health of the population linked to state divestment from public services created an opening for social activism that avoided overt politics. As such, charitable activities were generally supported (or at least tolerated) by regimes content to transfer these responsibilities to the private sector. No organization works independently of the state, but charities—particularly religious ones—were sometimes subject to more lenient restrictions than other kinds of civil society organizations. Further, work with religious charity organizations is, for many, a way to fulfill convictions about community development and social solidarity not allowed through other state-controlled channels.

The Experience of Collective Action

Contrary to the narrative that prevailed in the Western press, none of the revolts sprang spontaneously from a crowd of disaffected youth. The revolts were not the product of people who suddenly decided they had had enough, though public actions and confrontations with the police did energize and radicalize many who were not veterans of previous opposition activities. Rather, the uprisings grew out of varied histories of collective action. The perception of being pushed to the wall can spark riots on occasion. Humiliation and rage can bring about wildcat actions or foster demonstrations, but they do not build into full-scale rebellions without the experience of collective action provided by years or even decades of organizing to coordinate and carry out resistance. This experience included informal actions such as blockading roads, rallying for demonstrations, or organizing pots-and-pans protests and the more formal work of organizing strikes, work stoppages, or boycotts.

Some commentators have privileged the role played by new social media in promoting the collective action necessary to sustain the uprisings. The importance of Twitter and Facebook in organizing Egyptian and Tunisian demonstrations cannot be denied. The fact that the Syrian security forces make house-to-house searches confiscating cell phones so they will not be used to upload videos of the violence is further proof of the centrality of new media in the struggle. That all of the regimes involved have tried with differing success to slow or jam communication between groups on the inside and between demonstrators and those on the outside provides further evidence of the important role new social media have played.

On the other hand, revolts broke out in earlier epochs with a different mix of technologies available. Printing presses, for instance, often proved to be central to revolt coordination in the past, which was why regimes often sought to limit their number and control their output. And of course media employed to support uprisings can also be used to combat them. The disinformation campaigns waged on state-run Syrian television attest to that. Thus it seems fair to suggest that various media have played an important but not absolutely crucial role in the uprisings. What is crucial is the experience of collective action that knows how to make use of the organizing aid different media offer.

Campaigns by organized labor in Egypt and Tunisia served as key precedents for the uprisings in those countries. Egyptian laborers in particular had more experience taking action against their regime than did workers in any of the other countries in the run-up to the revolts of 2011. Between 2004 and 2008 over 1.5 million Egyptian workers participated in almost two thousand strikes across the country. Some of the most militant strikers, centered in the textile industries of the Nile Delta, linked their immediate demands for increased pay and fair working conditions to the corruption and autocracy of the Mubarak regime. In Tunisia, organized labor had been relatively quiet since the 1983-1984 bread riots that had swept across North Africa. Struggles with the regime tended to happen in closed meetings among senior union leadership rather than on the street. But in 2008, the mining town of Redayef near the western city of Gafsa exploded with protests over nepotistic hiring practices at the state-owned phosphate company and the persistent poverty in the region. The unrest spread to nearby towns, incorporating other trade unionists, teachers, and the unemployed. Despite the state media blackout, news of the protests traveled across Tunisia, inspiring solidarity actions in larger cities. The movement was finally crushed by state police after six months, but its example of open protest against Ben Ali's regime was a precursor to the 2010 protests.

Broader opposition movements had also gained strength in Egypt, Bahrain and Yemen before the 2011 uprisings. In 1994, protests against the Al Khalifa's discriminatory hiring practices for state offices snowballed into a larger movement for democratic reform. State repression against Shi'i activists, including mass arrests and forced exile, exacerbated sectarian social divisions and also precipitated anti-regime street violence between 1995 and 1997. The monarchy's violent reaction and mass arrests effectively suppressed much organized dissent until 2005 when alternatives to the established opposition groups began to emerge and organize cross-sectarian peaceful demonstrations against inequality and state violence. Egypt's strike wave of 2004-2011 was enhanced by the protests of professional associations and new middle-class activist groups like Kifaya and April 6 who organized solidarity protests as well as rallies against state repression of journalists, the blockade of Gaza and the continuing use of emergency laws. In Yemen, opposition activist Tawwakul Karman began leading weekly peaceful demonstrations against government repression in 2007. That same year, the southern al-Harak movement, a diverse coalition of Islamists, socialists, former military officers and unemployed youth, also began agitating peacefully for an end to corruption and the systematic impoverishment of the southern provinces. Their message resonated with many northerners, who had suffered the cronyism and lawlessness of Salih's regime for an additional two decades. Though these forms of organized dissent may not have achieved substantial gains against autocrats, their activities at least tilled the soil for the mass actions of 2011.

The Syrian regime, in contrast, had been much more successful in suppressing collective action through intimidation, brute force, and sowing social mistrust. Since Bashar's ascension to the presidency in 2000, two groups calling for democratic reforms emerged, drawing almost entirely on the intelligentsia and exiled opposition politicians. In both cases, the demands for an end to martial law, a truly independent legislature and judiciary, political pluralism, press freedoms and more market liberalization were met with arrests and prison terms for select leaders. This history makes the speed with which neighborhood organizations, both armed and unarmed, responded to state repression in the early days of protests even more remarkable. During the first months of the uprising, local coordination committees organized the daily demonstrations and funeral processions and tried to manage responses to regime violence as well as publicize the daily death tolls. In the face of escalating regime violence, however, these nonviolent committees were superseded in most areas by armed groups, a mixture of defected army members, ad hoc neighborhood militias and Salafis (fundamentalist Islamists), doing daily battle with the army and intelligence police. These groups operate simultaneously but without coordination, and the resulting chaos has put the benefits of a successful revolution in doubt for many Syrians.

First Steps

The obvious omission from our discussion of the uprisings is, of course, Libya. Prior to Qaddafi's fall, it was nearly impossible to conduct in-depth research in Libya because of the severe restrictions imposed by the state on journalists and academics, both Libyan and foreign. It was possible to write about Libyan foreign relations or prominent government decisions, and several authors did so in the pages of *Middle East Report*. But they could not offer the kind of bottom-up views of politics, society, and culture that were available for other countries, and so we do not have them for this volume.

The 2011 eruption of popular discontent in the Arab world has forever altered the Middle East and North Africa. Authoritarian regimes in the region have been either banished or put on notice that the old ways of oppressing and immiserating their subjects will no longer be tolerated. Yet not all of the uprisings turned out as planned: Syrians are locked in a ferocious conflict in which the outcome cannot be predicted; events in Bahrain are on hold. The states of the region, whether directly involved or not, are learning to perfect new strategies for the cooptation and containment of popular dissent. The United States, Saudi

Arabia and the Gulf States lurk at the edges as potential counter-revolutionary forces. Even the protesters who did cause regime change face enormous roadblocks on the way to building governments that can provide the decent jobs, wages, access to land, education, housing, food, democracy, and the respect and dignity for which their citizens originally rose in revolt. The economies of all six nations involved in the uprisings have been damaged. Plenty of pitfalls await the social forces struggling to gain control of the post-revolt situation.

The number of factors necessary for a revolt to take place is no doubt greater than the list of characteristics in common to the five Arab nations covered in this collection. But this is a start. No matter how these societies eventually emerge from the process of national transformation, they present valuable lessons in how to resist tyranny while struggling for democratic change and equitable economic development. Whatever the future holds, the dream unleashed by the 2011 uprisings is of a region remade into a new order guided by enforceable legal and constitutional guarantees, more economic equality, and greater social justice.

Notes

1. Mona El-Ghobashy, "Egypt's Summer of Discontent," *Middle East Report Online*, September 18, 2003.

2. Amy Aisen Kallander, this volume.

3. Human Rights Watch, "'Work on Him Until He Confesses': Impunity for Torture in Egypt," January 2011, p. 29.

4. Amro Ali, "Saeeds of Revolution: De-Mythologizing Khaled Saeed," *Jadaliyya*, June 5, 2012.

5. Human Rights Watch, "Torture Redux: The Revival of Physical Coercion during Interrogations in Bahrain," February 2010.

6. Middle East Watch, *Syria Unmasked*, (New Haven: Yale, 1991), p. 62.

7. Bassam Haddad, in this volume.

8. United States Department of State, "Tunisia: Country Reports on Human Rights Practices," (Washington, D.C., 2009).

9. Laura Ruiz de Elvira and Tina Zintl, *Civil Society and the State in Syria: The Outsourcing of Responsibility*, (Fife, Scotland: St Andrews Centre for Syrian Studies, 2012).

10. Issandr El Amrani, "Another Law Against NGOs in Egypt," *The Arabist*, April 12, 2012.

11. United States Department of State, "09MANAMA587 - Bahraini Civil Society Organizations," (Manama, 2009). Available: http://www.cablegatesearch.net/cable.php?id=09MANAMA587.

PART ONE

TUNISIA

Sidi Bouzid is a quiet burg located almost exactly in the middle of Tunisia. Its approximately forty thousand residents buy their produce from an open-air market ranged along a wide but sleepy street in front of a few single-story shops selling tea and other sundry goods. It was here on December 17, 2010 that Mohamed Bouazizi, a street vendor, had his produce confiscated by city officials during a minor altercation over paperwork. The humiliation and frustration he felt at this latest in a long line of incidents of petty harassment led him to set himself on fire later that day in front of the local police station. Reports of his act of desperation spread quickly across the country and proved the catalyst that launched demonstrations throughout Tunisia and eventually across the Arab world. His case became so famous that President Zine El Abidine Ben Ali felt obliged to visit him in the hospital at the end of December to pay his respects. Bouazizi never regained consciousness and passed away on January 4, 2011, unable to witness the fall of Ben Ali's regime on January 14 and the wider revolts this victory inspired.

Bouazizi's precarious employment was characteristic of many young people his age, particularly in Tunisia's rural interior. Youth unemployment there is estimated at around 30 percent, which is considerably higher than the national average of 14 percent and much higher than the 7 percent unemployment along the coast. Located far from the beaches and seaside tourist resorts, interior towns have missed out on the considerable sums invested in Tunisia's most important industry. The uneven development of the last four decades has exacerbated historical tensions and disparities between urban and rural Tunisians. What investment was earmarked for rural projects—millions in loans from the International Monetary Fund and the World Bank, among other sources—ultimately profited the agrarian elites who formed the backbone of Tunisia's post-colonial ruling class.

Following Tunisia's independence from France in 1956, the government led by Habib Bourguiba and his Socialist Destourian Party embarked on an explicitly liberalizing project, rewriting the Tunisian constitution and legal code to regularize rights for women and minorities and expanding access to public education. Despite early reforms, Bourguiba's rule became increasingly personalized over the subsequent thirty years as he managed political contestation and dissent through media censorship, legal maneuvers, and violent crackdowns on organized labor and Islamist political movements. In 1987, thirteen years after Bourguiba declared himself "president-for-life," he was ousted from power by Ben Ali (then prime minister) who had the aging president declared mentally and physically unfit.

Ben Ali renamed the ruling party but otherwise further entrenched one-man rule. The neoliberal economic reforms that had begun, slowly, under Bourguiba accelerated as Ben Ali and his extended family became the prime beneficiaries of privatization and the development of new export industries. The limited independence of civil society groups disappeared as they were forced to either integrate with state administrative structures or be dismantled. Organized labor had a variable relationship with the regime, but mostly refrained from street politics in favor of high-level bargaining with the regime on bread-and-butter issues. Though there were several legal political parties in the lower house of Parliament, many of them had ties to the ruling Rally for Constitutional Democracy and did nothing to challenge its dominance. Ben Ali consistently won reelection with close to 100 percent of the vote.

The police state also expanded dramatically under Ben Ali until over 1 percent of the population was employed by various policing and intelligence agencies. The police mediated daily life in Tunisia: They were the conduit for interacting with much of the state bureaucracy, as well as the regime's primary surveillance mechanism. At the pinnacle of the policing apparatus was the fearsome State Security branch, which was responsible for monitoring, arresting and torturing dissidents. Since Bourguiba's presidency, the most potent threat to the regime—whose secularism was both ideological and a method of political control—came from the Islamist party al-Nahda. Both Bourguiba and Ben Ali arrested, exiled or killed most of al-Nahda's cadres by the early 1990s but continued to use the threat of political Islam to justify authoritarian rule to international partners. After the attacks of September 11, 2011, Ben Ali took advantage of US funding for anti-terrorism iniatives to enhance the repressive machinery of the state. Ben Ali and Bourguiba also shared a mistrust of the armed forces as a potential threat to their rule. Rather than coopt the officer corps (as was the case with neighboring regimes), both men marginalized the military, keeping it underfunded and understaffed compared to the civil police.

Despite these barriers, there were several large demonstrations against the regime prior to the uprising of 2010-2011. In the early weeks of 1984, the end of state subsidies of food staples caused widespread anti-government riots. Thousands of Tunisians took to the streets, attacked stores and government buildings, and battled police and military units sent to put down the demonstrations. The violence ended when Bourguiba agreed to reinstate the subsidies and increase other welfare provisions. In 2008, mine workers in western Tunisia went on strike and took control of several towns, weathering government attacks for over six months before finally being crushed by the military. The regime claimed that Islamist terrorists were behind the unrest, but internet-savvy activists around the country publicized the workers' grievances against government corruption and organized solidarity demonstrations in several other cities.

Widespread dissatisfaction with the government's corruption—and the spectacular greed of the Ben Ali family—is part of what tipped the balance against the regime when protests erupted in 2010. Over twenty-three years, Ben Ali whittled away at the regime's political base among elites by directing more and more of the state's largesse into his own coffers. Institutionalized graft also threatened the social spending that had guaranteed well-paid jobs for the educated middle classes, who were increasingly under- or unemployed.

Unemployment remains one of the most pressing challenges facing the new coalition government led by the revived al-Nahda. Protests demanding swift economic reform in the early months of 2012 were met with riot police and a brief ban on demonstrations in Tunis. The new government also attempted to reinstate some controls over the press. These moves worry critics of al-Nahda, particularly those who view the censorship as motivated by the social conservatism of some al-Nahda officials. Women's groups in particular fear that al-Nahda's role in drafting the new constitution threatens many of the rights women gained over the last five decades. Nevertheless, the path of constitutional reform before permanent elections has allowed Tunisians a level of democratic control over the political transition absent in Egypt and Yemen. Two peaceful uprisings in 2011—the first to remove Ben Ali, and the second to abolish the system that backed him—and the continuing political ferment have inaugurated a new era of participatory politics in Tunisia.

1. TUNISIA'S WALL HAS FALLEN

NADIA MARZOUKI

For the first time in decades, Tunisia is free of one-man rule. The extraordinary events of December 2010 and January 2011 were nothing less than a political revolution: The consistent pressure of popular fury forced President Zine El Abidine Ben Ali first to make an unprecedented promise to relinquish power; then pushed him to step down; and finally halted an attempt at unconstitutional transfer of power, setting the stage for a transition to electoral democracy.

In the early months of 2011, the nature of this political transition was still in question. Three days after Ben Ali's January 14 departure to exile in Saudi Arabia, the caretaker head of government Mohammed al-Ghannouchi announced a "national unity" cabinet composed heavily of members of the long-time ruling party, the Rassemblement Constitutionnel Democratique (RCD), who initially retained the ministries of interior, defense, foreign affairs, and finance. Opposition parties classified as "legal" under Ben Ali also acquired posts. The announcement came after a night of gunfights reported around the presidential palace, opposition party headquarters, and major banks, as well as drive-by shootings elsewhere in the capital of Tunis. *The Guardian*, citing human rights activists, attributed the attacks to militias made up of security men loyal to Ben Ali, while Ghannouchi said on state television that "the coming days will show who is behind them."

Much more consequential were the protesters outside the presidential palace and the Casbah Square on January 17 voicing their anger at reports that RCD members would be part of the interim cabinet. The protests were dispersed with water cannons, but popped back up when the cabinet was named. Several opposition members of the interim cabinet, three of them affiliated with the countrywide labor federation, the Union Générale Tunisienne du Travail (UGTT), promptly resigned their posts amidst the renewed "RCD out!" demonstrations. Ghannouchi and others tried to quell the unrest by announcing their own resignations from the RCD, though not from the interim government; that event came three weeks later after larger demonstrations and the deaths of several protesters at the hands of the police. Despite the unrest, the original and remarkable achievement of Tunisian demonstrators prevailed: Ben Ali would not be back.

"Bread, Water, Yes; Ben Ali, No"

The fast-paced and utterly unexpected fall of Tunisia's dictator originated in what at first looked like a jacquerie of hungry, disenfranchised youths. Quickly, however, and spontaneously, the protests became overtly political as well as economic. They were certainly not the result of top-down manipulation by a specific party pursuing a ready-made political agenda, as the regime tried to pretend.

On December 17, 2010 Mohammed Bouazizi, a twenty-six-year old street vendor from the town of Sidi Bouzid, set himself on fire after police confiscated his merchandise, telling him he did not have a permit to sell his goods. The desperate gesture of this underemployed university graduate immediately sparked protests throughout the country. Anger at the status quo ignited within Tunisians of all generations, social classes, professional categories, and ideological sensibilities, despite the forceful police crackdowns, which likely killed some two hundred people. (The UN said on January 19 it could confirm some hundred deaths, including forty-two in a prison fire that claimed the lives of many protesters, but this number was almost certainly too low.) The uprising began as a movement against unemployment and high prices, particularly for food, but it rapidly transformed into a revolution demanding civil liberties and the ouster of the man who had long suppressed them. "Bread, water, yes; Ben Ali, no," the crowds chanted.

Accustomed to setting his own schedule, Ben Ali was compelled by the protests to address the people three times in one month. He first attempted, on December 28, to pass off the unrest in the usual manner of autocrats as the work of "extremists." On January 11, chastened, he pledged to create three hundred thousand jobs, hoping to calm the streets with state largesse. Two days later, he finally acknowledged the political nature of the protests, telling the country he would not run for reelection in 2014, freeing all protesters who had been arrested and lifting restrictions on the media. The unanimous verdict of the Tunisian people was: too little, too late. In the early afternoon of January 14, Prime Minister Ghannouchi announced that the president was temporarily unable to perform his functions and that he would take over until new elections could be organized. Opposition figures, however, immediately pointed to the breach of Article 57 of the constitution, according to which the speaker of Parliament, and not the prime minister, assumes the presidential role in cases of vacancy at the top. On the morning of January 15, the Constitutional Court, Tunisia's highest authority on such matters, declared that "the post of president is definitively vacant," leading Ghannouchi to give way to Fouad Mebazaa, the parliamentary speaker, who promised to hold elections within the constitutionally prescribed period of forty-five to sixty days. The opposition forces vociferously objected, and successfully lobbied to delay the elections for eight months to allow more time for logistical arrangements and campaigning.

The Tunisian events, though surprising to most everyone, were not a random outburst of frustration. Rather, they represented the logical consequence of an unsustainable formula for fake political and economic stability, the very formula that many Western policymakers lauded as the "Tunisian miracle." While dramatic, the self-immolation of Bouazizi (who later died of his burn wounds) was only the trigger rather than the cause of the protests, whose roots were much deeper and older.

Ben Ali's international backers often portrayed his rule as beneficent. In April 2008, on an official visit to Tunis, French President Nicolas Sarkozy declared that "some people are way too harsh with Tunisia, which is developing openness and tolerance in many respects." "The space for liberties is progressing," he continued.[1] Sarkozy was echoing the sentiments of his predecessor Jacques Chirac, who had argued when visiting Tunisia in December 2003 that "the first of human rights is the right to eat.... From this point of view, one has to acknowledge that Tunisia is in advance of other countries." Starting in the late 1990s, meanwhile, the World Bank, International Monetary Fund, European countries and the United States singled out Tunisia for systematic praise as a model of economic reform in North Africa. In 2008, for example, the World Bank called Tunisia a "top regional reformer" in the domain of easing access to credit and the Bank's country profile marveled that the Mediterranean nation had doubled its exports of goods and services over the preceding decade. Dominique Strauss-Kahn, president of the IMF, stated in November 2008 that the "Tunisian economy is going well" and that Tunisia is a "good example for emerging countries."[2] On both the political and economic counts, however, the reality was much darker.

Following his 1987 coup, which removed the long-time "president-for-life" Habib Bourguiba, Ben Ali methodically stamped out the few political and civil liberties that Tunisians had managed to attain. He was a master of staging demonstration elections that returned him to power with more than 90 percent of the vote. After two such sham electoral victories in 1994 and 1999, he amended the constitution in 2004, eliminating the three-term limit on the presidential mandate, so that he could run again in 2009. The RCD won every legislative election in this period in a landslide. Through the party apparatus, the regime carefully tracked the activities of labor unions, student associations, women's rights groups and media outlets, as well as dictated the content of cultural events. The program of state surveillance manifested itself at three levels: First, political activists were subject to severe repression and intimidation at the hands of the police. Tunisia was among the most heavily policed states in the world, with over one hundred thousand policemen in uniform in a country of 10.4 million. Torture of political prisoners was repeatedly documented and denounced by domestic and foreign human rights organizations. Second, the president's party established a very complex and pervasive regime of monitoring of ordinary citizens, described by the French political economist Béatrice Hibou as a "control grid" (*dispositif de quadrillage*). A Tunisian citizen had to take care not to incur the local RCD watchdog's wrath in order to conduct her ordinary life undisturbed. Officials might otherwise interfere with her enrollment at a university, her exams, her wedding or her desire to open a restaurant or shop, buy property, give birth in a hospital, obtain a passport or even buy a cellular phone. Third, and due to the intrusive state measures, paranoia spread among the populace. After twenty-three years of internalizing fear, Tunisians became their own censors.

Repression, however, was not the only factor accounting for the resilience of the regime. Rather, the longevity of the authoritarian system had come about through a combination of coercion and consent, what Hibou, in her book *La Force de l'obéissance* (2006), called a "security pact." By the terms of this tacit deal, in exchange for relatively easy access to credit and consumer goods, the Tunisian people were expected to acquiesce to the lack of civil and political liberties. Credit and consumption, indeed, were a large part of the "Tunisian miracle." The regime had compromised the old productive base of the economy by adopting the usual IMF and World Bank recommendations to sell off and downsize public-sector industries and agricultural cooperatives. In its place grew a more contingent economy of textile enterprises and call centers operated by foreign investors, who offered short-term and low-paying jobs, and tourist resorts on the country's sun-splashed beaches. Tourism and call centers, where Tunisians record the orders of Western consumers, were two of the main exports in the World Bank's accounting. The promise of credit, which as elsewhere was to have aided Tunisians in starting small businesses, proved ephemeral, in part due to rampant corruption: Persons with connections in high places took the most lucrative opportunities for themselves. Under Bourguiba there was a strong and dynamic middle class, highly educated and entrepreneurial. The corruption and bad governance of Ben Ali's reign contributed to the increasing pauperization of this middle class and the dramatic rise of unemployment, especially among university graduates. Forty-six percent of youth with university degrees, like Bouazizi, had no jobs commensurate with their education. The avarice of the president and his wife's relatives gradually alienated Tunisian and foreign investors, who were tired of paying a tithe to the reigning family, and preferred relocating to the more transparent Gulf countries. The so-called economic success story of Tunisia became a nightmare for the Tunisian people.

When the protests erupted in mid-December 2010, press coverage referred to them primarily as social movements, a "revolt against misery and corruption" or, as the satellite channel Europe 1 put it, a "revolt of the youth."[3] The protesters' motives were assumed to be limited to economic frustration and despair of social advancement. Initially, commentators insisted as well that the demonstrations were disorganized, almost random, lacking in structure and direction. Most important, the movement was alleged to be unsustainable: In the absence of leadership from formal opposition forces, many analysts argued that it could not succeed. As late as January 11, French journalist Christophe Ayad described an "alternative" to Ben Ali's regime as "difficult" to envision, explaining that "all the opposition formations, no matter how respectable, are anemic (exsangues)."[4] Earlier, on January 6, the reporter Marie Kostrz defined the Tunisian opposition as completely "disconnected from reality" and assured her audience that the "political void created by Ben Ali leaves no illusions for Tunisians: No one argues that the regime will collapse in a week or in a month." Her article quoted an analysis by the political scientist Vincent Geisser, who claimed that "change won't be radical, and will come from inside" the regime.[5]

These observers were perhaps comparing the protests of 2010-2011 to the unrest in Tunisia's western hinterlands in 2008. That January, violent protests took place in the town of Redayef, a town of twenty-six thousand located near the mining basin of Gafsa. The workers of this economically abandoned area took to the streets to express their anger at the fraudulent results of a hiring competition launched by the state-owned phosphate company. Most of the eighty-one positions opened by the company were given to workers with friends in high places, and not, as per an agreement between the company and the labor federation, to sons of workers who had died or been injured in work accidents and other inhabitants of the region. Despite its intensity and determination, which spread to the neighboring towns of Metlaoui and Moulares, and included a large number of women and unemployed graduates, the movement remained essentially about advocating the rights of mine workers of the Gafsa area. It did not translate into a wider mobilization demanding the comprehensive rights of the Tunisian people. Most Tunisians, again, chose the option of the "pact of obedience." On December 17, 2010, all that began to change.

Stereotypes Challenged

The events of December and January were propelled by an organic convergence of various currents of discontent. Successively joining the unemployed graduates who started the movement were students, lawyers, bloggers, artists, hackers, housewives, children, doctors, professors, and shopkeepers—each group harboring specific grievances and using its own symbolic vocabulary, but all united in overall purpose. These divergent clusters of protest coalesced into a movement of civil resistance with stunning speed, adapting along the way to the regime's tactics of repression.

The transformation of Tunisia's "First Family," as the US ambassador in Tunis called them in cables revealed by Wikileaks, into an extraordinarily predatory power is the key to understanding why the "security pact" identified by Hibou dissolved so rapidly and with such seeming ease after twenty-three years. The middle class and the professional bourgeoisie (among them, the lawyers, professors, and doctors who joined the protests) stopped accepting the pact as it became clear that one side was no longer honoring it. It may be argued that, in contrast to such countries as Syria, where the Asads and their relatives are also steeped in corruption, the reigning clans of Tunisia got so greedy that they lost their ability to redistribute even a small portion of the booty among the upper reaches of society. They neglected to keep the complicity of the bourgeoisie in place. Beyond the cross-class dimension, four aspects of the popular uprising were particularly critical.

The first, which attracted somewhat breathless coverage in the West, was information sharing. The state-run media was, of course, a fount of disinformation, and the regime exerted great effort to muzzle other media and prevent citizens from learning the details of what was happening. On several occasions in the past, the state blocked the websites of foreign media outlets and shut down the Internet reporting efforts of Tunisians themselves. Police intimidation of journalists and warnings to foreigners to stay indoors were largely effective on this occasion, as well, in keeping the foreign media mute. The major exception was the Qatar-based satellite channel Al Jazeera, which consistently braved the police in the streets and won over many Tunisians with its strong emphasis on the protest movement story from its very inception. The Tunisian events were not simply another illustration of the mighty "Al Jazeera effect," though, since much of what this and other channels broadcast was made possible by a unique collaboration with Tunisians. Al Jazeera had not had an official bureau in Tunisia since 2006, when, incensed by the channel's coverage, Ben Ali recalled the Tunisian ambassador from Doha. Especially at the outset, the channel had to rely on amateur videos, photos, and interviews sent in by Tunisian protesters themselves.[6] In December and January, more to the point, Tunisian youth managed to share critical information with each other, including live audio and video, about the exact unfolding of events. Using such Web 2.0 platforms as nawaat.org and other social media, the movement broadcast its own news of kidnappings of protesters and its own summaries of the analyses of international observers, as well as the time and location of upcoming demonstrations. The protesters also used these devices to compare notes on the respective roles of competing security institutions, such as the army and various police units, giving them insight into the progressive weakening of the apparatus of repression. The Tunisian events have accordingly been dubbed the first "Twitter revolution." In his last speech, delivered on January 13, Ben Ali offered to stop censoring YouTube and other Internet outlets, provoking a swift and dismissive response. The majority answer on Twitter and other social media platforms could be summarized as follows: "We don't want free YouTube or virtual democracy. We want a true regime change, conditioned upon the departure and eventual trial of Ben Ali, and the organization of free elections." Perhaps misled by years of complaints about Internet restrictions, Ben Ali appeared to believe that the protesters' demands were about means of communication, rather than politics and justice.

The intense public debates that characterized the month of protests did not take place solely on the Internet, however. They primarily occurred in the streets, which were transformed into a sort of large coffeehouse where excitement at the recovered freedom of speech coexisted with fear under the threat of state violence. Indeed, hundreds of people were killed and injured. Yet in addition to, and taking precedence over, the brutality, a remarkable sense of happiness, loquacity, and humor filled the streets of cities like Tunis, Gafsa, Sousse, and Sidi Bouzid. Each demonstrator tried to outdo her neighbor's story of regime depredations, not only describing her personal confrontation with deprivation and everyday corruption, but also proposing a line of political analysis and formulating predictions about the future. Institutions that had been de facto instruments of the regime adapted to this awakening of civil society in very short order. For example, the UGTT, which supported Ben Ali from the late 1980s forward, changed its attitude entirely. Beginning with postal workers and primary-school teachers, numerous local and regional chapters of the UGTT organized grassroots-level debates about the course of events. The sense of collective delight that emerged from this recovered right to speak was a challenge to the widespread notion that the "Arab street" is a space of little but anomie and diffuse anger.

A surprisingly under-covered aspect of the Tunisian demonstrations was the impressive visibility of women, also in contrast to stereotypes about the "Arab street" that propagate the image of a male-dominated public space. These stereotypes are closely tied to others about religion. Along with his fellow dictators, Ben Ali had long gulled his backers in the West with the idea that if the "Arab street" was ever opened, it would be filled with enraged Islamist men, calling for the imposition of *shari'a* law and the intensification of gender inequality, if not also jihad. Yet at all the major demonstrations leading to Ben Ali's flight from the country, men and women marched side by side, holding hands and chanting together in the name of civil rights, not Islam. The national anthem, not "*Allahu akbar*," was the dominant rallying cry, and the women were both veiled and unveiled. The tone of the protests was rather one of reappropriating patriotic language and symbols: Women and men lay in the streets to spell "freedom" or "stop the murders" with their bodies and worked together to tear down and burn the gigantic, Stalin-style portraits of Ben Ali on storefronts and street corners.

Rulers and Ruled

One of the most important elements of the uprising was the way in which "the people" (*al-sha'b al-tunisi*) came to be the decisive category of identity in the country. The slogan "The people want the fall of the regime" was, in part, a response to the misperception of Tunisians' demands. The numerous demonstrators who brandished loaves of bread, chanting "Bread, yes—Ben Ali, no," were objecting to analysis of their discontent in the Western press as purely economic, another "bread riot" to be quelled with minor subsidy adjustments. No, Tunisians argued, they represented not the hungry and downtrodden, but the entirety of the Tunisian people claiming their dignity. The emergence of the term *sha'b* was part and parcel of this collective *cri de coeur* and thus of the success of the revolution.

The normative dimension of the category of "the people" is novel in post-colonial Tunisia. Previous social movements, while often quite militant, did not take on an overtly political thrust. During the bread riots of 1983-1984, for example, the notion of *sha'b* ironically appeared mainly in the patronizing rhetoric of the regime, as when President Habib Bourguiba announced his decision to reverse planned increases in the prices of bread, sugar, and pasta. "O Tunisian people," said Bourguiba in his televised address, "I have decided that we are going back to the former situation." Neither these disturbances nor earlier ones were able to transform the relationship between ruler and ruled so that "the people" had agency as well as needs. After independence in 1956, Bourguiba promulgated an ideology based on the ideal of a homogeneous, united, modern, Francophile, and secular national body.[7] In the name of this ideal, he crushed his main rival Salah Ben Youssef, a proponent of pan-Arabism close to Nasserism, and methodically constructed the image of a leader (*za'im*) who was the sole legitimate benefactor and protector of the people.[8] While Bourguiba's era saw significant achievements in literacy, public health, and women's rights, the paternalistic relationship that developed between the *za'im* and Tunisians left little room for participatory politics. After Zine El Abidine Ben Ali seized power in 1987, this form of governance turned into a pervasive police state that restricted the space available for collective action even further.

"The people," like the nation, is what the scholar Benedict Anderson called an imagined community. One might point to various discrepancies between this imagined community and the real sociology of the Tunisian population—divisions of class, for example, or ideological affiliation. It is nonetheless important that the category of *sha'b*, and not Islam or workers or unemployed graduates, emerged as the rallying cry of the Tunisian revolution.

"The people" subsequently became the reference point that political projects had to adopt to be accepted as legitimate. This fact had the effect of making the projects more inclusive and, one may hope, broadening minds. On March 10, in an interview on Al Jazeera, Abdelfatah Mourou, second-in-command of the Islamist al-Nahada party, referred to the *sha'b*, not Islam or Muslims, as the central category of the Tunisian polity. When asked about al-Nahada's position toward partisan politics, often considered to contradict Islamists' ideal of unity, Mourou insisted on "the right of the people to its self" (*haqq al-sha'b li-nafsihi*). "The people may have different feelings," he granted, going on to contend, "the only parties that will win will be those chosen by the people." The concept of *sha'b* seemed to compel Mourou to acknowledge pluralism. The necessity of framing decisions in terms of the interests of the Tunisian people equally became apparent in a number of declarations by then-Prime Minister Beji Caid Essebsi, as well as members of the League for Defense of the Revolution party and association leaders. Every protest or strike—whether of journalists, railway workers or janitors—invokes not only the name of the demonstrating group, but also of the "Tunisian people." Within the Arabic and Francophone media, there has been major transformation, though the habits of the old regime are far from fully uprooted. Articles, op-eds, and forums about the expectations and needs of the Tunisian people proliferate. The notion of *sha'b* has established itself as the relevant signifier of consensus.

The transition away from Ben Ali showed that Tunisians were committed to a new model of political leadership. The explosion in the number of political parties (more than seventy) was regarded as a sign of fragmentation, but the plurality of voices was evidence that the normative power of the category of people could not be coopted by an opportunistic new *za'im*. The attitude of *dégage* or *irhal*—directed at Ben Ali and then two interim cabinets—was criticized as capricious and unconstructive, but it clearly showed that Tunisians were not ready to abandon their recovered rights to free expression to any pretender to the throne. The elections of the constitutional assembly, on October 23, 2011, has led to an unprecedented coalition of secular and Islamist parties. While al-Nahda secured eighty-nine seats out of the 217 of the Assembly, the Congress for the Republic, a center-left party won 29 seats and Ettakatol, a center-right party, 19. The compromise that the three parties have made, and that they have managed to uphold in the face of numerous political and social crises is a political experiment in the history of Tunisia. Despite their many ideological divergences, the three parties have promised to maintain the coalition until a new constitution is written and parliamentary elections are organized. In the meantime, the lively debates and frequent reorganization within many of the young or reformed parties are a testament to Tunisia's political energy and vitality.

The persistence of protest in the year following the departure of Ben Ali secured a momentous legacy for the events in Tunisia: In terms of political symbolism, this revolution is the equivalent for the Arab world of the fall of the Berlin wall in 1989. It showed, if nothing else, that the region's many dictators do not have to rule until they die, whether of natural or unnatural causes. No matter what happens over the coming years, the Tunisian revolution has set a dramatic precedent for how democratization from below might begin.

Notes

1. Quoted in Marc Semo, "La volte-face tardive de la France," *Liberation*, January 17, 2011.

2. *Oumma*, January 13, 2011.

3. *Politis.fr*, January 13, 2011.

4. Christophe Ayad, "Autour de Ben Ali, la politique du vide," *Liberation*, January 11, 2011.

5. Marie Kostrz, "Revolution de jasmin: qui pour remplacer Ben Ali en Tunisie," *Rue 89*, January 6, 2011.

6. *Le Monde*, January 19, 2011.

7. See Mounira Charrad, *States and Women's Rights: The Making of Post-Colonial Tunisia, Algeria and Morocco* (Berkeley, Calif.: University of California Press, 2001).

8. See Michel Camau and Vincent Geisser, *Habib Bourguiba, la trace et l'héritage* (Paris: Karthala, 2004).

2. TUNISIA'S POST-BEN ALI CHALLENGE: A PRIMER

AMY AISEN KALLANDER

The January 14 departure of Tunisian President Zine El Abidine Ben Ali amidst popular protests was a long overdue demonstration of the possibility for genuine democratization in the Arab world. Mohamed Bouazizi, the street vendor whose self-immolation set off the protests, tapped a deep vein of anger in Tunisian society at police harassment and the general arbitrariness of the state, but also at severe, endemic economic inequality sharpened now by rising global food prices. It remains to be determined, however, to what degree the toppling of Ben Ali will transform Tunisia into a representative democracy whose citizens enjoy greater economic opportunities. Ben Ali was the head of a system of one-party rule, and that system did not board a private plane along with him and his immediate entourage as they headed into exile.

As Ben Ali's personal grip weakened, the international headlines blared news of the deep corruption and extravagant privilege associated with the former dictator's clan. His family's extensive control of the economy, reaching into banking, telecommunications, import-export, cars, agriculture and food distribution, petroleum, tourism, real estate, and nearly every other sector, had long been an open secret in Tunisia. Two of the family heavyweights, Ben Ali's son-in-law Sakher al-Materi and his brother-in-law Belhassan Trabelsi, also fled the country in mid-January, and Tunisian authorities claimed to have rounded up others within days. Yet dismantling the structures that facilitated the concentration of political-economic power in the hands of Ben Ali will be a difficult task. In fact, while Ben Ali exploited the system to unprecedented personal and family benefit, the consolidation of one-party rule dates to the tenure of the first president of independent Tunisia, Habib Bourguiba (1956-1987).

Protesters from across the country continued to gather in front of the Interior Ministry and prime minister's offices in the capital of Tunis, demanding that Ben Ali's ex-lieutenants withdraw from government. Their hope was to secure a firmer guarantee of real change in how the country is ruled.

One-Party Rule

Notwithstanding the occasional bouts of nostalgia for Bourguiba, the hero of Tunisia's independence struggle from France, it was under his reign that the ruling party, the Neo-Destour (later named the Socialist Destourian Party), became synonymous with the state.

Bourguiba controlled the judiciary, placed arbitrary limits on press freedoms and allocated such minimal prerogatives to legislative assemblies that there were few checks on his power. He initially faced opposition within the Destour, and armed resistance led by Salah Ben Youssef, whose assassination he personally ordered in 1961. Secularization programs such as the nationalization of the Zaytouna mosque-university and the reform of family law reduced the influence of religious authorities. Labor unions and women's groups that had actively contributed to the anti-colonial movement were brought under state control and incorporated into the party apparatus. For instance, the National Union of Tunisian Women, founded in 1958, gathered together women from nationalist parties and independent women's groups, one of which voluntarily disbanded. Following the adoption of a 1959 law requiring civil associations to obtain a government permit, the remaining independent women's organization, affiliated with the communist party, was denied a permit and then outlawed in 1961. The first honorary president of the National Union was Wassila Ben Ammar, whom Bourguiba married in 1962.

After 1963, the Destour was the only legal political party. The membership rolls grew to some two million, and soon party branches became the only visible form of communal association. Electoral legislation, gerrymandering, intimidation, ballot stuffing, and selective distribution of voting cards promised Bourguiba winning margins of 90-98 percent. In 1975, Bourguiba revised Article 40 of the constitution, declaring himself "president of the republic for life." Despite this maneuver, and despite the absence of any credible opposition, Bourguiba's domestic practices were rarely questioned by his Cold War allies, who accepted his self-presentation as modern, Westernized, and democratic. Ben Ali, who served as prime minister and interior minister in the 1980s, took advantage of Bourguiba's weakness, ousting him in 1987 in what is often called a medico-constitutional coup. Ben Ali had Article 40 altered, adding the condition that presidency for life could last only as long as the president was mentally and physically capable to serve. He then called in doctors to affirm that Bourguiba was incapable. State propaganda subsequently glorified the coup as "the change."

When Ben Ali moved into the presidential palace, he promised to follow through with "change," starting with political pluralism and enforcement of constitutional limits on terms in office. To distance himself from the Destour and its legacy, he re-baptized the party in 1988 as the Constitutional Democratic Rally (in French, the Rassemblement Constitutionel Democratique, or RCD). Nonetheless, he was the only candidate in the 1989 and 1994 presidential elections, in both of which he received over 99 percent of the vote.[1] In 1999, he got over 99 percent again, despite having permitted two minor politicians to run against him in a sop to his mild foreign critics. With the constitution limiting the president to three terms in office, Ben Ali's parliamentary allies amended this clause in 2002, so that the only limit was the candidate's age, with the maximum set at seventy-five. Running in 2004 and again in 2009 with more handpicked opponents, he received 94.5 percent and 89.6 percent of the vote, respectively, and when the protests broke out he was preparing to modify the constitution yet again in advance of the 2014 poll. As for the parliament, the commission drafting the electoral lists was appointed by the RCD, which also ran the polling stations and counted the ballots behind closed doors.

In the wake of Ben Ali's flight to Saudi Arabia, interim premier Mohammed al-Ghannouchi, caretaker president Fouad Mebazaa and several of their minister colleagues resigned from the RCD, and the party's central committee was dissolved. In addition to demanding employment and economic change, the demonstrators called for the RCD to be dismantled completely and then banned. Even those steps, however, did not automatically consign the everyday practices of one-party rule to the past. The new government coalition between the al-Nahda party and Moncef Marzouki's Congress for the Republic (CFR) is an important step toward power-sharing, but both the transitional government and the al-Nahda-CFR coalition have sought to impose limitations on public demonstrations and periodically censored the internet. In order to sustain popular legitimacy, the new government must produce concrete solutions to high unemployment, invest in the impoverished rural interior, and make a clear break from the repressive policing tactics of the Ben Ali regime.

Patrons and Clients

Over the years Ben Ali also developed ways of consolidating power outside the realm of formal politics, seeking to capture economic resources, often at the expense of ordinary Tunisians. The best example of this phenomenon is the National Solidarity Fund, known by its account number 26-26. Founded by the president in 1993 as a program of rural development underwriting improvements to infrastructure such as electricity lines, roads, and health clinics, the Fund was kept afloat by an undisclosed portion of the state's annual budget as well as contributions from the general public. In principle, these contributions were voluntary. Civil servants paid the equivalent of one day's salary per year, farmers chipped in 1 percent of their annual profits and business owners contributed an amount tied to the number of people in their employ. The major trade union of artisanal craftspeople signed an agreement stipulating an annual contribution as well. In practice, the donations were not optional. Those who refused to donate faced all manner of difficulties in their routine dealings with the state bureaucracy, as well as the threat of audits of tax records and other forms of overt harassment.

Meanwhile, the Fund's record in the field is disappointing. Critics have pointed out the cracks in the hastily paved rural roadways and the holes in the expanded electrical grid: There is still no electricity for families who cannot afford to pay the monthly bills.

The main problem with the Fund, however, was its utter lack of transparency. The Fund was under the direct authority of the president, who alone managed it, and kept no accounts. According to official estimates, the Fund collected an average of $15-16 million per year in the late 1990s, yet the few economists who have attempted to calculate their own figures surmise that businesses alone contribute between $24-38 million on an annual basis. While state-run stations have televised the occasional home repair, and boasted of the number of families assisted, the better part of the Fund's income is thus unaccounted for.[2] Monies were also distributed in an arbitrary, clientelist manner under the aegis of the RCD. Committees of residents in the disenfranchised zones served in a consultative role, but the decisions about who received the funds were made by RCD deputies and elected officials who were members of the party.

Ghannouchi and old opposition figures returning from exile all vowed to take clear steps toward transparency in government and eliminate corruption from the highest echelons of power. Tunisians had heard these impassioned speeches before, and the proof of course is in the pudding. In a country where corruption and clientelism have governed behavior for so long, it is not obvious that even sincere political change at the top will be able to uproot them.

Cyber-Dissent

Perhaps the most encouraging front of the ongoing tumult in Tunisian society is freedom of expression. With Ben Ali and the RCD omnipresent, Tunisians have long struggled to make their voices heard. Newspapers were owned by members of the "First Family" and were self-censoring, while foreign dailies that were at all critical of the regime did not arrive at kiosks. Journalists who did speak out, such as Tawfiq Ben Brik, were hounded by the police, frequently arrested and often chose exile. The government, of course, wrote the content of most radio and television broadcasts, and even attempted to limit the programming accessible on satellite television. On one occasion in the summer of 2002, while an exiled opponent was speaking on an Arabic-language station based in England, power was cut throughout the capital. Tunisian dissidents increasingly turned to the Internet, but there a similar scenario applied, with the unique server in the country controlled by the government.

When Internet cafes sprang up in Tunis and other cities in the late 1990s, Zouhair Yahyawi created one of the first open forums online for discussion and debate. In mid-2001, his site TuneZine featured political cartoons, the occasional parody of the president (referred to by his initials as ZABA), commentary pieces from Tunisians across the political spectrum and an open letter to the president from his uncle, Mokhtar Yahyawi, an outspoken judge. The younger Yahyawi posted a poll asking visitors to the site if Tunisia was a democracy, a kingdom, a prison or a zoo. The majority said it was a prison. In response to Tunisia's first cyber-dissident, the regime arrested him in 2002, throwing him in jail, where he was subject to ill treatment and torture. Released late in 2003, in poor health due to prison conditions and a hunger strike he had undertaken while he was imprisoned, Yahyawi died of a heart attack in March 2005. He was thirty-six.

Over the past decade, the regime grew more and more adept at policing the Internet. Cited as one of twelve countries in the category of "Internet Enemies" by Reporters Without Borders, Tunisia was also ranked third on a Forbes magazine list of "the world's most Net-repressive regimes." The government regularly blocked access to the webpages of opposition groups, exiled dissidents, and human rights organizations, as well as a number of blogs, YouTube, and DailyMotion. Applying sophisticated software, the regime presented a user trying to view those sites with a standard "404 Error" message on the screen. More recently, the government adopted the tactic of "phishing," sending out fake e-mail messages designed to harvest the passwords for the Facebook pages and blogs of activists and then deleting the content.

The online censorship extended to the work of Tunisian rappers, who used their medium to complain of hunger, the unequal distribution of wealth and police brutality. In the spring of 2006, four teenagers in the western town of Kef were arrested for downloading an MP3 of a rap song critical of police violence. Though they were minors at the time, they received sentences of three to four months in prison. In January 2011, Hamada ben Amor, a twenty-one-year old rapper from Sfax, was arrested and detained for three days. One of his songs, "President, Your People Are Dying," had become the unofficial soundtrack of the protests, whose participants affectionately nicknamed him "El Général."

Despite the crackdown, the Internet was used strategically by the protesters to spread word of demonstrations, as with several in Bouazizi's town of Sidi Bouzid that were covered cursorily or not at all by state-controlled media. As was customary when there were protests in the south and west of the country, the police had closed off the roads leading in and out of the city. In response to the wave of state phishing expeditions, an anonymous hackers' collective threw its support behind Tunisian cyber-activism in an "Operation Tunisia" that successfully broke into and disabled several government websites. The government answered by making a number of webpages available only in Tunisia, and on January 6 arrested three bloggers, Hamadi Kalutcha, Slim Amamou and Aziz Amami, to dissuade others from writing personal online journals.

After Ben Ali's departure, Slim Amamou was released and accepted an interim cabinet position as secretary of youth and sports. Formerly blocked sites are now accessible, the newly promoted editor of the major newspaper al-Sabah is a person less known for being under the thumb of Ben Ali's son-in-law al-Materi, and formerly banned books published by Reporters Without Borders and Tawfiq Ben Brik had appeared in at least one bookstore before the end of January. Yet Tunisians continued to be skeptical of official media and the misinformation campaigns sponsored by the interim government. As for Internet censorship, Amamou tweeted from a meeting with the ministers of interior and communications that it may be harder to undo than he had imagined, since technicians who answered to Ben Ali personally had access to the infrastructure of the Internet. It is unclear what the precise technical problems are, but Amamou subsequently said that he was unblocking the censored websites one by one.

Islamists and the War on Terror

Both Bourguiba and Ben Ali were masters at exploiting the so-called Islamist menace to crush various forms of political opposition and garner foreign aid. In the 1980s, when Rachid Ghannouchi first organized under the banner of the Islamic Tendency Movement, the movement's base of support was middle-class, urban, and young. Ghannouchi, a schoolteacher with a degree in philosophy, took pains to make clear his support for democratic process. Accused by the regime of being Iranian agents, the movement was steadily alienated from the political system, however. Under Ben Ali, it removed any reference to Islam from its name (in accordance with state regulations banning religion from politics) and became the Renaissance Party, or al-Nahda. Still, it was denied official recognition.

After Ben Ali had orchestrated his first sham election as president, he offered a panoply of new excuses for not legalizing al-Nahda. And then Algeria's dirty war began. Similar to al-Nahda, Algeria's Islamic Salvation Front (FIS) voiced its intent to participate in democratic government. The FIS won a number of municipal elections in 1990, a clear sign of Algerians' dissatisfaction with their own one-party rule, which dated from their independence from France in 1962. In 1992, with national elections imminent, the FIS was poised to make major inroads into the ruling party's monopoly. The army intervened, canceling the elections and banning the FIS. Much of the ensuing civil war was a macabre performance directed by the state and the military. Not only did the regime label any opponent (such as the army sub-lieutenant who assassinated the president in 1992) an Islamist sympathizer, but security forces infiltrated—if not founded—the the Armed Islamic Group that was the Islamists' main combatant force. The military perpetrated attacks against civilians that were blamed on Islamists, of which the massacre at Bentalha is only one example. Eyewitnesses in Bentalha point the finger at the army, which was present during the massacre, refused to intervene on civilians' behalf and even prevented residents from fleeing.

Assassinations and full-blown civil war across the western border of Tunisia provided Ben Ali with ample reason to renew the crackdown on al-Nahda. Arson at the RCD's office in Bab Souika, a working-class neighborhood in the capital, was blamed on al-Nahda, though according to Amnesty International the guilty party was never solidly established. In any case, the regime used the fire to justify mass arrests, with an estimated eight thousand people imprisoned between 1990 and 1992. Many of them were tortured; at least eight deaths were reported.

After Algeria calmed down, the September 11, 2001 attacks in New York and Washington presented Ben Ali with another perfect opportunity to silence political opposition to Western applause. Tunisia enlisted in the US-led war on terrorism, and its activities stretched far beyond the domain of al-Qaeda and its supposed local affiliates. The regime deployed the police force to hassle women wearing the headscarf, for instance, denying entry to campus to veiled students. The police also followed men out of mosques and on one occasion blocked the streets surrounding the Sahib al-Taba' mosque in the Halfaouine neighborhood of Tunis in order to round up worshippers at Ramadan prayers. As Human Rights Watch wrote in its 2007 country report, "The government uses the threat of terrorism and religious extremism as a pretext to crack down on peaceful dissent." With the assistance of the Pentagon, which provides training to Tunisian forces, the regime arrested hundreds of youths on suspicion of involvement in terrorism, only rarely charging them with specific crimes.

As Jeremy Keenan has meticulously demonstrated, the Algerian regime has manu-factured much of the present "Islamist threat" in North Africa, which goes by the name of al-Qaeda in the Islamic Maghrib. Keenan has documented, for example, that the 2003 kidnapping of thirty-two European tourists in the Sahara, attributed to al-Qaeda's North African franchise, was coordinated with the complicity of the Algerian military and secret police. By opening a new front in the war on terrorism in northern and western Africa, the US intended to secure army bases and access to natural resources, including petroleum and natural gas in Algeria and Nigeria. The Algerian regime, for its part, hoped to increase its international standing and obtain sophisticated military equipment.[3] It was thus sadly predictable that when Mohamed Bouazizi's dramatic suicide sparked a series of demonstrations, Ben Ali claimed it was all the work of terrorists and radical Islamists. Though al-Nahda is now the largest bloc in the coalition government, the war on terror-ism remains a key US interest in North Africa, the Saharan front in particular, and thus holds out the promise of continued aid flows. A small but active Salafi minority, and bands of hooligans, have ensured that Tunisia's secular middle class can continue to wave the specter of a feared radical Islamist takeover, polarizing public debate, and perpetuating the simplistic binaries of the Ben Ali era.

Aftermath

The near-comprehensive surveillance of political activities that followed the September 11 attacks was accomplished thanks to the bloated police force maintained by Ben Ali. In 2002, one human rights association estimated that the number of police officers was around 130,000, in a country with a population of 10.4 million. The current force is more than three times the size of the police under Bourguiba (who were about forty-thousand strong), and comparable to the ranks of police in France, with its sixty million inhabitants. Since job creation was not keeping up with unemployment, Ben Ali opened the ranks of the police to most anyone who came calling. Policing was attractive to young Tunisian men who wanted to marry and move out of their parents' houses, but had no other marketable skills that would enable them to save the necessary cash. While salaries were not high (and a number of police officers took second jobs under the table, many as cab drivers), Ben Ali's de facto jobs program served to inflate the number of officers to the present level. The working-class basis of at least certain sectors of the police force is evidenced by their joining in protests against the interim government on January 22 and by their demands to be unionized.

Ben Ali's reliance on the police to control other Tunisians persisted to the detriment of investment in the military, the classic guarantor of regime stability in the Arab world. The army's role in the December-January unrest that led to Ben Ali's ouster is the subject of intense interest and contradictory information. Though the reasons why the army was deployed but did not shoot remain unclear, there were signs that the army had long been hostile toward the president. It seems that a plot brewed against the Ben Ali regime in the spring of 2002. A plane crash that year killed the army chief of staff, Gen. Abdelaziz Skik, as well as thirteen other senior officers. That so many of the top brass were traveling in the same plane is seen as more than fortuitous for Ben Ali and his clan. An official inquiry into the cause of the crash has still not made its findings public.

In the immediate aftermath of Ben Ali's overthrow, Tunisians were preoccupied with the lack of security in the towns and cities. Snipers, said to be Ben Ali loyalists, plagued the inhabitants of the capital and other towns. In the absence of a police force that truly existed to serve and protect, ordinary citizens formed local community patrols to watch over their neighborhoods. Though a reconstituted police force slowly returned to the streets, and trials against those responsible for the January 2011 violence are underway, tear gas and batons have been repeatedly used against protestors; whether the wounded of the revolution demanding proper medical attention, or journalists protesting censorship. With the tourist sector taking a significant blow in 2011, and promised foreign aid slow to arrive, many of the economic problems that fueled the revolution continue to plague the country. Unemployment remains high, disproportionately so among college graduates, and in the towns and villages of the Tunisian interior. Though Ben Ali and members of his extended family have fled, the revolutionary demand for dignity, and the hope of improved living standards remain elusive for many Tunisians.

Notes

1. Vincent Geisser, "Tunisie: des élections pour quoi faire? Enjeux et 'sens' du fait electoral de Bourguiba à Ben Ali," *Maghreb/Machreq* 168 (April-June 2000).

2. For details, see Eric Gobe, "Politiques sociales et registres de légitimation d'un Etat néo-patrimonial: le cas tunisien, "in Monique Selim and Bernard Hours, eds., *Solidarités et compétences: idéologies et pratiques* (Paris: L'Harmattan, 2003) and Béatrice Hibou, "Les marges de manoeuvre d'un 'bon élève' économique: la Tunisie de Ben Ali," *Les Etudes du CERI* 60 (1999).

3. See Jeremy Keenan, *The Dark Sahara: America's War on Terror in Africa* (London: Pluto Press, 2009).

3. AUTHORITARIANISM AND CIVIL SOCIETY IN TUNISIA

CHRISTOPHER ALEXANDER

A disturbing rumor made the rounds during the summer of 1997 at the Cafe de Paris, the Hotel Africa and the other haunts of Tunisia's *classe politique*. Word had it that a constitutional commission was considering legislation allowing the government to revoke the citizenship rights of some political opponents. True or not, the rumor's existence—and the widespread belief that the government started it—said much about political life on the tenth anniversary of Zine El Abidine Ben Ali's "tranquil revolution."

Ben Ali's November 7, 1987 coup inaugurated the heady period of political reform that swept across the Middle East and North Africa in the late 1980s. The new president promised to establish the rule of law, to respect human rights and to implement the kind of democratic political reforms that Habib Bourguiba had steadfastly refused. Along with Algeria, Jordan, and Yemen, Tunisia rode the leading edge of what many hoped would be a wave of democratic transitions in the region. Ten years later, it would be difficult to find another country that has moved so far in the opposite direction.

Back from the Democratic Brink

That Tunisia stood at the forefront of political reform in the late 1980s came as no surprise to many observers. Since the 1960s, scholars had held up the small country as one of the region's best hopes for democratic politics. Tunisia's tradition of reform and openness, its Western-oriented elite and its progressive social policies suggested the kind of trajectory that would culminate sooner or later in multiple political parties, competitive elections, and respect for human rights. Moreover, state and society in Tunisia had developed what the historian Mohamed Hedi Cherif describes as a unique form of "self-regulation." During periods of economic or political crisis, Tunisians accepted a strong state that intervenes to restore order and prosperity. But that state also generated countervailing social forces that kept it in check when it became too powerful.[1] Against this backdrop, the prospects for political reform under Ben Ali seemed good. If the president balked at his democratic promises, Tunisia possessed the kind of muscular civil society that would force him to follow through.

During his first year in power, Ben Ali seemed bent on establishing himself as the country's most dedicated reformer. He amnestied thousands of political prisoners, revamped Bourguiba's Parti Socialiste Destourien (PSD) into the Rassemblement Constitutionel

Démocratique (RCD), abolished the state security court and the presidency for life, reformed laws governing pretrial detention and ratified the United Nations' convention on torture. Ben Ali also supported new legislation that made it easier to form associations and parties, and he negotiated a National Pact with the country's principal social and political organizations.

By late 1988, however, the bloom had begun to fade. Ben Ali refused to legalize al-Nahda, the country's largest Islamist organization even though the party pledged to accept the rules of competitive democracy. And despite opposition demands for proportional legislative elections, the 1989 electoral code maintained the old majority list system. Those rules, combined with restrictions on media access and other interferences, allowed Ben Ali's RCD to win every seat in the April 1989 elections.

Those elections marked the end of Ben Ali's honeymoon and the beginning of Tunisia's slide into deeper authoritarianism. Angered by their exclusion from parliament despite strong support for their candidates who ran as independents, al-Nahda activists intensified protests at the university and in working class neighborhoods. The government, in turn, stepped up its repression against al-Nahda and the Tunisian Communist Workers' Party. Late-night raids and house-to-house searchers became commonplace in some neighborhoods. Stories of torture under interrogation and military court convictions multiplied.[2] The campaign to crush al-Nahda intensified in 1991 following an attack on an RCD office in the Bab Souika area of Tunis and after the government claimed that security forces had uncovered a plot to topple the regime. Susan Waltz reported that the government's extensive dragnet hauled in more than eight thousand individuals between 1990 and 1992.[3]

Most Tunisians tolerated the government's repression. As the press never ceased to remind them, a vigorous economy that could generate new jobs depended on Tunisia's ability to attract foreign investment in a competitive regional environment. Ben Ali and other officials pointed to Algeria and Egypt and argued that tolerating any kind of Islamist party would lead only to economic chaos. Better to be done with them quickly and create the kind of stable investment climate that Tunisia's neighbors could not provide. In terms of Cherif's model, the 1989-1992 period seemed to offer another example of Tunisians' willingness to accept a strong state that claimed to act on behalf of national wellbeing. By late 1992, Tunisia had reached an important crossroads. Economic growth had climbed above 8 percent, and most observers agreed that al-Nahda no longer posed a serious threat. Some portion of the rank and file certainly remained. But for all practical purposes, al-Nahda had become an offshore operation sustained by supporters in Europe and North America. By his fifth anniversary in power, Ben Ali could legitimately claim to have saved Tunisia from economic bankruptcy and civil war.

Many opposition figures had held their fire during economic and political crisis. Once those crises passed, they called on the government to make good on its earlier promises. This pressure did move Ben Ali and the National Assembly to pass a new electoral law in December 1992, but it only allowed the legal opposition parties a pitifully small share of seats.

At the same time, however, Ben Ali stepped up his campaign to quash any form of opposition. Some of the methods for coopting and manipulating the press, unions, and other organizations harkened back to the Bourguiba days. But Ben Ali's authoritarianism betrayed the kind of heavy-handedness that students of Maghribi politics generally associated with Algeria and Morocco rather than Tunisia. Between 1987 and 1997, Ben Ali dramatically expanded Tunisia's internal security apparatus. Critics claimed that much of this growth took place outside of the Interior Ministry and other official police forces. They argued that Ben Ali used a slush fund, labeled the "sovereignty fund" in the budget, to build up a parallel security apparatus run directly from the presidential palace.

Along with the Interior Ministry, this organization implemented a ruthless campaign whose tactics ran from surveillance and phone tapping to fabricated videocassettes, threats against family members, passport confiscations, beatings, and even assassinations.[4] In addition to rank and file workers, human rights activists, and university professors, this strategy targeted some of Tunisia's most prominent opposition figures.

Tunisia's growing authoritarianism challenged prevailing analyses of repression and state-society relations in the country. Why did a government that worked hard to establish a reputation as a bastion of human rights and civil liberties, and one that had eliminated serious political opposition, feel compelled to intensify its repressive methods? Why did this authoritarian turn fail to generate a countervailing "civil society" response? Had Ben Ali broken Tunisia's self-regulating system?

These questions relied on two pieces of conventional wisdom. The first was the widely held impression that Ben Ali was essentially Bourguiba redux. Although similarities existed, important differences distinguished the two leaders' strategies for consolidating and holding power.

The second piece of conventional wisdom was the equally popular notion that Ben Ali's political strategy—including the repression—was simply a product of the fight against al-Nahda. Although Islamists were the regime's single greatest preoccupation, it is misleading to reduce Tunisian politics under Ben Ali to a simple state versus Islamist dynamic. Ben Ali always viewed al-Nahda as part of a broader and more complex political game and there is good reason to believe that this game involved players that Ben Ali feared as much or more than al-Nahda.

A Tale of Two Regimes

In the struggle for Tunisian independence, Habib Bourguiba emerged as the nationalist movement's principal spokesman and negotiator. But he was not its only source of power and influence. Indeed, he survived a serious threat to his position as the Neo-Destour's leader in 1955-1956 only with the support of organized labor and other key party officials. As Tunisia's first president, Bourguiba consolidated control over the party and state bureaucracies by coopting and manipulating clientele networks in ways that would concentrate power in his own hands without alienating his bases of support. Rather than becoming Tunisia's sole political patron, he set out to become its chief patron.

Bourguiba accomplished much of this through an ongoing game of political musical chairs. He intentionally gave and withdrew important posts to powerful individuals who could use their positions to service their own clienteles. In this way, Bourguiba established himself as the maker and breaker of political careers. He created tangible incentives for loyalty that consolidated his personal power much more effectively than a system based solely on repression and fear. Bourguiba also recognized early on that protest and contesta-tion could play an important role in the effort to coopt individuals and organizations. In the 1950s and again in the mid-1980s, Bourguiba discreetly supported worker unrest designed to undermine the union leadership. On both occasions he supported breakaway unions, and then reunited the labor movement under leaders who owed their positions to Bourguiba rather than to the rank and file. He tried unsuccessfully to use this same tactic to bring the Tunisian Human Rights League to heel in the mid-1980s.

Bourguiba was not the only politician who exploited popular unrest. Indeed, the inter-mingling of elite politics and popular protest became a staple of Tunisian political life after the government established a prime ministership in 1969. Party elites also quietly encour-aged unrest as a way of discrediting competitors, then tried to negotiate alliances with the student and worker movements in order to secure a popular base for their own ambitions. Getting the militants to back off allowed politicians to demonstrate their ability to deliver social peace.

The onset of Bourguiba's health problems in 1967 sparked a great of deal of speculation and jockeying for position in a system that lacked a clear successor and a method for choosing one. In addition to relieving himself of the more technical tasks of government, Bourguiba used the prime ministership as a tool for turning this elite competition to his advantage.

At his direction, the National Assembly passed legislation that gave the president the power to select the prime minister and designated that person as the automatic successor if the president died or became incapacitated. By establishing his personal control over the succession, Bourguiba reinforced his power by creating what William Zartman aptly describes as "position politics."[5] Rather than building alliances against Bourguiba, party barons conspired against one another to earn his favor and a chance to become prime minister. As Bourguiba aged, Tunisian politics devolved into a collective wager on his mortality. Everyone wanted either to be prime minister or to be on good terms with the person who was when Bourguiba passed on. Through the early 1980s, this intricate politi-cal theater channeled elite competition away from Bourguiba. And while the radicalization of the labor movement in 1977 demonstrated that he could not completely control this messy game, two factors did help Bourguiba to keep social conflict from spinning totally out of control. First, strong economic growth in the 1970s supported a succession of wage increases and an extensive system of consumer subsidies. Second, the worker and student unions' reliance on public funds allowed Bourguiba to intervene in and manipulate their internal politics.

By the mid-1980s, these conditions no longer obtained. Economic deterioration eroded the government's ability to buy social peace. Bourguiba became less tolerant of labor's wage demands and cracked down hard on the General Union of Tunisian Workers (UGTT) in 1984 and 1985. The Islamic Tendency Movement—al-Nahda's precursor—stepped into the void created by the union repression and became the social force that politicians publicly reviled and privately courted. But the Tendency was an independent entity whose clandes-tine organization provided few openings for external manipulation. For Bourguiba, allow-ing it to become a force that elites courted was too risky. His campaign to destroy the Tendency set Tunisia on the course that brought Ben Ali to power in 1987.

Thus, the vibrancy of Tunisia's civil society and its ability to generate pressure on the state in the 1970s and early 1980s did not reflect a deep-seated political culture. Rather, it was a product of pragmatic political choices. Bourguiba's strategy for consolidating and holding power created new opportunities for protest, and workers, students, Islamists, and others tried to use them to their own advantage.

Ben Ali's strategy for consolidating and holding power produced a very different state-society relationship. Unlike Bourguiba, Ben Ali did not rise to power at the forefront of a well-organized movement. Prior to becoming interior minister in 1986, Ben Ali had spent his entire career in the military and security forces. When he seized power, he stepped into the void at the center of a paralyzed political system. The deepening economic and political crisis had discredited the ruling party's traditional elite. Internal divisions and government repression had crippled the opposition parties and other organizations.

These conditions gave Ben Ali a degree of freedom that Bourguiba did not enjoy. He faced no organized challenge and he did not have to court or compensate powerful constituencies that had contributed to his rise. Most Tunisians were simply relieved to see Bourguiba ushered offstage with minimal trauma.

At the same time, however, Ben Ali realized that this freedom from the entanglements of traditional party politics could be an important handicap. This fact raises a central point for understanding Ben Ali's authoritarianism. Battling al-Nahda was the government's primary focus during the first ten years of Ben Ali's rule. But this was precisely the kind of contest for which Ben Ali was eminently qualified. From the 1970s on, he had supervised Bourguiba's successive crackdowns on labor, students, and Islamists. This experience, and those of other countries in the region, suggested a simple, sober lesson. The Islamists would become a serious threat to his position if he followed Chadli Benjadid's example in Algeria and offered them access to the ballot box. But if he played to his strengths and remained committed to destroying al-Nahda, he could probably win.

A revival of position politics, on the other hand, would have posed a much more serious threat. Many long-time party barons resented Ben Ali for preempting their own plans for stepping into the presidency. From the beginning of his rule, Ben Ali feared that one of these established politicians, or one of his own ministers, would use their networks in the party, the state bureaucracy, and other organizations to undermine him. As a relative newcomer to ruling party politics, Ben Ali lacked the social bases and patronage networks so vital to Bourguiba's style of political management. He did not have the political resources to referee and manipulate effectively an ongoing competition between powerful politicians and the social actors they rallied to their camps.

To protect his own position, Ben Ali tried to do two things. First, he worked to prevent state and party officials from developing into centers of power that they became under Bourguiba. He abolished the office of party director—a position of considerable power in the 1970s—and reduced the autonomy of his ministers. His dismissal of Hedi Baccouche in 1989 after the prime minister's public criticisms of the structural adjustment program demonstrated that Ben Ali would not tolerate a subordinate who showed any sign of becoming a power in his own right. Throughout his cabinet, Ben Ali carefully selected individuals who were technically competent but came from non-political backgrounds or lacked extensive connections in the ruling party or the state bureaucracy. He involved himself in the operations of individual ministries much more deeply than Bourguiba ever had, and he used frequent cabinet shuffles to prevent ministers from establishing lasting clientele bases.[6]

Second, Ben Ali worked diligently to break the tie between elite and popular politics that was to vital in the 1970s and 1980s. Ill-equipped to play position politics, he tried to ensure that "civil society" remained unavailable as a political weapon.

Initially, Ben Ali relied on old fashioned cooptation, exercised with considerably less finesse than his predecessor, to put the opposition parties and other organizations on short leashes. Outright repression became more important after evidence emerged in 1989-1990 of a broad opposition front built around former Prime Minister Mohammed Mzali and other longtime Destour politicians. In April 1990, the political bureau of a group calling itself the Tunisian National Salvation Front issued a communiqué claiming to represent all opposition groups inside and outside of Tunisia. The communiqué condemned with equal vigor the government's repression of everyone from Bourguiba to the Communists and al-Nahda. It called on all democrats, regardless of ideology and affiliation, to unite in a common effort. From his new headquarters in London, al-Nahda's leader, Rachid Ghannouchi, made a similar comment that urged Ben Ali to establish a meaningful, multi-party democracy.

This challenge became Ben Ali's chief concern in the late 1990s. He became terribly afraid that this front, headed by former politicians with extensive ties throughout the country, was conspiring to unseat him. Ben Ali feared that this front would establish alliances with al-Nahda, the Tunisian Human Rights League, militant portions of the labor and student movements, the legal opposition parties, and anyone else who might provide a useful striking arm against him. From his perspective, then, a strike, a student demonstration, or an opposition communiqué could be much more than it appeared to be. Because any kind of contestation could be organized and manipulated by the opposition front it must be repressed.

This repressive strategy stunted Tunisia's formidable civil society. Most obviously, it elevated the risks of engaging in protest and made collective action much harder to organize. Beyond this climate of fear and intimidation, Ben Ali's effort to break the connection between elite and popular politics also created a profound strategic malaise for the organizations that long constituted the bedrock of associational life. As elsewhere in the region, the struggle for meaningful autonomy from state control dominated the lives of workers' and students' unions, human rights groups, women's groups, and Islamist organizations in post-independence Tunisia. At the same time, though, these organizations always understood that the line between state and civil society was blurry at best. For more than thirty years, establishing alliances with individuals and factions of the governing elite and playing on tensions within party and state bureaucracies had been a fundamental part of these organizations' strategies for influencing government policy. The dissolution of these ties, the end of position politics as it operated for so long, left Tunisia's traditionally vigorous civil society adrift.

To be sure, adrift does not mean broken. Pressure from the legal opposition parties helped to prompt electoral reform. The UGTT reduced some of the social costs of privatization and economic reform. The Tunisian Human Rights League fought valiantly to protect its independence and to make respect for human rights a value that the government must at least profess to support. These accomplishments are not trivial.

But the remaining years of Ben Ali's rule continued the schizophrenic combination of reform and repression that marked the first ten years. Ben Ali continued to repress criticism and contestation that he did not orchestrate. The legal opposition parties continued to participate in an electoral system that was stacked against them because it was the only game in town and because it gave them an opportunity to build their own organizations. They worked to slowly expand their foothold in the National Assembly, and the Tunisian Human Rights League continued to press the government on human rights. Ultimately, this scenario did not produce the kind of multi-party democracy that Ben Ali promised.

Notes

1. See Ridha Kéfi, "L'équilibre carthaginois," *Jeune Afrique* 1837 (March 20-26, 1996), p. 73.

2. For a revealing and disturbing account of this campaign, see Ahmed Manai's *Supplice tunisien: Le Jardin secret du Generale Ben Ali* (Paris: La Decouverte, 1995).

3. Susan E. Waltz, *Human Rights and Reform: Changing the Face of North African Politics* (Berkeley, Calif: University of California Press, 1995), p. 72.

4. The Tunisian National Salvation Front described the organization and activities of this parallel security apparatus in an April 1990 communiqué. A copy of the text appears in *Annuaire de l'Afrique du Nord* (1990), pp. 804-09.

5. See Zartman's introduction to I. William Zartman, et al., *Political Elites in Arab North Africa* (New York: Longman, 1982). See also Lisa Anderson, "Democracy Frustrated:The Mzali Years in Tunisia," in Reeva S. Simon, ed., *The Middle East and North Africa: Essays in Honor of J. C. Hurewitz* (New York: Columbia University Press, 1990), pp. 185-186.

6. In a surprisingly frank 1992 *La Presse* article, Mohsen Toumi openly criticized Ben Ali for becoming too involved in the daily details of government and for fearing a prime minister with a clear and decisive role. See "Nos mille huit cents jours," *La Presse*, November 9, 1992. I thank Chedly Ayari, former minister of national economy, for his insights on the difference in the status and power of ministers under Bourguiba and Ben Ali.

4. STRUCTURAL ADJUSTMENT AND RURAL POVERTY IN TUNISIA

STEPHEN JUAN KING

World Bank and IMF sponsored neoliberal reforms can have different effects on the political and social structure of receiving nations. Reforms may fortify a status quo unfavorable to the poor, or may even make a bad situation considerably worse, or they may undermine the existing economic system, empowering the poor to participate more actively in new market arrangements. Officially, World Bank policy supports rural projects leading to greater equality, including land reform, and denies aid to countries that have not instituted such policies. In Tunisia, however, the World Bank supported projects that concentrated land holdings and favored large landowners. Neoliberal reforms, in general, rendered Tunisia's peasantry less secure and more impoverished.

Conventional structural adjustment theory locates the greatest equity gains from economic reform in the countryside, primarily the privatization of communal and state-owned land, mechanization, and export-oriented crop production. Yet several factors contribute to growing inequalities within rural areas during agricultural economic liberalization. Land policies frequently increase the disparity of asset distribution. Agricultural policies fail to sufficiently integrate the landless and land-poor into export-led growth. Economic and political power figure strongly in the resolution of conflicts created by new tenure and other market arrangements. National government officials and local bureaucrats implementing reforms may place political considerations and rent seeking opportunities ahead of economic efficiency and equity. Truly representative farmers' organizations and other parts of civil society rarely participate in the process of determining economic reform policy, which transforms the lives of rural dwellers. Taken together, in many countries, these factors culminate in policies that favor rural elites, increase rural asset disparities, and make no serious efforts to alleviate rural poverty.

As early as the mid-1970s, the World Bank was well aware of the potential problems that accompany liberalizing reforms and produced many studies to address them. In 1975 the Bank published "The Assault on World Poverty," a document establishing that Bank policy should support rural projects that redistributed land downward and deny aid to those countries that did not pursue such policies. (The authors did, however, allow an exception for funding projects in which "a major share of the benefits [of land rights] accrue to high-income groups" if they dramatically improved agricultural production and the fiscal health of the government.) That same year, the Bank issued a land reform policy paper that laid out three key principles to guide its evaluation of projects: the desirability of owner-operated family farms on both efficiency and equity grounds; the need to promote markets to benefit more efficient producers; and the desirability of an egalitarian asset distribution and redistributive land reform.[1]

In spite of these policy guidelines, there was little evidence that land reform issues affected lending by the Bank. When it came to implementing liberalizing policies, officials realized that any reforms that helped the poor while imposing costs on the wealthy would encounter resistance whether or not they increased national income.[2] Ensuring the adoption of market reforms trumped considerations of those policies' impact on equity for most of the World Bank's funding activities.

Equity Versus Patronage

The Bank's theoretical emphasis on greater equality in rural assets as a macroeconomic good was based on extensive literature indicating that smaller holdings were more productive than larger ones in terms of output per unit of land. Extra human effort on small farms, through the use of cheaper family labor, was the main source of this superior productivity.[3] Family-operated farms did not bear the supervision costs of managing wage labor and enforcing effort required by large-scale operations.[4] Further, subsidy programs and greater access to credit for purchase of land and machinery, tended to favor large farms. Such structural advantages rendered the effective price of land higher for small farms than for large ones and reinforced the former's more extensive use of labor—often as a substitute for expensive equipment.[5] Policies that favored small producers could thus capitalize on the precarity of small farmers to produce more with fewer resources.

These same factors often encouraged large landholders to leave land fallow or otherwise not exploit agricultural land to its fullest. They might, for example, cultivate only those parcels that had the best soil. Large farms also limited production to avoid flooding a local market with a certain product (thus driving down prices) or to avoid unsellable surplus. Small farmers were much less likely to cut output, because they were rarely in a position to monopolize a market and any surplus could usually be consumed by the household. For elites, land also had uses beside production-based income, such as political power, prestige, or speculative gain. Large landholders did have their defenders among development economists. Advocates for large-scale agriculture argued that estates were better able to use machinery efficiently and that their owners, who tended to have more education, were better poised to employ new techniques and technologies. Pro-equity economists countered that this dynamism was the effect of market advantage, and that "the main policy implication is that the channels for credit and modern inputs to small farms should be improved—not that a large farm structure is essential for the adoption of new techniques."[6] The World Bank, which emphasized developing countries' need for agricultural productivity, shared this view and aimed to discourage land non-usage through policies that emphasized smaller farms.[7]

Yet from its start in 1986, the World Bank's agriculture lending in Tunisia favored the agrarian upper class. The rural bourgeoisie and their urban representatives were the most important clients of the Habib Bourguiba and Zine El Abidine Ben Ali regimes. Bourguiba and many cadre of the Neo-Destour Party belonged to a new generation of elites from the rural east whose liberal, technocratic education often put them at odds with the urban religious establishment of the Destour Party. Indeed, the creation of the Neo-Destour Party in 1934 was financed by large landowners and rural merchants who objected to the colonial government's fiscal policy during the global economic depression of the 1930s. This constituency was a crucial source of political support during the independence struggle and in the decades of postcolonial state-building. From the beginning of the structural adjustment program, this class dominated struggles over state patronage.[8]

Privatization

The World Bank's agricultural sector loan supported privatizing agricultural cooperatives under the rubric of improving the management of natural resources.[9] The dictates of structural adjustment thus offered Tunisian officials the opportunity to liquidate state-owned cooperatives that were draining public coffers, while also strengthening their bonds with rural notables by ceding them land. The program began with long-term leases of twenty-five to fifty years that were later converted into outright sales. According to the official narrative, the process of leasing public land involved three steps. First, a list was published in all major newspapers of production cooperatives available for leasing. An address was provided to which detailed project proposals could be submitted. Second, officials in the Ministries of State Land and Agriculture reviewed the applications and consulted at the local level in deciding who would win the contracts. Third, the state, with its administrative branches, supervised the implementation of the proposals by the *Sociétés de Mise en Valeur* (improvement companies). In practice, however, the review process was opaque and state landholdings were run with little if any supervision.

In all, nearly one million hectares of state land was transferred to large landholders between 1986 and 1996. Despite projections (and hope) of new employment opportunities on these privatized farms, there was no net job creation in agriculture under Tunisia's structural adjustment program.[10] Typically, the first step taken by the new managers of former state lands was to downsize by dismissing large numbers of agricultural laborers. Displaced peasants held no illusions about the root of these developments in state policy:

> The workers have become beggars! Why? The sun shines on everyone. Normally the state looks after us all. Why give the land to the rich? They already have land! If you give them more they will no longer think of the poor. What are they going to do with more, buy another car? It's no good. You find people with one thousand hectares while others won't even have one hectare. The poor wanted land. Some farmers before got land and they're doing well. In the early 1970s, a small amount of state land was distributed to former cooperative workers. If you have connections you can get land.... Those who were fired like me always go the administration asking for work. We tell them "you fired us, so give me something to buy bread." Nothing happens.

Estate owners also benefited from below-market input prices as well as credit and technological support from the state while only modest-to-poor efforts to improve small farmers' access to credit and inputs was undertaken. With these subsidies, large landholders were able to turn more easily to lucrative export crops such as garden vegetables, oranges, and dates. These crops typically required refrigeration and other resources that small farmers lacked. Indeed, the prices for rain-fed crops and livestock produced by the poor actually dropped during this period.[11] In the mid-1990s, poor farmers confronted a crisis in government price policy for olive oil. Prices were declining internationally, and it was difficult to find export markets. The state slashed the base price of olive oil by 40 percent in 1993. This not only erased the real price increases that producers had enjoyed since the mid-1980s, it also reduced the price to about 15 percent below the lowest real price since 1980. The impact on rural incomes was dramatic, affecting not only the owners of olive trees but also the seasonal laborers whom the orchard owners could no longer hire to harvest and prune.[12]

In addition to selling state-owned land, the structural adjustment program called for the privatization of the rural commons. There had been 2.7 million hectares of communal land in Tunisia, divided evenly between crop- and rangeland. As these properties were divided and sold, the informal land rights of the poor were superceded by a private titling system that did not recognize their claims. Procedures to resolve land disputes could be initiated at the local level, but their ultimate disposition occurred only at the top of the administrative hierarchy by the Director of Land Affairs, a branch of the Ministry of Agriculture in Tunis.[13] The Bank's acknowledgement that enclosing the commons removed an important "base of income stabilization and generation" for the rural poor, some of whom only farmed or raised animals in lean times, did not affect its lending policies.[14]

"Trickle Down" Development

Overall, the World Bank policies adopted in Tunisia supported successive regimes determined to favor the interests of large landowners over those of the small-scale, low-income peasantry. Amidst the typically robot-like language of Bank documents, one can even discern traces of Bank officials' frustration with Tunisian state agents in this regard: "The government is expressly not distributing these lands to improve the land assets of the rural poor."[15] Nevertheless, later Bank documents put a positive spin on the adopted land policy, arguing that leasing scheme was "extremely successful (more intensive cultivation, diversified production, exports, and profits). The authorities may wish to consider expanding the the leasing program and reassessing the costs and benefits of selling state lands to the private sector as another supporting measure in the establishment of an agricultural land market."[16]

In subsequent years, some of the theoretical justifications for the structural adjustment programs of the 1980s reverted to a "trickle-down" approach, arguing that any economic growth ultimately aided the rural poor. Some theorists went so far as to argue that there was little need for sensitivity to equity in adjustment policy. Since "almost everyone" in Africa "is poor on any objective basis...the fact that adjustment programs may not directly benefit the absolutely poorest should have far less policy and moral implications than if there were a bias in a rich country. If adjustment programs help a significant number of people...then inevitably a large number of the poor will be helped."[17] Government officials took advantage of donor agency and academic pronouncements that structural adjustment benefited all income groups in the agricultural sector; echoing these claims, they undertook a policy that in reality benefited their powerful allies.

Official statements indicate that the Bank partially accepted Tunisian officials' arguments that large-scale farms would increase productivity and modernize commercial farming techniques.[18] Yet Bank policy guidelines and a welter of statistical data contradicted this view. Bank documents only acknowledged that "unequal distribution of land, the lack of title and land rights, and the fragmentation of land contribute to the persistence of rural poverty"[19] to a degree. Where difficulties or failures were mentioned, the blame was placed on political elites, with little acknowledgement of the Bank's considerable leverage with regard to its own funds. Since these documents were abundant and easily available to Bank officials, the funding process reflects a substantial gap between rhetoric and practice within the Bank.

An interview with a Bank official revealed that the Bank conceded to Tunisian officials' desires to distribute state lands to wealthy Tunisians because the amount of land was relatively small and the Bank hoped to win other struggles with state agents. The primary goal for the World Bank in Tunisia into the late 1990s was to ensure the privatization of public enterprises, most of which were located in urban areas.[20] Ultimately, the World Bank's projects in Tunisia compromised on equity goals in rural areas in order to keep Tunisian economic and political elites on the path of privatization and a reformed market economy. The end result, however, was the enforcement of a development program of questionable efficiency that facilitated an increasingly neotraditional rural social order:

> How could they give all that land to those people? If I had one hectare, I could produce more than five or six hectares' worth! I work summer and fall only. How can I live on six months of work? I may work one week or two weeks with a cow owner until he sells the milk, and then I have to hit the road. He has 20,000 dinars and I have 10 dinars. I have a brain like you and him. Why is it that workers always stay workers? My boss may have 30,000 and when I ask for a loan I may get 20 dinars. Why should someone live below zero while others drive expensive cars? The owner's wealth, even his cars, came from us. I have a brain and blood and I work, but I can't even buy boots for the winter's rain.

Notes

1. Klaus Deininger and Hans Binswanger, "The Evolution of the World Bank's Land Policy: Principles, Experiences, and Future Challenges," *World Bank Research Observer* 14 (August 1999): p. 50.

2. World Bank, *World Development Report* (Oxford: Oxford University Press, 1990).

3. Michael Lipton, *Why Poor People Stay Poor* (Cambridge: Cambridge University Press, 1997).

4. M.C. Jensen and W.H. Meckling, "Theory of the Firm: Managerial Behavior, Agency Costs, and Ownership Structure," *Journal of Financial Economics* 3 (1976): 305-360.

5. R. Albert Berry and William Cline, *Agrarian Structure and Productivity in Developing Countries*, (Baltimore, Md.: Johns Hopkins University Press, 1979), p. 6-30.

6. Berry and Cline, *Agrarian Structure*, p. 27.

7. World Bank, *Republic of Tunisia: Growth, Policies and Poverty Alleviation* (Washington, D.C., 1995); World Bank, *World Bank Development Report 2000/2001*, (Washington, D.C., 2001).

8. For an argument to this effect, see Stephen J. King, "Economic Reform and Tunisia's Hegemonic Party: The End of the Administrative Elite," *Arab Studies Quarterly* 20 (Spring

1998).World Bank, "Republic of Tunisia, Agriculture Sector Adjustment Loan: Medium-Term Agricultural Sector Adjustment Program," (Washington, D.C., 1986).

9. World Bank, *Growth Policies and Poverty Alleviation.*

10. World Bank, *Republic of Tunisia Poverty Alleviation: Preserving Progress while Preparing for the Future,* (Washington, D.C., 1995).

11. Ibid, p. annex C.3,1.

12. Harold Lemel, *A Land Tenure Profile for Tunisia,* (Madison, Wis.: Land Tenure Center, University of Wisconsin, 1985).

13. World Bank, *Republic of Tunisia Poverty Alleviation,* p. annex C.3,7.

14. Ibid., p. annex C.3,6.

15. World Bank, *Tunisia's Global Integration and Sustainable Development,* (Washington, D.C., 1996), p. 39.

16. Jeffrey Herbst, *The Politics of Reform in Ghana* (Berkeley, Calif.: University of California Press, 1993).

17. World Bank, *Growth, Policies and Poverty Alleviation,* p. 7.

18. Ibid, p. 7.

19. World Bank, *Tunisia's Global Integration and Sustainable Development* (Washington, D.C., 1996), p. xv.

5. THE MAKING OF TUNISIA'S INTIFADA

LARYSSA CHOMIAK AND JOHN P. ENTELIS

As the waves of protest inspired by Tunisia rolled across the Middle East and North Africa, analysts were puzzled by the mysterious timing, incredible speed, and cross-national snow-balling of these uprisings or *intifadas*. In the six months following the electrifying scenes of thousands occupying Avenue Habib Bourguiba in downtown Tunis, directing the impera-tive *Dégage!* (Get out!) at President Zine El Abidine Ben Ali, the Tunisian "virus" spread across the region, unleashing apparently similar moments of resistance and revolution.

The back-door story is one focused on those who made the revolution, not those dealing with its consequences. In Tunisia, the nature of autocratic rule and its relationship to citizens created the environment in which challenges to regime incumbency would lead to protest, resistance or revolution. The deeper and more robust the authoritarian structure, and the fewer the opportunities for legal political opposition and participation, the more likely citi-zens are to rebel. The virtual absence of viable opposition social movements in Tunisia in the two and half decades of Ben Ali's rule smothered participatory politics to near extinction. When the autocratic state collapsed, it left a void in which demands for systemic reform were quickly transformed into revolution.

Tunisia Before Bouazizi

One of the distinctive characteristics of Ben Ali's Tunisia was the virtual absence of an effec-tive social movement. Almost from its inception, the Ben Ali regime outlawed the leading political currents on both ends of the ideological spectrum, the Islamist al Nahda party and the Tunisian Workers' Communist Party, building a de facto monopoly for its party, the Constitutional Democratic Rally (RCD). In so doing, the regime nearly eliminated any possibility for opposition movements willing to work within the system to operate legally and freely. Yet there was ample expression of dissent through the everyday activities of ordinary people. Tunisia's disenfranchised masses developed mechanisms for dodging the tentacles of the authoritarian state, including tax avoidance, illegal tapping of municipal water and electricity supplies, and illicit construction of houses. Within this atmosphere of circumvention, moments of contentious politics nonetheless occurred, eventually leading to the precipitous puncturing of Ben Ali's system of control.

The short history of Tunisia's revolution commonly begins with the self-immolation of a young Tunisian food cart worker by the name of Mohamed Bouazizi from the south-central town of Sidi Bouzid, just north of the mining city of Gafsa. It is thought that Bouazizi's dramatic public act was caused in part by the almost daily humiliation of ordinary Tunisians confronting an uncaring and often deeply corrupt bureaucracy. Bouazizi's plight, many believe, represented the frustration of thousands of Tunisia's young lumpen-intelligentsia, often overeducated but underemployed, facing an uncertain economic future at a time of rapidly increasing food prices.

Following Bouazizi's self-immolation on December 17, 2010, riots indeed spread across the rural south. Ben Ali ordered police to quell the unrest. Within days, documentation of police violence was disseminated via the Internet, including the social networking sites Vimeo, Facebook, and Twitter, while the pan-Arab satellite network Al Jazeera spearheaded in-depth television coverage of the disturbances. As these images swept across the country, Tunisians became incensed at the sight of unarmed protesters being brutalized by police. More social media challenges to the regime were unleashed, none more symptomatic of the character of the revolution-to-come than the song of the rapper El General, "Rais el Bled." After El Général posted the song on his personal Facebook page, authorities quickly arrested him. For their part, web-savvy residents of Tunis, Sfax, and other large cities quickly formed Facebook groups calling for solidarity against the Ben Ali regime.

By this time, protests had moved to the capital and the regime's end was imminent. The army's commander, Gen. Rachid Ammar, disobeyed orders from Ben Ali to shoot at protesters even as the army rumbled into cities and towns. Ben Ali tried to appease the populace, paying a visit to Mohamed Bouazizi's hospital room just before his death and delivering a series of three public addresses, each less combative in tone than the one before. He concluded with a pledge that he would not run in the 2014 presidential election and subsequently promised to reduce censorship, lifting restrictions on YouTube and DailyMotion on January 12. By then, however, hackers organized as "Operation Tunisia" had already shut down Ben Ali's presidential website, his Facebook page, the Tunisian stock market website and other government portals. Within hours, the General Union of Tunisian Workers (UGTT) called for a strike and two million Tunisian Facebook users changed their profiles to read, "*Ben Ali dégage!*" Many furiously stated that over one hundred protesters should not have had to die for YouTube to be unblocked. One day later, on January 14, thousands took to the streets in downtown Tunis and occupied the broad Avenue Habib Bourguiba. Facing the notorious Interior Ministry, opposite the towering, ultra-modern RCD headquarters, the inflamed crowd yelled epithets at the hated dictator. Within hours, Ben Ali had fled to Saudi Arabia, after both Malta and France denied him asylum.

The front-page version of Tunisia's revolution was accurate, but incomplete to the point of being somewhat misleading, in that it provided a mechanistic portrayal of a repressive state pitched against a quiescent population that suddenly exploded. To be sure, resisting Ben Ali, his one-party state and the mafia-like clan that surrounded him was no easy task. Deepening repression—from arbitrary economic barriers to jailing, disappearances, and torture—achieved a widespread political inertia just short of absolute submission. Nonetheless, courageous Tunisians engaged in episodic contention, notably in the southwestern mining town of Gafsa close to the Algerian border. The year 2008 was an especially hot one in Gafsa and nearby Redayef, as street protests began in January and February against unfair hiring and labor conditions imposed by the state-run phosphate company. In an area where unemployment hovers around 40 percent, people looking for work believed that the company had worked out nepotistic arrangements with the local UGTT branch in violation of an agreement with the national federation. Yet, the street protests, which began as labor actions, soon attracted unexpected levels of support and proliferated across the whole of the Gafsa governorate.

The weekly protests in Redayef were not reported in the state-controlled press, though opposition papers such as *al-Mawqif, al-Muwatin,* and *al-Tariq al-Jadid* gave full coverage to the events. The waves of protest also caught the attention of university students on campuses in Tunis, Sfax, and Sousse, as well as among the Tunisian diaspora in France and Montreal. Many of the supporters were members of the illegal Workers' Communist Party or its student wing, and committed to supporting the plight of Tunisians in the impoverished rural south. Within days, local schoolteachers, women, wives of miners, marginalized youth, and even local union branches joined in. A targeted demonstration against unfair hiring practices on the part of a local phosphate monopoly had expanded into a broad movement attracting local, national, and international adherents.

As was to happen in 2010-2011, Ben Ali ordered security forces to quash the 2008 protests, arresting hundreds of demonstrators, even children, and torturing jailed suspects. Catalyzed by the use of excessive force, greater numbers of Tunisians engaged in peaceful anti-government protests. For its part, the government justified its brutal tactics by branding opponents as "coup makers" intent on overthrowing the state—language that was to be repeated on the eve of the regime's collapse. In April 2008, wives of imprisoned workers, widows of others, and union members took to the streets in Redayef, while activists organized a day of solidarity in Tunis on April 4. As clashes continued sporadically over the spring, the military occupied Gafsa and Redayef, fatally shooting two protesters in June. Internet activists in Tunis, Gafsa, and Sfax began spreading the mining towns' story on Facebook, reacting to the virtual non-reporting in the Tunisian press and the blocking of all international news sites that covered the events. On August 18, Ben Ali ordered that Facebook be shut down, citing national security concerns. (The regime's narrative that Facebook in Tunisia was a tool used primarily by Islamist terrorists resonated among less critical observers for years, particularly following the April 11, 2002 bombing of a synagogue on the island of Jarba by al-Qaeda in the Islamic Maghrib.[1]) But the regime was compelled to unblock the social networking site less than a month later following an international pressure campaign on Facebook. By 2010-2011, activists in Tunisia were well schooled in Internet campaigns as well the Ben Ali regime's responses to them.

Tunisia in White

One of the last instances of contentious politics preceding the revolution was a protest organized by six young activists via Facebook and Twitter called Tunisie en Blanc (Tunisia in White) on May 22, 2010. "This Saturday," the participants promised each other on their Facebook pages, "I will dress in white and have coffee on the avenue," in a peaceful demonstration against Internet censorship in Tunisia. The plan consisted of two parts: a protest in front of the Ministry of Technology in downtown Tunis as well as something resembling a white-clad flash mob sipping coffee in one of the many cafés on Avenue Habib Bourguiba.

Tunisia in White was a bold initiative by young activists to mobilize around an issue that

affected the daily life of hundreds of thousands of Tunisians. So pervasive was the censorship that Tunisians created an imaginary character named Ammar as a metaphor for the
invisible gremlin impeding their online communications. One of the organizers of the campaign was Slim Amamou, who has devoted years to fighting Internet censorship in Tunisia.
His nickname "Slim 404" refers to the ubiquitous error message indicating that a site is
blocked or censored.[2] Amamou and others involved in the initiative were later prominent in
the revolution against Ben Ali. He was arrested on January 6, 2011 for dissident blogging,
but then appointed minister of sports and youth after Ben Ali's fall. Even earlier than 2010,
some of these activists had navigated the censorship and police harassment directed against
Internet mobilizations, for instance the nationwide support groups for the Gafsa protests.
Relying primarily on Facebook, the activists used a medium that was shielded from the government's censors. To ensure the wide dissemination of the Tunisia in White campaign, the
activists launched the event just days before the planned activities. On May 17, a Facebook
group named Day Against Ammar appeared, and approximately five thousand Tunisians
clicked on "Like" to spread the word, as did diaspora Tunisians in Paris, Montreal, New
York and other cities across the world. The page described the Tunisia in White event as a
peaceful and citizen-oriented effort pressing for a free Internet in the country. As Tunisians
were guarded under Ben Ali, the organizers stressed:

> Do not hesitate to invite your friends. There is nothing illegal about dressing in white and having coffee on
> the avenue. There is nothing illegal about demanding Internet access free of censorship. The demonstration
> will be held in front of the Ministry of Technology and Communication but if you do not want to or cannot
> attend, meet at a café dressed in white and simply have coffee.

On May 21, a day before the planned event, two of the organizers were detained at the
Interior Ministry, where they had attempted to obtain approval for the protest. Another
organizer's Facebook account was disabled, forcing peers to resort to Twitter to communicate with supporters. Tunisia in White never fully came about, as the police dispersed those
individuals who showed up at the avenue's cafes dressed in white. The event, nonetheless,
provided important training for future Internet campaigns and marked out a public forum
for political debate.

The unrest in Tunisia before the revolution reveals multi-faceted political mobilizations
that transcended the categories of ideology, formal organization and charismatic leadership
long associated with revolutionary transformations, whether democratic or not. Existing
opposition movements, legal and otherwise, were willing to collaborate to challenge incumbent rule. Most analyses of the uprisings, finally, begin at the moment when thousands of
ordinary citizens occupied central urban plazas in the glare of the global media. It is important to start the timeline earlier and enter the stories of the *intifadas* through the back door.

Notes

1. See, for instance, Saloua Charfi, "Tunisie: Terreur Intégriste sur Facebook," *Réalités*, April
22-28, 2010.
2. *Guardian*, January 18, 2011.

6. BEYOND GHANNOUCHI: ISLAMISM AND SOCIAL CHANGE IN TUNISIA

RIKKE HOSTRUP HAUGBØLLE AND FRANCESCO CAVATORTA

On October 23, 2011, for the first time since independence in 1956, Tunisians were called to the polls in free and transparent elections. They were to choose 217 members of a Constituent Assembly that for a year would play a double role: drafting a new constitution and governing the country.

For many Tunisians, as well as foreigners, the results were something of a surprise. First, the turnout was lower than expected, hovering just over 53 percent, despite serious efforts by the Electoral Commission to get out the vote. Many ordinary Tunisians, it appears, are skeptical of the political transformation in the country since the ouster of Zine El Abidine Ben Ali. Second, the victory of the Islamist party al-Nahda was much larger than antici-pated. Opinion surveys taken beforehand had predicted the party's first-place finish, but with a vote oscillating between 20 and 28 percent of the total. In the end, al-Nahda obtained 41.7 percent of the vote and, more significantly, won eighty-nine seats in the Constituent Assembly, by far the largest bloc. Third, secular, and leftist parties put in a solid performance (though not up to expectations), but their divisions split the secular electorate. No party except al-Nahda, therefore, garnered more than 8 percent of the ballot.

While these results were a bit startling, the subsequent negotiations to form a govern-ment were reasonably straightforward. al-Nahda ended up in a three-party coalition with the Congress for the Republic, led by Moncef Marzouki, a left-wing nationalist party that came in second with twenty-nine seats, and Ettakatol, a social democratic party that finished fourth with twenty seats and is helmed by Mostapha Ben Jaafar. Throughout the campaign, al-Nahda maintained it would seek a broad alliance with other political forces to signal Tunisians that partisanship would be put aside. It was the job of all political groups, sym-bolizing a unified nation, to draft the constitution and usher in the new era, said al-Nahda figures. On December 22, 2011 the new government was approved. The three-party agree-ment stipulated that Hamadi Jebali, secretary-general of al-Nahda, would be prime min-ister, Marzouki would be president and Ben Jaafar leader of the Assembly. The agreement also provided for the creation of forty-two senior and junior ministerial posts: nineteen slots would go to al-Nahda, including the Ministries of Interior, Justice, Education, Health, and Foreign Affairs, six to the Congress, six to Ettakatol, and eleven to independents chosen for professional ability in their respective fields. Finally, the coalition partners agreed to go their separate ways in constitutional debates without paralyzing the government. The Assembly quickly adopted a decree, the "small constitution," that will regulate government operations until a new national charter is drafted.

The immediate post-Ben Ali order in Tunisia has no exact parallel anywhere, but the French semi-presidential system was clearly influential on the provisional institutions while the Constituent Assembly debates the form of government to be adopted for the future. In practice, the president, chosen by the Assembly, appoints the prime minister and the two then work together on major policy decisions under the Assembly's scrutiny. This arrangement might slow deliberations at a time when very important decisions have to be made rapidly in several fields, particularly reform of the security services and the economy, but the advantage is that such major decisions will enjoy a reasonably broad consensus.

In any case, the election results and the institutional arrangements that followed leave al-Nahda in position to shape Tunisia's future.

Explaining al-Nahda's Sweep

That fact, combined with al-Nahda's religious references, makes many secular Tunisians and foreign observers uneasy. Many also wonder where al-Nahda's sweeping victory came from, given that the party was illegal before March 2011 and had been the target of relentless repression for three decades.

A number of explanations have been advanced to account for al-Nahda's success. First, it is said that al-Nahda was very quick and skilled in reorganizing its structures across the country after Ben Ali fell on January 14, 2011. This view found partial affirmation in a conversation with Abdelhamid Jelassi, a member of al-Nahda's Executive Committee, who argued: "Given that we are an old party, we have been able to revive our structures immediately after the revolution in January. Militants who were in prison for a long time started working for the party again, together with those who had operated underground." A second explanation refers to the party's reputation as an uncompromising opposition movement during the Ben Ali era. A third focuses on the weaknesses of the other parties, with one writer contending that "the large secular parties' reliance on advertising and reluctance to meet voters outside of the major cities made it difficult for undecided, rural voters to put their confidence in them. The majority of Tunisians showed…that al-Nahda not only understood their preferences, but also that Tunisian voters cannot be taken for granted and should be reached out to directly."[1] Fourth, some attribute the appeal of al-Nahda to its constant quest for a democratic national "consensus" on the key institutional matters. The party's emphasis on democratic principles may have reassured swathes of the population who might otherwise have doubted its commitment to pluralism. As Ali Laaridh, an Executive Committee member who is now minister of interior, said: "In terms of organization, the party's philosophy is about democratic principles, which are enshrined in our statute and the way in which the party is structured.…The whole structure of the party is very much the product of the wishes of the fee-paying members." Tunisia, he went on, should be governed in the same way. Finally, the party is said to have swayed many voters with pledges of job creation and replication of the successful Turkish model of economic development.

All these explanations are valid to a degree, but each has the shortcoming of being contingent upon the immediate circumstances of the elections themselves. Without a longer-term analysis, it is difficult to explain why the party did so well—and why it looks and acts as it does. The organizational skills theorem ignores two factors: First, many younger people with no connection to historical al-Nahda joined after Ben Ali fled the country, bringing their own interpretations of what it means to work for and support an Islamist political project. Second, other parties that had operated underground or in exile were not similarly effective. The personal histories of al-Nahda figures do not make them uniquely credible to Tunisians, as the cases of Marzouki and Ben Jaafar demonstrate; leftists also suffered years of jail and banishment. Secular parties campaigned competently enough to compel the tripartite coalition government that is in office today. As for campaign promises, al-Nahda's did not particularly stand out—all parties promised to generate economic growth and new jobs.

Analyses of al-Nahda's victory to date have missed the crucial element of long-term social change, in particular the unexpected return to religiosity by large sectors of Tunisian society since the 1990s.

New Social Forces and Islamic Value

al-Nahda is not a classic opposition actor or even a traditional political party, one run from the top down that takes advantage of a sudden opening in a political system that previously was tightly controlled. It was the bottom-up activism of ordinary citizens, much of it near spontaneous, that carried the party so far, so fast. Party leader Rafik Abdessalim, now minister of foreign affairs, recognizes this reality: "In 1989, many of the leaders and members went into exile, while four thousand were in prison....Before January 2011, there were no offices, no public activities, no visible signs of al-Nahda...so the structure of the party today is a product of people's engagement. You cannot explain everything based on the organization itself and on the idea that what should be done is dictated from the top. Local people are opening local offices of al-Nahda. It is not the top of the party opening these offices. It is based on people on the ground." From this premise, it follows that al-Nahda is best understood as a broad movement with multiple constituencies that subscribe to an Islamic ideal that developed during Ben Ali's rule, under the radar of the regime. These constituencies had few or no ties with the al-Nahda of the 1980s, the outspoken Islamist movement of Rachid Ghannouchi, the historical leader who flew home from exile shortly after Ben Ali's dictatorship ended. They have strong feelings, however, about al-Nahda as an idea of what public life and political engagement should be. The party's political project has been, and to some extent still is, built from below as a continuation of the re-Islamization of society under Ben Ali.

More than twenty-five years have elapsed since al-Nahda's last chance to operate openly—and the country has changed dramatically in that duration. Three phenomena are noteworthy in this respect: the emergence of a pro-market middle class at ease with much of Western modernity; the enunciation of a stronger Arab Muslim identity that deviates from the Western-inspired and particularly French-inspired project of modernization in post-independence Tunisia; and the parallel emphasis on Islam as personal piety.

During the twenty-five years of al-Nahda's proscription, Tunisia went through a neo-liberal economic transition, with much of the state sector turned over to private hands. Privatization and the wider embrace of market economics were profitable for Ben Ali's cronies from the beginning, and were implemented in part to strengthen authoritarian rule.[2] But these policies also managed to achieve considerable economic growth, leading to improvements in education standards, health, and other indices of human development, particularly during the first decade of Ben Ali's rule.[3] The French president, Jacques Chirac, may have been mistaken to speak of a "Tunisian miracle," but Tunisia did emerge from Ben Ali's reforms with a larger and newly entrepreneurial, globalized, and educated middle class. By the 2000s, however, the Tunisian economy had degenerated into a predatory system, with members of the presidential clan and close collaborators wielding both patronage and repression to acquire larger and larger slices of the pie. The middle class and businesses unconnected to the regime were squeezed. Tunisia, in many ways, became a mafia state—the workings of which are well described by journalists Nicolas Beau and Catherine Graciet in their exposé *La Régente de Carthage*, published in 2009. The avarice of the presidential elite not only undermined economic performance, but also aggrieved traditional merchant families, who were forced to share profits with the palace, and the emerging middle class, some of whom fell back into quasi-poverty. One response from the ranks of this middle class was fresh interest in Islamic values as a counter to the crass, corrupt, and soulless consumerism of their rulers.

Somewhat independently, Tunisia experienced a revival of the daily practices of Islam, in both rural and urban settings, in part because the regime frowned upon displays of religiosity. The regime's suppression of a strong Arab Muslim identity from 1956 onward was carried out in the name of modernization, but Islam's disappearance from public life did not mean that all Tunisians abandoned the faith as part of their identity. In fact, Islam was an important component of the independence movement itself, at least for the wing led by Salah Ben Youssef. The hardline secular Habib Bourguiba defeated Ben Youssef's faction, but many people retained a strong religious element within their interpretations of the country's history. Over time, Bourguiba's measures of French-style *laïcité*—the ban on the veil in public buildings, including schools and universities, the creation of an elitist, French-only education system based on *grandes écoles*, the state's absorption of the Zaytouna mosque-university—provoked increasing animosity in society. In the early 2000s, a religious reawakening began to offer a model of Arab Muslim identity that promoted values often associated with Western modernity, such as tolerance and self-improvement, and recast those values as forming the core of Islam. The new identity model was a rejection of both Bourguiba's, which excluded Islam from public life, whether policymaking or regular communal prayer, and the Ben Ali regime's, which seemed to celebrate conspicuous consumption and corruption in the name of progress.

Along with the revival of Islamic practice came careful attention to the moral issues raised by the modernizing efforts of the regime, as well as globalization. While such modernization brought about certain benefits, many Tunisians felt it also put on display a degree of amorality, notably that of the ruling classes. Since public space was monopolized by the regime, there was greater emphasis on personal morality and comportment, particularly in the form of stricter adherence to religious ritual like fasting during Ramadan or regular mosque attendance. Crucially, pious Tunisians also became more involved in social activism, which was perceived not only as a religious duty, but also as an ethical choice implicitly condemning the regime as unethical. This trend was strengthened by the spread of satellite dishes across Tunisia picking up speed around 2000 and the launch of Islamic satellite channels such as al-Majd and Iqra. For many, access to satellite dishes also meant access to interpretations of Islam that had previously been denied.

Circles of Conviction

Gradually, these vectors of social change came together in an attempt to influence public life. One powerful example is the Qur'an association called Riadh Ennasr, founded in 2007 in Cité An-Nasr, a middle-class suburb north of the capital of Tunis. The six co-founders, all men under forty, lived in Cité An-Nasr—an upper middle class area where many nouveaux riche moved to escape the increasing poverty of the capital[4]—but were alienated by what they felt was its hollow, consumerist culture. One of the founders explained that the spark for the association was the realization that the neighborhood "lacked values and warmth." The local imam parroted the regime's line and thus lacked the moral qualities that believers should expect and demand. To better themselves, and lead by example, they decided to create a space where people could meet, under the guidance of various religious scholars, to learn to read the Qur'an properly. This project reinforced their own identity as pious Muslims, but it was also social activism in the sense that they believed better training in the Qur'an would spur others to rediscover a genuine Muslim way of life and improve the neighborhood. Implicit in the association was a critique of what seemed to be the dominant values in Tunisia, namely consumerism, corruption, and a more general loss of self. The founders felt that Tunisians could cultivate an identity of their own—one that combined the best of what they saw coming from the West and the best from Islam. By April 2010, eighteen hundred people had signed up for reading classes, twelve hundred of them women.

In the battle with the regime for the soul of Tunisia, women were of course strategic terrain—with the veil or headscarf the immediate objective. A 1986 decree stated that it was forbidden to wear the veil in public. The ban was kept in force by the regime with regular campaigns directed against women who defied it. The controversy over the headscarf came to a head in 2006. That year, during Ramadan, the president and the minister of religious affairs declared that the veil was out of keeping with the Tunisian cultural heritage and national identity. Police stopped veiled women in the streets and told them to bare their heads. Many women kept on wearing the headscarf, however, presenting an increasing challenge to the regime.

The women attending the Qur'an classes in Cité An-Nasr range in age from twenty to sixty. Many are well educated, working as engineers, doctors or teachers. One woman, fifty-two, traced her motivation for attending the classes to practices she learned in her childhood: "My parents were practicing Muslims, so I have always heard the reading of the Qur'an and prayers in the house." Another woman of the same age explained, "Islam was present even then [under Bourguiba]. We learned the Qur'an at home because a sheikh came to our house." These memories recall a past when Arab Muslim identity was cherished; they also indicate that, under the radar, such practices always existed. The women felt a need to rediscover these practices to make sense of their own upbringing and identity. A woman in her late thirties emphasized that religious education was necessary "to really understand Islam. Before, we just practiced it. We prayed; we respected Ramadan; we knew the rules. But now we are also living within our convictions. My mother wore the veil, but I did not until two years before my wedding." All these sentiments are apolitical in isolation, but in the aggregate they highlight the yearning of many Tunisians to reconnect with an identity that they felt was being lost or misrepresented by the regime, particularly after the September 11, 2001 attacks, when Ben Ali seemed eager to equate Islam with terrorism as a means of pleasing the West. Together, therefore, the attendees of the Qur'an classes performed a political act.

The high attendance at the reading classes pushed Riadh Ennasr to branch out. They set up a kindergarten combining religious and other education with play. It met with over-whelming success, and the association had to acquire another building in the neighborhood to meet demand. Parents pressed the association to help them keep their children exposed to the kindergarten's educational approach. The solution was a cooperative agreement with an area private school to offer classes where children could continue to study Islam with their friends from the kindergarten. Previously, only state imams had given instruction in the Qur'an—at local *kuttabs* (Qur'anic schools) that pointedly scheduled classes on Sundays, which Bourguiba named the official day off to bring Tunisia into conformity with Western custom. The private school encountered considerable difficulties with the authorities when they applied for approval of a program including classes in the Qur'an. The principal, a woman, had previously been ordered to take off her veil if she wanted permission to run a private school. Rather than cancel the idea of Qur'anic instruction, the principal came up with the idea of offering the classes as "clubs" on a par with dance, drawing, and music clubs. It worked. One mother who chose the private school for her two children explained, "We know that our children will enjoy a good education if they are brought up within Islam and have solid moral values."

The 2011 revolution has freed these social forces that challenge the myth of Tunisian *laïcité*. An example is the Jarba Association for Solidarity and Development, which was established after the revolution by ten men and two women, many of them professionals, and all of them practicing Muslims in their forties with no experience of associational life. The founders explain that they had always talked about helping others as a duty at the core of their faith. Only after January 2011, however, did the law permit them to harness their spirit of social engagement, with a small initial budget of 24,000 Tunisian dinars (about $16,000). The group decided to use one third of the monies to help Libyans in distress during the war to topple the Qaddafi regime. One third would go to the poor during Ramadan, and the remaining third would be used to back entrepreneurs in Jarba.

Private Islamic activism has been on the rise in Tunisia for a decade, with a number of associations testing the monopoly of the regime over the public sphere and also, since the late 2000s, providing social goods. The civic engagement was partly a response to the state's retreat from welfare provision and widespread public corruption, but more importantly, it was a corrective to what Hamza Meddeb described as "the disappearance of the moral egalitarianism that the state had promoted under Bourguiba."[5] Left-wing secular forces the focused on economic woes, as during the 2008 uprising in mining district of Gafsa.[6] But for the rise of private Islamic activism, it was the linkage between ethics and Islam that mattered; their welfare provision was a counter to the immorality of the regime, a view shared by activists in wealthy areas such as Cité An-Nasr and in much poorer districts and towns. While the number of Islamic associations has grown after the revolution, the phenomenon is not a function of the fall of Ben Ali. It is characterized by an Islam that is deeply personal, centered on social activism rather than politics and dependent on local networks for support and expansion. The glue of these networks is a specific understanding and practice of Islam whereby religious precepts apply to those who choose them and are not imposed on the whole of the community. This shift in perspective has filtered up to the al-Nahda leadership, which has repeated professions of tolerance incessantly since being legalized, partly to reassure secular Tunisians, but partly to reflect the views and practices of its new members and supporters. As Tirad Labbane of Riadh Ennasr said: "Our commitment to Islam does not mean that we want to impose what we do on others. In that sense, you could say that we are anti-Salafi, because we do not approve of imposing behavior. If you want to wear a mini-skirt, it is not my problem; if you do not want to wear the veil, it is also not my problem. Choices have to be left to individuals; the state cannot impose behavior. From the state authorities we ask only that they let us do our work in peace."

Filtering Up

It would be misleading to draw a solitary bright line of causality between the Qur'anic associations and the Jarba charitable society, on the one hand, and al-Nahda's electoral triumph, on the other. But there is a clear resonance between the respective discourses and practices of the social activists and al-Nahda, and membership in the two circles overlaps. The social activism was flourishing years before al-Nahda was legalized and allowed to operate freely in 2011, suggesting that many party cadre and constituents come from the social activists' ranks and brought with them the experiences and values they had formed under Ben Ali's dictatorship.

It follows that there are echoes of the attitudes of the Islamist sector of society in the official positions of al-Nahda. The dimension of personal choice and individual piety, for instance, is notable in how al-Nahda members at all levels talk. "You cannot impose Islam on people. It has to be a personal choice, to come from the heart," explained a physician in Jarba, who supported al-Nahda. At the top, Jawhara Ehiss, a member of al-Nahda's office of women's affairs and a deputy in the Constitutional Assembly, underlines that Islam is a personal matter: "It is not the role of the state to give religious lessons and set religious rules." In this respect, the stated interest of al-Nahda coincides with that of many social activists, who simply want to be left alone by the state to pursue their task as they see fit. It is largely these younger middle-class activists, together with the older generation of militants returning from exile and coming out of prison, who have swollen the ranks of al-Nahda and contributed to its success. Their rallying to al-Nahda is not necessarily based on the party's policy statements or past record or on Ghannouchi's leadership, but on the assumption that it is the political actor whose beliefs are closest to their own.

These Tunisians are skeptical of any drive for a strong state. Young and old, the pious middle class rather supports the quest for a decentralized democracy with a thriving private sector. The new generation believes in free-market forces and wants to take advantage of the fall of the regime to expand the business opportunities they were denied under Ben Ali. (The anti-capitalist rhetoric for which al-Nahda was known in the 1980s has thus receded.) The older generation endured the repression of the strong, centralized state and wishes to break it up. It remains to be seen how these trends will weather the persistent economic challenges facing the country, which may require robust state intervention to solve. In a poll taken for the International Republican Institute in April 2012, 45 percent of Tunisians still believed that unemployment was the most important challenge facing the country.[7]

The other bond shared by old and new supporters is the attachment to religious values and practices that they believe should inform policymaking, but not dictate it. al-Nahda's decision to exclude references to *shari'a* in the new Constitution likely reflected this orientation, as well as the widely held belief that Tunisians must adopt shared rules as the country charts its democratic course.

Notes

1. Erik Churchill, "Tunisia's Electoral Lesson: The Importance of Campaign Strategy," *Sada*, October 27, 2011.

2. See Stephen King, *Liberalization Against Democracy* (Bloomington, Ind.: Indiana University Press, 2003).

3. See Antoine Sfeir, *Tunisie: Terre de Paradoxes* (Paris: L'Archipel, 2006).

4. We are grateful to Mohamed Zayani for pointing this out to us so clearly and effectively.

5. Hamza Meddeb, "La course à el khobza," *La Revue Economia* 13 (November 2011-February 2012), p. 50.

6. Amin Allal, "La 'reconversion' problématique du bassin minier de Gafsa en Tunisie: Réformes néolibérales, clientélismes et protestations en situation politique autoritaire," *Politique Africaine* 117 (March 2010).

7. This report is available at: http://www.iri.org/news-events-press-center/news/iri-releases-second-post-election-poll-tunisia.

PART TWO

EGYPT

"The people want the fall of the regime!" Over the course of eighteen days in January-February 2011, Egyptians made this slogan world-famous. In Tahrir Square in downtown Cairo, and in cities and towns across the country, millions of Egyptians rose up to demand the resignation of Husni Mubarak from the presidency, an office he had occupied for thirty years. Improbably, and after many twists and turns, they succeeded. Though the fuse of Arab revolt may have been lit by the events in Tunisia, it was the fall of Mubarak that fanned the flame.

Much of the groundwork for the Egyptian revolt was laid during the previous eight years of labor, student, and peasant strikes. Labor activism in Egypt has a long history, but a wave of strikes during the 2000s inaugurated a new era of militancy among Egyptian workers and professionals. Wildcat strikes in both public and private companies won a variety of concessions on pay, worker safety, and pension benefits. The cumulative pressure of thousands of strikes in a few short years led the state to raise the monthly minimum wage by 400 percent in 2010—though at $70, it was barely subsistence-level income. This period also saw the founding of four independent trade unions, signaling an important break with the state-run Egyptian Trade Union Federation.

The early 2000s also saw an increase in political demonstrations against the Mubarak regime's relationship to Israel and the United States in response to the wars in Afghanistan and Iraq, the physical re-occupation of the West Bank by the Israeli military, and Egypt's participation in the blockade of Gaza. These issues united diverse coalitions of activists including students, professionals, labor, and Islamist groups. A mass protest held in Tahrir Square against the invasion of Iraq in 2003 was a key precursor to the Square's occupation in 2011. Anti-war and Palestine solidarity activism spawned the Kifaya movement and other groups whose focus became domestic political reform.

As demonstrations took on an anti-government flavor, they were met with riot police and arrests. Yet the Mubarak regime tolerated a high degree of public dissent compared to other authoritarian regimes in the region. Egypt enjoyed a surprising level of press freedom and general access to media. There was little internet censorship and independent journals, magazines and satellite stations proliferated, though certain red lines limiting criticism of the government were enforced. Protests were usually confined to private spaces like universities and mosques, but the regime also worked to manage public demonstrations that did not target Mubarak or the government in order to give such frustrations a controlled outlet.

None of this relative openness negates the fact that Egypt was, and remains, a police state. Activists and journalists were arrested and tortured. The Interior Ministry oversaw a complex of police and intelligence agencies that dominated daily life, often by collecting protection money from local businesses, running drugs, and generally preying upon the population. The ministry also hired *baltagiyya* (plainclothes thugs) to terrorize protesters, intimidate voters, and otherwise supplement the organized violence of official security forces. Egypt's military, though an important element of regime power, operated with a degree of independence from Mubarak and his National Democratic Party (NDP). Many military officers were local power brokers capable of waiving compulsory military service or easing interactions with the state for the right price.

The law was another tool of repression under Mubarak, used to cudgel dissenting political voices and to institutionalize the power of the executive branch. Civil society groups were heavily restricted by laws controlling their funding and the nature of their operations. Anti-terrorism laws gave cover to the regime's attacks on Islamist groups such as the Muslim Brothers. (At other times, such as when the regime needed help containing popular protest, the Brothers often proved willing partners.) Constitutional amendments that strengthened Mubarak's power and undercut opportunities for political pluralism passed the NDP-dominated parliament easily. Egypt's semi-independent judicial branch provided a measure of resistance against the regime's aggressive legislating, but successful suits were rare and relied on a constitution drafted under Mubarak's predecessor Anwar al-Sadat.

An important legal victory for the opposition was mandated judicial supervision of elections beginning in 2000. Even with oversight, elections in Egypt were heavily scripted affairs: Sham opposition parties, ballot stuffing, and barricaded polling stations were par for the course. The only real opposition group in terms of popular base and organizational capacity was the Muslim Brothers, which was officially illegal. Brothers still managed to run for local and parliamentary elections as independents, and in 2005 won an unexpected eighty-eight seats (about 19 percent) in the People's Assembly. After this upset, the regime ensured that the 2010 elections returned a more definitive victory for the NDP, with the party and its "independent" affiliates winning 90 percent of seats in the lower house.

Presidential elections in Egypt were one-candidate referendums until 2005. During the first multi-party poll, the same irregularities and interventions that characterized parliamentary elections returned almost 90 percent of the vote for Mubarak. The next presidential election was to be held in May 2011, with Mubarak expected to run again. From the late 1990s forward, there was also speculation that Mubarak's son, Gamal, was being groomed to replace his father in the presidential palace. Gamal was integrated into the government and ruling party in various economic advisory roles, and was the public face of the regime's campaign of privatization and economic restructuring. Public distrust of Gamal was thus not motivated only by fear that Egypt might become a *jumlukiyya* (republico-monarchy), like Syria under the Asads, but also of the continuing neoliberalization of the economy that had impoverished so many in the preceding two decades.

Structural adjustment policies and privatization schemes begun under President Sadat and expanded under Mubarak left most Egyptians suffering from rising prices and stagnant or falling wages. Cutbacks in government spending weakened the public education and health systems, increasing costs for families. Price supports for staples such as bread and fuel shrank continuously. Unemployment compensation ended in the early 1990s at a time when over 8 percent of Egyptians (at the official, undoubtedly deflated rate) were without formal work. Unemployment only twice dipped below that rate over the next twenty years. State-owned companies were sold at a steady clip, with 40 percent of public enterprises fully or partially privatized between 1993 and 1999. Privatization of land for industrial agriculture and real estate development saw the consolidation of large tracts of land under wealthy families and corporations, both domestic and international. Traditional commons such as the lakes of the Nile Delta have also been subject to various enclosure schemes. Many of these reforms redounded to the benefit of high-ranking NDP members, the military (which operates a variety of industrial, energy, shipping, and real estate companies) and the business elite, while millions of ordinary Egyptians fell deeper into poverty.

The prospects for democratic reform in post-Mubarak Egypt are yet unknown. The military council that took power after Mubarak's departure moved to insulate its authority from any elected government through unilaterally-applied constitutional amendments that weaken the presidency and give the military veto power over the new national charter. The military was not able to engineer the presidential election of June 2012 for its preferred candidate, but the Muslim Brothers' acceptance of a largely disempowered presidency may be a more decisive victory in legitimizing the brass's backstage governing.

7. THE PRAXIS OF THE EGYPTIAN REVOLUTION

MONA EL-GHOBASHY

If there was ever to be a popular uprising against autocratic rule, it should not have come in Egypt. The regime of President Husni Mubarak was the quintessential case of durable authoritarianism. "Our assessment is that the Egyptian government is stable and is looking for ways to respond to the legitimate needs and interests of the Egyptian people," said Secretary of State Hillary Clinton on January 25, 2011.[1] With these words, Clinton gave voice to a common understanding of Egypt under Mubarak. Government officials, pundits, and academics, foreign and domestic, thought the regime was resilient—not because it used brute force or Orwellian propaganda, but because it had shrewdly constructed a simulacrum of politics. Parties, elections, and civic associations were allowed but carefully controlled, providing space for just enough participatory politics to keep people busy without threatening regime dominance.

Mubarak's own party was a cohesive machine, organizing intramural competition among elites. The media was relatively free, giving vent to popular frustrations. And even the wave of protest that began to swell in 2000 was interpreted as another index of the regime's skill in managing, rather than suppressing, dissent. Fundamentally, Egypt's rulers were smart authoritarians who had their house in order. Yet they were toppled by an eighteen-day popular revolt.

Three main explanations emerged to make sense of this conundrum: technology, Tunisia, and tribulation. Technological analyses celebrated young people who employed new media to defeat a stolid autocrat. By the second day of the Egyptian uprising, CNN correspondent Ben Wedeman was calling it a "very techie revolution." In the following days, every major news outlet framed the uprising as the work of wired, savvy twenty-somethings awakening the liberating potential of Facebook, Twitter, and the writings of American intellectual Gene Sharp. "For the world's despots, his ideas can be fatal," asserted the *New York Times* of Sharp.[2] A second category of explanation credited the Tunisian people's ouster of Zine El Abidine Ben Ali in mid-January with supplying a shining example to follow. Esam Al-Amin notes that the Tunisian revolution "inspired Egyptians beyond the activists or elites."[3] A third theorem focused on the many tribulations afflicting Egyptians, particularly soaring commodity prices, positing that hardship finally pushed the population to rise up against oppression. "Food: What's Really Behind the Unrest in Egypt," one Canadian newspaper headlined its story.[4]

None of these explanations are false. All of them correspond to interpretations of events forwarded by the participants themselves. And each has an impeccable intellectual pedigree, harkening back to two influential traditions in the study of popular collective action. One is the dramaturgical model, identifying a cast of self-propelled characters, armed with courage and a new consciousness, who then make an uprising. The second is the grievance model, by which an accumulation of social troubles steadily diffuses among the population and finally reaches an unforeseeable tipping point. The two models call attention to distinct but equally important forces: specific actors and generalized complaints. But both are oddly without context. Because aggrieved and heroic people exist under every type of political system, the models do not explain when such people will band together to challenge the conditions they deplore.

Egypt's momentous uprising did not happen because Egyptians willed it into being. It happened because there was a sudden change in the balance of resources between rulers and ruled. Mubarak's structures of dominion were thought to be foolproof, and for thirty years they were. What shifted the balance away from the regime were four continuous days of street fighting, January 25-28, that pitted the people against police all over the country. That battle converted a familiar, predictable episode into a revolutionary situation. Decades ago, Charles Tilly observed that one of the ways revolutions happen is that the efficiency of government coercion deteriorates. That decline occurs "when the character, organization, and daily routines of the population to be controlled change rapidly."[5] The organization and daily routines of the Egyptian population had undergone significant changes in the years preceding the revolt. By January 25, 2011, a strong regime faced a strong society versed in the politics of the street. In hindsight, it is simple to pick out the vulnerabilities of the Mubarak regime and arrange them in a neat list as the ingredients of breakdown. But that retrospective temptation misses the essential point: Egyptians overthrew a strong regime.

Strong Regime, Strong Society

Like his predecessors, President Husni Mubarak deployed the resources of a high-capacity state to cement his power. He handily eliminated all threats to his rule, from a riot police mutiny in 1986 to an armed Islamist insurgency in the 1990s to an over-ambitious deputy, Defense Minister 'Abd al-Halim Abu Ghazala, whom he sacked in 1989. He presided over the transformation of the economy from a command model with the state as primary owner to a neoliberal model with the state as conduit for the transfer of public assets to cronies. He introduced an innovation to the Egyptian authoritarian tradition as well, attempting to engineer the handover of presidential power to a blood relative, rather than a military subordinate. To manage social opposition to these big changes, Mubarak used the political arena to coopt critics and the coercive apparatus to deal with those who would not be incorporated.

Opposite this wily regime stood an ostensibly weak and fragmented society. Echoing the regime's own arguments, workers' protests, rural riots, electoral struggles, and any other forms of popular striving were explained away as economic, not political; local, not national; and defensive, not proactive. The little people had no politics. Thus spoke the political scientist and Mubarak loyalist 'Ali al-Din Hilal to a US diplomat, who in a 2009 cable reported that Hilal said, "Widespread, politically motivated unrest was unlikely because it was not part of the 'Egyptian mentality.'" Independent academics shared his view: "There could be a poor people's revolt if the state fails to provide food. But we must bear in mind that Egyptians rarely explode and then only in specific cases, among them threats to their daily bread or national dignity."[6]

The reality was that Egyptians had been practicing collective action for at least a decade, acquiring organizational experience in that very old form of politics: the street action. Egypt's streets had become parliaments, negotiating tables, and battlegrounds rolled into one. To compel unresponsive officials to enact or revoke specific policies, citizens blockaded major roads with tree branches and burning tires; organized sit-ins in factory plants or outside ministry buildings; and blocked the motorcades of governors and ministers. Take this small event in the logbook of popular politics from January 2001, one of forty-nine protest events recorded that year by just one newspaper. Workers at the new Health Insurance hospital in Suez held a sit-in to protest the halt of their entitlement pay. State security officers and local officials intervened, prevailing upon the authorities to reinstate the pay and fire the hospital director.[7] By 2008, there were hundreds of such protests every year, big and small. In June 2008, thousands of residents in the fishing town of Burg al-Burullus blocked a major highway for seven hours to protest the governor's abrupt decision to halt the direct distribution of flour to households. Police used tear gas and batons to disperse demonstrators, and ninety people were arrested.[8]

If one classifies Egypt's protests by the type of mobilizing structure that brings people out into the street, rather than the content of their claims, three sectors are salient, each with its own repertoire of tactics. The first is workplace protest, including collective action by industrial laborers, by civil servants, by students, and by trade practitioners such as auto mechanics and gold traders. The second is neighborhood protest, whether on the scale of a single street or an entire town. Protests by Copts, Sinai Bedouins, and farmers are often organized along residential lines. Associational protest is the third sector. The organizing mediums here are professional associations such as lawyers' and doctors' syndicates; social movements such as the pro-Palestine solidarity campaigns, the anti-Mubarak Kifaya movement, and the April 6 youth group; and the youth wings of political parties such as Ayman Nour's liberal Ghad, the Muslim Brothers, the liberal-national Wafd, the Nasserist Karama, and the Islamist Wasat.

Doing politics outdoors brought citizens face-to-face with the caste that rules the streets: Egypt's ubiquitous police. Mubarak's was not a police state because the coercive apparatus routinely beat and detained people. It was a police state because the coercive apparatus had become the chief administrative arm of the state, aggregating the functions of several agencies. Police not only dealt with crime and issued passports, drivers' licenses, and birth and death certificates. They also resolved local conflicts over land and sectarian relations; fixed all national and sub-national elections; vetted graduate school candidates and academic appointments at every level; monitored shop floors and mediated worker-management conflicts; observed soccer games and Friday prayers; and maintained a network of local informants in poor neighborhoods, to ensure that dispossession was not converted into political organization. Officers were free to work out their own methods of revenue extraction, sometimes organizing the urban drug trade.[9] Patrolmen routinely collected tribute from taxi and microbus drivers and shopkeepers, while high-ranking officers partnered with landowners or crony businessmen. When there was a riot or a road accident or a natural disaster, Egyptian police personnel were the first responders, not to aid the victims but to contain their rage.

By January 25, 2011, every protest sector had field experience with police rule, from Helwan University students to villagers in the Delta province of Daqhaliyya to Cairo lawyers to Aswan horse cart drivers. But no population group had come close to shifting the balance of resources in its favor, with the arguable exception of Sinai's Bedouins, who have been embroiled in fierce battles with police for years, ever since the Taba bombings in 2004 led to massive arrest campaigns targeting residents.

The first significant effort to link up Egypt's three protest sectors was easily aborted by the regime. On April 6, 2008, a loose coalition of Mahalla and Kafr al-Dawwar textile workers, town residents and groups in Cairo's associational landscape coordinated a general strike and national day of protest to demand a minimum wage and an end to corruption and police brutality. Riot police and state security officers dissolved the strike action at the Mahalla textile factory before it could take off. Then they easily broke up furious protests by thousands of Mahalla townspeople, lobbing tear gas canisters into crowds and arresting 150 residents. Smaller solidarity demonstrations in Greater Cairo were also effortlessly managed, and state security's plans succeeded in preventing the spread of protest to other provinces. But the event midwifed the April 6 youth movement, which would be a key organizer of the January 25 action.

Street clashes continued between locals and police in various spots throughout 2010, with some incidents leading to mass arrests and curfews. Although the triggers of these confrontations were particular to time and place, both police and citizens drew upon remarkably similar sets of devices, from Akhmim in Upper Egypt to Rosetta in the Delta to 'Umraniyya in Greater Cairo. Two signal events embedded these local patterns of friction into a national framework. In June 2010, a young Alexandrian named Khalid Sa'id was hauled out of his chair at an Internet café and beaten to death by plainclothes police officers on the street during an arrest for marijuana possession. Sa'id's death galvanized public opinion in disgust at police predation. Google executive Wael Ghoneim helped start a Facebook group called "We Are All Khalid Sa'id," and social movements organized several large demonstrations against police brutality at which the slogan "Leave! Leave!" was hurled at Husni Mubarak. The second occasion was the national legislative elections. Under complete police management, the elections in November-December 2010 were flagrantly rigged to return 97 percent of the seats for Mubarak's vehicle, the National Democratic Party (NDP). The elections outraged political elites and ordinary people alike, spurring a unified opposition protest on December 12, and leaving behind fresh memories of street battles in dozens of districts across the country.

By the time January 25, 2011 arrived, there was local resonance for the planned national "day of rage" in virtually every corner of Egypt. The political atmosphere was highly charged: Public opinion was inflamed by the Alexandria church bombing on January 1, which had led to numerous rumbles between police and Coptic protesters. The Tunisian people's toppling of Ben Ali electrified Egyptians. Riot police corralled a January 16 demonstration outside the Tunisian embassy, where activists had gathered to sing the Tunisian national anthem.

Unwittingly, the regime itself provided the calendar date for the "day of rage," having newly designated January 25 a bank holiday to mark Police Day. The holiday freed up citizens for assembly, practically inviting them to convert the official celebration into a popular harangue against police rule. Several get-out-the-protest clips on YouTube strung together notorious scenes of police brutality captured by cell phone video cameras. Members of all protest sectors announced their participation, including Mahalla workers, Sinai Bedouins, and civil servants employed by the cabinet. New actors joined in, such as hard-core fans of the two biggest national soccer teams and Khalid Sa'id's mother, who, in an interview uploaded by Nobel laureate Mohamed ElBaradei's reform campaign on January 21, also urged Egyptians to reclaim their rights in the streets.[10] The government felt compelled to counter-organize. State security officers warned Muslim Brothers in the provinces to stay home. NDP parliamentarians branded January 25 the "day of loyalty to the leader," paying for five hundred thousand posters featuring Mubarak's visage and pasting them in major squares.[11] The Coptic Church, seven tiny opposition parties, the Nasserist party, and Sufi orders spoke out against the protest action.[12]

In the days before the "day of rage," a little-noted disturbance prefigured scenes that would soon pop up all over Egypt. One afternoon in the Nile-side working-class neighborhood of Warraq, a brawl erupted between two detainees at the police station. Officers violently put down the fight. The detainees then set fire to the blankets in the lock-up, and the blaze soon engulfed the station, injuring the Warraq head detective and his lieutenant. Armored cars and riot police were dispatched to the neighborhood, as rumors spread that a detainee had died in the fire. Hundreds of residents and detainees' relatives descended on the station and tried to push their way in, pelting the building with stones and breaking four window panes. By 2 am, the standoff had ended. The Giza police chief had arrived to negotiate with residents, allowing them in one by one to ascertain their relatives' safety. "My brother is wrongly imprisoned. They accused him of stealing a cell phone," a resident outside the station told a reporter. "One of the officers framed him."[13]

Verdict of the Barricades

The January 25 protest started as a midsize demonstration and ended as a massive uprising against autocratic rule. But no one leaving their house that morning knew that they were stepping into the largest policing failure of Mubarak's tenure. The uprising was forged in the heat of street fighting, unanticipated both by its hopeful strategists and its watchful adversaries. "We went out to protest that day and expected to be arrested in the first ten minutes, just like usual," recalled Ziad al-'Ulaymi, an organizer with ElBaradei's campaign.[14] A lieutenant colonel in the riot police, who was monitoring events from the Cairo operations room, later noted, "Our preparations for January 25 were as per usual, and the instructions were not to molest demonstrators."[15]

Interior Minister Habib al-'Adli and his four lieutenants had met on January 24 to finalize their strategy. Cairo police chief Isma'il al-Sha'ir issued stern warnings through the media, threatening protesters with arrest and invoking the demonstrations law of 1914 requiring a permit for any public gathering of more than five persons.[16] Giza police chief Usama al-Marasi deployed twelve riot police trucks on Arab League Street, the main thoroughfare of Cairo's western half, and eighteen trucks outside Cairo University. The broad avenue and the campus were two of the pre-announced protest locations on the Facebook pages of the April 6 and Khalid Sa'id movements. For good measure, al-Marasi emplaced trucks along the entire stretch of the Warraq corniche.[17] Outside Greater Cairo, police set up checkpoints along the approaches to the large Delta towns of Tanta and Mahalla, block-ing the entry of delegations from Kafr al-Shaykh, Daqhaliyya, and Minoufiyya provinces that had been planned by protest organizers. Qalyoubiyya and Suez provinces were placed on high alert. Suez, in particular, had a recent history of troubles. In 2009, a high-ranking police general was assassinated in plain sight by a former informant; his 2010 trial turned into an exposé of the gendarmerie's brutal methods. And the heavy police hand was evident again during the 2010 elections. "The polling stations are under occupation. Suez has been turned into a military garrison!" cried an irate poll monitor on voting day.[18]

Zero hour, as announced by protest organizers, was to be 2 pm. The stated plan was to demonstrate in front of the Interior Ministry and then disband at 5 pm. Security forces therefore sealed off all the vital downtown streets leading to and from the Ministry, allow-ing pedestrians to pass only after checking ID cards. But it was a ruse. On the morning of January 25, organizers used cell phones and landlines to disseminate the real locations of the protests and the actual start time: noon. "The protest locations announced on Facebook and to the press were the major landmarks. The idea was to start marching down small side streets and pick up people along the way, so that by the time demonstrators reached the announced locations, they would be large crowds that security couldn't corral," explained organizer al-'Ulaymi.[19]

The crafty tactic worked in some neighborhoods, but not in others. Envision a sizable Kifaya demonstration walking down a tiny, picturesque lane in the inter-confessional neigh-borhood of Shubra, calling on residents watching them from the balconies to come down and join. Actor 'Amr Wakid is there, demonstrators are waving Egyptian flags and veteran sloganeer Kamal Khalil is providing the soundtrack with his unique sing-song rhymes.[20] By the time this group surged toward the announced rally point of Shubra Circle, they had collected one thousand bodies and police officers had started to chase them. Khalil was arrested, and the other legendary sloganeer and seasoned unionist Kamal Abu Eita just barely escaped. "That's when I realized that Abu Eita runs much faster than me!" said thirty-something activist Ahmad 'Urabi of Abu Eita, who is nearly sixty.

By that point at 2:30 pm, the Shubra people received calls and text messages that crowds were filling streets in the working-class neighborhoods of Boulaq, Imbaba, and Bab al-Khalq, and that Arab League Street in middle-class Muhandisin was overflowing with people marching toward Tahrir Square downtown. So they individually hopped into taxis and headed for the square. Meanwhile, outside the High Court building near Tahrir, middle-aged opposition parliamentarians and tweedy professors were scuffling with riot police. Lawyers from the bar association nearby had broken through the cordon and were approaching, as was a third roving group passing by the Judges' Club around the corner and chanting over and over again, "*Hurriyya! Hurriyya!*" (Freedom! Freedom!). The police were disoriented by the convergence of the three formations. State security officers negotiated with parliamentarians, trying to convince them to persuade the crowds that they could chant as much as they liked but had to remain stationary on the High Court steps. But there was another logic at work. The bodies gleefully broke through the cordons and rushed toward Gala' Street and from there to 'Abd al-Mun'im Riyad Square abutting the Egyptian museum, a stone's throw from Tahrir.

While security forces were trying to contain the court demonstration, Ghad party leader Ayman Nour and Wafd party members Muhammad Shurdi and businessman Rami Lakah were fronting an energetic group of Wafdist youth speed-walking from Ramsis Street to the Nile corniche. A couple of hundred strong and each member carrying a green party flag, the procession plucked off bystanders as it moved along, making its way to the NDP head-quarters where it stopped for some moments to denounce NDP leaders, promising them the fate of the Tunisian ex-president, Ben Ali. Before security forces could pen them in, a large group coming from the Qasr al-Nil bridge merged with the Wafdists and, together, they set off for the state radio and television building, completely encircling it for a few minutes with no security forces in sight. From there, they roamed the streets of Boulaq, reemerging at the intersection of Ramsis and July 26 Streets, and headed for Tahrir.

Nearby, on 'Abd al-Khaliq Tharwat Street, Khalaf Muhammad Mursi, a seventy-five-year old newspaper vendor, said, "Back in the days of the monarchy, I saw as many demonstrations as there are hairs on my head. Back then, they flipped over the trams and chanted against the king, and some of them wanted [Prime Minister Mustafa] Nahhas back in power. Demonstrating is good. They're marching and not doing anything wrong. The government should let them."[21]

In the provinces, there were also large demonstrations. Police containment varied in intensity, with some brigades tolerating the columns of protesters and others losing control of the crowds, as in Cairo. In Ismailiyya's Firdaws Square, police made rigorous preparations starting the night before. By early afternoon, rows of riot police were tightly hemming in six hundred demonstrators, who were performing the afternoon prayers outdoors and shouting, "Chant it, chant it! Raise your voice high! He who chants will not die!" By 6 pm, more people had joined in, enabling the protesters to break free of the cordon and ramble through the city. The labor stronghold of Mahalla was a different matter, the two demonstrations there having been violently put down, with eleven arrests. Alexandria's squares and landmarks saw several simultaneous, separate protests. Police ringed a large crowd outside the governor's office, chanting for the dissolution of the rigged parliament and demanding an audience with the governor, who refused. In the al-Asafra neighborhood, a procession flowed toward NDP headquarters, fending off the "karate companies," the state security musclemen who disperse crowds by striking demonstrators.

Back in Tahrir, shortly before 4 pm, security forces were resisting demonstrators' surge toward the national legislative headquarters from two directions. In the square, high-octane crowds led by soccer fans exclaimed "Egypt! Egypt!" in army-like cadence. They repeatedly rushed the thick layers of conscripts blocking the way to Qasr al-'Ayni Street, which leads southwest in rough parallel with the Nile, passing by the houses of Parliament. When the protesters succeeded in breaking through, panicked officers went in hot pursuit, pushing the discombobulated lower ranks in front of them to rearrange them again in a human blockade before the people could reach the People's Assembly, as Egypt's lower house is called. From the other direction on Qasr al-'Ayni Street, a now iconic scene saw light-footed young men sparring with an armored vehicle. In the footage posted online (where it has upwards of two million views), one of them then positions himself directly in the path of the moving lorry as it spouts water from a cannon. He stands there defiantly, hands on hips and drenched, as the vehicle brakes and the videographers wildly cheer him on from a balcony above.[22]

By then, something extraordinary was happening. The thousands of demonstrators who had been wending their way through different parts of the city were streaming through all the approaches to the square. Poet and Baradei campaign leader 'Abd al-Rahman Yusuf was running from security forces through the labyrinthine streets of chic Garden City, home to the US and British embassies. He and his fellows approached the square from underneath the Qasr al-Nil bridge. "It was one of the most profound moments of my life. The sight of the square filled with tens of thousands heralded the long-awaited dawn. As we entered the square, the crowds installed there cheered the coming of a new battalion, greeting us with joy. I wept."[23]

In the orange glow left by a setting sun, a skirmish unfolded outside the upper house of Parliament. Demonstrators had inched their way to that spot by making iterated advances into riot police formations, breaking them apart and gaining a tad more ground each time. Protesters clambered atop a red fire truck, and their jubilant fellows began to sing the national anthem. Tense riot police commanders herded their troops. The black-helmeted conscripts jogged in place and emitted the rhythmic grunts of soldiers revving up for close combat. When the order was given, the troops rushed into the crowd. "*Silmiyya! Silmiyya!*" roared the demonstrators, exhorting each other to non-violence and holding their ground as the troops retreated into position. An enterprising civilian knocked over a white-and-blue sentry kiosk. His fellows rushed to help him roll it to the protesters' side; a barricade had been made. When hotheads in the crowd started hurling rocks at riot police, a chant rose up from both the front lines and cheerleaders on the sidelines, "No stones! No stones!" In this army, the commanders and the foot soldiers were one.[24]

Night fell, but the people stayed put in the square. Huge speakers were procured from nearby Bab al-Louq, and a people's broadcast service was set up. Angry monologues, poetry couplets, and political demands were read out. A cardboard replica of a squat dictator hung from a lamppost. News was relayed that two citizens had died in Suez that day, solidifying resolve. Volunteers ranged across the square, collecting garbage in plastic bags. People built fires and danced around their light. Out of nowhere, food and blankets appeared, to the delighted claps and cries of the encampment. Memories of March 20–21, 2003 flitted through the minds of those who were there that evening, when the square was under the people's control for ten hours to express outrage at the US bombing of Baghdad. But on that occasion security forces had uprooted them by the next afternoon. Perhaps determined to avoid a reprise, the broadcast rallied everyone to spend this and every night in the square until their demands were met. As they had repeated over and over again throughout the day, they wanted: "Bread, freedom, social justice!" After sunset, as demonstrators realized their own power, this troika began to alternate with the Tunisian anthem: "The people want to overthrow the regime!" Reporters milled about, collecting stories. Sitting alone was Amal, a young nurse. Her friends had abandoned her, their parents refusing to let them join the demonstrations. Why did not her parents do the same? "My parents have passed away," she explained, "and I support five brothers and sisters. I'm here so that they can live a dignified life. I don't want them to be deprived because they're orphans."[25]

The riot police lieutenant colonel received the order at midnight. "The square had to be cleaned up," he recounted. "Absolutely no one was to spend the night there." The armored vehicles closed in, the riot troops were arrayed and the first tear gas canister was lobbed into the sit-in at 12:45 am. Nearly an hour later, following deployment of two hundred vehicles, fifty public buses, ten thousand riot police and three thousand special forces troopers, the people were expelled. Before scattering in all directions, knots of protesters encircled the vehicles that barged into the square at breakneck speed. A group ran to the NDP headquarters, where they smashed windows before being arrested. Another headed to the television building and blocked traffic in front of it. And a third group set fire to police kiosks and a police car near the 'Abd al-Mun'im Riyad bus depot. Holding up bloodied hands to the camera, one of the protesters said, "They shot at us! They shot at us! Who are we, the enemy?"[26]

Mubarak's Worst Fears

Habib al-'Adli and his adjutants were concerned by the day's events, especially the synchronized diffusion of protests across the country, the fluidity of crowd movement in the two major cities and citizens' euphoric sense of the weak points of the police. As the operations room lieutenant colonel recalled, "What we saw on January 25 was an uprising, not a demonstration. A young man standing in front of an armored vehicle, jumping on it to strike it, falling off and then doing it again? Honestly, there was no fear."[27] Both the Cairo and Giza police chiefs were in the field all day on January 25, and they saw the electrifying empowerment that seemed to course through Egyptians' veins. Both were experienced, hands-on officers who had proved their mettle in dicey situations. Cairo police chief al-Sha'ir won al-'Adli's trust by handily managing the large 2006 protests in support of reformist judges. And Giza police chief al-Marasi had been the head state security officer in Suez, seat of a sparsely populated province with multiple coils of social tension, from labor strife to drug running to Bedouin tribes with serious grievances, all sitting at the southern mouth of the Suez Canal, the country's prime generator of external revenue.

In the early morning hours of January 26, preparations were swiftly made to secure downtown Cairo against another popular takeover. State security instructed all downtown businesses to close before 1 pm on January 26. The two underground Metro lines converging on the major transfer hub at Tahrir announced that trains would not be stopping at the station. Police sealed off four entrances to the station, and three entrances to the July 26 station one stop to the northeast, outside the High Court building. Two thousand undercover policemen fanned out in downtown streets and government installations, and al-Marasi ordered the placement of multiple checkpoints on Nahiya Street, through which thousands of people had streamed the day before onto the Arab League boulevard. Labor commissar Husayn Mugawir, whose job was to control workers through the sole official union federation, instructed all union heads in the provinces to be especially responsive to the rank and file, lest any incipient job action happen to lend the demonstrations strategic depth.[28]

These measures indicated that Mugawir's superiors were feeling the worst fears of an authoritarian regime. For a capable autocrat like Mubarak, large protests are no cause for anxiety. The fears are diffusion and linkage. Indeed, the diffusion of collective action in time and space emboldened Egyptians, signaling the unwillingness or incapacity of the coercive apparatus to suppress demonstrations. The simultaneity of protests across very different locations, especially the filling of streets in neighborhoods entirely unused to such processions, revised citizens' calculations of what was possible and reduced uncertainty about the consequences of action. The second fear is the coordination between the three organizational infrastructures of protest. Indeed, the state security directorate existed to frustrate precisely this bridge building. It had done so quite successfully with the April 6, 2008 general strike, and had a stellar track record in branding each sector of dissent with a different label: Associational protest was "political," but workplace and neighborhood protest was "economic."

The diffusion of protests on January 25–27 shattered both the mental and material divisions between Egypt's three protest sectors, forcing the regime to confront them simultaneously, when for thirty years it had done so serially. In Cairo, there was a spontaneous sit-in on the tracks at the July 26 Metro station, with demonstrators halting the train. In Boulaq, a moving crowd of one thousand residents fought with police from early afternoon until past 2 am Friday morning, braving tear gas and rubber bullets, and setting up barricades on Gala' Street with dumpsters and carefully arranged burning tires. Undeterred by the traumatic routing of people from Tahrir Square, angry demonstrators by the hundreds continued to stride through the streets of downtown.

The picture in the provinces was much the same, with protesters refusing to empty the streets. Demonstrations in Daqhaliyya, Port Said, and North Sinai demanded the release of those arrested on January 25; in Sinai, residents used their signature tactic of blockading the highway with burning tires. On the third day of protests, a young Sinai protester named Muhammad 'Atif was killed in clashes with police, making him the fourth casualty nationwide. In Alexandria, state security broke up a planned lawyers' protest on the Manshiya court steps, arresting the first twenty people who showed up. The next day, two hundred lawyers returned and held their protest. In Qalyoubiyya, another two hundred lawyers marched down the streets on January 26 inveighing against price hikes and the export of Egyptian natural gas to Israel, so police cooped them up in the courthouse the next day. And Mahalla was still under lockdown, with security forces importing reinforcements to block renewed attempts by textile workers to start action. Percolating up from these varied locales was a decision to hold another round of protest on the next common-sense date: after Friday prayers on January 28, first dubbed "the Friday of the martyrs and the detained."

The situation in Suez developed rapidly. On January 25, security forces had been especially violent; the fighting resulted in 110 injuries and 3 deaths, as well as 54 arrests. The next day, hundreds of residents flocked to Suez General Hospital to donate blood, finding it so full that the injured were lying on sheets in hallways. Meanwhile, a large group of incensed relatives and citizens had gathered outside the morgue. The authorities insisted on handing over corpses without forensic reports, and security forces besieged the funerals with a ferocity that further enraged residents. "When you see this, you feel like you're in Palestine and Iraq," said the leftist Tagammu' parliamentarian for the city. "Security uses bullets and tear gas canisters and water hoses, and the residents can only confront this with stones."[29] But residents escalated their tactics, setting fire to a police post and the municipal council building on January 26, and trying to burn down the local NDP office. On January 27, hundreds of residents and detainees' relatives demonstrated outside the Arba'in police station, chanting, "Enough! We want our kids!" Demonstrators hurled petrol bombs at the station and ignited several police cars.

On the evening of January 27, police and protesters each held planning meetings to plot the second act of the confrontation. Police officials devised a comprehensive scheme to cut off physical and virtual means of linkage. They ordered a shutdown of Internet and cellular phone service for the next day; cell phones were especially important for demonstrators to spread news of protest diffusion in real time, and to share spot instructions or eleventh-hour location changes. Cairo was sealed off from the provinces and put under lockdown. All of the arteries and bridges leading into Tahrir Square from east and west were closed to traffic—even to pedestrians. Additional Metro stops were closed, not just the two nearest the square. And mosques were carefully primed in advance. The 'Umar Makram mosque in Tahrir was ordered shuttered. Friday preachers all over the country were instructed to deliver sermons denouncing assembly and disobedience of the ruler. At the Giza mosque where Mohamed ElBaradei was set to attend prayer before joining the protests, the preacher of twenty years was replaced with a government pick. For their part, the youth groups and opposition forces coordinating the protest added new locations and reacquainted themselves with landlines to cope with the cellular shutdown. Opposition parties who had sat out the January 25 action—the Tagammu' leftists and the Nasserists—scrambled to join up. And the Muslim Brothers threw their organizational weight behind the Friday gathering, revising their calculus of risk after seeing the momentous events of the previous three days. The players readied themselves, and the world watched.

On January 28, shortly after noon, a majestic scene unfolded all over Egypt. Grand processions of thousands upon thousands of people in every province made their way to the abodes of the oppressive forces that controlled their lives. Beckoning those watching from their windows, they chanted, "Our people, our people, come and join us!" When the crowds reached town and city centers, they encircled police stations, provincial government buildings, and NDP headquarters, the triad of institutions emblematic of the regime. The syncopated chorus that had traveled from Sidi Bouzid to Tunis now shook the Egyptian earth: "The people...want...to overthrow the regime!"

In Tanta, fifty thousand people blockaded a major highway, encircled the provincial government building and ripped down its billboards. In Kafr al-Dawwar, twenty-five thousand did the same. In Damietta, the people called for the dissolution of Parliament, torching the NDP building and defacing the façade of the governor's offices. In Minya, whose governor had bragged that his middle Nile province had not seen demonstrations on January 25, people ignored the entreaties of the police chief and barricaded the Cairo-Aswan highway, braving rubber bullets to chant outside the NDP headquarters: "Corruption caused this country's destruction!"

Everywhere, the rising of the commons was met with superior force. Police fired tear gas canisters, rubber bullets, and—the ultimate escalation—live ammunition. The goal, to be reached at any cost, was to prevent separate crowds of demonstrators from fusing together in city centers. State security commandeered ambulances to arrest the unsuspecting injured, and hospitals were pressured into falsifying the cause of death for demonstrators who were shot at close range. Residents provided first aid to demonstrators leery of getting into ambulances, and tossed water bottles, vinegar, and onions (homemade tear gas remedies) to the civilians fighting below. On Ramsis Street in downtown Cairo, as a crowd of ten thousand crashed into a security formation and was hurled back with copious tear gas, a woman cried out from her balcony, "God be with you, men of Egypt!"[30]

Communications between Alexandrian field commanders that day record the shock and awe police experienced in Egypt's second city. "We are still engaging very large numbers coming from both directions. We need more gas," a squadron head radioed to a superior. "The people have barged in and burned a security vehicle. The situation here is beyond belief. I'm telling you, sir, beyond belief," says another. By mid-afternoon, Alexandrians had laid siege to three police stations. In other parts of the city, police had run out of ammunition and resorted to throwing stones. A high-ranking commander got on the line to sternly instruct a field officer, "Stop engaging and secure the police stations! You don't have sufficient forces to calmly engage these numbers. Go and batten down the hatches!"[31]

And Suez? Security forces had isolated the Canal town from the rest of the country, closing off all access points. Massive reinforcements had arrived daily since January 25. At 1 am on January 28, the top police brass met at the Arba'in police station, which only a few hours before had been ablaze, to set the plan for the "Friday of anger." The showdown in Suez started after noon prayers. Gen. Ashraf 'Abdallah, commander of the riot police in the Canal Zone, later prepared an internal report:

> After Friday prayers, no fewer than five thousand people began a procession that was joined by large numbers of citizens from all mosques. The procession grew to forty thousand people, and the police chief ordered that it be allowed to proceed to the provincial capital building. Once there, the numbers exceeded fifty thousand. The masses remained outside the building for many hours, chanting hostile slogans. At the same time, large numbers of no less than twenty thousand had gathered in front of the Arba'in police station and assaulted the forces with rocks and Molotov cocktails. The forces used only tear gas. Due to the density of the crowds, the forces were unable to deal with them. The crowds burned the station, released the detainees and burned all the police vehicles in the area, among them ten lorries and an armored car belonging to the Ismailiyya force.[32]

In five compact hours, from noon to 5 pm, the police battled the people in all areas of the capital, desperate to thwart the amalgamation of multitudes in Tahrir Square. A climactic battle erupted on the Qasr al-Nil bridge, as surging crowds from the west sought to cross the river to join their brethren converging on Tahrir from the east. Qasr al-Nil has rightly been memorialized in word and video.[33] But there was another climactic Cairo fight in the east, where at least fifteen citizens died (the youngest of them aged fourteen) and ten troop carriers parked in a row burned. The battle of Matariyya Square, to the east of the suburb of Heliopolis, raged as police sought to stop residents from merging with crowds in the adjacent, densely populated 'Ayn Shams neighborhood. The people's insistent anthem, as outside

Parliament on January 25, was "*Silmiyya! Silmiyya!*" and "No stones! No stones!" When police used overwhelming force, including live rounds, the people switched tactics, forming a barricade with overturned dumpsters, seizing the shields of riot police, and burning the vehicles and the police station. The mother of 'Imad al-Sa'idi, twenty-four, killed by one bullet to the heart and one to the side, wondered, "If there was no way out for a policeman but to fire, then fire on his hand or his foot. But to shoot him in the heart and end his life—why?"[34]

The Egyptian uprising telescoped the daily encounters between people and police that had played out for more than ten years. Al-'Adli's police force did not melt away in the face of a popular onslaught. It fought for four straight days on nearly every street corner in every major city, before finally being rendered inefficient by the dynamism and stamina of exceptionally diverse crowds, each with their own know-how in the art of interfacing with gendarmes. At 5 pm on the afternoon of January 28, when reports started rolling in of police stations burning down, one after another, al-'Adli capitulated and ordered the removal of his forces from the streets. It was a sight unseen in modern Egyptian police rule—the one and only time that Egypt's three protest subcultures were able to jointly defeat the coercive apparatus that had existed to keep them apart.

By the end of the street fighting, preliminary estimates were that 365 citizens had died and some 5,000 had been hurt. On the police side, there were 32 deaths and 1,079 injuries, while ninety-nine police stations and three thousand vehicles had burned. Al-'Adli stayed bunkered inside the Interior Ministry until January 31, when he was transported out sitting huddled in an army tank. In a six-hour interrogation by the prosecution, on charges of responsibility for the deaths and injuries, al-'Adli shunted blame upward and downward. He accused his four top assistants of providing him with false intelligence, and demanded that Husni Mubarak be held accountable for the decision to fire on demonstrators, in his capacity as head of the Supreme Police Council. But he did concede defeat.

> The situation was beyond imagination. The faces of the demonstrators showed how clear they were in challenging the regime and how much they hated it, how willing they were to resist with their bodies all attempts to divide them with truncheons and water cannons and all other tools. They outnumbered security forces by a million or more, a fact that shocked the Interior Ministry leaders and the president. Those government officials all sat at home watching the demonstrations on TV. Not one of them devised a political solution to what policemen were facing—confrontations with angry people and indescribable hatred of the government. All of us were astonished.[35]

The prosecutor-general referred al-'Adli and his four lieutenants to Cairo criminal court, on charges of murder and endangerment of public property.[36] The lieutenants' acquittal on these charges in June 2012 sparked a revival of mass demonstrations around the country and a reoccupation of Tahrir Square.

The People's Choice

When Husni Mubarak appeared shortly after midnight on January 29 to announce his appointment of a new government, it was the first time in his tenure that he had been summoned to the podium by popular fiat. But he was enacting a familiar script written by autocratic rulers past, offering concessions to a population that had beaten the police and gained control of a country's streets. An offering that if made only four days earlier would have been considered shrewd—a cabinet reshuffle—was now foolhardy. It simply sharpened the population's apprehension of imminent victory, spurring them to stay outdoors and demand nothing less than the ouster of the president. Since Mubarak had made it impossible to remove him from office through elections, Egyptians resorted to the streets to relay the people's choice.

The liberation of the streets from the occupation forces of the Mubarak regime was only the opening act. Next was the symbolic public acquisition of Parliament, filling the avenue outside with peaceful protesters and plastering the building's gates with the people's insignia. Then came the branding of public goods; "our money," read a scrawl of graffiti on an army tank. With remarkable focus, citizens targeted the structures of rule that had disenfranchised and dispossessed them for decades. The police stations and NDP headquarters were the first targets, but the nascent revolutionaries did not stop there, hitting municipal councils, governors' offices, state security buildings, police checkpoints, traffic departments, toll booths, utility buildings, and other institutions that had taken their resources without giving in return. In Fayyoum, residents stormed the public utility company and destroyed the water bills that charged them exorbitant rates. In Ismailiyya, among the government institutions stormed was the Electricity Administration. In Alexandria, youthful demonstrators grabbed files from the main provincial building that they said showed evidence of corruption. In Isna, a town in Upper Egypt, one thousand demonstrators stormed a brand-new administrative building that had yet to be formally opened, paid for with their monies.

The genius of the Egyptian revolution was its methodical restoration of the public weal. The uprising restored the meaning of politics, if by that term is understood the making of collective claims on government. It revalued the people, revealing them in all their complexity—neither heroes nor saints, but citizens. It repaired the republican edifice of the state, Mubarak's hereditary succession project being the revolution's very first casualty. It compelled the police to bring back their old motto, erasing al-'Adli's sinister "police and people in service to the nation" and returning "the police at the service of the people." The countless public institutions branded with the names of Mubarak and his wife are now being rechristened in the names of regular people who died for the revolution. The referendum, a procedure disfigured beyond recognition by authoritarianism, on March 19 regained meaning as a matter for adjudication by the people. The revolution will have realized its emancipatory promise if it achieves one great task: constructing institutional checks against the rule of the many by the few.

Egypt's revolution is still in progress. It must be expected, however, that the revolution will undergo phases of setback, real or apparent. The apparatus of coercion, indeed, has been quickly rehabilitated and is gingerly reinserting itself into civilian life. But on what terms? For Egypt's revolutionary situation to lead to a revolutionary outcome, existing structures of rule must be transformed. Citizens must be free to choose their presidents, governors, parliamentarians, faculty deans, and village mayors, their trade union, student, and professional association leaders. They must have a binding say in the economic decisions that affect their lives. The coming years will reveal how much of that will happen and how.

Notes

Author's Note: Thanks to Evelyn Alsultany, George Gavrilis, and Mandy McClure for sympathetic and tough-minded feedback.

1. Reuters, January 25, 2011.

2. *New York Times*, February 16, 2011.

3. Esam Al-Amin, "When Egypt's Revolution Was at the Crossroads," *Counterpunch*, March 9, 2011.

4. *The Globe and Mail*, February 9, 2011.

5. Charles Tilly, "Does Modernization Breed Revolution?" *Comparative Politics* 5 (April 1973).

6. Interview with Muhammad al-Mahdi, professor of psychology at al-Azhar University, *al-Shurouq*, October 15, 2010.

7. *Al-Ahali*, January 3, 2001.

8. *Al-Ahram Weekly*, June 19–25, 2008.

9. *Al-Misri al-Yawm*, March 18, 2011. [English]

10. This interview is online at: http://www.youtube.com/watch?v=UgZMz3encLE.

11. *Al-Shurouq*, January 22, 2011.

12. *Al-Misri al-Yawm*, January 23 and 24, 2011.

13. *Al-Shurouq*, January 12, 2011.

14. *Wall Street Journal*, February 2, 2011.

15. *Al-Misri al-Yawm*, March 12, 2011.

16. *Al-Misri al-Yawm*, January 25, 2011.

17. *Al-Shurouq*, January 25, 2011.

18. *Al-Shurouq*, November 29, 2010.

19. *Al-Shurouq*, February 18, 2011.

20. This scene was in fact captured on camera: http://www.youtube.com/watch?v=1HfkUJrSMoM.

21. *Al-Misri al-Yawm*, January 27, 2011.

22. The scene can be viewed at: http://www.youtube.com/watch?v=kWr6MypZ-JU.

23. 'Abd al-Rahman Yusuf, "Diaries of the Revolution of the Patient," *al-Misri al-Yawm*, March 7, 2011.

24. See footage from this battle at: http://www.youtube.com/watch?v=pgh1iOXl6sQ.

25. *Al-Misri al-Yawm*, January 27, 2011.

26. These moments are recorded at: http://www.youtube.com/watch?v=g58Sl_4GN0E.

27. *Al-Misri al-Yawm*, March 12, 2011.

28. *Al-Shurouq* and *al-Misri al-Yawm*, January 27, 2011.

29. *Al-Misri al-Yawm*, January 28, 2011.

30. *Al-Misri al-Yawm*, January 30, 2011.

31. The transcripts of these communications were published in *al-Misri al-Yawm*, March 15, 2011.

32. The report was obtained by *al-Misri al-Yawm*, March 16, 2011.

33. *New York Times*, January 28, 2011.

34. *Al-Misri al-Yawm*, February 15, 2011.

35. *Al-Shurouq*, March 19, 2011.

36. *Al-Shurouq*, March 23, 2011.

8. WORLDS APART: AN EGYPTIAN VILLAGE AND THE INTERNATIONAL TOURISM INDUSTRY

TIMOTHY MITCHELL

Ayman wanted a job in tourism. But he did badly on his high-school language exams and spent two years at a school in Luxor, across the river from his village, struggling to master enough rudimentary English and German to get into the hotel school at Qina. His most vivid memory from his two years in Qina was the night when he and the other front-desk trainees played the role of guests in a restaurant for the final exam of the student waiters and cooks.

The meal began with soup. He burned his mouth on the first spoonful and it was cleared away before it had cooled enough for him to eat it. Next was "Russian salad," containing raw egg which made him choke on the first mouthful. Silverware was brought and taken away faster than he could figure out how to use it. The main course was veal too tough to cut with a knife but which they were not allowed to pick up with their hands. The desserts looked appealing but there were not enough to go around. The meal ended without him having eaten a thing. Back at his parents' house in the village, without a job or a future, he told and retold this story. Life was a meal you never got to eat.

Ayman's father, a guard in the Pharaonic tombs, was nearly crippled with chronic asthma caused by dust from the tombs and a cigarette addiction. His wages of 100 Egyptian pounds per month (about a $1 a day) barely covered cigarettes and medicine. Ayman's younger brother, also out of work, carved Pharaonic stone motifs to sell to the alabaster factories, as the shops are called, on the main road where tourist buses stop.

The family was supported by Ayman's mother, who raised rabbits, chickens, sheep, and water buffalo. With the older children, she harvested sugarcane in winter for the large land-owners, taking the stripped leaves for the buffalo to supplement the clover she grows on the family's own half-acre. They were lucky still to own the land: In 1982, the World Bank drew up plans to convert their field into a parking area for tour buses. Fortunately, when the government implemented the plans it spared the field, although several other households lost land to tourist industry expansion.

Outside Development

Ayman's difficulty in finding a tourism job was linked partly to the activities of jihadist groups, veterans of the US-backed anti-Soviet jihad in Afghanistan who had returned home and launched a terror campaign in southern Egypt aimed at tourist sites. A series of attacks in the mid-1990s culminated in a massacre in November 1997 at a tourist site near Ayman's village in which fifty-eight tourists and four Egyptians died. Prior to that attack, Luxor's local religious leaders, popular sentiment, and a pervasive secret police had created a safe haven for sightseeing. But tourists had stayed away, nonetheless, and hotel and tour operators responded by laying off unskilled workers—the easiest part of their budget to cut.

By the mid-1990s, tourists were slowly returning to Egypt, but difficulties continued.[1] For one thing, tourism was a volatile industry. Before the jihadists there was an earthquake; before the earthquake there was the Gulf war; and before that the fire at the Heliopolis Sheraton, stretching back through the 1980s. But even if there had been no more riots, earthquakes, killings, fires or wars, Ayman and others like him would still have found it hard, to benefit from the industry that surrounded them and affected far more than the relative few it employed. Ayman's hamlet is one of about twenty communities opposite Luxor on the west bank of the Nile, where the majority of Luxor's archaeological sites are located. Government decrees of 1976 and 1981 prohibited the building of hotels and other enterprises on the west bank, to preserve the touristic quality of the villages and Pharaonic sites. Building of any sort had to be mud brick and was severely restricted. No new commercial or workshop licenses were issued.[2] Developing Luxor tourism required the "de-development" of these villages.

The 1982 World Bank program, drawn up by the US consulting firm Arthur D. Little, suggested one or two remedies to these problems: a cooperative to improve the quality of homemade souvenirs, and the building of a new village to the north, which would ease the housing shortage but remove people even farther from the tourist industry. It would also remove them from their fields and other places of employment.

The consultants' brief was to increase tourism revenue, from better visitor management (new roads, bus parks, and other facilities) to increase the flow of tourists and from a new airport terminal, increased water and electric supplies, and other infrastructure to enable the development of luxury hotels and Nile cruise ships. Since there was a limit to the number of tourists who could be squeezed in and out of King Tut's tomb each hour, income growth was to come from a shift toward wealthier tourists.

More than half of the Luxor development budget—$32.5 million out of a total of $59 million—was to be spent abroad, for foreign contractors, consultants, and equipment.[3] The Egyptian government borrowed this $32.5 million from the World Bank. Following the usual practice, the development assistance was actually money paid by the Third World to the West.[4] The balance of incurred local costs was paid directly by the government. The major local construction project, building a new river embankment at Luxor, which might have employed local labor, was awarded to a military work force from China.

These investments generated a phenomenal growth in tourism. From 1982 to 1992, the number of visitors to Egypt and their estimated expenditures more than doubled.[5] In Luxor most of the growth, as planned, was in luxury hotels and cruise ships. Across the river, the few who had established small hotels or other tourist enterprises before the development ban was imposed did well. But for others, there was almost no way of breaking into the tourist business, except for the handful who found jobs as unskilled workers at below-subsistence wages in Luxor hotels. Half a dozen young men did better by marrying foreign tourists—usually much older women, who visited for a few weeks each winter and with luck were wealthy enough to set up the husband in business. One woman, an enterprising California divorcée named Happy, began to build a small hotel on the edge of the village before being stopped by the authorities.

The hotel stood half-finished. Most of the husbands settled for something less, such as an imported car to use as a tourist taxi. Cruising in their air-conditioned Peugeots, past those working in the sugarcane fields, these men underlined the separation of the tourist world from the village.

Enclave Tourism

The World Bank's program for Luxor tourism was designed to increase this separation. The Bank's consultants conducted a survey in Luxor and reported that tourists' biggest complaint was of being bothered continually by locals trying to take them somewhere or sell them something. The consultants recommended that no further peddler licenses be issued, and devised a visitor management scheme to minimize unregulated contact between tourists and the local community. Separate ferry and bus facilities were to be improved to isolate the movement of tourists from local traffic. An enclosed visitor center would have its own restaurant and shops. In Ayman's village, plans called for an elevated walkway through the middle of the village so that tourists could cross from the bus park to the Pharaonic temple without setting foot in the village itself.

This kind of enclave tourism arrangement became typical of tourist development in the Third World, required by the increasing disparity between the wealth of tourists and the poverty of the countries they visit. The Egyptian Ministry of Tourism appealed to foreign capitalists considering ventures in hotels or other enterprises in Egypt with the claim that investors were "enjoying outstanding profits in the tourism field," thanks to easy repatriation and "labor costs that are more than competitive on a worldwide scale."[6] The ministry calculated that each tourist spent on average $100 a day in Egypt—more than most hotel employees earned in a month.[7]

There was a larger reason for the creation of enclave tourism. As the industry became concentrated in the hands of luxury hotels, mostly under the management of American or European chains, managers sought to increase their profit by channeling more and more tourist expenditure within their own establishments.[8] The grand Egyptian hotels that used to provide little more than accommodation and a dining room were replaced by complexes that offered three or four different restaurants, several bars, shopping arcades, a swimming pool and fitness club, cruises and excursions, business facilities, and evening lectures and entertainment. The Nile cruise ships and the walled "tourist villages," popular where space is plentiful such as the Red Sea coast, are even more self-contained.

Except for a small and wealthy elite, the local population is excluded from these enclaves, kept out by the prices and the guards posted at the gate. The result is almost total segregation. Most Luxor tourists have no contact with the local street, except, perhaps, for occasions of brief shopping excursions in the Luxor bazaar or a five-minute walk from the cruise ship to an archaeological site through a village strip. These encounters become frenzied scenes in which local peddlers, merchants, and entrepreneurs scurry to secure some small share of the tourist business.

Traveling Expenses

Driven by the plans of international hotel chains, this process of segregation was further encouraged by Egyptian government and World Bank policy. In the 1980s the Bank directed Egyptian public funds into building the infrastructure for tourist development, with projects like the one in Luxor. In the 1990s the Bank began pushing for the profits from this public investment to be switched into private, and especially foreign, hands. Supported by Fu'ad Sultan, a former Egyptian banker appointed minister of tourism, the World Bank in 1992 paid the consultants Coopers and Lybrand Deloitte to draw up plans to sell off the country's luxury hotels, managed by international hotel chains but still owned by the state.

Selling off state-owned assets was usually justified by the need to eliminate subsidized or inefficient enterprises. But the hotels were highly profitable, providing returns of up to 50 percent or more of revenue.[9] The consultants justified the proposed sale as a "flagship privatization," a public relations venture to encourage the privatization process in general by offering lucrative assets for sale, mostly to corporate investors from Europe and the Gulf.[10] (The consultants also claimed that the sale would raise funds for further tourism development, but offered no analysis of the need for such funds or reasons why the lump sum from a sale was more beneficial than the annual income from assets held in perpetuity.) "Flagship privatization" followed the discredited model of Thatcherite Britain, where Coopers and Lybrand Deloitte gained their expertise. As the consultants acknowledged, again based on British experience, the investors may enjoy prospects for windfall profits from the future resale of grossly undervalued properties.[11]

Increased control by international capital sent not just the profits abroad, but tourist expenditure in general. Increasing international integration of the tourist industry decreases the proportion of tourist expenditure that remains in the host country.[12] The integration of the hotel industry was being followed by that of the tour operators.[13] Those who purchased these assets, moreover, increased the pressure on local managers to build their share of a limited market, intensifying the segregation of tourists within their luxury enclaves. For Ayman and his fellow villagers, both developments decreased the proportion of tourism income available to the local community.

Mode of Consumption

A conventional industry, whether in manufacturing or agriculture, involves organizing people to produce. Mass production relies upon all the well-known methods of recruiting and disciplining a work force, organizing their use of time, their movement and their arrangement in physical space, and developing systems of instruction, supervision, and management.

Mass tourism, by contrast, involves organizing people to consume, although it relies upon similar methods of managing, instructing and supervising to maximize the process of consumption. Tourism is usually defined, from the tourist's point of view, as a form of leisure, in contrast to work. It is better seen as a particular form of capitalist industry, organized around the maximization not of production but consumption and not of individual goods but of a more complex commodity-experiences. No object of capitalist consumption is ever just a thing. One pays not just for food, clothing or cars, but for a certain taste, lifestyle or experience that the thing signifies. With tourism, this consumption of signification is taken

79

to the extreme. The tourist industry sells not individual objects but entire worlds of experience and meaning.

In Luxor, the tourism experience is created out of archaeological sites, but also by organizing the contemporary society to appear as a reflection and extension of the past. The 1982 World Bank report on visitor management explained that "the creation of an overall environment is needed on the west bank [of the Nile] in order for Luxor to reach its full market potential."[14] Although very few west bank residents were to be directly employed in tourism, all were inevitably part of the overall environment of donkeys and horse-drawn carts, mud brick houses, and peasant ways—a life scarcely changed in the last five thousand years, as a popular American study of the area published at the same time actually claimed.[15]

In 1981, half a million tourists visited Luxor and each stayed for an average of only 2.1 nights. By 1995, the number of visitors in a good year had more than doubled, but the average length of stay had declined.[16] The local tourist industry had less than forty-eight hours to maximize the tourist's consumption. This required a meticulous planning of meals, drinks, sleeping, and entertainment, plus the requisite trips to the Karnak and Luxor temples, the sound and light show, the felucca ride, the Luxor bazaar, plus King Tut's tomb and other sundry tombs and temples of the Theban necropolis across the river.

This mass production of experience produced a curious common interest between tourism's over-organized consumers and some of the local community. In the 1982 World Bank survey, alongside the complaint about the behavior of peddlers and local merchants, the most frequent tourist request was for more meaningful contact with the local population. Many tourists to Luxor were anxious to meet "real Egyptians." Many of the local population, interested in diverting tourist expenditure in their direction, were keen to help. Ayman's aunt, for example, had a house directly in front of the parking area for buses. Her children hung around, out of sight of the tour guides, and caught the eye of tourists lagging behind the main group as it headed off toward the temple. They then invited them into the house to watch their mother baking bread at an earthen oven. In exchange, the kids expected a tip of a pound or so.

Another Place, Another Restaurant

The Luxor region is not necessarily typical of Third World tourism, or even of Egypt. The industry takes different forms in different places. But patterns are similar from place to place. In Egypt, antiquities-based tourism is concentrated in Upper Egypt and Cairo, and draws foreign tourists primarily from North America, Europe and East Asia (as well as domestic tourists and busloads of local children on school trips). Domestic tourism, traditionally centered on Alexandria, now stretches along the entire Mediterranean coast. The Red Sea region, offering beaches, diving, and windsurfing, is marketed locally and in Europe and Israel.

In the 1990s, Cairo was a growing center for conference and business travel, but its largest market consisted of Arab visitors from the Gulf—a market so big that summer became Egypt's peak tourist season. The city's five-star hotels became another kind of tourist enclave. The gambling casinos, the hotels' most profitable venues, were legally off limits to Egyptians, creating little zones of extra-territoriality within the heart of the capital city. To enter the gambling hall one had to show a passport.

Another kind of enclave was created in response to the actions of the Islamist groups. To deflect the image abroad of Egypt as a terror-ridden place too dangerous to visit, the tourism ministry and tour operators began a marketing campaign for resorts of Sinai and the Red Sea coast making no reference to the fact that they are in Egypt. "Business is booming…we are expanding the hotel," reported a satisfied European hotel manager in Sharm al-Sheikh. "Most of the tourists who come here are under the impression that they are coming to some separate entity called Sinai, which has nothing to do with the rest of Egypt."[17]

With the Red Sea resorts far less affected by the political violence of 1992-1994, many people from the Luxor region sought jobs there. Ayman went looking for work in Hurghada, the resort on the mainland coast. So, too, did Happy, the California divorcée, and her husband from the village.

Ayman managed to get himself a job in a small hotel. At first he was employed to clean the rooms, earning 85 pounds a month (about $26 at the time). It was filthy work, he said, the kind of thing no person from his village would normally do. He started to smoke, and half of his pay went to cigarettes. Within a few weeks he managed to get the front desk job, work for which he was trained. But he found that nothing he had learned at hotel school applied. He had been taught that the customer is always right. If, for example, the room a guest had reserved was unavailable, you gave him a better room at that same price. At his hotel, there was only one better room, with air conditioning. The hotel owner liked to use that room for himself and was so annoyed with Ayman for giving it to low-paying guests that he fired him. "It's no good being honest," Ayman said, back in the village, "In the tourist business you have to be tricky. I went to Hurghada with 100 pounds in my pocket. I came home with 7."

Happy opened a small restaurant on the main shopping street of Hurghada. She chose an American menu, featuring several kinds of hamburgers, and called the place Happy's. It attracted the town's European tourists and, with the American navy putting into Hurghada after the Gulf war, a steady stream of US military personnel. Leaving her husband in charge of the place, Happy made a nice return on her investment.

Notes

Author's Note: The author wishes to thank Rania Fahmy for research assistance and Lila Abu-Lughod for sharing research notes. The names of people in the village have been changed to protect their identity.

1. During the first half of 1995, the number of tourists to Egypt increased by about 24 percent over the same period in 1994. *Financial Times*, July 21, 1995.

2. Arthur D. Little et al, *Study on Visitor Management and Associated Investments on the West Bank of the Nile at Luxor* (Washington, D.C.: World Bank, April 1992), p. VIII-9.

3. World Bank, "Staff Appraisal Report: Arab Republic of Egypt Tourism Project" [mimeo], April 26, 1979, pp. 19-22.

4. See Tim Mitchell, "America's Egypt: Discourse of the Development Industry," *Middle East Report* 169 (March-April 1991), pp. 18-36.

5. Egyptian Ministry of Tourism, Development Authority, Information Management Department, *1992 Tourism Data Bulletin*, January 1993.

6. Egyptian Ministry of Tourism, "Taba Touristic Development Company" [mimeo], Cairo, 1991, pp. 54-55.

7. *Egypt: Profile of a Market in Transition* (Geneva: Business International, 1989), p. 75.

8. See Tilman G. Freitag, "Enclave Tourism Development: For Whom the Benefits Roll?" *Annals of Tourism Research* (1994), pp. 538-553.

9. Coopers and Lybrand Deloitte, "Egyptian Hotels Privatisation Study: Interim Report" [mimeo], June 19, 1991. The management companies typically take 15-20 percent of profit.

10. Coopers and Lybrand Deloitte, "The World Bank-Egypt Privatisation: Private Sector Financial Operations Group: Privatisation of Hotels in Egypt: Technical Proposal for Consulting Services" [mimeo], London, October 1990.

11. The scale of private profit is staggering, the latest British example being a public utility company, the South Western Electricity Board, which the Thatcher government sold in 1990 for 400 million pounds. After paying themselves "bloated salaries and share options" for five years, in July 1995 the Board directors were considering selling the industry to a US giant, the Southern Company, for more than 1 billion pounds. *The Observer*, July 16, 1995.

12. John Urry, *The Tourist Gaze: Leisure and Travel in Contemporary Societies* (London: Sage, 1990), p. 64. Studies of the exact proportion of tourist expenditure that remains in the host country are inconclusive, in part because circumstances differ dramatically from one economy to the next. E. Philip English, *The Great Escape? An Examination of North-South Tourism* (Ottawa: The North-South Institute, 1986), pp. 17-45. Another reason is because the very nature of the industry, organized around the consumption of experience, makes conventional economic measurement impossible.

13. In Britain, for example, three companies (the largest of which was Canadian-owned) control 60 percent of the tour industry. *The Observer*, July 16, 1995.

14. Arthur D. Little, *Study on Visitor Management*, p. VII-9.

15. See Tim Mitchell, "The Invention and Reinvention of the Egyptian Peasant," *International Journal of Middle East Studies* 22 (1990).

16. Arthur D. Little, *Study on Visitor Management*, p. VIII-2; Government of Egypt, *1992 Tourism Data Bulletin*. Since 1981 the average visitor length of stay has declined steadily for Egypt as a whole, except for a sudden increase in 1986-1988 caused largely by long-stay summer tourists from the Gulf, very few of whom visit Luxor.

17. *New York Times*, October 21, 1993.

9. STRIKES IN EGYPT SPREAD FROM CENTER OF GRAVITY

JOEL BEININ AND HOSSAM EL-HAMALAWY

In the last decade of President Husni Mubarak's rule, the longest and strongest wave of worker protest since the 1940s rolled through Egypt. In March of 2007, the liberal daily *al-Misri al-Yawm* estimated that no fewer than 222 sit-in strikes, work stoppages, hunger strikes, and demonstrations had occurred during 2006. In the first five months of 2007, the paper reported a new labor action nearly every day. The citizen group Egyptian Workers and Trade Union Watch documented fifty-six incidents during the month of April, and another fifteen during the first week of May alone.[1]

From their center of gravity in the textile sector, the strikes spread to mobilize makers of building materials, Cairo subway workers, garbage collectors, bakers, food processing workers, and many others. Like almost all strikes in Egypt in the preceding forty years, these work stoppages were "illegal"—unauthorized by the state-sponsored Egyptian Trade Union Federation (ETUF) and its subsidiary bodies in factories and other workplaces. But unlike upsurges of working-class collective action in the 1980s and 1990s, which were confined to state-owned industries, the wave that began in late 2004 also pushed along employees in the private sector.

Around the same time the first strikes broke out, the most outspoken pro-democracy street protests in years—including in their ranks leftists and secular nationalists and sometimes Muslim Brothers—also appeared. Having spent three years trying to contain the pro-democracy ferment, the Mubarak regime launched a counterattack on the workers' movement as well. The counterattack came as many activist workers shifted their gaze from wages, benefits and working conditions to the explicitly political question of their relation, through the ETUF, to the state.

Workers and Brothers

Notable among the April 2007 actions were repeated work stoppages by 284 workers at the Mansura-Spain Company, at which a 75 percent female work force produced quilts and ready-made clothes. These workers were protesting the sale of their enterprise without a commitment from the prospective new owner, the private sector bank al-Masraf al-Muttahid, to pay supplemental wages and profit shares due them since 1995.

The largest private-sector strikes occurred in the coastal city of Alexandria at Arab Polvara Spinning and Weaving, a fairly successful enterprise privatized in the first tranche of the public-sector selloff during the mid-1990s. On March 24, 2007, and again on April 2, nearly half of the firm's twelve thousand workers struck to protest discrimination between workers and managers in the allocation of shares when the company was sold, failure to pay workers dividends on their shares, and the elimination of paid sick leave and a paid weekend. Workers last received dividends on their shares in 1997, when they were paid 60 Egyptian pounds (about $10.45 at the time).

The demands of the Arab Polvara workers indicated that public-sector workers were correct to suspect that, even if privatized firms initially agreed to offer pay and benefits similar to those in the public sector (in some cases, the pay is even higher), the requirements of competing in the international market would eventually drive down wages and worsen working conditions. Since there were few trade unions in the private sector, workers lacked even the weak institutional mechanism of the state-sponsored union federation to contest the unilateral actions of private capital.

The government charged the Muslim Brothers with inciting the Arab Polvara strike, but there was no evidence that they played any role in this or any other labor action that year. Labor solidarity was an unusual stance for the Brothers, who had never had a strong base in the industrial working class and, in the past, had assisted the government in breaking strikes. While some Muslim Brothers acted to encourage the spate of worker activism, it appeared there were differences within the organization between the affluent businessmen who dominated the leadership and rank-and-file members from the lower middle classes and working poor.

In February 2007, the Muslim Brother MP 'Abd al-'Aziz al-Husayni announced his backing for the walkout of the Misr Spinning and Weaving workers in Kafr al-Dawwar, south of Alexandria. His parliamentary colleague Sabir Abu al-Futouh, from Alexandria, followed up by issuing several statements supporting the Arab Polvara strike. Earlier, Abu al-Futouh had been coordinator of the Brothers' campaign to run candidates in the fall 2006 trade union elections. The government disqualified thousands of Muslim Brothers, leftists, and independents from running in those elections—consequently judged "undemocratic and non-transparent" by independent observers.[2] Abu al-Futouh had declared that if the elections were rigged, the Muslim Brothers would establish a trade union independent of the regime, similar to the independent student unions they founded in cooperation with the Trotskyist Revolutionary Socialist group at several universities.

Yet on November 21, after the first rounds of voting were over and their undemocratic character was apparent, the Brothers' Deputy General Guide Muhammad Habib sounded more reserved. In an interview at the American University of Cairo, Habib said: "Establishing an independent labor union requires a long period of consistent organizing. Workers are different than students because they have family responsibilities and will not lightly risk their livelihoods."

The Alexandrian Brothers were generally considered more militant, more confrontational toward the regime and closer to the popular classes than the organization's other branches. Even if Abu al-Futouh was serious in his initiative, however, it was spurned by would-be partners the Nasserists and the so-called legal left National Progressive Democratic Union Party (Tagammu'), who rejected an alliance with the Islamist opposition.[3] There was no indication that the Muslim Brothers were involved anywhere in setting up trade union structures on the ground.

Ideas of Independence

The fresh momentum for the idea of an independent trade union federation came from among the striking workers themselves, particularly those in the mills of Nile Delta towns. In December 2006, the local union committee at the Misr Spinning and Weaving facility in Mahalla al-Kubra declined to back the rank and file when they halted production. Angered, the Mahalla strikers demanded that federation bosses in Cairo remove the union committee and, when this demand was ignored, protested by handing in their resignations from ETUF. In early February 2007, strikers at the Shibin al-Kum Spinning Company echoed the Mahalla workers' call for mass resignations from the federation.[4] Workers in other localities also adopted the idea of an independent network of trade unions, most prominently in Kafr al-Dawwar.[5]

The idea of an autonomous national union to supplant the state-sponsored General Federation had circulated among trade unionists for over a decade and was supported in principle by many progressives. Among them were the Center for Trade Union and Workers' Services (CTUWS) and its general director, Kamal 'Abbas, veteran trade union organizers like Sabir Barakat and labor lawyer Khalid 'Ali of Hisham Mubarak Law Center and the Coordinating Committee for Workers and Trade Union Rights and Liberties (and later the founding director of the Egyptian Center for Economic and Social Rights); 'Abd al-Ghaffar Shukr, a leader of the Socialist Alliance, which sought to forge a coalition among all the Egyptian socialist forces; Socialist Horizons, the labor center affiliated with the Communist Party of Egypt; and Workers for Change, an offshoot of the Kifaya movement for democracy. Yet government repression and internal divisions over tactics and strategy produced great uncertainty among the opposition forces over whether they had the organizational capacity to launch a parallel trade union.

While the Revolutionary Socialists backed an independent national trade union in principle, they were more cautious than the other political forces involved. Fearing elitism and recognizing that grassroots support for such a project did not yet exist, they focused on the preparatory steps of supporting the demands of Nile Delta activists to impeach their factory-level union committee officials and establishing channels of communication between strike leaders.

Notably, Tagammu' appeared not to support the establishment of an independent trade union federation, though it used such rhetoric during the labor union elections in an attempt to deter the government from mass vote rigging. 'Abd al-Rahman Khayr, a Tagammu' representative in the upper house of Parliament and president of the General Union of Military Industries, is the only non-ruling party member who won a seat on the state-affiliated federation's executive committee. In February, Khayr assembled ETUF bureaucrats to disrupt a press conference at the Journalists' Syndicate called by the CTUWS and other trade unionists to denounce government attacks against labor activists. Many believed he had made a deal with the regime.

Legacy of Leftist Retreat

These working-class struggles erupted without any politically organized leadership. Tagammu', which was much more closely connected to workers in the 1980s, publicized and offered material support to such struggles. It began to issue a workers' magazine and to cover labor affairs regularly in the pages of its weekly *al-Ahali*. In addition, several independent workers' newspapers based on industrial regions or sectors were established.[6] Tagammu' was unable to strike deep roots among insurgent workers, however. During the 1990s the party lost most of its popular base, amidst a general retreat of leftist politics, because of the party's strategic decision to support the Mubarak regime in its battle against the Islamist insurgency based in southern Egypt and the urban slums of Cairo and Alexandria, and eventually against the non-violent Muslim Brothers as well. This strategy was the brainchild of Tagammu' chief and former Communist Party of Egypt member Rif'at al-Sa'id. It was embraced by the underground Communist Party, the remnants of which worked actively inside Tagammu'.

Clampdown

Despite the retreat of the "legal" and much of the underground left from engagement with industrial workers in the 1990s, the career of CTUWS director Kamal 'Abbas was marked with relative success. 'Abbas got his start as a leader in the upsurge of labor activism in the 1980s, culminating in two fierce strikes at the Egyptian Iron and Steel Company in 1989. He was fired for participating in these "illegal" strikes that had no support from the official trade union. In 1990, 'Abbas founded CTUWS with advice and support from the late Yusuf Darwish, a veteran communist and labor lawyer who had represented many trade unions in Shubra al-Khayma and Cairo from the 1930s through the 1950s. Darwish had also recruited many union leaders into the Workers' Vanguard organization, one of the three main trends in the communist movement that eventually united in the Communist Party of Egypt in 1958. At one point, 'Abbas joined Darwish and another veteran communist militant, the late Nabil al-Hilali, in the leadership of the People's Socialist Party, a small group that left the Communist Party objecting to Rif'at al-Sa'id's iron grip on party affairs and the strategy of supporting the Mubarak regime against the Islamists.

Despite 'Abbas' early association with underground Marxist politics, by the mid-2000s he abandoned overt political demands, and the CTUWS focused on bread-and-butter issues. This strategy, however, did not save CTUWS from the attacks of the Mubarak regime. On April 25, 2007 the Ministry of Social Solidarity ordered the closure of the CTUWS headquarters in the industrial suburb of Helwan, south of Cairo. The center's two regional offices in southern and northern Egypt had already been shut down, on March 29 and April 11, respectively. 'Adil Zakariyya, editor of the CTUWS magazine *Kalam Sinaya'iyya* (Workers' Talk), told a reporter, "The authorities are clamping down on the center now because they don't know how to deal with the waves of strikes that have rocked the country over the past six months. They need a scapegoat, so they are accusing us of inciting the workers to strike. But how can they accuse us of inciting all 220 of the strikes estimated to have occurred in 2006?"[7]

The closure of CTUWS was the climax to a month of escalating aggressiveness by security forces in attempting to break up strikes and other forms of collective action. On

April 15, a delegation of one hundred workers from Misr Spinning and Weaving in Mahalla al-Kubra, including thirty-six-year-old CTUWS activist and December 2006 strike leader Muhammad al-'Attar, was prevented from traveling to Cairo to protest at the ETUF head-quarters. Police first confiscated the license of the driver of the bus they had hired, and then physically blocked the workers from boarding a Cairo-bound train. The intended demonstration was a further step in the Mahalla workers' campaign to resign en masse from ETUF. On May 6, at the behest of State Security Investigations, Misr Spinning and Weaving management ordered al-'Attar's summary transfer to the company's branch in Alexandria.

Many Egyptian non-governmental organizations could have been shuttered on the same pretext that the regime used to close CTUWS—that they were not properly registered with the Ministry of Social Solidarity in accordance with the extremely restrictive regulatory legislation. The ministry refused to grant CTUWS recognition as an NGO, so it registered as a civil company. Because the closure of CTUWS was perceived as a potential assault upon all advocacy NGOs, the center received strong support from thirty NGOs in a statement released at a press conference on April 24. Representatives of over a dozen NGOs occupied the CTUWS office the next day. Hundreds of riot police gathered outside and eventually implemented the closure decision. CTUWS later reopened as a legal office of its counsel and program director, Rahma Rif'at, but the regime had sent its message.

Though the Mubarak regime showed signs of desperation, internal division, and weakness, lashing out at Muslim Brothers, bloggers, journalists, striking workers, and NGO activists alike, the opposition was even weaker and more divided. The leadership of the Muslim Brothers, the largest opposition force, was embattled by a full-scale security crackdown. With its senior members facing trial in military courts, the Brothers decided to avoid a direct confrontation with the regime. While the relationship between the Brothers' leaders and the secular opposition was fraught with contention and mistrust, on the ground there were signs of gradual rapprochement among the youth who made up their respective bases. A common strategy, however, was not established at that time. Kifaya, which showed so much promise from late 2004 through mid-2005, had been unable to mobilize effectively since the end of the Lebanon war in August 2006. Primarily a movement of students, intellectuals, and middle-class professionals, Kifaya had only tenuous relations with the insurgent workers' movement. The few candidates from its labor affiliate Workers for Change who were not banned by the security forces from running in the fall 2006 union elections performed poorly.

While Kifaya and the rest of the oppositional intelligentsia remained incapable of providing the technical and logistical support required to launch an independent trade union federation in the face of fierce opposition from the regime, the strike wave opened a channel of communication for radical activists in Cairo with those in the provinces. Following the December 2006 strike in Mahalla al-Kubra, leftist elements in Kifaya worked to establish links with the industrial centers in the Nile Delta by organizing solidarity trips, mobilizing media support and raising strike funds. The Misr Spinning and Weaving workers' planned trip to Cairo on April 15, though aborted by security forces, was nonetheless a landmark. Some of the strike leaders contacted leftist Kifaya activists in Cairo to ask for their support on that day, suggesting that they were beginning to consider political issues beyond their immediate economic demands, perhaps including regime change.

Militancy at Mahalla

A second strike at Mahalla al-Kubra in September 2007 was key to the emergence of more trenchant political critiques alongside workers' demands. The 2007 strike was impelled by unfulfilled promises made at the conclusion of its December 2006 antecedent. At that time, workers said they would accept annual bonuses equal to forty-five days' pay rather than the two months' pay they had been promised the previous March. In exchange, Minister of Investment Mahmoud Muhi al-Din agreed that if the firm earned more than 60 million Egyptian pounds in profit in the fiscal year that ended in June 2007, then 10 percent of that profit would be distributed among the employees.

Egyptian statistics being malleable, it is possible to say only that Misr Spinning and Weaving had reaped somewhere between 170 and 217 million pounds of profit in the fiscal year 2006-2007. Consequently, workers claimed that they were due bonuses equal to about 150 days' pay. But they had received only the equivalent of 20. They also demanded increases in their clothing allowances and production incentives. Finally, the workers contended that CEO Mahmoud al-Gibali took extravagant trips abroad, a manifestation of the corruption and mismanagement that was squandering the company's resources. The workers were acutely aware that this was their money, since Misr Spinning and Weaving is the flagship public-sector firm in Egypt. "Save us! These thieves robbed us blind!" read one placard held aloft before the cameras and shown on Al-Jazeera English. The strikers called for Gibali to be suspended pending an investigation.

As in the past, government mouthpieces claimed that the Mahalla workers were "incited" to action by the Muslim Brothers and other opposition political parties. When representatives of the regime-sponsored National Council for Human Rights visited Mahalla to investigate, several workers displayed their NDP membership cards. Strike leaders repeatedly said that theirs was a workers' movement and that the opposition parties, which were discredited and have little to offer the workers in any case, had nothing to do with it.

Indeed, the workers did not have a unified political position. Some remained hopeful that Husni Mubarak would intervene to compel the paying of bonuses and incentives, perhaps banking on the regime's record of meeting economic demands in many of the strikes of the wave. Others were more militant and identified the regime as their enemy. Twenty-three year old worker Karim al-Buhayri, who writes a widely read Arabic blog called Egyworkers, said, "Find us another society to live in. Or find us other rulers to rule us. Or find us our rights." He uploaded video clips (unfortunately no longer available) featuring workers chanting, "We will not be ruled by the World Bank! We will not be ruled by colonialism!" On September 28, veteran unionist Sayyid Habib told Voice of America radio, "We are challenging the regime."

Throughout the strike, the workers remained barricaded in the hulking mill. Eight strike leaders were arrested on the third day of the action. The sympathetic local police released them two days later to thunderous chants of approval from their colleagues. But the compromise proposal of an immediate payment of a forty-day bonus they presented to the strikers was derisively rejected. The leaders, who may have been compelled to present this offer as a condition of their release, then announced that the strike would continue indefinitely. There was broad support for a long and militant struggle, the threat of which brought ETUF head Husayn Mugawir (breaking his earlier pledge) and company officials to the negotiating table in Mahalla, according to a statement released by the Workers' Coordination Committee. Such high-level negotiations could not have occurred except at the behest of State Security.

After halting production for less than a week, the Mahalla workers scored a huge victory for the Egyptian textile industry and beyond. They won a bonus equivalent to ninety days' pay, payable immediately. A meeting of the company's administrative general assembly increased this to at least 130 days' pay. In addition, a committee was formed in the Ministry of Investment to negotiate increases in extra compensation for the hazardous nature of their work and clothing allowances. Incentive pay became linked to basic pay and subject to a 7 percent annual increase. The executive board of the company was dissolved and al-Gibali was sacked. The days of the strike were treated as a paid vacation.

No doubt the expressly political rhetoric of the strikers worried the state as much as the millions of dollars company managers claimed to be losing every day the strike ground on. On September 27, after strike leader Muhammad al-'Attar had been released from jail, he reiterated his demand for greater accountability inside the Egyptian labor movement. He told the *Daily News Egypt*, "We want a change in the structure and hierarchy of the union system in this country.... The way unions in this country are organized is completely wrong, from top to bottom. It is organized to make it look like our representatives have been elected, when really they are appointed by the government." Addressing a pre-iftar rally after his release from prison, al-'Attar said, "I want the whole government to resign.... I want the Mubarak regime to come to an end. Politics and workers' rights are inseparable. Work is politics by itself. What we are witnessing here right now, this is as democratic as it gets."

Notes

Authors' Note This chapter was drawn from "Strikes in Egypt Spread from the Center of Gravity," *Middle East Report Online*, May 9, 2007; and "The Militancy of Mahalla al-Kubra," *Middle East Report Online*, September 29, 2007.

1. The Egyptian Workers and Trade Union Watch report for the month of April (in Arabic) is available at http://arabist.net/arabawy/wp-content/uploads/2007/05/aprilreport.pdf. The report for the first week of May (in Arabic) is available at http://arabist.net/arabawy/wp-content/uploads/2007/05/1stmay.pdf.

2. Interview with Jano Charbel posted at http://www.arabawy.org/2006/11/29/ndp-abducts-the-egyptian-trade-union-federation/#more-268.

3. *Al-Masri al-Yawm*, November 12, 2006.

4. Mohamed El-Sayed Said, "Silent No More," *al-Ahram Weekly*, February 8-14, 2007.

5. See the Kafr al-Dawwar Workers for Change statement, posted at http://www.arabawy.org/2007/04/18/kafr_dawwar_workers_for_change_mahlla/.

6. Joel Beinin, "Will the Real Egyptian Working Class Please Stand Up?" in Lockman, *Workers and Working Classes: Struggles, Histories, Historiographies*, (Albany, N.Y.: State University of New York Press, 1994), pp. 262-266.

7. Faiza Rady, "Workers Remain Undaunted," *al-Ahram Weekly*, May 3-9, 2007.

10. STRIKING BACK AT EGYPTIAN WORKERS

HESHAM SALLAM

The earliest mainstream narratives of the 2011 Egyptian revolution centered around a "crisis of the state." Among the elements of the crisis were the utter failure of top-down political reform, as shown in the shamelessly rigged 2010 legislative elections; mounting corruption and repression; emerging opportunities for collective action offered by networking sites like Facebook and Twitter; and the advent of neoliberal economic policies and the resulting constraints on the state's capacity to deliver on its traditional obligations, such as social services, subsidies, price controls, and guaranteed employment for college graduates. There was considerable consensus that the revolution was—at least in part—a backlash against the exclusionary economic order that the deposed president's son Gamal Mubarak and his associates helped to erect over the preceding decade. Yet over a year later it remains unclear if post-Mubarak Egypt can succeed in addressing the socio-economic grievances that helped to spark the January 25 uprising.

The prevailing discourse among Egyptian elites and opinion makers, however, signaled early on that the answer is no. The ambivalent, if not hostile, rhetoric directed toward demands for more humane standards of living pointed to the potential for continuity in the highly uneven economic order. While most believe that there will be no return to the pre-January 25 political system, even if post-Mubarak Egypt is not fully democratic, workers may continue to be marginalized by the economic liberalization begun under the previous regime.

Let the Wheel Turn

Shortly after the resignation of Husni Mubarak on February 11, Egypt witnessed the rise of what Egyptian authorities and media outlets began describing as *ihtijajat fi'awiyya* or small-group protests. The Arabic term *fi'a* simply means "group," but has acquired negative connotations and might be compared with how the term "special interest" is used to disparage American labor. In the first weeks and months of post-Mubarak Egypt, officials used its adjectival form *fi'awi* in reference to any demonstration, strike, or sit-in advancing demands related to distribution of wealth, whether the protesters were blue- or white-collar employees, and whether they were calling for higher wages, greater benefits, improved working conditions or replacement of corrupt management personnel. The term's usage encompassed the public and private sectors and applied to collective action as limited as a protest in a single state-owned enterprise and as broad as a national strike by disgruntled members of a professional syndicate.

Over the course of 2011, the Supreme Council of the Armed Forces (SCAF), state officials, and other elites built—wittingly or not—a consensus around a narrative that condemned this class of political action and designated it a challenge to Egypt's future security. Only three days after Mubarak's resignation, the SCAF released Communiqué 5, which outlined the negative impact of continuing protests on the economy and called on labor and professional syndicates to help bring about a return to normalcy in everyday life.[1] A few days later, an army statement described "*fi'awi* demands" as illegitimate, pledging to deal with the agitators through legal means in the name of "protecting the security of the nation and its citizens." On March 23, the government of Prime Minister 'Isam Sharaf approved a law banning protests, assemblies, and strikes that impeded private and public business, and rendering such actions punishable with up to a year in prison and a fine that could reach a half-million Egyptian pounds.

Vocal figures outside of government also took a leading role in denouncing labor actions. Two days after the release of Communiqué 5, the Muslim Brothers' then-spokesman Essam El-Erian accused *fi'awi* protests of undermining national consensus and expressed "understanding" for the army's point of view.[2] Usama Haykal, editor-in-chief of the liberal Wafd Party's daily, warned that the demonstrations could "destroy" the gains of the revolution. In March, a group of correspondents in al-Fayyoum announced that they would not cover *fi'awi* demonstrations because "while legal, they are poorly timed."[3] In April, Egypt's grand mufti, 'Ali Gum'a, went so far as to say that "instigators of *fi'awi* demonstrations violate the teachings of God."[4]

The dangers of *fi'awi* demands were said to be three. First, the workers who made them were accused of seeking to exploit the revolution to serve their own financial interest. Wahid 'Abd al-Magid of the al-Ahram Center for Political and Strategic Studies articulated this perspective on a number of televised occasions, chiding labor protesters for slaving away in silence for thirty years and then choosing a moment of crisis to press their case. Mainstream portrayals usually drew a contrast with the Tahrir Square gatherings that preceded the downfall of Mubarak, juxtaposing the selfless motives of Tahrir to *fi'awi* protests that put particular agendas ahead of the greater good. According to the columnist Khalid Muntasir, "Tahrir demonstrations raised a political slogan, 'The people want to bring down the regime.' All the slogans revolved around the meaning of freedom, as demonstrators set aside their *fi'awi* demands and summoned forth the spring of liberty. They did not ask for a raise or a bonus. They looked at the wider context and at the nation as a whole. The contagion of narrow viewpoints did not spread among them, as it did among those who engaged in continuous, hysterical, and vengeful *fi'awi* demonstrations."[5]

Second, bread-and-butter demands were presented as a major challenge to Egypt's economic prosperity and, therefore, national security. Finance Minister Samir Radwan claimed that *fi'awi* demonstrations cost the treasury 7 billion Egyptian pounds and the tourism sector 13.5 billion—making them largely responsible for Egypt's budget deficit and decline in foreign direct investment. Critics of strikes in 2011 regularly invoked the expression "the wheel of production must turn" as a means of telling protesters to go back to work. Supreme Council head Field Marshal Husayn Tantawi himself sounded this note in one of his few public appearances. Similarly, a week after Mubarak's resignation, prominent Salafi preacher

Muhammad Hassan used the phrase in calling for an end to strikes and sit-ins. Even opinion makers who proclaimed sympathy with the strikers' demands often deferred to elite consensus on this point. "Despite the legitimacy of these demands," wrote journalist and talk show host Lamis al-Hadidi, "I believe that this is not the time for settling accounts or self-interest. Now Egypt must come first and this is not simply a slogan.... Now the wheel must turn."[6] Interestingly, during the lead-up to the March 19, 2011 constitutional referendum those who advocated the "yes" vote also referred to "turning the wheel of production" to argue that approving the amendments would help bring normalcy to the country's economic life.

Third, so-called *fi'awi* protests, the narrative went, took their cues from affiliates of the formerly ruling National Democratic Party (NDP) stirring up trouble to reverse the gains of the revolution. Eight days after Mubarak's resignation, unidentified "informed sources" told *al-Misri al-Yawm* that three former regime figures were behind the "*fi'awi* demonstrations" in the state sector.[7] The same week, the official news website of the Muslim Brothers reported that NDP members were inciting labor unrest, citing an unidentified source claiming that a dentist who held a leading position in the former ruling party had been calling on his colleagues to stage demonstrations. Government officials corroborated claims of NDP involvement in inciting these activities, though they did not present any concrete evidence to back up the allegations. In March, Justice Minister Muhammad al-Gindi said that labor demonstrations were not spontaneous but a manifestation of an organized "counter-revolution" staged by remnants of the old regime. As the spring wore on, and sectarian tensions began to preoccupy the national political debate, it became standard practice for pundits and commentators to list *fi'awi* protests together with sectarian strife as the two main channels through which forces of darkness were attempting to undermine the January 25 revolution.

Convenient Omissions

What was most striking about the conventional narrative of *fi'awi* protests was not what it revealed, but rather what it concealed. While media reports took for granted the premise that "*fi'awi* protests" emerged after Mubarak's ouster, what was new was not the phenomenon but the terminology. Labor strikes, demonstrations, and sit-ins had been on the rise in Egypt for a good part of the previous decade. According to the Land Center for Human Rights, the number of labor protests in Egypt rose from 222 in 2006 to 756 in 2007 and exceeded 700 in 2009. Stated differently, well before January 25, 2011 the victims of economic liberalization among workers and civil servants had been loudly voicing their grievances, sometimes in highly visible locations, such as before the parliamentary building in downtown Cairo. Interestingly, the end of 2010 witnessed a number of high-profile strikes that were similar in character to what were later described as *fi'awi* actions, but the stigmatizing term *fi'awi* was rarely invoked. One prominent example was the weeks-long strike by cargo truck drivers in December 2010, just two months before Mubarak's ouster. Strikers were protesting new laws that, among other things, raised taxes and imposed hefty fines on truckers for carrying excess cargo. Because many industries relied on truckers for transportation of their raw materials and products, the strike imposed massive economic losses on the government and many businesses, and threatened to raise prices of basic food items and construction and agricultural material. The strike resulted in daily losses of 500 million Egyptian pounds, according to the Land Transportation Association. The stakes for key economic sectors were not negligible, given that the strike effectively froze significant imports and exports, as many companies that rely on truckers were unable to transport shipments from and to ports. Despite these serious economic repercussions, however, there was no talk among opposition elites of the urgent need to "turn the wheel of production" or for the strikers to set aside their demands for the sake of economic security. Instead, the blame was placed almost entirely on the incompetence of former Prime Minister Ahmad Nazif's government in dealing with the dire situation. For example, while acknowledging the severe impact of the strike on Egypt's economy, a former parliamentarian belonging to the Muslim Brothers criticized the government for dealing with the striking truckers in a "pedestrian way." In fact, some NDP members openly blamed the government for the impasse and supported the strikers' position.[8] Five weeks before the January 25 uprising, the Popular Campaign to Support Mohamed ElBaradei, the Nobel laureate and opposition politician, described the strike as "an inspirational lesson" that showed how "Egyptians can in fact change their current conditions if they really want to." The national consensus was so favorable to the strikers that Ahmad 'Izz, the infamous businessman and ruling-party boss, complained of unreasonable bias toward truckers who were refusing to abide by the law.[9]

The absence of criticism of the limited character of these strikes, despite the serious challenge they posed to Egypt's economy, was quite revealing. While job actions were an important part of contentious politics in pre-January 25 Egypt, they were not demonized as *fi'awi* protests. Before the release of the army's Communiqué 5, the mainstream media relied on terms like "demands-based protests" (*ihtijajat matlabiyya*) or labor sit-ins (*i'tisamat 'ummaliyya*) when discussing worker unrest. Yet the sudden proliferation of the phrase "*fi'awi* demands" in post-Mubarak Egypt began to obscure the long-standing nature of the grievances in question. Perplexed by the backlash, prominent blogger 'Ala' Sayf al-Islam wrote on May Day 2011: "Although labor strikes and demonstrations have been on the rise since 2006 and have not stopped since, and even though workers played an important role in bringing down Mubarak, we find the term '*fi'awiyya*' being used as an insult. And suddenly we find that demands for just wages and respectable working conditions are portrayed as selfish…. Others go so far as to portray the strikes of Egyptian workers and employees as part of the counter-revolution and a conspiracy by the National Democratic Party."[10]

The Illusion of Parochialism

By reinforcing the impression that the demands of discontented workers for more humane wages and working conditions were the mere product of parochial employee-management disputes inside various factories and bureaucracies, the term *fi'awi* did more than just stigmatize and dehistoricize these demands. Characterizing so-called *fi'awi* claims as the sum of a variety of disjointed narrow interests masked the serious national economic problems that these demonstrations and sit-ins collectively underscored.

The illusion of parochialism perhaps stemmed from the way that labor actions appeared as chaotic efforts isolated from one another and from any national political agenda. The fragmentation of these efforts, however, was not an expression of insularity as much as it was a reflection of the long-standing absence of meaningful national advocacy for Egyptian workers' rights. For decades, the state-controlled Egyptian Trade Union Federation enjoyed a legally sanctioned monopoly over the formal representation of workers and did more to rein in its members at the state's behest than to lobby on their behalf. At the level of elite politics under Mubarak, there was scant opportunity to channel the needs of Egyptian workers into a coherent platform because licensed opposition parties that claimed to speak for labor, like the Tagammu' Party, were dominated by regime allies who sought to keep workers quiet. Since the January 25 revolution there has been some progress in overcoming this challenge, including the founding of the Independent Federation for Egyptian Workers in January 2011 and the formation of new parties proclaiming commitment to labor rights. Such efforts, however, remain a work in progress.

Meanwhile, the fact that workers' protests and sit-ins in early post-Mubarak Egypt were disconnected from each other did not reduce the problem at hand to a set of opportunistic attempts at rent seeking by special interests. The problem, first and foremost, was and still is a national one, stemming from the failure of the state to deal with rising prices of basic goods such that a significant segment of Egyptian society remains stuck in a constant struggle to make ends meet. With inflation rates in the 2000s having reached levels not seen since the early 1990s and 40 percent of Egyptians living on less than $2 per day, the visible signs of socio-economic discontent, which so-called *fi'awi* protests epitomized, were not surprising. In fact, labor unrest was not the only expression of hardship: Riots over shortages in subsidized bread were widely reported in 2008 when bread sold at private bakeries became virtually unaffordable to many Egyptians after its price increased fivefold.

The decline in quality and quantity of state social services forced many families to spend a good chunk of their paychecks on services that Egyptians used to take for granted, such as health care and education. For example, it was estimated that Egyptian families were spending 10-15 billion Egyptian pounds per year on private tutoring in order to compensate for the shortcomings of formal instruction at public and private schools.[11] Estimates showed that two thirds of schoolchildren in Egypt were privately tutored and 60 percent of families that relied on these services spent at least one third of their incomes on the lessons.[12] It was not surprising, therefore, to observe chronic expressions of grievances revolving around the inadequacy of wages to keep up with rising prices and the cost of living. Further inflaming these grievances were frequent reports about the extreme disparity in pay across management and junior staff within individual organizations, notably in the banking sector, where angry employees objected.[13] The proliferation of the term *fi'awi* and its supporting assumptions diverted attention from the need for inclusive deliberation upon the urgent economic problems that touched people's everyday lives. The unreflective deference that many opinion makers awarded to "the wheel of production" helped to sideline these pressing concerns even as millions of Egyptians were crushed under the wheel's grinding rotation. A lonely dissenting voice appeared in an opinion piece titled "The People Want Another Wheel of Production" by *al-Shurouq* writer Wa'il Gamal: "Egyptians have revolted to replace the old wheel of production because it is oppressive and creates poverty, ignorance and illness."[14]

In other words, the surge in worker unrest following Mubarak's resignation highlighted the extent to which labor rights had deteriorated during the preceding years of crony capitalism. Mass layoffs and slashing of wages and benefits took place during the post-2004 rush toward economic liberalization under the Nazif government, particularly in the privatization of public-sector enterprises. More and more workers were contingent and temporary: It was estimated that in 2010 three million Egyptians were employed under contractual arrangements that gave their employers the de facto right to dismiss them at any moment. One common practice was to compel new employees literally to sign a "resignation letter" at the outset of their employment. The absence of benefits such as health insurance in these contracts was quite alarming, since temporary employment was most concentrated in fields involving high-risk physical labor, including the agriculture, construction, and mining sectors.[15] Many Egyptians decided to enter into these insecure contractual arrangements in the state sector and put up with monthly salaries not exceeding 100 Egyptian pounds in the hope that eventually they would be hired as full-time state employees, affording them a higher salary, more benefits, and—someday—a pension check. While the interim government announced steps to grant temporary workers full employment rights in state agencies, little was done to address the difficulty that millions of Egyptian employees continued to face due to the state's ambivalence. The grievances of temporary employees, moreover, were but a sample of a broader problem in which considerable sectors of the economy are untouched by laws regulating labor rights. For example, the government's decision in 2010 to raise the monthly minimum wage from its 1984 level of 35 to 400 Egyptian pounds, slightly above the poverty line at $67, was meaningless from the perspective of the seven million Egyptians (including half the women in the work force) who work in the informal economy outside the reach of government scrutiny.

In the aforementioned May Day column, there was a powerful list of ordinary people from all walks of life enduring hardship: a "big-shot engineer with a masters degree" who had to sign a resignation letter on her first day of work; a high-school mathematics teacher of eighteen years who "still rides a Vespa motorbike" and "would die of hunger" without the supplemental income from private tutoring; an assistant manager at a Kentucky Fried Chicken store who worked from 9 am until 10 pm every day; a Ministry of Health doctor whose pension after a thirty-year term of service was 900 pounds ($151); women who got only three months of maternity leave. These people were not unlike the protesters dismissed in the press as selfish, except that many of the "*fi'awi* demonstrators" were even more beleaguered.

Finally, the popular assertion that labor unrest was at the root of Egypt's post-Mubarak economic woes, as Egyptian officials often alleged, was unpersuasive, to say the least. Official claims that an end to *fi'awi* protests would have immediately steered foreign direct investment and tourists back to the Nile ignored the lawlessness following the disappearance of police from the streets during the January 25 uprising; the uncertainty of Egypt's political future; sectarian tensions; travel advisories issued by foreign governments; and the inconvenience of living under curfew and martial law.

Rewriting History

Opinion makers who popularized the term "*fi'awi* demands" seemed to be writing an unusually selective historical account of the unfinished January 25 revolution.

In response to public outcry over the government's decision to ban strikes and demonstrations, Prime Minister Sharaf told journalists in March that the purpose of the new law is to protect the revolution from *fi'awi* demonstrations. A week later, a political activist told a newspaper that Sharaf assured the Coalition of the Youth of the Revolution that the new law would not infringe upon their right to convene the mass demonstrations they usually hold in Tahrir Square almost every Friday.[16] Implicit in the government's approach was that the Tahrir rallies were an extension of the revolution, whereas labor demonstrations referred to as *fi'awi* supported counter-revolution. The dichotomy drawn in these government statements reinforced the belief that demands for distributive justice played a limited role in bringing about Mubarak's demise. This claim, while common, was flawed for three main reasons.

First, the month of January before the uprising witnessed an intensification of labor demonstrations and strikes. Whether these activities provided the impetus for mass participation in the uprising warrants further investigation, but at least these trends showed that many signs of public discontent revolved around redistributive demands immediately before the uprising—let alone years before it. A few examples of these activities included: a sit-in by fifteen hundred Mansoura University Hospital workers who demanded permanent employment after having worked more than fifteen years as temporary employees; a strike of three hundred workers in a wood factory in Dashna in demand of unpaid wages; a strike by 20 percent of the railway workshop employees in Cairo; a strike by two hundred nurses and X-ray technicians at Ashmoun hospital in protest of slashed benefits; and a sit-in by al-Karakat Company workers in Ismailiyya and Port Said in protest of disparities in working hours among employees.[17]

Second, working-class regions like Mahalla and Suez that had undergone major labor unrest saw demonstrations of thousands during the January 25 uprising, not to mention intense battles with security forces. This fact indicates that redistributive demands later characterized as *fi'awi* played a role in moving the masses in support of the revolution. It also suggests that workers participated in the uprising, albeit as individuals and not as organized labor, as leading labor historian Joel Beinin and others have argued.[18] Even though it is not possible to evaluate the role of redistributive demands precisely, the wide distance that certain opinion makers projected between the revolution and calls for humane standards of living seems at the very least overblown. It is one thing to argue that demonstrators set aside their socio-economic demands and rallied behind a unified message calling on Mubarak to step down. It is another thing to argue that economic hardships were irrelevant to why people chose to take to the streets in the first place.

Third, the understandable focus of media reports on Tahrir Square and the cross-class unity there must not detract from the importance of labor unrest outside of the major squares during Mubarak's final days. For example, after businesses reopened on February 7 for the first time since January 28, workers' strikes and demonstrations became widespread throughout the governorates of Egypt. The demands of these protests were not unlike the "*fi'awi* demands" that many rushed to condemn shortly after February 11. Signs of labor unrest that occurred on February 9, one day before the SCAF released its first communiqué, included: demonstrations by thousands of workers in Helwan, Kafr al-Dawwar, and Kafr al-Zayyat; a demonstration by temporary employees in front of the General Authority of Health Insurance building in Cairo in demand of permanent employment; a demonstration by over five hundred employees of the Red Crescent on behalf of temporary workers on provisional contracts for twenty years; a strike by the Boulaq railway workshop's workers who gathered to prevent trains from passing through; and a march by thousands of street cleaning personnel down Sudan Street in the Cairo neighborhood of Muhandisin to demand higher wages and better working conditions.

Some close observers, like the activist and blogger Hossam El-Hamalawy, believe that labor strikes in the last week of the uprising were the tipping point that forced Mubarak's resignation.[20] There is no credible account as yet of the exact chain of events that pushed Mubarak out of office. Yet the fact that one of the first things the SCAF tried to do after taking power was to bring an end to strikes suggests that work stoppages were a source of deep concern for the generals who surrounded Mubarak in his last days. The claim that these activities hastened Mubarak's ouster is, therefore, quite plausible.

The proliferation of the term *"fi'awi"* to describe Egyptian workers' demands and reduce them to parochial, even counter-revolutionary interests was more than just a denial of the right to a humane living standard. There was more at stake than just the absurdity of the assumptions on which the usage of this term was based. The ubiquity of the term signified a mounting elite consensus that worked to rewrite the history of the Egyptian revolution, its meaning and its goals—with the purpose of sidelining pressing socio-economic problems and the millions of Egyptians who suffer from them. While many believe that Egyptians revolted largely out of socio-economic discontent, the speed with which influential figures clung to the derogatory term *fi'awi* indicates that addressing these grievances in post-Mubarak Egypt—let alone putting them on the national political agenda—may not be as easy as one would have thought. It remains to be seen whether the emergence of new parties and independent unions and syndicates will give workers and their allies among advocates of distributive justice a shot at countering this wave of unreflective elitism. But, in any event, the trends suggest that what awaits Egyptian workers after the end of a decades-long bad romance with Mubarak's authoritarianism is not a happy ending, but new challenges and greater uncertainty.

Notes

1. The statement appears online at: http://www.sis.gov.eg/Ar/Story.aspx?sid=44125.

2. *Al-Misri al-Yawm*, February 16, 2011.

3. *Al-Wafd*, March 9, 2011.

4. *Al-Yawm al-Sabi'*, April 1, 2011.

5. Khalid Muntasir, "Tahrir Contagion," *al-Misri al-Yawm*, March 4, 2011. [Arabic]

6. Lamis al-Hadidi, "Good Morning, O Country," *al-Misri al-Yawm*, February 15, 2011. [Arabic]

7. *Al-Misri al-Yawm*, February 20, 2011.

8. *Al-Yawm al-Sabi'*, January 11, 2011.

9. *Al-Misri al-Yawm*, December 29, 2010.

10. Quoted in Bilal Fadl, "When Will the Workers Win?" *al-Misri al-Yawm*, May 1, 2011. [Arabic]

11. Ahmed Zewail, "Reflections on Arab Renaissance," *Cairo Review of Global Affairs* (Spring 2011).

12. *Al-Ahram*, September 21, 2011.

13. *Al-Ahram* April 28, 2011.

14. Wa'il Gamal, "The People Want Another Wheel of Production," *al-Shurouq*, April 26, 2011. [Arabic]

15. *Al-Misri al-Yawm*, October 22, 2010.

16. *Al-Dustour al-Asli*, April 6, 2011.

17. See http://www.id3m.com for a full list of news stories about labor protests in Egypt since December 2010.

18. Joel Beinin, "Egypt's Workers Rise Up," *The Nation*, March 7, 2011.

19. The full list is in Husayn 'Abd al-Wahid, *Thawrat Misr: 18 yawman hazzat al-'alam* (Cairo: Dar Akhbar al-Yawm), pp. 50-54.

20. "Interview with Hossam El-Hamalawy," *Jadaliyya*, April 9, 2011.

11. SIGHTINGS OF THE EGYPTIAN DEEP STATE

ISSANDR EL AMRANI

The turbulence that hit Egypt starting in November 2011 seemed, at first glance, mostly a testament to the poor performance of the Supreme Council of the Armed Forces (SCAF) in handling the transition away from the rule of Husni Mubarak. Having assumed power on February 10, 2011, the SCAF moved quickly to attain the stamp of popular legitimacy through a March 19 referendum on constitutional amendments. In the following months, however, the conclave of generals stumbled over the flawed logic of its own plan for the transition, as well as ad hoc decision making and a high-handed, dismissive attitude toward the new politics of the country. The SCAF's plan, in brief, was to engineer a restoration of civilian rule that shielded the army's political and economic prerogatives from civilian oversight, and perhaps bolstered those roles, yielding a system not unlike the "deep state" that prevailed for decades in Turkey. Such was the system in Egypt, in fact, under Mubarak.

By the end of 2011, the SCAF was far from securing such behind-the-scenes dominance for the military and was much further from winning popular consent to that arrangement. Indeed, for much of the political class and a not inconsequential slice of public opinion, the violence of the early winter reduced the military's moral authority to a level unseen since its defeat at Israel's hands in 1967.

In some respects, this delegitimization was not unlike the erosion of Mubarak's authority over the 2000s: Just as the deposed president, once deemed untouchable, became the butt of activist and media scorn from late 2004 onward, the military found itself subjected to unprecedented criticism and scrutiny. The difference was that the SCAF's fall from grace occurred at an accelerated pace, propelled by the new faith in participatory politics unleashed by the January uprising and the army's own bungling.

Fateful Triangle

In the eyes of some, the protest movement and the political class shared blame with the SCAF for the stalling of the post-Mubarak transition—the former for taking to the streets without a clearer long-term agenda, the latter for failing to elaborate a coherent counter point to the SCAF's misadministration. Instead of working together, politicians of all stripes engaged in time-wasting arguments about the identity of Egypt, eventually turning to the SCAF for arbitration.

Egypt's largest and closest-knit political party force, the Muslim Brothers, cozied up to the generals, who were comforted by the Brothers' supposed ability to control the streets. The Brothers, officially outlawed under Mubarak and his predecessors, obtained a degree of "normalization," as well as a transition plan that favored them. An Islamist intellectual luminary, the former judge Tariq al-Bishri, chaired the commission tasked with redrafting the six constitutional articles for the March 19 referendum. This body included no representatives of secular parties or revolutionary youth groups, and only one politician, the Brothers' former MP from Alexandria, Subhi Salih. The Brothers and other Islamists campaigned for the amendments' approval, at times presenting a "yes" vote as a religious duty. After 79 percent of voters said "yes," the amended clauses were incorporated into a sixty-two article "constitutional declaration" that was simply decreed by the SCAF. But the Brothers were attracted by the generals' blueprint putting parliamentary elections first—ahead of a completely new constitution that would allocate Parliament's powers—because their superior numbers and organization made them most likely to succeed.

Secular politicians, for their part, strove in vain to get the SCAF's imprimatur upon the outlines of a new constitution. Some of them, particularly the newly registered parties that chose to recruit from the ranks of the formerly ruling National Democratic Party (which was dissolved by court order in April 2011), sought the tacit backing of the *ancien régime*.

Formation of this Islamist-SCAF-secularist triangle naturally redounded to the generals' benefit. The ruling brass positioned themselves as umpires of what was, for the most part, a non-dispute over how such terms as "Islamic" and "civil" ought to figure in the definition of the post-Mubarak polity. The secularists had fallen into the Islamists' trap of debates over identity, where they could never win, rather than respond to the public's demands for social justice, prosperity, and law and order.

In the meantime, the politicians lent little succor to the protest movement—a motley crew of liberal youths, seasoned radicals, and many thousands of unaffiliated sympathizers for whom the January uprising remains an indelible memory. Those activists who rejected formal politics or wished to work independently found themselves the target of reinvigorated security services; a state media machine that painted them as troublemakers and, increasingly, traitors; and the SCAF-led project to promote "stability" over "chaos" and "sectoral (*fi'awi*) demands," code for supposedly parochial concerns whose expression was detrimental to national progress.

In mid-February 2012, several activists were sent before military tribunals, which offer no possibility of appeal. The SCAF also continued to field civilian security services under the hated Emergency Law in place since 1981. In the autumn of 2011, other provisions of this law were invoked, such as the prohibition upon public gatherings of more than five persons. The murder rap faced by blogger Alaa Abdel Fattah was only one of the ludicrous charges thrown at well-known protesters. It is unclear what effect the expiration of the Emergency Law in May 2012 will have on the SCAF's security operations.

Dark Clouds Over Cairo

The military's claim to be guardian of the revolution began weakening soon after Mubarak was toppled. The SCAF was slow to arrest kingpins of the old regime, and its military police maltreated protesters in March and April 2011, as with the infamous "virginity tests" of women. The protest movement's mounting dissatisfaction culminated in the reoccupation of Tahrir Square that July. Another turning point was the October 9 confrontation at the state broadcasting headquarters, known as Maspero, in which twenty-five protesters for Coptic rights died at the hands of army troops. (The SCAF claimed that an unknown number of soldiers were also killed; Abdel Fattah was accused of murder in this connection.) If many Egyptians accepted that these deaths resulted from panic among the soldiers, the SCAF's grip on public sympathy slipped badly amid the clashes of November and December.

Unlike previous instances, Maspero and a few others excepted, the winter confrontations—in Cairo, Alexandria, and Suez—were very bloody, claiming at least fifty-seven lives and wounding over fifteen hundred. The clashes began on November 19, the day after a peaceful "million-man march" in Tahrir Square, led by Islamist groups but which also attracted significant secular participation. The protesters focused their ire on "supra-constitutional principles" drafted by then Deputy Prime Minister 'Ali al-Salmi, an attempt to predetermine basic tenets of a new constitution as well as rules for the composition of the future constitutional assembly. Among the proposed measures: guaranteed secrecy for the military budget and SCAF authority to impose its own constituent assembly should the body appointed by Parliament fail to agree upon a draft national charter. The day of protest against the army's power grab passed without incident.

The decision by Salafi groups and the Muslim Brothers to back the November 18 demonstration marked the Islamist forces' first public break with the SCAF. Coming less than two weeks before the start of parliamentary elections, it was an important challenge to the military. The Islamists were confident in their electoral chances, however, and their participation was not a sign of a divorce between them and the army. The Brothers had resorted to protest only on rare occasion: Indeed, for most of the transition period, their cadre stood aside, a decision many frequenters of Tahrir Square saw as evidence of a deal with the SCAF. Strengthening this analysis was the fact that the Brothers, as well as Salafis, largely withdrew from Tahrir at 6 pm on November 18, leaving other activists behind. By the next morning, only a few hundred diehards stayed with the small encampment of families of victims of the January uprising. The families had set up their tents several weeks previous to demand investigations into the deaths of their loved ones and delivery of the promised compensation.

The November-December violence stemmed from the state's decision to send in riot police to clear out these remaining demonstrators. The police used considerable force, prompting the full reoccupation of Tahrir Square and a fracas on the adjoining Muhammad Mahmoud Street that claimed forty lives and wounded hundreds, many of them critically. Police snipers were found to be aiming for protesters' heads; several activists lost an eye, including one who had lost a first eye in January. The massive use of tear gas over the ensuing week shrouded much of central Cairo in an acrid cloud, afflicting hundreds, if not more, with serious ailments. Doctors at the field hospital set up by volunteers witnessed several case of seizures brought on by tear gas inhalation. Whether, as many suspected, a substance other than ordinary CS gas was used remains unknown. Some activists alleged that military-grade chemicals were deployed when normal tear gas proved ineffective.

The circumstances of the decision to order the unnecessary police intervention of

November 18 were puzzling. Several cabinet ministers stated that they opposed such a step, including, oddly, the minister of interior, who officially oversees the riot police, the Central Security Forces. The SCAF or other security officers may have overruled them. Equally strange was that the fighting was allowed to go on for several days before the army intervened, taking advantage of a truce to build a wall to separate the riot police from the protesters.

The Muhammad Mahmoud Street clashes, which recalled the scenes of police brutality in late January, outraged the public. The SCAF made some important concessions, agreeing to hold presidential elections by July 2012 (previously they could have been held as late as mid-2013) and sacking the ineffectual government of 'Isam Sharaf, the former Mubarak-era minister of transport whose early pro-revolutionary stance had won over protesters in February. Attention shifted quickly away from Tahrir Square as parliamentary elections began on November 28, drawing large crowds to polling stations.

Over the next two weeks, Tahrir Square reopened and its occupiers launched a satellite sit-in three blocks south, in front of the prime minister's office on People's Assembly Street, where Parliament is also located. The protesters advanced multiple demands, some of long standing and others of fresh provenance. They called for an end to military trials and accountability for police brutality, for instance, as well as opposing the appointment of Kamal al-Ganzouri, a Mubarak-era prime minister (1996-1999), as the new caretaker premier. After Sharaf's firing, there had been hope that the military would share power with a civilian presidential council. The sit-in perdured through the first weeks of December with no problems aside from a dozen cases of food poisoning. The country was riveted by the elections and, in particular, by the success of the Muslim Brothers and the Salafis, who respectively garnered some 40 percent and 20 percent of seats in the first round.

The second round of street fighting began early on the morning of December 17, by most accounts when a member of the cabinet sit-in kicked a football into the gardens of Parliament and climbed over the gate to fetch it. After being detained by military police for several hours, he was returned to the protesters bruised and beaten. By the next morning, a makeshift barricade blocked People's Assembly Street from the major artery of Qasr al-'Ayni Street, which leads to Tahrir Square. On one side, protesters threw rocks, and on the other, men in civilian clothes and uniformed soldiers did the same. The authorities described the plainclothes combatants as irate residents, though there is no housing on that particular street; activists retorted that they were undercover police officers. Groups of soldiers and other men also stood on the roofs of nearby buildings, hurling rocks, makeshift Motolov cocktails, office furniture, and debris down upon the protesters' heads. Occasionally, each side stopped to shout insults and give their opponents the finger.

Their detractors, and many sympathizers, accused the protesters of throwing rocks for thrills or to get revenge. Most astonishing to Egyptians, however, was the behavior of military police and other soldiers. Never, they shook their heads, had men in khaki uniforms been allowed to behave so wantonly. Snipers were apparently used to kill protesters, including a prominent al-Azhar sheikh, 'Imad 'Iffat, who had come to broker a truce. Soldiers were captured on camera urinating on protesters from atop buildings and assaulting women, such as the "girl with the blue bra," a volunteer doctor at the Tahrir Square field hospital whose brutal stomping was gasped at worldwide. For most of this time, riot control troops and other regular police were absent. There was no information as to why the Ministry of Interior did not handle the protests, as was custom. The soldiers were not only ready to treat Egyptians as poorly as the police did, but also to forgo the discipline one might expect of military men, and certainly of those so fulsomely praised for declining to fire on protesters in January and February.

The battle in front of the cabinet office petered out over the next few days, with deadly army raids pushing protesters back toward Tahrir Square. Two major streets near the plaza, Sheikh Rihan and Qasr al-'Ayni, joined Muhammad Mahmoud in being walled off by twelve feet of concrete, further scrambling Cairo's already messy traffic. To the government and much of the pro-SCAF media, the protesters were hooligans far removed from the "true revolutionaries" of January. This line retained some credence with the public, which was weary of disturbances. But it was undeniable that the credibility and legitimacy of the SCAF, and indeed the military institution as a whole, suffered severe damage.

Below the Surface

Coming as they did in the middle of the elections, the protests had the potential to divert the road back to civilian rule. Among Islamists, in particular, the protests were deeply worrying. Most disquieted of all were the Muslim Brothers, who feared that prolonged unrest could lead to cancellation of the elections. Having lifted their moratorium on participation in large protests on November 18, the Brothers refused to support any subsequent ones. Their publications—the Arabic- and English-language websites and the daily newspaper of their new Freedom and Justice Party (FJP)—adopted a deliberate ambiguity on the subject. Leading Brothers who had been prominent in the January uprising, like the former MP Mahmoud al-Baltagi, were visibly distressed by the organization's reticence toward mass politics, but eventually acquiesced.

Many spoke of a trap set by the SCAF, particularly during the second wave of protests near the cabinet building, when the military appeared to provoke and perpetuate the street battles. These observers noted the proximity of the People's Assembly Street incidents to the Islamists' gains in the first round of elections. If the Brothers had joined in the melee, they said, the SCAF would have had the excuse it was seeking to scotch the remainder of the balloting. The killing of the highly respected scholar Sheikh 'Iffat, a member of Dar al-Ifta', the authority empowered to issue fatwas on behalf of the Egyptian state, was particularly traumatic for Islamists. Abu al-'Ila Madi, head of the Wasat Party, an offshoot of the Brothers since 1995, was booed away from 'Iffat's funeral at al-Azhar mosque because he was serving on a body appointed after the Muhammad Mahmoud Street protests to advise the SCAF. Madi resigned the next day.

The Brothers' decision to stay out of the streets, their insistence on elections being paramount, their disdain for the protest movement, which at times echoed SCAF talking points—all this earned them the opprobrium of many activists. In the view of many, the Brothers were overly concerned with elections that they had, in essence, already won. They were suspected of preparing, as the incoming legislature's largest party and probable kingmaker in the presidential election, for coming negotiations with the army over Parliament's powers and the writing of a new constitution. It was likely that the Brothers were thus preoccupied, and indeed some of them may have tacitly approved of crackdowns on mostly secular protesters, but the Islamist factor does not explain why events took such a grim turn. If the SCAF and the Brothers were in cahoots, the army would not have needed to flex its muscles as it did on People's Assembly Street. If, instead, the SCAF intended to assert its monopoly of violence as a message to the Brothers, as well as other political forces, it did so at the tremendous cost of shattering the reputation of its leader, Field Marshal Muhammad Husayn Tantawi, and sullying the image of the army both at home and abroad.

Apart from gross incompetence, the army's actions had another explanation: reassertion of a "deep state" that was badly bruised during the January uprising and took some time to regain its footing. While the army may have been the bedrock of the post-1952 Egyptian state, the country's array of security agencies now crosses the boundaries between civilian and military. The Ministry of Interior's agencies were particularly battered by the uprising and the fall of the ex-minister, Habib al-'Adli, who had amassed unmatched clout in his long years on the job. It was not clear who controlled the Ministry at the time, but it was almost certain that the police veteran in charge when the wintertime clashes broke out, Mansour al-'Isawi, was not master of his own house.

The strongest security agency in post-Mubarak Egypt continues to be the General Intelligence Services (GIS), which gleans its senior staff from the military and whose only loss in January was its head, 'Umar Sulayman, who briefly served as Mubarak's first and last vice president. Sulayman was heir apparent from his appointment as vice president on January 29 until February 5, when an assassination attempt (most likely carried out by elements of the military) against him failed. He mostly disappeared from public view after Mubarak's departure (which he announced), aside from a visit to Mecca when he met Saudi Arabia's Crown Prince Nayif, until his death from a heart condition in July 2012.

Sulayman's successor at the GIS was one of his former deputies, Murad Muwafi, a veteran of Egypt's mediation in the Israeli-Palestinian conflict. Muwafi was made a full member of the SCAF and played a key role there alongside the "big three" generals believed to run the body: Tantawi, Chief of Staff of the Armed Forces Sami 'Inan and Commander of the Army's Central Command Hasan Ruwayni. The GIS is the SCAF's main source of information—including, according to foreign officials who have met with SCAF members, the reports the generals frequently cited throughout 2011 hinting at a foreign conspiracy against Egypt. The GIS, in other words, is the SCAF's eyes and ears. Egypt's ruling clique is unusually dependent on a single source of intelligence, one that appears to have taken over the Interior Ministry's demoralized and sometimes vengeance-bent assets. Muhammad Ibrahim, the minister of interior in the Ganzouri cabinet, was rumored to be close to the GIS.

It is worth recalling what the SCAF is, or rather, what it is not: The SCAF is not modeled on the chain of command in the armed forces, and its members have widely different degrees of interaction with, and influence upon, civilian affairs. Only half of the body is composed of military officers who occupy top billets in the army's organogram, such as commander of the air force or navy. The rest are political officers, mainly lieutenants of Tantawi who held senior positions at the Ministry of Defense (and who often appear on television as spokesmen), or officers drawn from the GIS or the military's own intelligence service (often a career precursor to a GIS assignment). The method by which the SCAF makes decisions, its frequent slowness in doing so, and the confusion that prevails (or is allowed to linger) over the manner in which it handles security issues, in particular—all these things are a mystery, even by the army's customary standard of opacity.

In elite Egyptian circles, among the Muslim Brothers and amid an increasing number of activists, concern grew over 2011 that the SCAF's right hand did not know what the left hand was doing. A bumbling SCAF provided one explanation for the army's spectacular mishandling of protests after months of building its popularity on declining to fire on protesters to defend the Mubarak regime. But while incompetence was a tempting explanation—it was easy to picture the generals as a coterie of out-of-touch old men—the events of late 2011 rendered this answer insufficient and unconvincing. For many activists, the leading interpretation became that the SCAF had always been intent on restoring the practices of the Mubarak regime. But this theory, too, fell short, as the inner mechanisms of the SCAF's decision-making, its dependence on intelligence agencies with their own agenda and the likelihood that the generals were not all on the same wavelength had to be factored in.

Next Generation

The dramatic moves by newly-elected President Muhammad Mursi on August 12, 2012—retiring Gens. Tantawi, 'Inan and Muwafi and and promoting a younger generation of officers; and canceling an amendment to the Constitutional Declaration issued by the SCAF on the last day of the presidential election in June 2012 that castrated the incoming president and gave the SCAF wide continued powers—were, in a sense, confirmation that the military is not a unitary actor. It was notable that the new Defense Minister, Abdel Fattah El-Sisi (formerly head of Military Intelligence), is the second- youngest general in the SCAF and his second-in-command, Chief of Staff of the Armed Forces Sedky Sobhy (formerly Commander of the Third Army) the youngest. The military leaders in ascendance received training in the United States and did not participate in any of Egypt's major wars with Israel.

Their rise does not tell us, however, that they are democrats, even if they appear to have decided that the armed forces should retreat from the front-line political role they have played since the fall of Husni Mubarak. Nor does it resolve in itself questions of reform and accountability in the military and the security services, and their relationship with elected civilian leaders. Indeed, the arrangement between these generals and President Mursi appear to be based on a guarantee that the military will not be subject to inquiry over its handling of the post-Mubarak transition: retired generals have been decorated and publicly praised, and some have landed in cabinet posts and other civilian positions. It appears unlikely, for now, that there will be accountability for the clashes of Maspero, Mohammed Mahmoud Street and parliament of late 2011 and early 2012 (which claimed dozens of lives), and other abuses of the transition period.

12. EGYPT'S GENERALS AND TRANSNATIONAL CAPITAL

SHANA MARSHALL AND JOSHUA STACHER

Before and after the ejection of Husni Mubarak from office, the size of the Egyptian army's share in the economy has been a subject of great debate. The army is known to manufacture everything from olive oil and shoe polish to the voting booths used in Egypt's 2011 parliamentary elections, but no one knows for sure how much of the country's economy the military industries control. News reports have cited "expert" estimates that are all over the map, from 5 percent to 40 percent or more. Pushed by the *New York Times* to venture a guess, the former minister of trade, Rashid Muhammad Rashid, now in exile, offered "less than 10 percent."[1] The broad range of figures drives home the impossibility of measuring the footprint of what scholar Robert Springborg calls "Military, Inc."[2] Not only are army holdings classified as state secrets—reporting on them can land a journalist in jail—but they are also too vast and dispersed to estimate with any confidence.

The military's oldest commercial interests are the factories run by the Ministry of Military Production, the Arab Organization for Industrialization (AOI) and the National Service Projects Organization. But the army also oversees numerous subsidiaries of state-owned holding companies and owns shares in public-private ventures. In many cases, these smaller operations are embedded in transnational conglomerates that reach into several economic sectors, from construction and maritime shipping to weapons manufacturing.

High-ranking army officers were once trustees of "import substitution industrialization" and other statist policies pursued by President Gamal Abdel Nasser. Conventional wisdom is that the Egyptian military seeks to uphold such Nasser-era legacies as a sizable public sector and a protectionist trade policy. The 2011 uprising strengthened this belief, particularly after the defenestration of Gamal Mubarak and his circle, masterminds of the aggressive neoliberal reform carried out under Prime Minister Ahmad Nazif from 2004-2010. That program, had it continued, might have dismantled the last public-sector enterprises in Egypt, many of which the army runs. The army is thought to have pushed out Gamal partly in order to preserve these operations. US officials had telegraphed this analysis years before: In a September 2008 State Department cable published by WikiLeaks, then-Ambassador to Egypt Margaret Scobey called the military's conglomerates "quasi-commercial," concluding that the government's privatization schemes were viewed "as a threat to [the military's] economic position" and that the military "generally opposes economic reforms." Scobey's predecessor Frank Ricciardone had made a similar argument in a March 2008 cable: "[Field

Marshal Hussein] Tantawi believes that Egypt's economic reform plan fosters social instability by lessening [government] controls over prices and production."

After the Mubarak family's ouster in February 2011, the United States tried to nudge the Supreme Council of the Armed Forces (SCAF), Egypt's de facto rulers, onto something like Gamal's path. In his May 19, 2011 speech on the Middle East, President Barack Obama claimed the US had already asked the International Monetary Fund and World Bank to devise a plan to stabilize and modernize the Egyptian economy. Obama said the US had written off $1 billion of Egyptian debt and would "work with our Egyptian partners to invest these resources to foster growth and entrepreneurship." Under social pressure, however, the SCAF spurned the initial IMF loan package, making many observers anxious that Egypt would return to a more statist model of economic management.

But the SCAF's subsequent actions suggested that those concerns were misplaced. The army was diligent in disciplining striking workers, while the SCAF dragged its feet on draft laws setting minimum and maximum wages and legalizing independent labor unions. These moves might have invoked the spirit of Nasser, who himself hanged two strike leaders less than a month after the coup that brought him to office, except that the army paired the crackdown with other measures being promoted by the IMF and World Bank. Egypt's interim military rulers issued tranches of dollar-denominated treasury bills to guard against inflation and reassure investors, for instance, and refused to lift Egypt's debt ceiling. They replaced Finance Minister Samir Radwan—an old NDP stalwart who had put forth an expansionary budget that increased social expenditures and wages—with Hazim Biblawi, a strong advocate of free-market liberalism and the "rationalizing" of state subsidies on staples. To soften up the public for cuts in fuel subsidies, the SCAF was rumored to have orchestrated fuel shortages and delays in gasoline delivery—even at the military's own Wataniyya gas stations. Finally, in December the SCAF "grudgingly" agreed to a $3.2 billion IMF loan facility. The funds were scheduled to be disbursed around the time the Egyptian Central Bank would run out of currency reserves, narrowly averting economic disaster and allowing the army to claim the credit. At the same time, the SCAF favored political players who viewed Egypt's interests as synonymous with those of the military's economic planners. Acquiescing to this logic was rewarded with entry into the state's reconfigured institutions. Voices that rejected this vision, such as independent labor organizers and protesters for social justice, were derided as *fi'awi*—divisive and parochial.[3]

In retrospect, it seems clear that while the military-industrial complex resisted the privatization pursued by Ahmad Nazif's cabinet, their recalcitrance was predicated on two fears: first, that military operations would be next on the chopping block and second, that the private-sector oligarchs close to Gamal would eclipse Military, Inc. in Egypt's political economy. Tenders of privatization are excludable goods, and the more of them were granted to Gamal's cronies, the fewer remained for military companies, which sought them just as assiduously.

After a year with the SCAF as executive, and many of Gamal's associates facing investigation or in exile, Egypt's economic trajectory looked remarkably similar to its position in 2010. No longer did silk-suited technocrats enjoin Egyptians to forgo living wages, safe working conditions, and political accountability in pursuit of "economic growth." Instead, khaki-clad officers echoed the argument that social justice must wait, accusing those who demanded it of scaring away tourists and foreign investors. Proximity to political power continued to be the primary path to economic privilege, and the traditional constituencies of the interventionist state—civil servants, peasants, and the urban poor—remained marginal. In tandem with transnational capital, the army sought to corner markets even as it espoused free-market nostrums. And Military, Inc. may do the Mubaraks one better: With Gamal's crony capitalist allies out of the way, there is no longer any competitor whose ambitions are a counterweight to the army's appetite for economic expansion.

Expanding the Portfolio

Its Nasserist aura notwithstanding, the Egyptian military's foray into the private sector was some two decades in the making. Military companies are best known for making war materiel, and despite a historically small foreign market, weapons systems continue to roll off the army's assembly lines at rates exceeding what even a robust police state can absorb. Warehouses bulge with inventory. Some arms manufacturers believe that "export is our future,"[4] but the overall health of the army's portfolio requires that it diversify its economic operations.

Military, Inc. has accordingly inaugurated projects in sectors ranging from maritime transport to oil and gas exploration and renewable energy. Contrary to the army's reputation as a pillar of protectionism, these projects are collaborative, bringing in Gulf conglomerates, as well as Western and Asian multinationals, as partners. Like Egypt's civilian private-sector oligarchs, the brass exploited their political influence and privileged access to economic inputs to attract foreign investors whose capital infusions and technology transfer agreements beefed up the balance sheet. The military's investment strategy appeared to reap significant dividends: Not only did the SCAF "loan" the Egyptian Central Bank $1 billion in December 2011, but it also managed to dole out sizable monthly bonuses (about 2,400 Egyptian pounds, or $400) to mid-ranking army personnel in the year following Mubarak's ouster.[5]

The military had been diversifying its holdings long before the uprising, through expansion into sectors like real estate development and heavy equipment leasing, in which the military's enormous land holdings, infrastructure, and capital provided major advantages, as well as the privately owned businesses that constitute what became known as the "officer economy." The army's tentacles also grasped large shares of the civilian public sector as part of the "privatization" process in the 1990s. Alexandria Shipyard, for instance, was turned over to the Ministry of Defense in August 2007. It now produces large merchant vessels and warships and offers its repair services to private shipping companies. Likewise, the army-controlled AOI eventually acquired 100 percent of the General Egyptian Company for Railway Wagons and Coaches, initially offered up for privatization in 2002. But the joint investments with Gulf conglomerates and multinational corporations gave the army's diversification project an unprecedented boost.

The Kuwaiti group M. A. Kharafi and Sons—whose late patriarch ranked seventh on the 2010 Rich List of the magazine *Arabian Business*—proved a particularly eager partner. Beginning in 2001, it joined the Egyptian military in a number of ventures, including the Arab Company for Computer Manufacturing, Egypt's only producer of computer hardware and laptops, in which Kharafi owns 71 percent of shares and the AOI and a Ministry of Military Production subsidiary each own 5 percent. The company, which draws on the Taiwanese firm Aopen for technology inputs, had start-up capital of $140 million and produces 750,000 computers per year.[6] Via a subsidiary, Kharafi controls approximately 60 percent of the International Pipe Industry Company, of which the Ministry of Military Production owns 10 percent. This company is the largest manufacturer of oil and gas piping in the region, reporting sales of $104 million in 2008, and former Minister of Military Production Sayyid Mish'al has described it as a "model of cooperation" between the state and private sector.[7] The military and Kharafi also run an operation called Maxalto, which relies on technology from the German firm Schlumberger to manufacture smart cards. In addition, there are a number of joint ventures between Kharafi's Egyptian subsidiaries and divisions of state-owned holding companies widely perceived to be under the army's aegis.

Joint Ventures

Egypt's military is well situated to attract foreign investment partners, in large part because the economic sectors where its influence is strongest are also those that have great profit potential. These sectors include maritime and air transport, oil and gas, and industrial-scale environmental projects like wastewater treatment and renewable energy generation. The Egyptian military has actively pursued partnerships with overseas firms in all of these sectors, primarily under the rubric of public-private partnerships—a mechanism of development economics that also meets the strictures of neoliberal policy planners. Large infusions of capital from state-owned banks, along with loans from international financial institutions and stepped-up privatization under the Ahmad Nazif cabinet, converged to facilitate the army's efforts to establish joint ventures with Gulf conglomerates and foreign multinationals.

Historically, the military often validated its role in the economy by highlighting the strategic nature of certain sectors, like maritime transport, which long remained immune from privatization imperatives. In the late 1990s, Public-Sector Enterprise Minister 'Atif 'Ubayd restricted privatization of shares in maritime companies to 10 percent after the Israeli ambassador revealed that Israeli companies were interested in purchasing one of Egypt's state-owned (and likely army-run) stevedoring companies. Amid perceptions that Israeli owners would deliberately block the acquisition of new technologies in order to keep Egypt underdeveloped, the military was able to pose as guarantor of vital national assets. Ultimately, the government decided to postpone privatization of maritime transport altogether.[8] But renewed pressure from World Trade Organization members with major shipping interests led the government to adopt a master plan (2001-2017) to extend the liberalization of maritime activities. This plan included the introduction of the "landlord model," whereby private-sector firms fulfill many port functions, but remain under the supervision profit-oriented and nominally independent (but still state-owned) entities.[9] By the middle of the decade, Egypt's ports were experiencing what a 2008 USAID report termed an "investment stampede," which included sizeable new investments from four of the world's largest maritime conglomerates: the Danish Moeller-Maersk, the French CMA CGM, and Cosco Pacific and Hutchison Port Holdings, both of Hong Kong. Though such overseas firms now hold majority shares in Egyptian maritime companies, the military was able to secure significant minority shares, as well as top executive posts, primarily through the state-owned Holding Company for Maritime and Land Transport, the various port authorities, and the Ministry of Maritime Transport, all of which are heavily staffed by naval and other officers. (Military, Inc. also controls other parastatals involved in maritime shipping, such as the Arab Federation of Chambers of Shipping, whose chairman is Adm. Hatim al-Qadi.)

These joint ventures represent tens of billions of dollars in investment from foreign firms, state banks, and international lenders; even the military's minority share in these companies is a substantial asset. The new port operators include Damietta International Port Company, in which private French, Kuwaiti, and Chinese firms own a combined 70 percent alongside an unknown holding by the United Arab Shipping Company (a roughly fifty-fifty joint venture between the military-dominated Holding Company and the Kuwaiti government) and a 5 percent holding by the Damietta Port Authority, whose chairman is also a military officer.[10] Likewise, the Suez Canal Authority—headed by Adm. Ahmad 'Ali al-Fadil—owns 12 percent of the shares in the Suez Canal Container Terminal Company, which began operations in 2004, and whose other shareholders include Maersk and Cosco Pacific.

Alexandria International Container Terminals, majority-owned by Hutchison Port Holdings of Hong Kong and a UAE-based private equity fund, is another major joint venture. The project was inaugurated under Gen. 'Abd al-Salam Mahgoub, a former chief intelligence officer who became a vocal advocate of coordination between the state and private sectors after being appointed governor of Alexandria in the late 1990s. The primary vehicle for this collaboration was an agreement signed by Mahgoub and the local Chamber of Commerce, which gave businessmen hefty privileges—including free access to land for commercial development—in exchange for a portion of their profits, which were deposited into a special city development account that allowed the governorate to avoid sending its tax revenues to Cairo.[11] Military interests maintained a measure of ownership (5 percent) in this instance as well, through the Alexandria Port Authority. The port authority's chairman, Adm. Muhammad Yusuf, praised the introduction of foreign shipping interests, stating that the government's policy to "attract foreign direct investment by partnering with multinational companies" would benefit the transport sector through the transfer of "management expertise and best practices," as well as the introduction of new technology and more container traffic.[12]

The various port authorities also have shares in individual maritime infrastructure projects and complementary sectors (such as shipping insurance) alongside foreign investors. One such project is a dredger assembly deal with the Dutch company Damen Group; another is Suez Canal Insurance, which is now majority-owned by Green Oasis Investments, a joint Chinese-Egyptian investment fund. The military stands to benefit handsomely from this influx of investment, equipment, and technology, not only because it controls shares in both the joint venture companies and their state-owned competitors, but also because it exerts substantial control over associated industries. For instance, the military (via the aforementioned General Egyptian Company for Railway Wagons and Coaches) provides much of the hardware and labor for Egypt's rail construction, which is being expanded in order to link new maritime port terminals with inland rail networks, which in turn will increase the volume of business for the joint venture port operators. The revenue of Military, Inc. from

EGYPT | EGYPT'S GENERALS AND TRANSNATIONAL CAPITAL

the maritime sector may also explain the degree of violence meted out to strikers and other protesters around Egypt's ports, which are often incorporated into "special economic zones" where regulation is minimal and tax incentives are high.

Petrochemicals and Renewables

Between 2000 and 2010, the proven gas reserves in Egypt doubled in size, from 36 to 76 trillion cubic feet, and in 2009-2010 proven oil reserves reached an all-time high.[13] These finds sparked a dramatic rise in foreign direct investment; Egypt signed 176 oil and gas agreements between 1999 and 2010, but more than half of the deals were struck in just the last two years of the decade.[14] The petroleum sector (including downstream processing) accounts for almost half of the state's export earnings.

As with maritime transport, the military is in a good position to benefit from overseas investment in Egypt's energy sector, where it exercises nearly as much formal control as the Ministry of Petroleum. The military has holdings in Tharwa Petroleum, the only state-owned oil company in Egypt that engages in the upstream activities of exploration and development. Tharwa has several joint ventures with foreign firms, including Sino Tharwa (a drilling operation with China's state-owned Sinopec); Tharwa Breda Petroleum Services and Thekah Petroleum Company (joint ventures with the Italian firms Breda and Eni, respectively); and the Egyptian-Chinese Petroleum Company for Manufacturing Drilling Rigs (a consortium of Egypt's Petrojet, Tharwa and Enppi, and Sichuan Honghua Petroleum Equipment). China and Italy are also key states in maritime transport, since most Chinese exports bound for Europe are unloaded at the southern Italian port of Gioia Tauro. Increasing the share of traffic headed to Italy that passes through the Suez Canal would therefore represent a huge source of revenue for the military. In 2006, the three governments signed an agreement designed to ease traffic through the Canal, which officials from the Suez Canal Authority said might be further encouraged by "tariff incentives" granted by the Ministry of Finance, according to a WikiLeaked State Department cable.

Foreign firms have also pursued partnerships with Egypt's military producers in order to secure a piece of Egypt's growing market for renewable energy and environmental cleanup projects. China signed a memorandum of understanding with the AOI for collaboration in solar and wind energy projects. European firms have also been active in this area. German and Danish companies have concluded licensing agreements and technology transfers with the AOI to generate wind energy, while Spanish and Canadian firms are partnering with the AOI to build a photovoltaic plant near Cairo. Other environment-related projects in which Military, Inc. is involved include wastewater treatment, waste incineration, and kits for converting vehicles to operate on natural gas. A report compiled by Cairo University's Faculty of Engineering highlighted the military's capacity to manufacture the components necessary for a renewable energy industry, and many commercial attachés at foreign embassies also stress the investment potential in these areas. Such marketing devices have paid off: Germany invested fifty million euros in rice straw recycling, building two factories in collaboration with the AOI.[15] The rice straw is to be pressed and transported under a contract concluded with another military institution, the National Service Projects Organization.[16]

The army's drive to gain access to transnational capital was further reflected in the rhetoric of the SCAF-appointed minister for military production, Maj. Gen. 'Ali Sabri, who oversaw the expenditure of 1 billion Egyptian pounds (about $166 million) to expand the military's fertilizer production and water treatment and sanitation operations in 2006-2008. Although Sabri made many of the same pronouncements as his predecessor regarding job training for young graduates and industrial development in remote areas, he was especially fond of pointing to the numerous foreign partnerships the military had secured with the US, Russia, Great Britain, China, South Africa, France, Germany, and Italy. In a barrage of press interviews following his appointment in July 2011, Sabri cited a long list of the military's economic successes, including a 5 percent growth in production in the period after the uprising began, the completion of Egypt's first (and according to Sabri's statements, the region's only) hot steel rolling mill, the scheduled completion of an industrial complex on a desert road northeast of Cairo, and the intensification of commercial joint ventures with major international companies that were "keen" to move ahead with planned expansion despite continued political unrest.

The SCAF also succeeded in restarting talks on some of the public-private partnerships that were put on hold when foreign investors demanded enhanced guarantees against currency fluctuations and political risk. The primary sectors targeted for public-private financing—hospitals, wastewater treatment plants, and roads—are also the traditional purview of the military and were featured prominently in Sabri's media pronouncements.

Betting with the House

The payoff for foreign conglomerates that go into business with Military, Inc. is largely the same system of benefits that Egypt's civilian oligarchs have enjoyed, including preferential treatment in bidding for state contracts, privileged access to infrastructure and services, and advance notice of pending projects. The biggest perk, however, is being able to rely on Egyptian soldiers to secure corporate assets—a type of insurance no other state actor can provide. During the course of 2011, Kharafi National (part of the eponymous Kuwaiti group) was given an armored guard to ensure safe delivery of equipment to its al-Shabab power plant project, part of a public-private partnership venture awarded in 2010. According to a Kharafi National newsletter: "The Egyptian military provided forces, reinforced with tanks, to protect the client's major power sites in al-Shabab and Damietta.... The Egyptian military also used armed military personnel to escort the transportation of large pieces of equipment for the gas turbines from al-Ismailiyya port to the al-Shabab site." In the wake of the uprising, when several Gulf states announced aid packages to Egypt in hopes of containing popular anger, the Kharafi Group announced it was borrowing another $80 million to expand its infrastructure investments in Egypt, adding to the estimated $7 billion the Kuwaiti conglomerate already has invested there.

From the outset of the uprising, army leaders went to great lengths to assure outsiders that ports, oil and gas facilities, and other critical sites were operating normally under the watch of armed forces and police.[17] As the army consolidated the additional leverage it accrued as Egypt's transitional government, its merits as a business partner became clearer: Not only do foreign investors get soldiers to safeguard their assets, but they also get the political connections that have always been the path to economic gain in Egypt. Future foreign investment may be even more concentrated in ventures where the military has a stake.

The army, for its part, will likely reinforce its incursion into the private sector as its overseas allies increase in number. In the past, the military was able to block new commercial ventures on "security" grounds, but not without expending precious political capital. With several civilian oligarchs at the mercy of corruption probes after the uprising, the military was freer to dictate its terms. With the power to determine the winners and losers at the commanding heights of Egypt's capitalism, the SCAF will retain unchallengeable clout long after the formal return of civilian rule.

Choosing Autocracy

Much of the speculation over the Egyptian military's role in the economy has been misleading. The generals' antipathy for Gamal Mubarak led many to assume they also disdained all neoliberal projects. The guessing similarly obscured the fact that, in an era of transnational capital, the army's footprint is found in many places outside the formally state-owned holding companies. The military has broadened its portfolio by launching joint ventures and executing share purchases in private operations, exploiting its monopoly over lucrative sectors, and granting exclusive access to foreign companies in order to burnish its pro-business bona fides. While the SCAF's lust for direct political power is in doubt, the centrality of military-run industries to Egypt's economic future is not. The generals had over twelve months in which to anchor their enterprises so firmly as to make them immovable.

From the moment of Mubarak's resignation, it was apparent that the SCAF was no disinterested arbiter of the political transition. The furor over the obscene wealth of Mubarak's private-sector cronies presented the military with a golden opportunity to eliminate rivals. The SCAF proceeded to shape the electoral field to advantage those politicians who would not infringe upon the military's economic prerogatives. Chief among its tactics was a showy, but highly selective anti-corruption campaign. By jailing big businessmen like Ahmad 'Izz, an intimate of Gamal's, and unpopular officials like the former housing minister, Ibrahim Sulayman, the SCAF channeled the public's demand for justice. Not surprisingly, civilian businessmen with strong links to military companies were passed over by prosecutors—another signal to politicians to accept the military's role in the economy or be shut out altogether.

The SCAF also crafted a new electoral law designed to advantage supporters of the status quo. In the lower house of Parliament, one third of the seats still belong to single-member districts, giving a leg up to the same local power brokers who had benefited from NDP-sponsored patronage. The remaining seats are allotted according to proportional representation, and although this system might have allowed for contests reflective of party-based platforms, the SCAF's demand to hold elections so soon after Mubarak's resignation meant that most potential challengers were too weak and disorganized to mount a meaningful campaign. Old NDP clients were thus the winners here, too. The SCAF's law also maintained a provision requiring that half of the seats in the lower house be reserved for "workers and peasants," although in reality these slots are often filled by retired military and police personnel. These men then take up membership in the parliament's defense and national security committee, the only body with even nominal responsibility for overseeing the military.[18]

The military's election management techniques appeared to pay off. The army's most powerful potential adversary—the Muslim Brothers' Freedom and Justice Party—continues to toe the SCAF line on salient issues, including adherence to the peace treaty with Israel, the *sine qua non* for continued US military aid. The Brothers' deputies also voiced their support for shielding the details of the military budget from prying fellow parliamentarians (who will have access only to a single, aggregated figure). And the Brothers mobilized their members to stand alongside security forces confronting large demonstrations, such as on the "Tuesday of Determination" in January 2012, when protesters marched to the parliamentary building demanding an accelerated transfer of power to civilians.

The result was a parliament in near lockstep with the military on economic governance. Although the parliamentarians will certainly have power struggles with the generals, the parties that command almost 87 percent of the assembly—Freedom and Justice, the salafi Nour Party, the Wafd and the Egyptian Bloc—all endorse the continued pursuit of neoliberalism. Groups rejecting that framework, such as The Revolution Continues, won a paltry 2.5 percent of the seats. It would be simplistic to suggest that the SCAF manipulated the results with precision, but they did design a system likely to produce their preferred outcome.

In addition to electoral engineering, the SCAF engaged in both overt repression and legal chicanery to quiet those excluded from the political arena in the months following the elections. Not only did the generals make it a crime to organize protests that disrupted the economy, deftly exempting "thuggery" from the list of acts that are no longer punishable under emergency law, they also encouraged the notion that labor strikes were undermining the national economy. The SCAF's civilian allies went to dramatic lengths to remind the population of the worsening economic situation, with Prime Minister Kamal al-Ganzouri literally shedding tears on camera.[19] Meanwhile, dissenters were subject to arbitrary imprisonment, military tribunals and torture. Together with the sowing of fear and discord, such coercion served as a deterrent to labor actions and street demonstrations that challenged the neoliberal program. The aim was not to imprison every demonstrator, but to dissuade the discontented from protesting in the first place.

Egyptians were thus offered a familiar Hobson's choice: Acquiesce to a slightly adapted status quo in order to restore "stability," or return to the streets and invite the resumption of chaos. Elections, whatever their benefits, gave the authorities a broader mandate to repress dissent and recruit new enablers of the military's rent-seeking behavior. Military, Inc. is determined that its holdings and operations remain beyond public scrutiny. The real Machiavellian turn in Egypt is just how many Islamists, liberals, nationalists and unaffiliated actors are content to watch the military's economic empire grow at the expense of those clamoring for political change and social justice.

Notes

1. *New York Times*, February 17, 2011.
2. *Egypt Independent*, October 26, 2011.
3. Hesham Sallam, in this volume.

4. Shana Marshall, "Egypt's Other Revolution: Modernizing the Military-Industrial Complex," *Jadaliyya*, February 10, 2012.

5. *Guardian*, December 28, 2011.

6. *Daily News Egypt*, December 26, 2005.

7. *Al-Ahram*, April 2, 2005.

8. Marsha Pripstein Posusney, "Egyptian Privatization: New Challenges for the Left," *Middle East Report* 210 (Spring 1999), p. 39.

9. "Maritime Transport and Related Logistics Services in Egypt," ICTSD Program on Trade in Services and Sustainable Development (December 2007), pp. ix, 8.

10. "Major Lines Join Damietta Project," *Lloyds List* (via NewsEdge Corporation), December 7, 2007.

11. Samer Soliman, *The Autumn of Dictatorship* (Stanford, CA: Stanford University Press, 2011), pp. 88-89.

12. "Contract for a New Company to Upgrade Container Terminal Quays at the Ports of Alexandria and El Dekhelia," March 13, 2005.

13. *Los Angeles Times*, August 16, 2010.

14. *Egypt Oil and Gas* 47 (November 2010) and 50 (February 2011).

15. "Egypt: Business in Brief" (Royal Netherlands Embassy in Cairo, January 2006).

16. "Sector Review on Environment and Energy" (Royal Netherlands Embassy in Cairo, April 2008).

17. Ashraf Ghazy, "Back to Normality: How Egyptian Ports Are Settling Back into the Old Routine," *Port Technology*, February 7, 2011.

18. Jeff Martini and Julie Taylor, "Commanding Democracy in Egypt," *Foreign Affairs* (September-October 2011).

19. Associated Press, December 11, 2011.

PART THREE

YEMEN

Thousands of Yemenis took to Sanaa's Tahrir Square on January 27, 2011, to demand an end to the thirty-three-year rule of President 'Ali 'Abdallah Salih. After being driven from the square with tear gas and batons, protesters relocated to Sanaa University Square (redubbed Taghyir Square) in February 2011 and turned it into ground zero of the Yemen revolution. They set up tents and art exhibits and debated the best way to defeat Salih's autocratic regime. The uprising survived a year of regime brutality, resulting in scores of injuries and deaths, before Salih, by then the longest-serving president in the region, agreed to step down in November 2011 in a deal brokered by the United States and the Gulf Cooperation Council.

For most of Yemen's citizens, 60 percent of whom are younger than twenty-five, Salih's regime was the only government they had known. Salih became president of North Yemen in 1978 and was elected president of the unified Republic of Yemen in 1990 when the conservative Yemen Arab Republic in the north and the nominally-Marxist People's Democratic Republic of Yemen in the south merged into one nation. Plans for unification had existed in various forms since the early 1970s, and by the time the unified constitution was put to a popular vote in 1991, it won overwhelming approval. Yet the dominance of northern political and economic interests under the new arrangement angered and alienated southerners. A civil war broke out in 1994 from which the north emerged victorious, after which discrimination against the south became further entrenched.

Following the north's triumph over southern secessionists, the Yemeni Socialist Party, which had been a major partner in the unity government, was politically marginalized. It was eclipsed by Islah, a Sunni Islamist grouping, as the primary, though minority, opposition to Salih's General People's Congress (GPC). Several other small opposition parties, including liberals, socialists, and Shi'i Islamists from the north have also won seats in the lower house of parliament. In 2005, these groups joined with Islah to form the Joint Meeting Parties coalition to strengthen the opposition's bargaining position vis-à-vis the regime. Even in union, opposition parties represent a minority of the elected representatives. The GPC's predominance in the legislature—like Salih's reelection margins—is inflated by ballot-stuffing and other irregularities, but the party and president do have popular backing in large parts of the north and among some southerners as well. In addition to the tribal, religious, regional, and commercial affiliations that shape Yemeni politics, patronage networks have been key to consolidating support for the regime.

Institutionalized corruption under Salih's rule is a grievance shared by millions of Yemenis. The country's limited resources have been channeled into enriching the regime's political base and buying off opponents. The openness with which government officials steal from the public purse has led to rebuke and reduced aid packages from international donors. Meanwhile Yemen's tiny oil reserves, which provide over 60 percent of the government's revenue, are dwindling, along with the country's water table. The industrial and service sectors are quite small; the economy is based largely on fishing, herding, and agriculture. Migrant work in neighboring countries' oil sectors was once an important economic stimulus, but foreign employment has not recovered since Yemen's isolation for opposing the US invasion of Iraq in 1991. Unemployment is estimated at 35 percent and roughly half of Yemenis live below the poverty line.

These crises have come to the fore in recent years as the government has reduced subsidies on food and fuel. Because the population is predominately rural, petroleum is essential to the movement of people and goods. When Salih announced an end to fuel subsidies in the summer of 2005, riots erupted in cities and towns across the country. After three days, several dozen people had been killed by security forces and Salih was forced to reinstate the price controls. Water scarcity has sparked local conflicts over control of wells and has caused mass migration to the cities. Over the last twenty years, Sanaa has doubled in size to two million inhabitants, many of whom live in the expanding slums that ring the city.

Frustration with the government has ignited two movements against the regime since 2004. In the northwest of the country, an armed rebellion by Zaydi (Yemeni Shi'i) groups allied with the prominent Houthi family has fought to overthrow the Salih regime. The conflict has engulfed large parts of the northwest, killed thousands and displaced many more. A ceasefire agreement signed in 2010 decreased tensions temporarily, though the rebels have not formally ended their struggle. In the south, a movement known as al-Harak has held non-violent demonstrations against northern oppression of the southern provinces and against Salih's regime since 2007. Al-Harak contains a variety of political elements with divergent visions of the movement's ultimate goal, but the youth who form the movement's core advocate for southern secession.

As in the north, Salih responded to the southern political challenge with military attacks on cities and a campaign of arrests, torture, and assassinations. Regime-affiliated media outlets promoted the government's propaganda about al-Harak's ties to al-Qaeda. Salih's cooperation with US anti-terror initiatives secured military equipment and training that was deployed against both the southern and Houthi movements, as well as other regime critics. Press freedoms deteriorated following the 1994 civil war, and the unrest throughout the country in the 2000s prompted more severe crackdowns on independent journalists, publications and websites.

Despite this repression, Yemenis turned out in the hundreds of thousands to protest the corruption and violence of Salih's rule. Protests continued into 2012 over unemployment and southern independence, and a large part of the camp at Taghyir Square still stands. Salih's successor (and former vice president), 'Abd al-Rabb Mansour al-Hadi, began to replace Salih loyalists in in the security services and the government, but change remains incremental. The military has resumed repressing secessionist demonstrations in the south, and several protesters have died under military fire. Two suicide bomb attacks in Sanaa in the summer of 2012, claimed by jihadist group Ansar al-Shari'a, highlight the lack of security and political divisions that Yemen continues to face.

13. NO EXIT: YEMEN'S EXISTENTIAL CRISIS

SHEILA CARAPICO

A venal dictatorship three decades old, mutinous army officers, dissident tribal sheikhs, a parliamentary opposition coalition, youthful pro-democracy activists, gray-haired Socialists, gun-toting cowboys, veiled women protesters, northern carpetbaggers, Shi'i insurgents, tear gas canisters, leaked State Department cables, foreign-born jihadis—Yemen's demi-revolutionary spring had it all. The mass uprising in southern Arabia blended features of the peaceful popular revolutions in Egypt and Tunisia with elements of the state repression in Libya and Syria in a gaudy, fast-paced, multi-layered theater of revolt verging on the absurd.

President 'Ali 'Abdallah Salih stalled and contrived to avoid signing a late April 2011 deal brokered by Gulf Cooperation Council (GCC) neighbors desperate to restore a semblance of stability in the most populous corner of the Arabian Peninsula. The GCC extracted a verbal promise from Salih to resign the presidency after a period of thirty days. But convincing him to make good on his pledge under conditions satisfactory to Yemeni elites, the pro-democracy movement and interested foreign parties was a gargantuan task, requiring more diplomatic legerdemain than had been brought to bear. On April 30, instead of signing onto the proposed agreement, Salih sent tanks firing live ammunition to clear some fifteen hundred campers from a central square in the Mansoura district of the southern port city of Aden. 'Abd al-Latif al-Zayani, secretary-general of the six-nation GCC, who had flown to the Yemeni capital of Sanaa to meet with Salih, returned to Saudi Arabia red-faced and empty-handed.

Under the Bush and particularly the Obama administrations, the United States became deeply implicated in Yemen, which emerged in the late 2000s as a haven and launching pad for the Arabian Peninsula branch of al-Qaeda. In the year after the Christmas 2009 "crotch bomber" attempted to detonate an explosive device hidden in his underwear on an airplane in Detroit, the US spent up to $300 million upgrading counter-terrorism, military, and internal security forces loyal to Salih. The Pentagon provided helicopters, armored vehicles, ammunition, surveillance technology, Humvees, night-vision goggles, and other military equipment, as well as training, to its Yemeni counterparts. Classified cables released by WikiLeaks show that this assistance increased despite the Salih regime's widely recognized backsliding from democratization and toward repression, as well as plentiful red flags in 2009 and 2010 that American-made weapons were being used against domestic enemies. Gulf and French officials were also frank with the State Department in their assessments of the regime's shattered legitimacy.[1] Indeed, as early as 2005, the US ambassador in Sanaa wrote a cable envisioning scenarios including Salih's fall to the legal parliamentary opposition, plotters among his inner circle or mass popular protests.[2] No one could have predicted the confluence of all three. But Washington, forewarned, might better have hedged its bets. It has yet to do so.

Over $1 billion in additional US military assistance already in the pipeline in the spring of 2011 was frozen in light of the government's attacks on citizens. Hesitant to distance itself from Salih and low on sympathy for the protesters, the US was upbeat about the prospects for the face-saving GCC agreement to be sealed by the end of April. The Embassy in Sanaa announced that it was "distressed" and "disturbed" by the "violence, April 27, that killed [twelve] and injured hundreds of Yemeni citizens...on the eve of signing an historic agreement...that will achieve through peaceful, democratic, and constitutional means a transition of authority leading to new presidential elections in July 2011." Its press release urged "Yemeni citizens" to show good faith by "avoiding all provocative demonstrations, marches, and speeches in the coming days," adding coyly: "We also urge government security forces to refrain from using violence against demonstrators."

The Central Players

At center stage in the Yemeni potboiler was President 'Ali 'Abdallah Salih, barricaded in a fortified palace compound in the capital behind Revolutionary Guards and US-armed Special Forces commanded by his son and one-time heir apparent Ahmad. Peeping over the parapets, Salih delivered nearly nonsensical speeches in his trademark not-quite-literate Arabic inveighing against Zionist instigators and fornicating demonstrators. The revolt against his rule was coordinated from "an operations room in Tel Aviv," he ventured on March 1. On April 18 he denigrated the popular movement as an un-Islamic "mixing of sexes." To these and other pronouncements the throngs jeered and hurled their shoes at the giant video screen in the plaza outside Sanaa University: In video footage of the scene, the footwear looked like flies buzzing around the president's face.

Defiant if not oblivious, Salih announced in late April fifty thousand new, unfunded civil service jobs and vowed to relinquish power only "through the ballot box," calling, spuriously, for elections monitored by international observers. "People who resign from their posts and join the revolutions are the symbols of corruption and they do not have agendas for reforming the economic, cultural, social, and developmental situation in the country," he told military cadets on April 25. Next, presumably enraged by Al Jazeera coverage of the demonstrations, he accused Qatar, one of the GCC states sponsoring the exit deal, of "inciting and financing chaos."

The partners to the proposed exit deal were the leaders of the so-called Joint Meeting Parties or JMP, a motley coalition of Socialists, Sunni Islamists, and other conservatives affiliated with the party known as Islah, and partisans of Nasserist, Baathist, and liberal platforms, as well as Islamists from the Zaydi branch of Shi'ism practiced in (northern) Yemen. This legal, parliamentary opposition coalition had been bargaining with the ruling General People's Congress (GPC) over the rules of the suspended electoral process for several years. It includes prominent national figures like former South Yemeni Prime Minister

Yasin Sa'id Nu'man, human rights activist and Sanaa University professor Muhammad 'Abd al-Malik al-Mutawakkil and Islah spokesperson 'Abd al-Wahhab al-Anisi, among others with a measure of "street cred."

Comprised of politicians from both of the two Yemeni polities that unified in 1990, this important group has extensive experience in Yemen's unique National Dialogue of Popular Forces and in electoral and parliamentary politics. With its rotating chairmanship keeping any one star out of the limelight, the JMP played a pivotal yet ambiguous role in the 2011 political crisis, embracing the demonstrations after they were well underway, refusing Salih's belated February offer to form a coalition government and now conferring with the GCC and other international actors to find an exit from the impasse. The JMP leaders accepted the deal whereby Salih would step down in return for immunity from prosecution for his many crimes and the promise that they would gain substantial parliamentary representation.

The Plotters

When Salih accused his opponents of sedition, he was referring explicitly to defectors from his inner circle. Two were tagged by US Embassy officials who detected dissension within Salih's original "triumvirate" at least as early as 2005 and again in 2009. One was Gen. 'Ali Muhsin, Salih's henchman since 1978, head of the First Armored Division and the Northwest Military Command who prosecuted merciless campaigns that vanquished southern secessionists in 1994 and scourged Sa'ada province in the far north in order to contain Zaydi Houthi rebels and their tribal allies in 2010. In both battles, the general called upon radical Sunni jihadis to join the fight against godless Socialists in the south and Zaydi partisans in Sa'ada. US Ambassador Thomas Krajeski described him in 2005 as a sinister arms smuggler whose name was spoken in hushed tones because he was feared and mis-trusted by the Houthi rebels, southerners, leftists, and others.[3] Subsequent cables revealed the rumor that he was assigned the nearly impossible task of fighting the Houthis in order to ruin his military reputation and thus his political ambitions. There is strong evidence, as well, that during its intervention in the conflict in 2010 the Saudi Air Force was given tar-geting recommendations to strike coordinates that turned out to be 'Ali Muhsin's command headquarters.[4] The general's March 2011 defection and deployment of tanks to protect the demonstrators from forces loyal to the president was thus no surprise.

In blogs, interviews, and Facebook postings, pro-democracy spokespersons made it clear that they were not fooled by cynical turncoats jockeying for power but hardly inter-ested in liberal democracy. When 'Ali Muhsin's troops deployed to the square outside Sanaa University, the demonstrators initially cringed, thinking he was coming to destroy them.

The other power broker, who broke ranks after at least fifty peaceful protesters were murdered on March 18, was Hamid al-Ahmar, the most politically ambitious of the ten sons of the late 'Abdallah bin Hussein al-Ahmar, paramount chief of the Hashid tribal confed-eration, long-time speaker of Parliament, and stalwart of the original triumvirate backing Salih's rule. Although not his Reaganesque father, as a member of Parliament, part of the Supreme Committee of the Islah party, a millionaire businessman, and a prominent figure in the Hashid confederation, Hamid is able to draw large crowds in the family's hometown of 'Amran. Salih is himself a Hashid.

US embassy cables made available by WikiLeaks indicate that Hamid al-Ahmar has been maneuvering against Salih since soon after his father's death in late 2007. One cable from August 31, 2009 quotes him calling Salih "the devil" and his son Ahmad and nephews "clowns." According to the same State Department missive, he promised to organize anti-Salih demonstrations if and when he could persuade 'Ali Muhsin to go along and also enlist Saudi assistance. A second cable dated the same day put al-Ahmar among a small group of insiders blaming Salih for "wrong-headed policies" contributing to "Yemen's myriad problems" who may be "truly concerned about the fate of Yemen, or, smelling blood in the water…positioning themselves for a post-Saleh era." In April 2011, the US Embassy in Sanaa felt compelled to issue a terse denial of rumors of its support for Hamid al-Ahmar.

Fifty Thousand Pairs of Clasped Hands

State-run Sanaa television ran continuous tape of people jumping up and down, yelling "the people want 'Ali 'Abdallah Salih," and filed footage of marches celebrating his leadership. Yet neither he nor the dissident counter-elites could contain the unprecedented, sustained, spontaneous grassroots uprising. The crowds clamoring for change (*taghyir*) were diverse, and dispersed among at least a dozen cities and towns. At the core were the youth, the demographic plurality between the ages of fifteen and thirty who have never known another government leadership: university students, graduates, dropouts, and wannabes grasping at straws of hope for a better future in the Arab world's poorest country. They have turned their daily marches and sit-ins into performance art with music, dancing, skits, caricatures, posters, chants, and collective gestures of defiance like fifty thousand pairs of clasped hands held high. Women, most prominently the eloquent and outspoken Tawakkul Karman, head of the NGO Women Journalists Without Chains, raised their voices more and more, in solidarity with demands for change and in outrage at the president's sleazy innuendo directed at "ladies" who march or speak in public. The freedom struggle went viral and virtually nationwide.

A peaceful *intifada* had been in motion since the summer of 2007 in the south, the territory known as the People's Democratic Republic of Yemen and ruled by the Yemeni Socialist Party (YSP) from 1967 to 1990. In 1990, the south unified with the north, already ruled by Salih, and then attempted secession four years later. During the short civil war, the president called in assorted tribal militias and "Afghan Arabs"—Salafis returned from the anti-Soviet jihad in Afghanistan—to assist the regular army under the command of Gen. 'Ali Muhsin. A beer factory and civil service administration offices in Aden were torched and looted, while the erstwhile southern Socialist leadership fled by boat to Oman. Northern military officers and gangs of scalawags installed themselves as governors, administrators and landowners. Men deprived of their jobs and pensions and women stripped of the rights enjoyed under the old Socialist administration seethed under what they regarded as occupation. Oil revenues from wells on what had been Southern soil flowed into the coffers of Salih and his cronies. After more than a decade of economic collapse and political repression, the youth and some of the old YSP cadres launched what became known as al-Harak, a movement for change.[5] By late 2010, their protests had become commonplace, although Salih and the official media succeeded temporarily in presenting their grievances as secessionist gripes that would destroy Yemeni unity. On April 26, 2011, they marked the anniversary of the start of the 1994 civil war in which the former South attempted to reestablish its independent sovereignty.

Whether or not they harbored genuinely separatist sentiments, residents of the former South Yemen had good reason to feel they have been punitively targeted and deprived of basic liberties and entitlements.

Yet, by the same token, many southern tribulations resonated in every province of the republic: the grotesque enrichment of regime cronies at the expense of the many; deteriorating standards of living; obscenely bad schools, hospitals, and roads; the skyrocketing price of meat, staples, and even clean water; the lack of jobs for college and high-school graduates. Ambassador Krajeski had already seen prospects for revolt in the 2005 riots prompted by the lifting of fuel subsidies. Then, dissatisfaction was particularly acute among the perennially restive tribes of the eastern provinces of al-Jawf and Ma'rib, where truckers and pump farmers consider cheap fuel their lifeblood. Grandiose pageants of presidential power, half-truths in the official media, indignities at military checkpoints, arbitrary arrests and imprisonments—these and other daily insults fed popular alienation, despair, and frustration, most notably among the youth. While a privileged few cooled off in swimming pools in their luxury compounds, the water table plummeted, decimating the farm economy that remains the livelihood of the rural majority. Farmers and ranchers facing starvation flocked to the cities where water supplies and social services were swamped. Misery became the new normal; millions barely survive on the equivalent of a dollar or two per day.

Misery Loves Company

Without a doubt, Yemenis were inspired by the revolutionary movements in Tunisia and Egypt in early 2011. Gatherings in Sanaa and other cities in January, as the spirit of Tunisia diffused in the Arab world, were relatively restrained affairs, replete in some cases with folding chairs for various JMP dignitaries.[6] In February, as Egyptian President Husni Mubarak began to proffer concessions under the sustained pressure of the street, the timbre of the Yemeni rallies rose in intensity. On the evening of February 11, the date of Mubarak's resignation, thousands of joyful youth converged on Sanaa's Liberation Square. There, they were confronted by uniformed security forces and regime-supporting agitators armed with sticks.[7]

Thus prevented from occupying the central Tahrir Square, the youths nevertheless eventually found their own iconic protest locale: the plaza before the gates of Sanaa University, which they have redubbed Taghyir Square in homage both to their core demand and the rhyming name of the epicenter of revolt in Cairo. The first tents were set up there on February 21. People who gathered in Taghyir Square echoed the slogans of Tahrir Square, which in turn had traveled to Egypt from Tunisia: *Irhal!* (Leave!) and *al-sha'b yurid isqat al-nizam* (the people want to overthrow the regime). Salih's men borrowed the failed tactics of Mubarak, sending thugs wielding batons into the crowds and rounding up known regime opponents. On March 18, 2011, in a pitch of fury or panic someone ordered snipers overlooking Taghyir Square to open fire on the assembled protesters. By the following day at least fifty were dead and more lay dying. In disbelief, fury, and sorrow, a record 150,000 marched in Sanaa's biggest "day of rage" so far. Ministers, ambassadors, civil servants, members of Parliament, and military officers including 'Ali Muhsin declared their sympathies with the protesters. On March 23 a state of emergency was declared. Within a month, a tent city housing men and boys (and sometimes whole families) from around the country stretched, by some accounts, for miles along the streets leading to Sanaa University. Other camps were pitched in other cities and towns.

In provincial cities, where hundreds or thousands had attended rallies, tens of thousands seized public spaces. In Ta'izz, a large commercial and industrial city in the verdant southern mountains of the former North Yemen, and the neighboring city of Ibb, simmering discontent erupted. The Ta'izz-Ibb area, a rich agricultural zone of peasants and sharecroppers often called the "middle regions," served as a bridge between the southern al-Harak and the revolutionary movement centered in Sanaa. People from Ta'izz traveled, telephoned and tweeted with family and compatriots in Aden, Hadramawt, Abyan, and other parts of the former South Yemen already in ferment. Youth and parents in Hudayda, the Red Sea port that is the hub of the Tihama coastal plain where Afro-Yemenis suffer the country's highest rates of poverty and political disenfranchisement, filled the public square with banners and chants: *Irhal!* In mid-April protesters were shot dead by security forces in Ta'izz, Hudayda, and other cities, as well as in Sanaa. Each funeral—at least 145 by May 2011—provoked more angry or grief-stricken dissenters to call for the downfall of the regime.

Insurrectionary sentiments fueled patriotic solidarities and unifying sympathies. These spread to the vast plains, mountains, and deserts north, northwest, east and somewhat south of Sanaa, in the provinces of Sa'ada, al-Jawf, Ma'rib, 'Amran, and Dhamar. In these rather sparsely populated, semi-arid regions analogous to Texas or Wyoming, the so-called tribal heartland where ranchers, cowboys, truckers, and hillbillies carry Kalashnikovs or even bazooka launchers and historically harbor deep mistrust of the central government, conventional protests were mixed with "traditional" acts of civil disobedience, such as road blockages and commercial stoppages. In a heavily tribal area further south, al-Bayda, men threw down their arms in April 2011 to march to another popular slogan: *Silmiyya!* (Peacefully!) Bear in mind: Armed tribesmen and villagers could have resorted to open rebellion but elected to keep their powder dry.

The Impasse

As April moved into May, scenarios were buzzing like the shoes tossed at Salih's visage on the giant screen. The accord that was supposed to be signed May 1 remained a work in progress up to the eleventh hour. The basic plan was for President Salih to transfer power to his vice president, the relatively impotent 'Abd al-Rabb Mansour al-Hadi, within thirty days. Under a new power sharing arrangement, the ruling General People's Congress would retain 50 percent of the 301 seats in Parliament, the opposition JMP would acquire 40 percent and 10 percent would go to independents, including, presumably, representatives of the youth movement. Within a week a transitional unity government expected to be lead by a JMP prime minister, preferably from the former South, was to be formed. Senior statesman 'Abd al-Karim al-'Iryani, the current secretary-general of the GPC, having until recently remained aloof from the fray, was dispatched to the Saudi Arabian capital of Riyadh to participate in negotiations with the GCC. Crucially, but vaguely, the proposal specified an end to the demonstrations. The remaining seventy loyalists in Parliament further demanded that Salih retain his leadership of the GPC. It was not clear if a popular opposition demand that he and family members resign their military posts was really part of the deal.

The arrangement was too ambiguous and riddled with loopholes for either Salih or the protesters to accept by the May 1 deadline. In the end, only the GCC monarchies and the JMP leaders were ready to sign. Salih first offered to have either al-'Iryani or Vice President al-Hadi verify the accord on his behalf in Riyadh, and then promised to sign in Sanaa in the presence of the GCC's al-Zayani. At the last minute, he acquiesced to sign in his capacity as head of the ruling party but not as president. This refusal scuttled the negotiation. Salih scoffed at a basket of carrots that left him with his arsenal of sticks.

Although Salih was the one who nixed the deal, it was clear that the GCC plan did not have popular backing, either. It had not been negotiated so much as cobbled together. On April 24, a group signing itself as the Youth Popular Revolution Committee already rejected the provision of immunity from criminal prosecution for the president and his family, which could have easily amounted to carte blanche for excessive force during the month-long transition. Amnesty International and Human Rights Watch shared these concerns. It was unclear, moreover, how the JMP could have dispersed the sit-ins and roadblocks; as commentator Jamila 'Ali Raja told Al Jazeera, the formal parties could invite their own members to abandon the barricades, but not give orders to the tens of thousands they did not represent.

Long Denouement

The US-backed GCC push to reach an accord in May 2011 turned out to be the opening gambit in a complex negotiation that took nine more months to bear fruit. Severely injured in a bomb blast inside the mosque in his vast presidential compound in June 2011, Salih was evacuated to a Saudi hospital for treatment only to return that September. Three times he promised to sign the GCC document but found excuses at the last moment, eventually insisting he would surrender power only "through the ballot box."

All the while, tens of thousands of protesters stayed camped in Sanaa, Ta'izz, and other cities. Their spirits were lifted when a Yemeni woman, Tawakkul Karman, was awarded a Nobel Peace Prize in October 2011, to symbolize the work of Arab activists for social justice and human rights. Salih was finally coerced to sign a modified GCC agreement in November 2011 that arranged for a referendum, of sorts, that offered voters a single choice, Salih's Vice President 'Abd al-Rabb Mansour al-Hadi. On December 22, 2011 some three thousand anti-regime activists marched the 150 miles from Ta'izz to Sanaa to protest the agreement's granting Salih immunity from prosecution.

After formally assuming the presidency in February 2012, Hadi—with the support of Saudi Arabia, other Arab Gulf monarchies, and the Obama administration—began attempting to dislodge Salih's son and other family members and loyalists from key military commands and political posts. So far they have only been partially successful, with the Republican Guards and parts of the military still outside government control.

The new Yemeni administration has also continued Salih's cooperation with the US counter-terrorism agenda in the southern provinces. Throughout 2011, as peaceful demonstrations against the Salih kleptocracy gained momentum only to be met with brute force, a string of American political actors declared that the Yemen-based "al-Qaeda in the Arabian Peninsula" posed a grave peril, including to the American homeland. New CIA chief Gen. David Petraeus dubbed it "the most dangerous regional node in the global jihad" in testimony before Congress in September 2011. AQAP, as this group has been dubbed by the US military, is actually less a unified command than a motley handful of preachers, militants, and misfits including the group Ansar al-Shari'a, which took control of several cities in Abyan province when Salih withdrew forces to protect his regime against mass demonstrations elsewhere in the country. It is difficult to imagine a more effective recruitment tool for al-Qaeda wannabes worldwide than this mantra and, sure enough, scores of jihadis and frustrated youth from Somalia, Pakistan, and elsewhere sneaked into Abyan to fight the good fight against the imperial infidels and their Saudi-sponsored lackeys.

The crackdown on jihadi groups in the south—including US airstrikes and remote-control drone assassinations—has sparked a war that is in danger of spreading throughout the country. For the 2012-2013 budget, Washington upped its security assistance package of weapons transfers, training, and joint operations. The Yemeni military will receive a boost from heavy weaponry, surveillance drones, and two new bases in Aden province. Despairing that the political process in Sanaa will address their concerns, many southerners abandoned the unified protest movement to renew calls for independence. In Ta'izz and other cities north of the former inter-Yemeni border activists vowed to continue their struggle but with dimming prospects for government accountability. Clearly President al-Hadi, the Pentagon, and the GCC states had other priorities than addressing the legitimate concerns of peaceful demonstrators calling for social justice.

Notes

1. *Washington Post*, April 9, 2011.

2. The cable was published in the *Guardian*, March 11, 2011.

3. Ibid.

4. *Guardian*, April 8, 2011.

5. Susanne Dahlgren, in this volume.

6. Stacey Philbrick Yadav, "No Pink Slip for Salih: What Yemen's Protests Do and Do Not Mean," *Middle East Report Online*, February 9, 2011.

7. Nir Rosen, "How It Started in Yemen: From Tahrir to Taghyir," *Jadaliyya*, March 18, 2011.

14. THE ECONOMIC DIMENSION OF YEMENI UNITY

SHEILA CARAPICO

To the outside world, the unification of the two Yemens in 1990 resembled the German experience in miniature. North Yemen (the Yemen Arab Republic, YAR) was considered a *laissez faire* market economy, whereas the South (the People's Democratic Republic of Yemen, PDRY) was "the communist one." When, weeks ahead of Bonn and Berlin, Sanaa and Aden announced their union, Western commentary assumed that in Yemen, as in Germany, capitalist (Northern) firms would buy out the moribund (Southern) state sector and provide the basis for future economic growth.

In theory, and in Germany, capitalism and socialism are distinguished by patterns of private and public ownership of the means of production. In North and South Yemen, however, differences in ownership patterns were largely evened out by comparable access (and lack thereof) to investment capital. Disparities in the relative weight of private and public enterprise were far more subtle than the designations "capitalist" and "socialist" indicate. Indeed, available data on private and public participation revealed common patterns of spending. The North's state sector invested more than did the private sector, while the South's socialist policy statements belied the increasing role of domestic and foreign private firms.

Relatively poor countries situated on the periphery of the Arabian Peninsula's oil economy, both Yemens relied on labor remittances and international assistance. Both Yemens faced austerity when falling oil prices, compounded by a drop in Cold War-generated aid, reduced access to hard currency—until the discovery of oil in the border region in the mid-1980s attracted a third type of international capital from multinational petroleum companies. These forces cumulatively reduced the differences between the two systems and added an economic dimension to the political incentives for unification.[1] In contrast with Germany, their marriage was more a merger than a takeover, for neither was in any position to buy the other out.

Two Economies

Historic Yemen was a cultural entity rather than a political unit; its formal division stemmed from British imperialism in the South. Unlike the relatively isolated, independent North, where a semi-feudal agrarian society persisted, the South developed capitalist classes, markets, and enterprises. The major port between the Mediterranean and India, Aden's modern infrastructure and services attracted a small indigenous capitalist group, a working class of stevedores and industrial labor, and a small urban middle class, including shopkeepers and intellectuals. Sanaa, by contrast, was a center of Islamic conservatism ruled by a Zaydi Shi'a imam. Strict trade and investment restrictions protected a few monopoly import-ers and large landowners. Would-be bourgeoisie and working class aspirants escaped this restricted environment for the free port at Aden. The North was ripe for a kind of bourgeois revolution, opening the door to capitalist development, just when the South's radical anti-imperialism slammed the door to foreign investors.

After the 1962 revolution and 1962-1968 civil war, the North (the YAR) became a "no doors" economy, with few legal barriers to either trade or investment. Revolutionaries in the South after 1968 nationalized or collectivized many foreign enterprises, large estates, and fishing boats. Whereas the South (the PDRY) was subsequently governed by a single Soviet-style Marxist party, in the absence of legal parties politics in the North were domi-nated by fluid tribal, Islamic, and leftist "fronts" covertly supported by other Arab regimes.

The two Yemens shared a physical environment where household-scale cereal and livestock production employed most men and women. Both governments were unsure of their authority in the countryside, and each backed elements of the other's opposition. The economies remained intertwined. In the early 1970s, the Southern bourgeoisie, some of them originally Northerners attracted to Aden's port economy, moved back north to Ta'izz, Hudayda, and Sanaa, where they established businesses and held government posts. After the rise in oil prices in 1973, worker remittances fed consumption (imported goods, residen-tial construction) rather than productive investment, despite both regimes' efforts to mobi-lize these funds for agriculture and industry.

The North was more affluent and enjoyed higher consumption of imports, but it also had far worse current account deficits. Although the labor force was still predominantly agricultural, especially in the North, over half of gross domestic product in both systems was generated by services; the rate of new investment in services, especially government services, indicated that this trend would continue. The level of education and health ser-vices—slightly better in the South, especially for women—put both countries among the world's least developed nations. While central planning was a goal of the leadership in the South, in the North planning was not an ideological commitment but rather part of the documentation required by the International Monetary Fund and the World Bank.

Property Relations

The South, with its colonial legacy, entered the 1960s with many more capitalist enterprises than North Yemen. South Yemeni nationalizations and land reforms created a modern state sector, and dramatically equalized land ownership, but the economy retained many fea-tures of a traditional agrarian economy comparable to that of North Yemen, which was just embarking on its first commercial and industrial projects.

Production systems in the South included subsistence agriculture on family land mixed with herding on commons, sharecropping on pre-capitalist estates, and wage labor on modern farms. In Aden and Lahij, where ownership was most distinctively class-divided, the revolutionary regime expropriated the largest holdings as well as religious endowments (*waqf*). The number of expropriated estates increased from eighteen to forty-seven between 1975 and 1982 with the addition of some smaller properties of unpopular landlords. These

129

state farms, with modern equipment and wage labor, managed most farm land in Aden governorate and nearly a third in Lahij just to the north.[2] Redistributed land, nearly two thirds of the South's cultivated area, was classified as cooperative. Over a quarter, mostly in the east, remained private.[3]

By contrast, the revolution in the North nationalized only the royal family's prime tracts. Over half of the large farms were private and were conservatively managed, frequently employing sharecrop labor and moving only slowly toward capitalist farming. Most dry land in both systems consisted of family-cultivated parcels or open range. Well into the 1980s, at least half of Yemeni farms produced cereals and livestock for cultivation. The only popular, profitable cash crop in the highlands was the narcotic leaf, qat, outlawed in the South and discouraged by the North's Ministry of Agriculture.

Both regimes advocated farm mechanization, yet typical Yemeni farmers planting sorghum or millet with their own draft animals on small, scattered, often terraced parcels were unable to profitably invest in pumps, tractors or trucks, even with remittance income. Each regime turned to "cooperatives" around 1974, hoping to combine petty savings and remittances for investment in nurseries, equipment, repair stations, storage facilities, and marketing services. Southern holders of redistributed land formed purchasing and marketing cooperatives. Sixty-odd cooperatives helped up to fifty thousand members acquire inputs in the mid-1980s, but instead of moving toward full-scale cooperative farms, twenty-nine state farms abandoned group farming and only two produced collectively.[4]

In the North, although groups known colloquially as "cooperatives" built stopgap rural infrastructure, the twenty-odd agricultural, fishing, and craft cooperatives foundered on difficulties in both credit and marketing.[5] Unlike in the South, participation was purely voluntary, and often made no sense as an investment. While a few cooperatives profitably ran diesel stations or rented drilling rigs, most failed to mobilize and manage share capital.

After nationalization, public ventures controlled 60-70 percent of the value of industry in the South, including power and water and the oil refinery (the single largest employer). Mixed companies produced cigarettes, batteries, and aluminum utensils; wholly private firms were either small-scale plastic, clothing, glass, food, and paper goods manufacturers or traditional carpentry, metal, pottery, or weaving industries.

Whereas the South inherited modern plants and offices, the North embarked on its first modern enterprises only in 1970. Despite liberal investment incentives, private manufacturing grew slowly. An industrial complex near Ta'izz producing sweets, soaps, and plastics, owned by the Hayel Sa'id Group, dominated large-scale private industry. The remaining large private factories were mostly food processors or bottlers. Light industry consisted mainly of repair and construction "workshops" and crafts.

Unlike in other Third World countries with a large pool of labor, the proximity to the Persian Gulf's oil economies drove wage levels up. Roughly a third of adult males were absent for at least a year or two during the oil boom decade (1974-1984). The North imported not only teachers and health professionals but construction and hotel workers. While planners and international experts were initially optimistic about the investment potential of remittances, the class that benefited most from *laissez faire* were Northern-based moneychangers and importers, middlemen to the migration-and-consumption cycle.

The North's open import markets attracted a commercial bourgeoisie from the lower Red Sea region, resulting in a predominance of service sector investments. Those with cash to invest—local traders, North Yemeni migrants to the Gulf, and entrepreneurs from Aden, Asmara, Djibouti or Mombasa—were lured to the North's currency, real estate, and import markets, where they profited from the hefty share of remittances spent on consumer goods.[6]

Extraordinarily unfettered currency and import markets worked better for the North during the boom than the bust cycle. Global recession and depressed oil rents slashed remittance and aid levels, undermining, postponing or eliminating private and public projects by the thousands. The Yemeni riyal, having been kept artificially high at a uniform rate of 4.5 riyals to the dollar for over a decade (stimulating imports), plummeted to 18 to the dollar in the winter of 1986-1987. Facing balance of payments and currency reserve crises from 1982 onward, Sanaa temporarily banned all imports, blocked rampant smuggling, reformed and enforced tax codes and, in late 1986, took over currency markets and halted new investment projects.[7] The secondhand bonanza in the North was gone, and with it the "hands-off" policy of economic non-management.

Ownership and Investment

Ideologies differed from plans, and plans from outcomes. At best, the North's capitalist orientation and the South's socialism represented tendencies or goals, for both were really "mixed" economies.

The relative contribution of private and public capital can be measured in several ways. The North experienced a trend during the oil boom away from private capital formation towards public investment. In 1975, the private sector provided two thirds and the state only one third, but these proportions were reversed by 1982. By 1987, the North Yemen government financed three quarters of investments in agriculture, fisheries, transport, and communications, and nearly all utilities and mining development—amounting to two thirds of all investment. Individuals funded most new construction, trade, and hotel business, and 70 percent of manufacturing. Private investors' preference for real estate speculation over agricultural production was particularly disconcerting to planners; whereas overall growth was a healthy 6.6 percent, in agriculture it was only 2.4 percent.[8]

Nor was the South ever an entirely state-owned economy. The nationalizations of 1969 affected foreign financial, trade, and services businesses. Between 1973 and 1976, consolidation of state and joint industrial ventures continued, reducing the contribution of private domestic firms to industrial production from 51 percent to 38 percent, and the contribution of foreign firms from 36 percent to 10 percent. In fishing, however, foreign investors replaced some cooperative production. By 1976, private domestic and foreign firms held about 40 percent of the construction market, and local private transportation had over half the market. Cooperatives were credited with 71 percent of agricultural output, and the state with the rest, but livestock production was over 90 percent private.[9] This was as "socialist" as the South got.

In Aden's plan for 1981-1985 targets for private investments increased, and during the first three years of the plan private sector participation exceeded expectations by 8 percent, mostly in agriculture and local private fishing.[10] The 1988 census reported that of nearly thirty-five thousand establishments, 75 percent were private, 21 percent governmental, and the remainder cooperative or joint ventures. Just over a quarter of the work force was in the government sector.[11]

All these figures are estimates that probably understate subsistence, smuggling, and some informal trade. Cumulatively the evidence is sufficient to conclude that state and private sectors each played significant roles in both economies. There is little sign of sharp contrasts between centralized public ownership in the South and private enterprise in the North. Although their revolutions committed them to divergent paths, twenty years of practice produced convergent patterns. The explanation lies in the development projects supported by foreign donors.

Foreign Finance

Before the first Yemeni oil discovery in 1984, Yemen depended on aid rather than foreign companies for capital investment. International "soft" loans to the public sector represented the largest single source of new capital formation between 1970 and 1990. International companies participated either as contractors on donor-financed or nationalized state projects, where they earned profits but committed no capital, or as minority partners in public enterprises, to which they brought both capital and expertise. Once the oil industry began to take off, foreign private and public firms competed for roles in Yemen as contractors, partners, and investors.

The foreign-owned private sector in the PDRY had been slight. BP and Cable & Wireless did contract work for state corporations. BP, Mobil, and a joint Yemeni-Kuwaiti company supplied petroleum. Planners spoke of foreign firms as a source of capital for development, and a few Arab, Asian, and Eastern European firms entered the market.[12]

In the North, the Arab world's most liberal foreign investment policies attracted only a few foreign ventures, which raised much of their capital locally. Canada Dry, Ramada, and Sheraton were the most visible; since the hotels imported their own staffs, only the locally owned bottler was a source of significant jobs. Other companies bought shares of Yemeni public corporations: A subsidiary of British Rothman had a 25 percent partnership and five expatriate employees in the National Tobacco & Matches Company, and the Saudi al-Ahli Commercial Bank and Bank of America together owned 45 percent of the International Bank of Yemen.[13] Citibank found an economy where two thirds of the cash circulated outside the formal banking system to be an unprofitable market. Scores of American, Arab, Asian, and European contractors were active with donor projects: In roads, for instance, American and European engineers, Lebanese contractors, and South Korean and Chinese work forces (cheaper and more skilled than Yemenis) were not unusual.

By the 1980s, the overall patterns of external financing in the two Yemens were remarkably similar. For more than a decade, the West and the conservative states of the peninsula had shunned the South, while the Soviet Union, its allies, China, and radical Arab regimes were the main benefactors of both North and South. The global and regional multilateral agencies did work with the South, however, led by the World Bank's International Development Association (IDA). After 1980 the easing of tensions on the Peninsula prompted Saudi Arabia, Kuwait, and Abu Dhabi to offer assistance; by the middle of the decade, Arab funds surpassed assistance from socialist countries.[14] In North Yemen the Arab oil monarchies were the most visible donors in the 1970s, and the IDA exercised the most influence in economic policy. North Yemen's development assistance peaked in about 1981 at over $1 billion, and declined to half that amount in 1985 and to less than $100 million in 1988.

By that time, both countries relied on a similar list of donors and creditors. Grants were normally limited to small-scale technical assistance programs from the UN or European donors, or showy "gifts" from wealthy Gulf monarchs. Most new capital formation came from "soft" loans with low interest charges and long repayment schedules. Thus debts accumulated against the accounts of international benefactors roughly in proportion to the amount of aid provided.[15] The extent of polarization between "socialist" and "capitalist" trends was mitigated by the fact of Arab, IDA, Soviet, Chinese, and European loans for both development programs. Infrastructural projects were the bedrock of government development investment. Bilateral donors chose their own design, engineering, and construction firms, and global and Arab multilaterals applied the World Bank bids and tender system.[16]

Utilities—immense industrial plants supplying urban water and power nationwide—were also financed from diverse sources. After studying the South's poorly functioning Soviet-built system, World Bank economists recommended an all-Yemen electrification grid to maximize economies of scale, and IDA initiated financing for this joint grid in the mid-1980s. While not the first joint North-South venture, this involved unprecedented inter-Yemeni coordination.

Integrated rural development (IRD) was the Western and multilateral agencies' strategy to equip rural regions with roads, utilities, and some social services. The most prominent IRD projects in Yemen followed the World Bank model, whereby infrastructure, credit, and technical assistance stimulate rural investments by individuals or cooperatives. They were introduced in the areas of North Yemen best suited to intensive cash farming: the semi-tropical Tihama plain and the temperate southern uplands. By 1987 integrated projects, with different components from IDA, UN organizations, several Arab funds, and the European Community, at least theoretically covered most of rural Yemen.

These schemes followed a similar pattern in both countries. The South's largest IRD project, the Wadi Hadramawt project, stressing road construction, groundwater studies, deep wells mechanization, and credit through cooperatives for fertilizers and pesticides, was modeled on the Tihama Development Authority project.[17] The only difference was that in the South credit was available exclusively to cooperatives, whereas in the North, private loan applications were also accepted. Had farmers flocked to mortgage their land for bank loans (other than for qat, disallowed from loan applications), this might have been a significant difference; instead, credit officers in both systems bemoaned the lack of applications, and public spending in agriculture far outpaced private and/or cooperative financing.

Petroleum

The last stage in the convergence of the two Yemeni economies occurred in the nascent petroleum industry. Here the convergence was literal: Deposits discovered in the North/South border region were jointly developed by the two states in cooperation with international firms.

Both state petroleum companies relied on foreign expertise. Soviet petroleum companies conducted on- and off-shore studies for the South, and by the late 1970s concessions were won or under negotiation by British, French, Italian, Spanish, Kuwaiti, and Brazilian firms. Thirteen international firms had explored in the North. In 1984, Yemen Hunt, then a wholly owned local subsidiary of Texas-based Hunt Oil, made the first significant discovery, beyond Marib near the joint border. Soon Exxon, and then a consortium of South Korean firms, bought into Yemen Hunt; Texaco, Elf Aquitaine, Total, Canadian Occidental, and Soviet firms negotiated and paid to drill for Yemeni oil. The Soviet company Technoexport made a major find in 1986 at Shabwa, across the intra-Yemeni border from Marib. Discoveries in turn created scores of sub-contracting opportunities for suppliers and builders from around the globe, such as the US firm that built a small modular refinery near Marib and a Lebanese-Italian-German group that laid the pipeline. There were new commercial finds in 1987, 1988 and 1989.[18]

Realization of the commercial potential of the Marib-Shabwa basin required both inter-Yemeni cooperation and foreign capital and expertise. Not only was security around oil fields astride their common border improved by joint production, but the North hoped to use existing facilities at Aden, including the port and the refurbished BP refinery, which in turn needed the business. Cooperation avoided both conflict and duplication. The two national petroleum companies merged their operations into a joint Yemen Company for Investment in Oil and Mineral Resources, which signed a production agreement in late 1989 with an international consortium consisting of Hunt and Exxon (with 37.5 percent between them), the Kuwait Foreign Petroleum Exploration Corporation (25 percent), Total (18.75 percent), and two subsidiaries of Technoexport, Machinoexport and Zarughgeologia (18.75 percent).[19]

This commercial agreement culminated the twenty-year convergence of two ideologically different systems on a common, and eventually joint, pattern of public-foreign partnership on the "commanding heights." A more "mixed" venture could hardly be imagined, for the whole package included not just the joint Yemeni corporation but two of the largest capitalist oil giants, Exxon and Total, and Soviet and Kuwaiti state corporations. Destined to overshadow the value of property and investment in other sectors, this technically public venture was shortly followed by the political unity accord.

Thus the flow of capital into Yemen as aid and remittances created systems dominated by "development projects," on the one hand, and "uncaptured" farming, migration, and informal sector trade, on the other. Recessions in international oil prices and worldwide assistance cutbacks seriously disrupted both economies, leading to draconian austerity measures in the North and contributing to the outbreak of factional strife in Aden in early 1986. The discovery of oil gave Yemen access to a new source of foreign financing, corporate investment, and the promise of hard currency revenues. Oil rents, unlike aid, strengthened the power of Yemeni policymakers by financing the general account rather than earmarked projects.

Many of the arguments advanced for unity stressed the economic advantages, such as combining Aden port facilities with the North's private transport network, utilizing both the South's professional cadres and Northern-based entrepreneurs, taking advantage of larger markets and economies of scale and maintaining all existing foreign trade and aid relationships. The prospect of economic improvement offered considerable popular appeal because of widespread political unease and economic dissatisfaction in both polities, personal and social ties of the northern bourgeoisie to families or places in the South, political leaders' cross-cutting ties, and a common sense of nationalism.

Articles 7 and 8 of the constitution approved in popular referendum in May 1991 called for a mixed economy based on "Islamic social justice in production and social relations," a developed public sector "capable of owning the basic means of production," "the preservation of private ownership," and "scientific planning which leads to the establishment of public corporations engaged in exploiting the national and public resources, developing capabilities of and opportunities for the public, private, and mixed sectors."[20] The government budget approved in February 1991 listed recurrent and capital expenditures for ninety-one production-oriented public firms, forty service-oriented public companies and boards, and seventeen mixed ownership corporations.[21] More "socialist heritage" has been retained in Yemen than in Germany.

Before any economic benefits of unification could be realized, the Gulf crisis disrupted the flow of remittances and aid from Kuwait, Iraq, and Saudi Arabia. Newly unemployed migrants and their families, numbering upwards of a million, streamed into the cities just as operating funds in many social services sectors drained away.[22] By early 1991, the value of the riyal, having stabilized at about thirteen to the dollar, collapsed to twenty-six to the dollar. The government suspended civil service salaries to cover the costs of currency support and vital operations. By that summer, unemployment, inflation, and the strains on housing and services prompted public marches and demonstrations. Oil revenues were not only insufficient to cover the losses of foreign exchange, but they were threatened by Saudi claims to oil in the border region.[23] Once again, politics abroad and changes in the world economy disrupted Yemen's economic plans.

Notes

1. See Charles Dunbar, "The Unification of Yemen: Process, Politics and Prospects," *Middle East Journal* 46/3 (Summer 1992); and Robert D. Burrowes, "Oil Strike and Leadership Struggle in South Yemen: 1986 and Beyond," *Middle East Journal* 43/3 (Summer 1989).

2. World Bank, *People's Democratic Republic of Yemen: Special Economic Report Mid-Term Review of the Second Five-Year Plan, 1981-1985* (Washington, June 4, 1984), p. 19.

3. International Fund for Agricultural Development, *Report of the Special Programming Mission to People's Democratic Republic of Yemen* (Rome, June 1985), Table 16, p. 142, citing the Ministry of Agriculture and Agrarian Reform in 1985.

4. Helen Lackner, *PDR Yemen: Outpost of Socialist Development in Arabia* (London: Ithaca Press, 1985), pp. 176-179.

5. Hammoud al-'Awdi, *Al-Tanmiya wa Tajrabat al-'Amal al-Ta'awuni fi al-Yaman* (Sanaa: Kitab al-Ghad, 1977); 'Abdu 'Ali 'Uthman, "The Cooperative Movement in Yemen and Development: Participation of Cooperative Organizations for Development in Projects of the First Five-Year Development Plan," Report for the Council of Ministers and the Central Planning Organization, 1985.

6. See Kiren Aziz Chaudhry, "The Price of Wealth: Business and State in Labor Remittance and Oil Economies," *International Organization* 43/1 (Winter 1989).

7. *Middle East Economic Digest*, November 7, 1987, reports that the moves "backfired" by discouraging remittances, but Chaudhry argues that austerity measures were much more efficient in Yemen than in neighboring Saudi Arabia, where the state-owned oil-rent and direct subsidy system was less amenable to reform.

8. Faysal Sa'd Far'i, "Recent Economic Developments in Yemen," paper delivered to the Contemporary Yemen Conference, May 21-23, 1990, School of Oriental and African Studies, London, pp. 7-8. Data on the broader trends is in the World Bank Country Economic Memorandum of 1986.

9. World Bank, *People's Democratic Republic of Yemen: A Review of Economic and Social Development* (Washington, March 1978), Table 2.1, citing Ministry of Planning and World Bank estimates.

10. World Bank, 1984.

11. A. A. El-Sherbini, "An Analysis of Public-Sector Management Development in the People's Democratic Republic of Yemen" (Desk Study for UN Development Program, December 1989), p. 12, citing preliminary census results, and p. 15. Even in Indian Ocean fishing and trawling, where the public sector generated nearly three quarters of the value of production, the movement was toward privatization. By 1987, government, domestic firms and foreign firms each contributed about a fifth of sectoral production, the cooperatives had 28 percent and the mixed sector had a tenth.

12. *Middle East Economic Digest*, December 5, 1969, December 1971 and April 21, 1978; World Bank, 1978, Table 10.2.

13. See the account of Tobacco Exporters International's relations with the national tobacco company in Colin Morgan, "Joint Ventures: A Case Study," in *Focus on Yemen Arab Republic* (London, 1982), pp. 13-17.

14. World Bank, 1984, Table 2.3; Gerd Nonneman, *Development, Administration and Aid in the Middle East* (New York: Routledge, 1988), p. 103; and *Middle East Economic Digest*, January 19, 1990.

15. Data on "Percentage of External Public Loans from Major Donors" released by the Bank of Yemen, Aden, December 12, 1983; and the Central Yemen Bank, Sanaa, June 30, 1987, are several years apart, but the data is consistent with the World Bank (World Debt Tables, 1986-87 [Washington, DC, 1987], pp. 410, 414), which also shows nearly identical official credits of about $2.5 billion owed by both countries. The North owed more to the multilaterals, and the South owed more to other governments.

16. Virtually all projects, tenders and contracts are reported in *Middle East Economic Digest*.

17. Tareq and Jacqueline Ismael, *PDR Yemen: Politics, Economics and Society* (London: Frances Pinter, 1986), pp. 94-95.

18. On the Yemeni oil industry, see *Middle East Economic Digest*, July 22, 1983; *World Oil*, April 1988; *Oil and Gas Investor*, March 1988; and the *Middle East Economic Digest* special report of April 3, 1992.

19. *Middle East Economic Digest*, January 19, 1990 and March 19, 1990; *Gulf News*, March 15, 1990. Later, the Soviet firms withdrew and other US and international private corporations bid for their rights.

20. English translation by *Yemen Times*, July 1991.

21. *Yemen Times*, February 27, 1991, pp. 6-7, lists each company by name and two categories of expenses.

22. See Thomas Stevenson, "Yemeni Workers Come Home: Reabsorbing One Million Migrants," *Middle East Report* 181 (March-April 1993).

23. See "Yemen: Border Disputes and Relations with Saudi Arabia," a special study by the Petro Finance Market Intelligence Service (Washington, DC, May 1992).

15. TRACING THE CRACKS IN THE YEMENI SYSTEM

SARAH PHILLIPS

The sudden announcement in July 2005 by Yemeni President 'Ali 'Abdallah Salih that he would step down in 2006 in favor of "young blood" set the country and the region abuzz. Having led the northern Yemen Arab Republic from 1978, and then assumed the presidency of the whole of Yemen following the country's unification in 1990, Salih had enjoyed one of the longest reigns in the Arab world, behind only Libyan strongman Muammar Qaddafi and Oman's Sultan Qaboos bin Said al Said. As speculation raged that either the "young blood" was his son Ahmad, or that Salih's announcement was only a ploy to maintain power, one thing was certain: Yemen was in the midst of a prolonged security and economic crisis that had exposed the fragility of the state and widened cracks in the country's political system.

Two days after the president's announcement on July 17, the government lifted a set of popular state subsidies of fuel. The resulting riots, which the regime quashed with soldiers and tanks, killed 22 people and wounded 375, according to government figures. Unofficial estimates put the number of fatalities at 39 or more. These disturbances highlighted Yemen's dire economic straits and the deep suspicions of the public about uncontrolled regime corruption. They also took place against the backdrop of the government's then year-long fight against a Zaydi (Shi'i) insurgency, the leaders of which the regime once supported but who began raising once dormant questions about the right of Salih's regime to rule Yemen.

Two Rounds of Fighting

Starting in June 2004, government forces and tribal forces paid by the government waged a sporadic though unexpectedly bloody battle with a group calling itself the Believing Youth based in the province of Saada on the border with Saudi Arabia. The Believing Youth, whose numbers were estimated to be between one and three thousand by 2005, were originally the followers of the Zaydi cleric Hussein al-Houthi, a former Member of Parliament for the Zaydi party Hizb al-Haqq (1993-1997). Zaydism is a form of Shi'i Islam that is prevalent in northern Yemen's highlands.

While the government tried to downplay the conflict—Salih declared it "practically overcome" in mid-April 2005—various media and eyewitness accounts attested that people were still being killed in significant numbers. Although accurate figures were impossible to obtain, the government claimed in May 2005 that the number of soldiers and civilians killed in two rounds of fighting had been 525, with 2,708 wounded. The real figure was likely to be much higher than this, and did not include the number of rebels killed. Amnesty International reported that civilian targets were attacked by "security forces reportedly [using] heavy weaponry, including helicopter gunships." A large number of houses were destroyed during the conflict, some intentionally and others as a result of indiscriminate shelling.

The first round of fighting was centered in Saada, where al-Houthi and his followers were able to pound away at government troops from mountainous redoubts, inflicting many casualties. Mass arrests were carried out in the province, and Amnesty International reported that an unknown number of suspected al-Houthi followers were being held incommunicado by the government. Hussein al-Houthi was killed in the fighting in September 2004. Tensions eased during the six months following al-Huthi's death, whereupon the leadership of the Believing Youth was passed on to his elderly father Badr al-Din.

In early 2005, Badr al-Din al-Houthi was invited by Salih to the capital Sanaa to discuss a permanent settlement that was to include the release of prisoners and compensation payments for lives and properties lost during the fighting. The government had hoped to obtain assurances that the rebellion would not resume. Badr al-Din stayed in Sanaa for about two months. Accounts vary as to the exact outcome of the talks. The government claimed that he was granted immunity, while al-Houthi claimed that the government reneged on its promise to release prisoners and stop pursuing suspected sympathizers with the uprising. Two weeks after he returned to Saada in March, a police station and a military vehicle were attacked in surrounding areas. Serious fighting erupted and spread to other cities, including the streets of the capital. While there was relative calm in the early summer of 2005 and negotiations continued over the possibility of his surrender, Badr al-Din al-Houthi remained still at large. Another of his sons, Abd al-Malik, was quoted in the July 6 edition of the Yemeni weekly *al-Wasat* vowing that the remaining militants would "stay in the mountains" until the prisoners were released.

Murky Origins

The origins of the Houthi rebellion were murky. Fighting broke out in Saada in the summer of 2004, shortly after the regularly televised Friday sermon at Sanaa's Grand Mosque appeared via satellite with a banner in the background reading "death to America, death to Israel." The banner was a clear, if hardly unique challenge to the regime, whose cooperation with US anti-terrorism efforts had been more public than the regime would have liked. But while Hussein al-Houthi had a record of strong statements against US policy in the Middle East, it was not the Yemeni state's relationship with the US that truly drove his revolt. The March 9 edition of *al-Wasat* quoted Badr al-Din as saying that his son was motivated by the need to "protect Islam." As always, this begged the question of whose interpretation of Islam required protection and to what political ends?

The regime charged that the Believing Youth called for the reestablishment of the Zaydi imamate that governed northern Yemen for over one thousand years (with brief interruptions) until 1962. As a *sayyid*—one who claims descent from the Prophet Muhammad through his daughter Fatima and her husband Ali—al-Houthi would theoretically have been eligible to claim the title of imam for himself. According to another charge that circulated, al-Houthi did in fact proclaim himself imam. The Houthis and their former political party Hizb al-Haqq deny both of these politically explosive accusations.

Revival of the imamate is an idea that is rejected by Yemen's Sunni majority and many Zaydi tribespeople, and which stands in contradiction to the goal of the 1962 revolution to weaken the age-old power of the *sayyids* over other Zaydis who are not members of the religious elite (often referred to as "tribal"). As a secular former military officer and a Zaydi tribesman who is not a *sayyid*, President Salih embodied that goal. In 1990, Zaydi religious leaders, including figures now involved in Yemen's two Zaydi political parties, held a conference in Sanaa, where it was declared that the leader of the state was not required to be a descendant of the Prophet and agreed that "the fair and the strong" should rule Yemen. The declaration was, of course, issued under pressure from Salih.

There was some ambiguity in the Houthis' denials of aspirations to bring the imamate back. Badr al-Din was quoted in the March 9 *al-Wasat* to the effect that the imamate is the "most preferable" system of government for Yemen if the "true and legitimate" imam is present. "Any just believer" can rule the country, he said, if the imam is not present. When asked whether he considered Salih a legitimate ruler, Badr al-Din declined to answer, telling the interviewer: "Do not put me in a difficult position." It is this broader objection to the regime, rather than talk of the imamate, that resonated with disenchanted Yemenis.

Complex Web of Alliances

The persistent fighting in Saada drew accusations from Shi'i religious luminaries in Iran and Iraq that the government of a majority-Sunni country had launched a sectarian campaign against the Shi'a minority. In May 2005, Grand Ayatollah Hossein Ali Montazeri of Iran said: "It is not acceptable that the Shi'a be persecuted for their faith in a country which defines itself as Islamic." The same month, Montazeri's counterpart in Najaf, Ali al-Sistani, reportedly accused Yemen's government of waging "a kind of war" against the Zaydi population. Though the Houthis themselves spoke of sectarian divisions, to frame the conflict as simply a Sunni-Shi'a one was to misstate the issue.

Prior to 1990, the Republic of Yemen was divided into two states, the Yemen Arab Republic (or North Yemen) and the People's Democratic Republic of Yemen (or South Yemen). The Sunni former south and its largest city, Aden, had been a part of the British Empire since 1839. Not long after the British were removed in 1967, the state declared itself Marxist. The large majority of the Sunnis of Yemen follow the moderate Shafi'i school of jurisprudence. Although there was a small Sunni majority in the former north, rulers have almost always been of the Zaydi sect. Since 1962, only one Sunni president has held office (1967-1974). In the unified republic that exists today, Zaydis account for roughly 20-25 percent of the population but have continued to dominate the country's political system, Salih being the most obvious case in point.

Sheikh 'Abdallah bin Hussein al-Ahmar was another prominent but non-*sayyid* Zaydi who played a key role in overthrowing the Zaydi imamate and establishing the Yemen Arab Republic. As the preeminent tribal leader in Yemen, the speaker of Parliament, and the head of Islah, the largest opposition political party until his death in late 2007, he was widely considered to be the second most powerful person in the country. Despite his being

Zaydi, the party that he led is largely inspired by Sunni doctrine as espoused by the Muslim Brotherhood. Zaydi republicans like Salih and Ahmar relied on Sunni Muslims, particularly the Brotherhood, to counter threats from the formerly Marxist south.

Along with religious leaders, the Zaydi northern tribes have, since the 1962 revolution against the imamate and the end of the resulting civil war in 1970, generally formed the other major base of support for northern governments. Shortly after the Egyptians withdrew from the war in 1967, the northern tribes consolidated their position in the military and extended their political influence, giving them unprecedented power. The northern tribal confederations (particularly the Hashid confederation) fought for the Salih regime against the south before unification and afterward during the 1994 civil war. The divisions in national Yemeni politics are not religious sectarian divisions per se, but are based on a complex web of tribal, social, religious, and politically expedient alliances.

"Salafi Attack"

On the very local level, however, sectarian divisions were related to the Houthi rebellion. The province of Saada is part of the Zaydi tribal area that has traditionally been the heartland of the Yemeni regime. After the 1962 revolution, Saada remained loyal to pro-imamate "royalists" until 1970. The region did not, however, really come under state control until late in that decade and early in the next, at which time it saw the introduction of the "scientific institutes," religious schools propagating the ideas of the puritanical Sunni Islam adhered to in neighboring Saudi Arabia. The scientific institutes were state schools informally controlled by the Muslim Brotherhood and financed by Saudi Arabia. These modern, Salafi (often termed "Wahhabi" to suggest their links to Saudi Arabia) institutes competed with the older Zaydi parochial schools, as well as public state schools, but did not replace either. However, the number of Zaydi schools decreased as youths from ordinary Zaydi families became attracted to the scientific institutes' emphasis upon the social equality of all Muslims—as opposed to the special status claimed by the *sayyids*.

Hussein al-Houthi's initial rise to prominence was a direct product of Salih's style of playing both sides against the middle. After favoring Salafi upstarts in the 1980s against the *sayyids*, some of whom retained pro-imamate sympathies, Salih backed al-Houthi throughout the 1990s in an attempt to offset the growing strength of Salafism as taught in the scientific institutes and some of the mosques of Saada. Salih adopted this strategy as part of a balancing act against Saudi influence (and reportedly also a check upon the power of regime crony, military strongman, and Salafi sympathizer Ali Muhsin). After the 1994 civil war, Salih supported the establishment of a Zaydi militia under the command of al-Houthi, who also revived the Zaydi parochial school system in the northwest of the country. These are the schools that the regime began closing in the mid-2000s for allegedly teaching intolerance. While this was in some cases, a reasonable claim, the Zaydi schools were pursued far more seriously than the equally intolerant anti-Shi'a scientific institutes.

During the early months of fighting, Badr al-Din accused the government of stirring up sectarian sentiment against the Zaydi religious elite, telling *al-Wasat* that the puritanical Sunnis' "enmity toward us is as strong as can be." His son Abd al-Malik broadened the charge, saying that the governor of Saada had "continued the Wahhabi attack" on Zaydism by replacing the prayer leaders at Zaydi mosques and tolerating the statements of some Salafis that the Zaydis are not Muslims at all.

Badr al-Din hinted at another line of ideological attack on the regime when he was asked by the *al-Wasat* interviewer for his opinion of democracy as provided for in the Yemeni constitution. While the regime did not adhere to the constitution in any consistent fashion, the idea that Yemen was in the midst of a transition to democracy was an idea from which the regime derived a considerable measure of legitimacy internationally and, to an extent, domestically as well. Badr al-Din answered only: "We are for justice and we know nothing else."

Economic Woes

Despite the charges of wanting to restore the imamate, and despite its possible hostility to broad political inclusivity, the Houthi movement struck a chord with segments of society extending beyond its own members simply because it stood up to a regime seen as feckless and corrupt.

Yemen remains one of the poorest countries in the Arab world. The World Bank estimated at that time that just over 40 percent of the population lived in poverty—a figure that has increased substantially in the intervening years. This condition was widely perceived to have been exacerbated by the government's decision on July 19, 2005, in accordance with an economic "reform" package recommended by the International Monetary Fund in 1995, to remove state subsidies on diesel fuel and fuel products. Overnight, the price of gasoline nearly doubled while the price of diesel rose by nearly 150 percent. Many farms in Yemen pump ground water using diesel that, prior to the subsidy removal, was sold to the public for approximately 50 percent of its international market price. With the production of market crops so directly dependent on pumped irrigation, prices of many basic commodities move up and down with the price of diesel. In the days following the removal of the subsidies, prices of non-fuel products appeared to have increased by around 20 percent. On July 26, Salih slightly reduced the fuel prices in an effort to ameliorate the criticism being leveled at the government in the aftermath of the July 20-21 unrest.

Rumors of even larger price increases ran rampant leading up to the subsidy removal, as did the claim that many of the protests had been orchestrated by factions within the military leadership that derived benefits from diesel smuggling. The regime undertook no public information campaign to dispel the rumors of further increases, perhaps because they did not wish to call attention to diesel prices at all. According to a well-informed ex-parliamentarian from the ruling General People's Congress (GPC), high-ranking regime officials smuggled large quantities of subsidized diesel from Yemen's southern ports to the Horn of Africa, transferring at least 20 to 30 percent of the public money used to pay for the subsidies into their own pockets. Further transfers were widely believed to have occurred on paper, without the need to physically transport the subsidized diesel at all. Concrete evidence of the extent of smuggling was impossible to obtain, but the rapid increase in Yemen's diesel imports made a circumstantial case.

Though Yemen has its own small oilfields, 70 percent of the diesel consumed per annum must be brought in from elsewhere. While the amounts of other commodities imported remained fairly constant between 1998 and 2003, imports of "petroleum and petroleum products" (the vast majority of which is diesel) leapt from 6.44 percent of all imports in 1998 to 14.86 percent in 2003. The fact that all other categories of imports (including equipment that uses diesel such as power-generating machinery and transport vehicles) actually decreased slightly in this period, combined with the fact that Yemen had no strategic civil or military diesel reserve, made smuggling the only explanation for the increase, or at least a great deal of it. In any event, much of the Yemeni public was convinced that the regime was smuggling diesel. As Islah member Nasser Arman asked some months before the subsidy was lifted, "When the government admits that the subsidies on the oil derivatives go to the pockets of smugglers, why doesn't it audit even one of them?"

Confusion

The deteriorating economy was only one of the regime's problems. In the eyes of most Yemenis, the spate of explosions, demonstrations, assassinations, and gunfights witnessed throughout the spring and summer of 2005 were likely related to the uprising in Saada—and were signs that the regime was losing its grip on the country.

In mid-March there were two days of strikes and demonstrations across the country over the introduction of a sales tax that articulated anger over the government's failure to respond to rising poverty. The closure of the US and British embassies for a few days in early April coincided with reports of several attacks on government installations and personnel. On March 29, there was a hand grenade attack on uniformed security guards outside the gates to the old city (Bab al-Yemen) in Sanaa. There were subsequent unconfirmed reports of a grenade attack on the Ministry of Defense on April 5, followed by a second attack in Bab al-Yemen, and one in central Tahrir Square. On April 25, there was an attempted assassination of a military official as he rode in a Defense Ministry vehicle past the Customs Office. The would-be assassin, who authorities said was a member of the Believing Youth, threw a grenade at the car but was quickly shot dead. The intermittent gun battles between government forces and alleged al-Houthi supporters, in Sanaa and beyond, and the almost daily low flyovers by military jets all added to general public unease.

In the prevailing tension, the al-Houthi rebellion came to mean many things to many people. Some Yemenis latched onto President Salih's claim that the Saada uprising was a "foreign conspiracy." They might have cited the fact that well-known Zaydi preacher Yahya Hussein al-Dailami was sentenced to death in late May 2005, after being found guilty of supporting the Houthi rebellion. The government-run *Yemen Observer* reported that al-Dailami was found guilty of "having contacts with the state of Iran with the aim of harming the diplomatic and political position of Yemen." The report quoted the trial judge as saying that al-Dailami had "traveled to Iran and made contact with the Iranian state seeking support for an Islamic revolution in Yemen." Some Yemenis believed the president's other claim that domestic opposition groups, namely the two Zaydi parties, the Union of Popular Forces (UPF) and Hizb al-Haqq, were backing the Houthis in an attempt to destabilize the regime. Still others saw it as the potential unraveling of a delicate balance of religious and tribal interests that had been the regime's source of power for so long.

The confusion surrounding the causes and effects of the uprising was due to the virtual media blackout imposed by the government on the topic of Saada. At least two foreign journalists trying to gain access to the area were briefly jailed in the summer of 2005 and international organizations were restricted from entering the area. Local journalists had little more success. Misinformation therefore abounded in both the official and independent media. Some endeavored to provide accurate reporting, some resorted to guesswork and rumor, and others simply traded insults. The independent *Yemen Times* published an article in June 2005 that labeled a foreign journalist writing about events in Saada "a docile pupil of a…mentally retarded monkey" (with reference to the leader of the UPF).

Meanwhile, the regime harassed members of the UPF and Hizb al-Haqq, raiding the UPF's offices and arresting several leaders on the grounds that they were inciting forces to overthrow the government. Both of these parties are quite small, and the UPF is little more than a handful of urban intellectuals. One of the UPF's leaders argued that the real reason for the attacks on his party was the president's concern over the strength of their efforts to consolidate democracy in the country. While this was an unlikely suggestion, it indicated the opposition was holding onto the hope that, despite evidence to the contrary, their desire for greater political inclusion was having an impact upon the regime, and indeed, Yemen's future.

In the wake of the July 20-21 riots, the opposition was careful to condemn both the government and the damage done by the rioters. In an official statement, a coalition of six opposition parties including Islah and the ruling party of the former South Yemen, the Yemeni Socialist Party, said that the government bore the responsibility for the chaos resulting from the removal of the subsidies. Highlighting the opposition's generally reactive stance on political reform, the statement said the parties would "suspend dialogue with the ruling party until these measures are reviewed and until a proper reform process is implemented."

In the atmosphere of confusion that prevailed in Yemen, al-Houthi's implied claim that the government was illegitimate made his rebellion a symbol of the country's extensive problems and the regime's narrowing support base. While most Yemenis (including the Zaydi community) considered the views of the Believing Youth to be extreme, their ability to recruit and inspire sympathy was a testament to the increasing unpopularity of the government.

16. THE SNAKE WITH A THOUSAND HEADS: THE SOUTHERN CAUSE IN YEMEN

SUSANNE DAHLGREN

In the summer of 2007, a lively and non-violent movement sprang up in the southern provinces of Yemen to protest the south's marginalization by the north. The movement was sparked by demonstrations held that spring by forcibly retired members of the army, soon to be accompanied by retired state officials and unemployed youth. The deeper roots of the uprising lay in grievances dating to the 1994 civil war that consolidated the north's grip over the state and, southerners would say, the resources of the country.[1] Southerners soon took to calling their protests al-Harak, a coordinated campaign against a northern "occupation."

The ethos of the national revolutionary movement that began in January 2011 was pre-figured by al-Harak: it met brutal violence with peaceful resistance and relied on flexible organisation instead of hierarchies. As Yemenis from across the country came together to demand the end of President 'Ali 'Abdallah Salih's regime, it almost seemed as if the call for reestablishment of the independent southern state would be put on hold. When Salih finally signed the Gulf Cooperation Council plan for political transition in November 2011, there was a brief celebration before protests resumed in "Change Squares" across the country and a "parallel revolution" fought to oust corrupted functionaries in state bureaucracy and the army. In post-Salih Yemen, al-Harak continues to struggle for the rights of southern Yemenis.

Al-Harak should be understood as a broad-based popular movement demanding sounder and more just governance. As such, the southern cause commands widespread support (including from some outside the south). The movement encompasses elements that want to secede and, in a country long forecast to become a "failing state," if not the "next Afghanistan," these are the actors who are featured in the international media. To the extent that the southern movement was noticed amidst Yemen's multiple problems prior to the uprising of 2011, it was mostly dismissed as secessionist or, following the preference of the government, cast as a potential ally of al-Qaeda in the Arabian Peninsula and a threat to Yemeni stability. Indeed, in the midst of the movement to oust Salih in May 2011, jihadist group and al-Qaeda affiliate Ansar al-Shari'a managed to take over major towns in Abyan province in the south. According to the Bureau of Investigative Journalism, the following six months saw more than a dozen US airstrikes in Abyan. Rumors at the time attributed the militants' success to the withdrawal of army units from the area, allowing around two hundred jihadists to walk in and declare their "Islamic Emirate." These cities were later recaptured by the government in the spring of 2012. Though the Yemeni Army claimed credit, local people said Ansar al-Shari'a was driven out by "People's Committees" made up of local tribes and southern activists. 2

The southern uprising was a completely new type of social movement in this part of the world and, even inside Yemen, many old-guard activists failed, in the beginning, to understand it. In a country where about 60 percent of the population is under twenty-five years of age, the movement reflected the aspirations of youth for opportunity and openness to the outside world. It also advocated peaceful resistance rather than armed struggle. As the protests proliferated in 2007 and after, however, Salih vowed to crush them. His security forces and the army obliged with blockades of entire provinces—such as Radfan, where the 1963 revolution that brought independence for the former South Yemen was launched—use of live ammunition against unarmed demonstrators, air raids upon entire cities, assassinations, and arbitrary detentions. Still, the southerners persisted in attempts to foster a new political culture in the poorest Arab country.

Salih and his regime propagated a narrative whereby the southerners, about one sixth of the Yemeni population, suffered in equal measure with residents of the more populous north. Because of Yemen's pre-1990 history, however, the southern cause is unique. The southerners yearn for reestablishment of the rule of law they recall from the days before unification with the north. Some hope to remain united with their northern brothers under better rule; others would just as soon split the country once more.

Unified and Divided

From 1967 to 1990, the southern provinces of Yemen—Aden, Lahij, Abyan, Shabwa, Hadramawt, and Mahra—comprised a self-declared socialist state known for most of its existence as the People's Democratic Republic of Yemen. The new republic was governed by the Yemeni Socialist Party (YSP), which became increasingly divided along lines of ideology and tribal affiliation. In the north, Salih emerged as leader of the Yemen Arab Republic and its ruling General People's Congress (GPC), a nonideological party-like structure similar to those led by Nasser and Sadat in Egypt. Both Yemens were poor, undeveloped, and dependent on foreign assistance. Both were best described as mixed economies; the north had a large public sector, while the south (its socialist label notwithstanding) welcomed foreign private investment and in 1988 employed only 25 percent of the work force in state-owned enterprises. In the late 1980s, there were several joint companies and oil was discovered on the north-south border.[3] In 1988, the border was opened so that Yemenis on either side could visit the "other part of the homeland." It was not so strange, therefore, when the south entered enthusiastically into unity with the north in 1990.

But southerners' contentment soon turned to worry about the failing economy, rising poverty, and abuse of power by Salih and his loyalists. The YSP figure 'Ali Salim al-Bid was made vice president of unified Yemen, junior partner to Salih in an arrangement southerners felt was mirrored all down the ranks of state. Salih had majority control of the presidential council and the Ministry of Finance. Southerners complained as well of clientelism, corruption, and centralization of power around personality rather than political institutions in the unified state. The northern and southern army commands, for example, did not merge, but remained loyal to Salih and al-Bid's faction of the YSP, respectively. Negotiations over the mechanics of unification began to break down amidst a "war of declarations" from both sides in Yemen's newly rambunctious press. Meanwhile, "Arab Afghans" returning from the anti-Soviet jihad, among them the Abyan tribal figure Tariq al-Fadli, were used to assassinate more than one hundred of the YSP's cadre—apparently with the northerners' blessing.[4] Southern cries for bolstering the rule of law date from the assassination campaign. Many notables on both sides genuinely desired unity, as did the bulk of the population, but hardliners in Sanaa and secessionists within the YSP prevailed in the internal struggles.[5] A secession front emerged behind al-Bid and his party colleague Haydar al-'Attas, significantly including two former enemies of the YSP, 'Abd al-Rahman al-Jifri of the Sons of Yemen League and 'Abdallah al-Asnag of the Front for the Liberation of South Yemen.[6] The result was the 1994 civil war, which ended in a decisive victory for Salih's forces.

On July 7, 1994, northern forces took Aden, trashing and looting government offices and public-sector companies. The leaders of the secession front, having retreated before the advancing northern army, escaped abroad. To add to the humiliation of defeat, southerners were made to celebrate July 7 as a day of national unity. Southern activists have since renamed it the "day of rage."

Over the past decade, the rifts in the southern political establishment began to heal as the population soured on the policies of Salih's government. Southerners protested with special vehemence against what they viewed as large-scale land theft and reallocation of southern wealth and resources to the northern elite. During the 1994 fighting, 'Ali Nasir, a former president of South Yemen ousted in a 1986 intra-regime bloodbath, had directed his partisans to fight on the side of the north. In 2006, speaking from Syrian exile, he declared that Yemeni politicians had been overly hasty in pursuing the original unification. Two years later, on January 13, 2008, his loyalists and their allies in a tiny communist party joined YSP rank-and-filers and al-Harak supporters in a reconciliation rally held in the Aden district of Shaykh 'Uthman. The following spring, al-Bid acknowledged and apologized to the southern people for his role in unification. Al-Bid, who remains in exile, now heads the Supreme Southern Movement Council, one of the many groups that form al-Harak.

A third personage to rally behind the southern cause was Tariq al-Fadli, son of the sultan who ruled the Fadli sultanate in part of what is today the Abyan province during the British era. As a former jihadi in Afghanistan, Tariq al-Fadli had advocated the establishment of an Islamic state in the Arabian Peninsula, and violently opposed the YSP, but he said his old mission was in the past.[7] All these forces stood united in opposition to Salih's government though not all were in favor of secession. While al-Bid, al-Asnag, and al-Fadli supported separation, 'Ali Nasir, al-Jifri, and al-'Attas were either non-committal or favored a federation. The coming together of bitter foes, across the ideological spectrum, spoke both to the urgency with which the southern cause was felt and to the absurdity of conflating al-Harak with al-Qaeda.

The Southern Movement

In any case, the popular movement in the south was much larger and more diffuse than the councils of politicos. It was built on the idea of fairly autonomous local units, each of whose leaders arose organically. As one Adeni man with roots in Abyan said, "It is a snake with a thousand heads. The authorities cannot stop it, as when local leaders are detained or go undercover, new ones replace them. It is the strength of the movement that it does not have a national leadership that can be liquidated." Many of the local cadres were youth, and the signature tools of al-Harak were new communication technologies and social media such as text messaging, Facebook, and independent websites that the government was not able to close down. To keep up weekly demonstrations amidst the army sieges and road closures, activists were flexible about the location of rallies, which they scheduled by text message on short notice. This "just-in-time" production of protest was possible because the rallies were local and the demonstrators all lived in the vicinity. To obtain information on airstrikes in blocked-off areas, some of which the government claimed were home to "al-Qaeda camps," young Internet wizards devised means of circumventing state-censored servers and gaining access to foreign-based websites.

The situation in the southern provinces started to resemble the independence struggle of the 1950s and 1960s. As the British did then, the Yemeni regime faced its fiercest resistance in Radfan and al-Yafa'. As an old-guard women's activist says she told a dismissive northern official, "Do not think we cannot throw you out of our country. We did that to the British, who had a much bigger army than you do."

Most al-Harak activists wanted to establish an independent state and cancel the unification accord. In January 2010, the Yemeni Center for Civil Rights found in a poll that 70 percent of southern Yemenis were in favor of secession. However precise this number was, the proportion of southerners who backed secession certainly grew rapidly, as state violence and suppression of press freedom escalated. The violent response to the protests of 2011, as well as the prominence of northern elites in the political process, convinced ever more southerners to rally behind the idea of independence.

There are two vital social strata of southerners that prefer federation with the north with regional autonomy, even as they support the rallying cries of al-Harak—the rule of law, transparency, and respect for human rights. These two groups are, first, Yemenis of northern origin and, second, old-guard urban intellectuals and activists, the men and women who fought for independence from British colonial power. Even without the opposition of the mighty northern tribes, who will never countenance the loss of the south and its natural resources, secession is unlikely as long as these groups of southerners back a federal solution. As for the surviving cadre of the YSP, they voice vague support for al-Harak's goals while continuing to play politics in the capital, through the dialogue between the ruling GPC and the opposition Joint Meeting Parties (JMP) coalition, which encompasses the southern socialists as well as the religious conservative Islah party.

It was easy to understand why people with roots in the north oppose secession. To them, the vision of a border that would once again separate families is anathema. But they also fear that northerners will be persecuted in a rejuvenated southern state. In modern Yemeni history, roots and origins have been sources of social division in times of crisis and instability. Today's divisions take colloquial form in the suggestion by northerners that all southerners are "Somalis and Indians," a reference to the centuries of migration and commerce between Aden and those countries. Southerners, meanwhile, are apt to deride northerners as *mutakhallifin* (country bumpkins) or *dahbashin*, a pejorative taken from a popular TV series.

Amidst southerners' anger over property issues, northern shop owners have been harassed and urged to leave the south while they can.

Why do the old-guard freedom fighters support federation with the north rather than a sovereign state? One reason is that al-Harak lacks a manifesto or a central committee, elements that have characterized political movements in this part of the world. As an Adeni male intellectual stated, al-Harak cannot be trusted to bring change since it has no single political program and its leaders are self-nominated. Local al-Harak leaders, particularly Tariq al-Fadli, arouse suspicions among the secular-minded urban elite, who consider him, at the least, a turncoat. Some al-Harak figures have built nationwide support by penning columns in opposition newspapers; one was the Aden-born Ahmad 'Umar bin Farid, but he was jailed in 2008 and then forced to leave the country. Another is Hasan Ba'um, also Adeni, who was jailed and held incommunicado with his son in 2010. In addition, reports of violence came from areas blocked off by the army and from rallies that security forces disrupt, casting doubt upon the movement's peaceful nature. But non-violent actions, like road blockages and strikes, are viewed with equal disdain by the old guard, who search in vain for the hierarchical, tightly organized cells of 1960s revolutionary movements.

Women's rights activists are also suspicious of al-Harak, particularly of those elements that endorse the idea of secession. Over the last twenty years in unified Yemen, women's issues have been pushed to the margins, and activists are able to raise them only with the aid of a handful of sympathetic male politicians. In both the north and the south, these male politicians happen to be skeptical of secession. Still, women's groups are following events closely and some have already switched horses. Al-Harak has a small women's section unaffiliated with the mainline movement, the Yemeni Women's Union, which has its roots in the late colonial period.

Three years into the southern uprising, the regime in Sanaa had learned its lessons about how to disseminate its version of the truth. The offices of *al-Ayyam*, the premier press outlet for movement sympathizers, were shuttered. Army blockades ensured that little detailed reporting of any sort leaked out of the south. Government officials in southern provinces were regularly briefed in mass meetings to keep them on message, which the state also propagated via "independent" newspapers with more or less open links to the security apparatus. Foreign reporters, meanwhile, were gulled by seemingly firsthand information about al-Qaeda in the Arabian Peninsula, which after the failed underwear bombing in Detroit on December 25, 2009, was easy to sell as the "number one threat in Yemen." Part of regime propaganda tactics was to hint that al-Bid and other southern leaders were in cahoots with al-Qaeda or—as they accuse the Houthi rebels in Yemen's northern highlands—Hizballah and Iran. These insinuations found a ready audience in the United States, in particular, and military aid continues to flow to Sanaa. The regime's manipulation of Western fears of al-Qaeda angered southerners, who know the US-made weaponry was deployed against them, as well as the Houthis.

Privatization Gone Bad

While all of Yemen is rife with poverty and unemployment, the south is its own case. To start with, southerners were less inured to the corruption and nepotism of the Salih regime than their northern brethren, who endured it for an additional two decades. During the long years of colonial rule—the British kept Aden for 130 years—there were many crises of governance, but official corruption was not one of them. When the south was an independent state, there was likewise no pocketing of public funds. Though the state was cash-strapped, the political elite did not live upon state funds and so the budget more or less corresponded to the real national accounts.

After unification, and more intensively after the 1994 civil war, the Salih regime introduced a patronage system whereby political loyalty was bought with deeds to lucrative land, concessions to start businesses, houses, jeeps, and expensive consumer goods. Such largesse was bestowed upon state functionaries who were willing to join the GPC. While in the north these privileges were enshrined by dint of practice as an entitlement of government service, however much ordinary northerners may have objected, in the south there was a stronger taboo against using the state treasury as a milking cow. In meetings with foreign donors, Sanaa officials rebuffed criticism by saying that what outsiders (and southerners) viewed as corruption was needed to unify the country and incorporate southerners into the system prevalent in the north.

In the 1990s, like developing countries around the world, Yemen embarked upon the privatization of its public-sector industries and agricultural ventures, as recommended by the World Bank and the International Monetary Fund. While neither the north nor the south was a worker's paradise before unification, privatization was more haphazard in the south and social dislocation was more severe. Aggressive privatization started after 1994 civil war. Machinery and raw materials were looted in the chaos that followed the arrival of northern troops in Aden and other cities. In Aden, most industrial enterprises were closed down because looting had left them unable to function and the employees, most of them women, were sent home with a state pension. The factories were then put up for sale. Some of them were simply turned into real estate, affording investors access to huge tracts of land. In actual terms, therefore, privatization meant idling Adeni industries and freeing up market share for producers located in the northern industrial zones of Ta'izz, Hudayda, and Sanaa. After a few years, former factory workers in the south lost their pensions and joined the swelling ranks of the unemployed.

There were also several well-connected northerners who showed up in the south after 1994 bearing forged deeds to property. In rural areas, privatization of state farms and cooperatives meant that lands were simply given to members of the northern elite. The workers were left entirely without income. These desperate people and their teenaged children form the backbone of the southern movement in the countryside.

Too Much, Too Soon

The southerners' grievances are mostly political and economic in nature, but cultural and religious concerns have also come to the fore. According to common sentiments in the south, northern ways of life were imposed upon the south by the government, pushing the south one hundred years back in time. Tribal customs like child marriages and summary executions are two examples that southerners cite; the official patronage system is another. The idea that the Salih regime—and now its successor—was tribal and "backward" is one that many northerners share. As one human rights activist from the northern town of Ta'izz explained his support for al-Harak, "First the tribal-based rulers of Sanaa destroyed all initiative and marginalized Ta'izz; now they are doing the same in the south."

These alleged cultural differences were increasingly linked in the popular consciousness to religion. After the 1994 war, the conservative Islah party took over the reins of southern governorates and launched a "re-Islamization" campaign.[8] The campaign was mostly unsuccessful. When Islamists headed by the ill-reputed Islah leader 'Abd al-Majid al-Zindani proposed a Saudi-type morality police for Yemeni streets, for example, the government was quick to refuse it any authority. Still, the mere attempt at establishing such a religious watchdog stirred Yemeni Women's Union leaders to say it "undermined women and the fundamental role they play in building Yemeni society."[9] The era of unification coincided with the tide of religious conservatism that swept over every country in the Middle East. Almost all Yemeni women, for example, have donned cloaks and headscarves, and an increasing number wear the *niqab*, the full-face veil that leaves only the eyes visible. Hardline religious schools have proliferated. In earlier times, these phenomena were certainly present, but they were not criticized in the same terms. Today many men say the *niqab* is too much. As one male government official explained, "If this is religion, I don't want it." Southerners often claim that northerners have a shallow, materialistic view of modernity, rushing to buy the latest model of sports utility vehicle but failing to send their daughters to university.

Modernity, in general, is something that southerners associate with themselves and their region's history of European colonization, nationalist rebellion, and Marxist-inspired governance. Many southerners would agree with the view of a YSP official in 1982: that unity with the "backward" north will be possible only when the latter develops to the level of the south. Today the YSP's official stance is much softer, of course. In March 2010, the party endorsed the Vision for National Salvation, the opposition's program for a democratic system of federal autonomy, drafted by the Preparatory Committee for National Dialogue on which the YSP sits. This document has not won widespread support in the south, as many perceive that full unification is premature.

As the southern uprising grew, more and more families in the south tuned in to Aden TV, the satellite channel that broadcasts live from London. Aden TV showed footage of al-Harak demonstrations, as well as newsreels from the good old days of southern independence, inviting viewers to sing along with the popular entertainer 'Abboud Khawaja's ode to al-Harak. "People of the south, be ready—this is the revolution of the old and the young."[10] While the opposition parties quarreled with the regime over elections and Salih threatened to make southerners "drink from the sea," the younger generation longed for a fair political system and a sound economy.

These struggles continue following Salih's formal resignation in February 2012. Salih's successor, former Vice President 'Abd al-Rabb Mansour al-Hadi, hails from Abyan and has undertaken some civil sector reform, and the government he heads is a coalition between the GPC and JMP. Some al-Harak figures now advocate a five-year test period to allow the new regime to address southern concerns. But for many southerners, the unity government is just another trick to entice the south to stay in a dysfunctional relationship. As in the 1960s, when there was no going back to kinder and gentler colonial rule, and hasty attempts to allow locals entry into administration came too late, the time for restructuring unified Yemen into a more equitable system has passed in the minds of many young people. They are eager to take their lands into their own hands.

Notes

1. For background, see Franck Mermier, "Yémen: la menace du séparatisme au Sud," *EchoGéo*, June 15, 2008; and Susanne Dahlgren, "The Southern Movement in Yemen," *ISIM Review* 22 (Autumn 2008), pp. 50–51.

2. *Yemen Times*, June 4, 2012.

3. See Sheila Carapico, "The Economic Dimension of Yemeni Unity," in this volume.

4. Abdul Rahman al-Jifri, "Yemeni Unification: Crisis and Solutions," in E. G. H. Joffé, M. J. Hachemi and E. W. Watkins, eds., *Yemen Today: Crisis and Solutions* (London: Caravel Press, 1997), p. 186.

5. See Sheila Carapico, "From Ballot Box to Battlefield: The War of the Two 'Alis," *Middle East Report* 190 (September-October 1994).

6. For background on the various southern factions, see Fred Halliday, *Arabia Without Sultans* (Harmondsworth, UK: Penguin, 1974); Fred Halliday, "Yemen's Unfinished Revolution: Socialism in the South," *MERIP Reports* 81 (October 1979); and Joe Stork, "Socialist Revolution in Arabia: A Report from the People's Democratic Republic of Yemen," *MERIP Reports* 15 (March 1973).

7. Al-Fadli's star faded somewhat in 2011 as it was rumored his son had joined Ansar al-Shari'a.

8. See Susanne Dahlgren, *Contesting Realities: Morality and the Public Sphere in Southern Yemen* (Syracuse, N.Y.: Syracuse University Press, 2010).

9. Adnkronos International, July 18, 2008.

10. The video for the song is available online at: http://www.youtube.com/watch?v=2YeAw2PRZUc.

17. TAWAKKUL KARMAN AS CAUSE AND EFFECT

STACEY PHILBRICK YADAV

Political activist Tawakkul Karman brought Yemen's revolution to New York in October 2011, speaking directly with Secretary-General Ban Ki-Moon and organizing rallies at the United Nations headquarters in lower Manhattan. The purpose of her visit was to keep pressure on the UN Security Council to adopt a resolution that reflected the aspirations of the overwhelming numbers of Yemenis who had sustained peaceful calls for change for the nine long months since protests had begun in late January. Arriving newly anointed by the Nobel Committee, which named her as one of three recipients of the 2011 Peace Prize, Karman feared—as did much of the Yemeni opposition, in its many forms—that the UN would merely reiterate the approximate parameters of the Gulf Cooperation Council (GCC) initiative put forth in April. That plan, which enjoyed support from the United States, as well as Yemen's GCC neighbors, gave legal immunity to President 'Ali 'Abdallah Salih, whose crimes against Yemeni protesters had multiplied in the months since the spring. Her fears were well founded: The UN resolution announced on October 21 demanded that Salih sign the GCC resolution immediately. Karman thus ended her week in New York as she had ended so many weeks in Sanaa in previous months—at the head of a protest.

That the Yemeni revolution was being led symbolically by a woman was an attractive concept to many international observers. Karman's biography, however, and her record of activism were more complex than the Nobel Committee's citation suggested. She was unquestionably worthy of the international recognition attending the Peace Prize, but not necessarily for the reasons given. The Committee recognized Karman, along with two Liberian activist women, Ellen Sirleaf Johnson and Leymah Gbowee, "for their non-violent struggle for the safety of women and for women's rights to full participation in peace-building work." Yet Karman was at the UN demanding trenchant political reform, of the kind that would enhance the political freedoms of Yemeni men, women, and children, and produce a new regime more accountable to the public. She was decidedly not calling for "women's rights." In its citation, the Committee reduced the scope of the work of a multi-dimensional activist whose efforts had been resisted inside and outside the party from which she emerged. Without understanding Tawakkul Karman as both a cause and an effect of change in state-society relations in Yemen, it is difficult to see precisely what she represents or why so many Yemenis from different backgrounds were so responsive to her call for sustained non-violence.

Partisan Origins

Yemen's revolution developed into a post-partisan affair, but its origins undoubtedly lay in the decade of partisan opposition and alliance building that preceded it. Whereas the revolutionaries of 2011 were calling, first and foremost, for the end of the Salih regime, the partisan opposition was primarily focused on procedural reforms that would expand their opportunity to hold the country's leadership accountable. There was good reason for drawing this distinction between reformist and revolutionary activism, because the failures of the reformist project fed the frustrations that sustained the revolutionary movement, even as partisan actors stepped in to help organize (and, according to some, attempt to coopt) the momentum of the youth.

The partisan opposition is composed of several small leftist and nationalist parties, as well as the Yemeni Socialist Party, which has performed poorly in elections, but nonetheless carries weight as the ruling party of South Yemen prior to its 1990 unification with the north. But by far the largest opposition party is the Islamist Yemeni Congregation for Reform, or Islah.

Beginning through a series of informal linkages between mid-level and senior leaders of the Socialists and Islah as early as 2002, a robust (if procedure-minded) political opposition named the Joint Meeting Parties (JMP) alliance became an important feature of Yemen's political landscape in the succeeding decade. After running a candidate against Salih in the 2006 presidential election, however, the grand coalition was unable to achieve most of its political aims. Its letdowns stemmed largely from divisions among (and within) the constituent parties, and what critics viewed as a preoccupation with the court politics of Sanaa, at the expense of constituencies in the periphery, particularly in the south. Feeling neglected by their nominal representatives in the capital, southern activists mounted massive popular demonstrations beginning in 2007, demanding greater autonomy and redress of perceived inequality with the north.[1] The grassroots Southern Movement, also known as al-Harak, caught the JMP leadership in the capital by surprise and contributed to its internal divisions, with party chiefs uncertain about whether and how to support the independently developed movement.

The eventual postponement of the 2009 parliamentary elections—a delay agreed upon by Salih's government and the JMP—was probably the most poignant sign that the opposition was unlikely to reach its goals through status quo institutions. The JMP had lobbied for a series of electoral reforms that would level the playing field, allowing the opposition parties a fighting chance against the ruling General People's Congress. The government, unwilling to level that field, was concerned that a boycott by the JMP would tear apart even the few shreds of democratic credibility that it hoped to retain. So government and opposition agreed to a postponement—the JMP to avoid going forward without reforms, and the government to avoid going forward without opposition. For many Yemenis, the deal marked the end of hopes that political change could occur through elections, at least if the Salih regime was a participant.

The Rise of (Centrist) Islahis

Laid against this backdrop of partisan opposition disappointment is the story of Tawakkul Karman's success. Like Islamist parties elsewhere in the region, Islah contains distinct "trends," but its political organization has increasingly come under the control of a centrist group of Muslim Brothers, a process facilitated by the activism of women within the party, including Tawakkul Karman. With a parallel set of institutions for women at all levels of the organization, the Islah party produced a powerful cadre of activist women over its first two decades, and these women have left a clear mark on the "gender agenda" of the opposition.[2]

Islah's position on women's rights—to the extent that it is possible to speak of a single position, given the deep cleavages within the party, among tribal, Muslim Brother, and Salafi factions—is equivocal. On the one hand, the party has been more successful than any other Yemeni party in mobilizing women as voters. And its parallel institutions have afforded them (gender-segmented) opportunities for leadership far greater than those enjoyed by women in the secular and leftist parties. From the perspective of many women (and men) from the south, where there was a tradition of state feminism under the Marxist regime before unification,[3] Islahi activism has meant a regression in political rights and freedoms for women, evidenced in educational segregation, an Islamized family law and a general Islamization of public space. At the same time, for many women in the north, Islah has been central to advancing a "rights consciousness" whereby women have been encouraged to know and seek "their rights" and to view the state, in theory if not in practice, as the guarantor of those rights.[4] That does not mean, however, that these rights are always conceptualized by Islahis as equal rights, in the sense meant by many women's rights advocates in the secular and leftist parties, or by those in government. Indeed, disagreements over this question within Islah and among the opposition parties helped to widen the gaps among the parties making up the JMP.

The push for greater women's representation within the party and the right of women to stand for national election has been particularly divisive. As an advocate of women's political leadership, Tawakkul Karman has faced considerable resistance within her party and from conservatives outside of it as well. As Houriyya Mashour of the Yemeni Women's National Committee explained, much of this pushback came from Salafi Islahi women: "The women of al-Iman University opposed her, 'Aisha al-Zindani [daughter of the prominent Salafi Islahi cleric, 'Abd al-Majid al-Zindani] opposed her, but she is the best of them."[5]

And indeed, a majority of active party members agreed. At the 2007 party conference, Karman was among thirteen women voted into leadership positions on the party's Shura Council. Their election represented the rise of centrist Muslim Brothers within the party organizational structure, a group who vocally supported female candidates to the Shura, one of whom (not Karman, but the head of the Women's Directorate, Amat al-Salam Raja') received the tenth-largest vote share of the 130 delegates who were elected. This affirmation of women's leadership within the party pointed to a way in which the work of Islahi women, and the reputations and relationships they built within the party, helped to change Islah. The change in the party, in turn, helped the centrist trend to marginalize some of its most hardline conservatives and cement the JMP alliance. At the same time, the changes were slow, too slow for some, like a number of party members who defected in 2009, citing Islah's refusal to support female candidates for public office at the national level. Taken together, the divisiveness of the issue inside Islah and among the member parties of the JMP has produced a pervasive "silence" on gender issues, which the party leaders prefer to the risk of rupture in the coalition.[6]

Instead, the politics of the JMP have focused not on women's rights, but on citizen rights, with implications for women. The procedural reforms of the JMP platform have been transformed in the post-partisan context of the revolution into a more forceful version of the same—those who are protesting are doing so for their dignity as Yemeni citizens.

Why Women Are Essential to the Revolution

In retrospect, despite the fractiousness of the partisan sphere (and, arguably, Yemeni society) regarding the rights and roles of women, it should not be entirely surprising that a woman activist played such an essential role in mobilizing the post-partisan revolutionary movement. As the opposition parties became mired in internal debates over women's rights (among other issues), many Yemeni women—including Tawakkul Karman—shifted some of their energies to the associational sector, taking up the cause of reform through their work as journalists or through various civil society organizations, and building dense networks of personal and professional alliances. Growth in the number of women leading such organizations helped to shift the substantive focus of "women's rights" work: Whereas, in the 1990s, this work strove for reforms that would improve the lot of women as wives and mothers, the new activities sought to frame women's rights as human rights or to expand the reach of civic and economic freedom in general.

Tawakkul Karman's organization, Women Journalists Without Chains, founded in 2005, reflects this shift in its commitment to freedom of expression and civil rights. Staging weekly protests each Tuesday from 2007 until the beginning of the revolution in 2011, Karman called for inquiries into corruption and other forms of social and legal injustice; the lifting of limitations on press freedoms; and more. When the partisan opposition of the JMP came under fire from the government, Karman and her associates rallied to their aid, often working with other Yemeni and international organizations. And when she and other opposition journalists faced pressure, even arrest and detention, the partisan opposition did the same for her. The migration of women into associational sector activism and the ties they forged—illustrated by Karman's own multi-faceted persona as Islahi, journalist, and activist—have been central to laying the groundwork for the network-reliant post-partisan opposition movement that sustains the ongoing revolution in post-Salih Yemen.

That Tawakkul Karman is the public face of this movement—and has become, perhaps, the most recognized Yemeni after Salih himself—may have a lasting impact on the ultimate inclusivity of conceptions of citizenship and equality in the future. This question remains unresolved, however, just as the success of the revolutionary movement itself is very much in doubt amid the ongoing violence in Yemen and withdrawal of international support for the insurrection since Salih's resignation in February 2012. Throughout the revolution, Karman has embodied the fraught question of women's rights and roles. She has been a lightning rod for criticism: from Salafis within Islah for her public role and unseemly visibility; from those on the secular left who distrust her Islamist leanings; from those who resent what they see as Islah's effort to dominate the revolutionary movement.

For these reasons and more, the language of unity and the focus on areas of procedural agreement seem to be taking pride of place in Karman's approach to the revolution, as well they must in these movements of great uncertainty and risk. Her work has been essential to the revolutionary movement and she is a resonant exemplar of the vision of Yemeni women. But recognizing her for work on behalf of Yemeni women was a controversial gesture, one which bypassed the other ways in which Yemeni women have pursued progress for their sisters over the two decades since unification (and still others under the distinct regimes of North and South Yemen before then). Two of these women died in 2011: Fawziyya Nu'man, who worked within the system to pursue essential reforms in girls' and women's education, and Ra'ufa Hasan, who worked at great personal cost to retain her independence in the associational sector, as both the regime and Islah launched campaigns against her. Both of these women, and the many others who have followed their respective trajectories, might take issue with the idea that Tawakkul Karman was being honored for her work on behalf of women's rights, but they would probably also join Mashour and the many others who carried Karman's image at the celebration in Sanaa's Taghyir (Change) Square following the Peace Prize announcement. These men and women, in the tens of thousands, admire Karman for the work she has done in transforming Islah, as a party, and advancing the rights of all Yemenis, regardless of gender or political creed.

Notes

1. See Susanne Dahlgren, in this volume.

2. Stacey Philbrick Yadav, "Segmented Publics and Islamist Women in Yemen: Rethinking Space and Activism," *Journal of Middle Eastern Women's Studies* 6/2 (Spring 2010).

3. Susanne Dahlgren, *Contesting Realities: The Public Sphere and Morality in Southern Yemen* (Syracuse, N.Y.: Syracuse University Press, 2010).

4. Interview with Amat al-Salam Raja', Islah Women's Directorate, Sanaa, October 6, 2004.

5. Interview with Houriyya Mashour, Women's National Committee, Sanaa, January 2009.

6. Stacey Philbrick Yadav and Janine A. Clark, "Disappointments and New Directions: Women, Partisanship and the Regime in Yemen," *Hawwa: International Journal of Women in the Middle East and Islamic World* 8 (2010).

PART FOUR

SYRIA

"The people want the fall of the regime" appeared in spray paint on the walls of the southern agricultural town of Daraa, Syria, over the night of March 13, 2011. A band of young teenagers was emboldened to paint the slogan by the events in Tunis and Cairo, news of which had dominated media outlets and no doubt excited some hope of change, even in the dusty provinces of this repressive police state. The regime responded swiftly and mercilessly to the graffiti. Members of the political security branch of the *mukhabarat* (intelligence services) swept up approximately a dozen Daraa residents between the ages of ten and fifteen and tortured them in the local detention center. In the days that followed, distraught parents and relatives went to the police to demand the boys' release and eventually protested in the streets. On March 18, security personnel opened fire on the demonstrators, killing four. The brutality was enough to swell the protestors' ranks in Daraa and to spread the demonstrations to nearby towns and villages. The security forces continued their repression in the area, combining mass arrests with lethal force.

What happened to the teenagers in Daraa was in keeping with the Syrian state's longstanding treatment of dissent. Even in a region known for police states, Syria stood. For decades, the government blocked political parties (other than the ruling Baath) and an independent press; violently suppressed Kurdish cultural activities; held membership in the Muslim Brothers to be punishable by death; subjected activists and their families to travel bans; and censored websites. The permanent state of emergency institutionalized the power to arrest without a warrant (arrests usually happened in the middle of the night) and several opposition intellectuals, lawyers and journalists spent more time in than out of prison. The thousands in detention were likely to suffer ill treatment, torture, or even death while in custody.

Syria's *mukhabarat* is a vast network of agencies spread across the civilian and military branches of the state. The agencies are headed by men with close links to the regime of President Bashar al-Asad, whether of blood, marriage, or ethnicity (the Asad family are 'Alawis, a heterodox Shi'i minority concentrated in northwestern Syria). In addition to the tens of thousands of official employees, the *mukhabarat* rely on an equal—perhaps larger—number of informants, both voluntary and involuntary. The level of surveillance over everyday life confines most political talk to small groups of trusted friends or family. One of the distinct aspects of Syria's political policing is its reach into all levels and sectors of society;

members of the military, the government, and elite business families have also been arrested for political reasons.

Though the *mukhabarat* has its origin in the intelligence services of the French colonial government (1920-1945), the current institutions were built under the rule of Bashar's father, Hafiz al-Asad. The military wing of the Arab Baath Socialist Party seized control of the Syrian government in 1963. Hafiz served as minister of defense under this regime, presiding over the purging of internal opposition within the party and the military. In 1970, Hafiz took over the presidency in a bloodless coup and further engineered the upper echelons of the government and military around his personal rule, drawing primarily (though not exclusively) upon family and friends from his home region in the Latakia governorate. He also began the transformation of the army into a tool of the security services, a process enhanced under Bashar, who acceded to the presidency in 2000, with the appointment of close family allies to key positions within the military. Today, the Syrian regime is a Gordian knot of the military, security services, the party, and the administration.

The regime is also bolstered by a spoils system that rewards loyalty with access to government jobs, state assets, and business opportunities. During the privatization campaign of the 1990s and 2000s, regime allies were able to corner markets and build profitable enterprises from formerly nationalized industries. A handful of powerful individuals and families control the Syrian economy. Rami Makhlouf, a cousin of Bashar, is one of the richest people in the country and the head of a sprawling commercial empire with tentacles in nearly every sector of the economy. While the well-positioned few expanded their wealth, 30 percent of Syrians (5.1 million people) are estimated to live at the poverty line, with 2 million unable to meet basic daily food needs. Severe droughts beginning in 2003 have increased the pressure on food supplies and caused over a million people to migrate to cities.

Despite rising poverty and continuing political repression, the regime does have a popular base. The Asad regimes convinced many Syrians (and foreign governments) that the state's secularism—even if corrupt and oppressive—was necessary to protect religious and ethnic minorities from the Sunni majority, which forms roughly 70 percent of the population. Outlawed and in exile since an armed rebellion in 1982 was crushed by the regime, the Syrian Muslim Brothers are not a significant political force within the country. But since the majority of Syrians are devout Sunnis, the regime has used the specter of a "Salafist" government to consolidate the support of most 'Alawis (about 10 percent of the population), various Christian sects (another 10 percent) and Druze (about 4 percent). The Kurdish minority, the largest ethnic minority at two million people, does not support the Asad regime, but also clashes with opposition parties that echo the regime's Arab nationalism. Faced with ongoing violence and instability, even those who dislike the Asad regime—including many middle-class Sunnis—have preferred the regime's promise of restored stability to the fragmented and uncoordinated opposition. The pro-regime demonstrations, particularly in the centers of Damascus and Aleppo, of tens—or even hundreds—of thousands of people likely represent a mix of stalwarts and conscripted participants. But probably 30 percent or more of the population is either opposed to or wary of the opposition forces.

Weak civil society institutions have hampered the formation of a united opposition to the Asad regime. The Baath Party came to dominate all associational bodies after its takeover in 1963, installing party loyalists in leadership positions of labor and peasant unions, professional organizations and women's groups. Though restrictions were loosened for charitable and development groups under Bashar, they were still subject to state intervention in their operations and governance. Much of the day-to-day coordination of the resistance is carried out by a relatively decentralized group of youth known informally as "local coordination committees" that organize demonstrations and funeral processions and manage responses to regime violence (such as medical care) as well as publicize the daily death tolls. A couple of different umbrella groups claim to represent these more local branches of the resistance, though it is hard to know to what extent because information about them is limited. The most public face of the opposition is the Syrian National Council (SNC), a group of exiled dissidents formed in Istanbul on September 17, 2011. Its members are mainly intellectuals and politicians, including Muslim Brothers, and it enjoys growing support from—or at least credibility with—Western governments, as well as Arab Gulf states.

The armed resistance is staffed mainly by average Syrians, joined by thousands of defecting—mostly low-ranking—army troops. Some identify themselves as the Free Syrian Army, but this is a decentralized series of forces operating more or less on their own around the country. There are also armed groups not affiliated with the Free Syrian Army, some of whom are funded by exiles linked to conservative Islamist agendas.

Though the violence and hardships of life (food shortages, deteriorating social services and infrastructure) in Syria have weakened support for the uprising, the iron-fist, zero-tolerance policy toward dissent has not cowed the civilian population. Use of torture by the security services—not to gather information, but to teach the victim a lesson—the shelling of whole cities and the unleashing of *shabbiha* (thugs) on the civilian population has fueled hatred of the government rather than fear. The savagery of the Asad regime's response to calls for change has irreversibly shifted the balance of power in the country. It remains to be seen what shape a resolution to this bloody stalemate will take, but the Asad regime is unlikely to emerge from the conflict intact.

18. ASAD'S LOST CHANCES

CARSTEN WIELAND

On January 31, 2011 the *Wall Street Journal* printed words that Bashar al-Asad must have winced to recall. In an interview with the newspaper, the Syrian president said that Arab rulers would need to move faster to accommodate the rising political and economic aspirations of Arab peoples. "If you didn't see the need for reform before what happened in Egypt and Tunisia, it's too late to do any reform," he chided his fellow leaders. But Asad went on to assure the interviewer (and perhaps himself): "Syria is stable. Why? Because you have to be very closely linked to the beliefs of the people. This is the core issue. When there is divergence…you will have this vacuum that creates disturbances."

Not even two months later, confrontations between protesters and security forces across Syria shook the Baathist regime harder than any challenge since the 1980s. No matter what the course of the upheavals, the Syria that many knew for decades will never be the same. The protests tore asunder the delicate fabric of rules, explicit and implicit, that for decades determined the relations between the regime and the citizenry. By Syrian standards, the political concessions promised by regime representatives to quiet the early months of unrest were far-reaching; long years of civil society activism were unable to achieve them. By the yardstick of the times, however, the moves were inadequate. Following a presidential speech to Parliament on March 30, it looked like sweeping reform was an empty promise. And a rising number of Syrians did not swallow their disappointment. The pervasive fear for which this police state is infamous gave way to unpredictable bursts of popular anger, as well as hope for a better future.

President Asad, for his part, likely feels twinges of nostalgia for the days when Syria's main source of dissent was a group of intellectuals of the Civil Society Movement, most of them elderly, who for ten years had called for political pluralism and civil rights. He may miss the occasions on which he was presented with elaborate declarations, lists of signatures and critical articles appearing in the Lebanese press but meant for Syrian consumption. Many of the authors shared the Baathists' pan-Arab orientation and hardline stance toward Israel; they could have been secular partners to build bridges to Islamist and other more radical forces.

Just after the US invasion of Iraq, in May 2003, many observers pricked up their ears in surprise when a central regime figure commended the Syrian opposition for its prudence. Bahjat Sulayman, the powerful former head of Syrian intelligence, wrote in the Lebanese newspaper *al-Safir*, "In Syria, the regime does not have enemies but 'opponents' whose demands do not go beyond certain political and economic reforms such as the end of the state of emergency and martial law; the adoption of a law on political parties; and the equitable redistribution of national wealth."[1] Forcible regime change, Sulayman knew, was only on the agenda of select exiles and US politicians.

But President Asad treated the Civil Society Movement intellectuals, with their debating clubs and talk of a soft landing for Syria's transition away from authoritarianism, like a gang of criminals. By March 2011, the days were long gone when obstreperousness was defined as discussion in the back rooms of teahouses suffused with the aromatic smoke of water pipes. Now the Syrian president faces tumult in the streets and the whiff of gunpowder.

Patterns of Unrest

Information about the demonstrations and clashes has been scarce since the beginning of the uprising. Much of the country outside of Damascus has been a no-go zone for journalists, with most forms of communication cut. Reporting from anywhere in Syria has been scanty throughout the crisis.

Yet the outlines of a minimum outcome quickly emerged: Power relations will be renegotiated. Inside the regime, key posts were reshuffled amidst rumors of open discord between Bashar al-Asad and the security services, between Asad and the army, between Bashar and other members of the Asad clan and, possibly, between 'Alawis, Sunnis and members of other sects in the upper echelons. The regime will have less leeway in its social, economic and political decisions going forward; that have been (until his assassination in July 2012). But the current round is far from over, in any case, and its maximum outcome is regime change. For years, Asad quelled demands for fundamental change with piecemeal, sometimes cosmetic reforms. Some strata of the public considered him part of the solution; the danger is that he will lose these people and become part of the problem.

In its foreign policy, ideological makeup and social composition, Syria differs greatly from Tunisia or Egypt, so the momentous events of 2011 in those countries cannot simply be replicated. Yet the pattern of Syria's early crisis was quite similar to those in other Arab countries. The protests were sparked by a minor incident: Teens in Daraa were detained for spray-painting buildings in town with graffiti inspired by the Tunisian and Egyptian uprisings, including the famous slogan, "The people want to overthrow the regime." A "day of rage" was declared. The police, unused to civil unrest, overreacted and shot several protesters dead. Anger rose countrywide and triggered more widespread demonstrations, which were met with more brutal force, in turn fueling more protest.

Bashar al-Asad mostly kept a low profile, feeding the early gossip that he and his family were feuding over how to respond. The president behaved like the leader of a "*jumlukiyya*," as the Syrian opposition calls the country's political system, melding the Arabic words for republic and monarchy. Rather than assuming responsibility for the crisis, the "republico-monarch" shunted the blame downward, offering to replace the cabinet and sack the lieutenants responsible for the hot spots around the country. In terms of public relations, the regime tried to make do with sending advisers, deputies or ministers before the cameras to explain its point of view, trotting out the president only in extremis. Much of the regime's verbal response aimed to criminalize the protests or portray them in sectarian terms; in tandem, the regime resorted to lethal force to suppress the agitation. As the protests spread, the regime turned to attempts at political accommodation, then measures of appeasement before finally abandoning false-note diplomacy in favor of war against the opposition and civilians.

In Tunisia and Egypt, presidential concessions had no conciliatory effect upon the crowds because they always came a few days or weeks too late. In Syria, as well, the concessions appeared poorly chosen for the circumstances. On April 7, 2011, Asad granted citizenship to some 150,000 of Syria's Kurds who had been stateless, answering a long-time demand of Kurdish advocacy organizations. The measure was so overdue that Asad got little credit. "Citizenship is the right of every Syrian. It is not a favor. It is not the right of anyone to grant," retorted Habib Ibrahim, leader of a major Kurdish party. Other concessions, like permitting schoolteachers to wear the *niqab*, or full face veil, and closing a casino, were meant to placate Islamists but meant little to the wider base of opposition demonstrators calling for real political reform.

In the initial weeks, the demonstrators' wrath did not, by and large, target Bashar al-Asad himself. But the hits drew closer and closer to home over subsequent months. Great fury is directed toward Bashar's brother Mahir, who has a reputation for personal cruelty and, as head of the Fourth Division of the Republican Guard, is a bulwark of authoritarian rule in the country. Other names heard in the protesters' chants are 'Asif Shawkat, husband of Bashar's sister Bushra and deputy chief of staff of the army, and, above all, Rami Makhlouf, who owns Syria's cell phone companies, duty-free shops and almost everything else that promises quick profits. Like his counterparts in Tunisia and Egypt, Makhlouf is beneficiary of a classic predatory arrangement, whereby his unquestioning political loyalty buys him commercial monopolies bestowed by the state. The stories of Makhlouf's corruption incense ordinary Syrians, from the working poor to the endangered middle class. No wonder the first wave of protesters in Daraa burned down the local cell phone company outlet, as well as the court building and the Baath Party offices.

Sitting It Out

As late as January 2011, Asad thought he could sit out the season of Arab revolts. As supportive Syrian columnists tirelessly point out, Asad is a relatively young man at forty-six, unlike the aging Arab leaders in trouble elsewhere. He has made no pact with the US or Israel, keeping him close to public opinion on regional issues. His backers adduce additional pillars of legitimacy: Asad maintained law and order in times of great turbulence in the bordering nations of Iraq and Lebanon; his secular Baathist regime safeguarded an atmosphere of relative religious and ethnic tolerance, which many in the region admire; and the president successfully cultivated a humble public persona, in contrast not only to dictators like Saddam Hussein or Muammar al-Qaddafi, but also to their uncouth sons. In the eyes of many Syrians, the junior Asad has not lost his image as a reformer frustrated at every turn by an irascible old guard.

The country indeed made progress during the first ten years of Asad's rule in areas that were not directly related to democracy or human rights. Syrian media outlets were more numerous and plainspoken than under Bashar's father Hafiz, from whom he inherited power in 2000, although red lines persisted in the areas of politics, religion, and sex. Arts and letters benefited from more freedom of expression. Though several Internet sites were permanently blocked, Syrians had (prior to the uprising) far more access to information and the outside world, through satellite TV, blogs, and foreign media. Cell phones and other modern equipment became accessible to a wider range of people. Women's organizations gained strength and were granted room to maneuver even if they were not legally registered or explicitly supportive of the government.

There is, in fact, considerable sympathy for Bashar al-Asad among the population, though some of it stems from fear of the unknown. The manifestations of pro-regime sentiment that popped up alongside the spring 2011 protests, particularly in Damascus and Ladhiqiyya, may have been orchestrated by the state, but they were also emotionally real for the participants. Many members of religious minorities, such as Christians and the Druze, not to mention 'Alawis, watch the present upheavals with distinct unease, as they contemplate possible backlash from the Sunni majority. The 'Alawis, from whose tribes the Asads and their inner circle hail, worry they will suffer communal retribution for the ruling clique's ways. But much of the Sunni merchant class, as well, has so far stuck to an alliance with the Asad regime. As minorities and middle-class Sunnis make up more than 50 percent of the population, they are not a negligible constituency.

No Damascus Spring

Here lay an opportunity for Asad shortly after he took power in June 2000: Had he mustered the courage to curtail vested interests and dismantle obsolete Baathist structures in the early years, he might have called for free elections and won them. As a leader with a genuine social base, he could have confronted the militarist policies of President George W. Bush without falling back upon dusty pan-Arab themes or Islamist-sounding rhetoric. His position would be correspondingly stronger today. But Asad chose not to put his rule to a popular test.

The Civil Society Movement of Syria claims the mantle of intellectual pioneer of the 2011 Arab revolutions, with the addendum that Tunisians turned out to be the champions in practice. The short-lived heyday of this opposition movement that started in September 2000 was known, indeed, as the "Damascus spring." That fall, the writer Michel Kilo headlined a group of intellectuals who published the "manifesto of the ninety-nine," followed that December by the "manifesto of the thousand." The distinguished secular philosopher Sadiq al-'Azm was a key signatory. The intellectuals' aim, to paraphrase the pointed words of Alan George, was both bread and freedom.[2] Riyad Sayf, an entrepreneur and outspoken member of Parliament, went the furthest, putting forward social-democratic ideals of a "fair market economy" that he upheld with decent labor practices in the companies he owned. Politically, he called for a constitutional state, an independent legislature and courts, and a free press. But Sayf crossed a red line when he announced his intention to found a party of his own. He was arrested, and the "Damascus spring" turned cold as the debating clubs in Damascus teahouses closed down.

The regime might introduce political pluralism (or a semblance thereof) under the pressure of the street. A new party law meant to break the stranglehold of the Baath Party has been gathering dust in a presidential desk drawer for years. But it is one thing for the regime to introduce such reforms under circumstances of its own choosing and quite another to do so under duress, with the latter step likely to embolden the opposition to press for more. The same dynamic holds for the regime's various other promises, like tackling legal discrimination against citizens of Kurdish ethnicity, erecting a legal framework for the activities of NGOs or promulgating a new media law. It even holds for declaring an end to martial law, a step that, rhetorically, has always been tied to liberation of the Golan Heights from Israeli occupation and the end of hostilities with Israel. Now it is purely domestic stresses that are bringing such measures to the forefront of regime calculations. The regime is losing one trump card after another.

Waves of Suppression

The massive street protests reached Syria precisely when the regime was in a phase of increased suppression of opposition forces, whether the older Civil Society Movement or the bloggers and Internet activists of more recent vintage. Several well-known human rights defenders are languishing behind bars. The unrest also arrived at a time when Syria had managed to extricate its head from the noose of international isolation.

The successes in establishing better international relations were rooted in a series of decisions since 2008 that, on the one hand, reflected a break with the past, even paradigm shifts, and, on the other hand, displayed the growing maturity of President Asad in foreign policy matters. A new Syrian pragmatism emerged after a phase of ideological encrustation during the early phases of the Iraq war that can be explained by both *raison d'état* and desperation amidst the bellicose talk emanating from Washington.

In the past, it was plausible to advance the thesis that Syria's isolation and the regime's feeling of existential threat from outside was making the regime reluctant to open up the political system and apt to crack down heavily on opposition movements. Many had hoped that Syria would adopt domestic reforms when the foreign threat abated. Instead, the reverse arguably occurred. One experienced Syrian analyst who has worked inside the government conceded in an interview: "I made the same mistake. I thought there was a correlation between foreign and domestic policy.... With or without external pressure, we have no political change in Syria. Domestic pressure is a continuity not a contradiction."

Three waves of suppression have swept through Syria during Bashar al-Asad's eleven years in power. The first began in 2001 with the completion of the clampdown on the debating clubs of the Civil Society Movement. Asad adopted the Chinese model: The regime would pursue economic reform, but political and administrative reforms would be discarded. No democratic experiment was in the offing as US threats of regime change began to emerge in 2002, and the Baathist regime subsequently entrenched itself in harsh ideological opposition to the Iraq war. Pressure mounted on Syria, especially from Saudi Arabia, France, and the United States in subsequent years, culminating in the autumn 2003 passage of UN Security Council Resolution 1559, calling upon "all remaining foreign forces to withdraw from Lebanon," and then the assassination of Rafik Hariri in February 2005, which eventually compelled Damascus to summon its troops in Lebanon home.

In the face of the regime's obvious weakness, and with the encouragement of Western diplomats, the opposition picked up momentum. It took a historic step toward unity with the Damascus Declaration of October 16, 2005. For the first time, all major opposition groups—ranging from the secular civil society movement to Kurdish activists to the outlawed Society of Muslim Brothers in their London exile—issued a manifesto for democratic change in Syria. The lengthy document called for an end to emergency law and other forms of political repression, a national summit on democracy and a constitutional convention to draft a charter "that foils adventurers and extremists." The head of the Civil Society Movement, Michel Kilo, composed the Declaration. Under this document, Asad could have been part of the solution. No Asad statues were toppled in Syrian cities. But, again, he chose to crack down.

The second wave of persecution followed in the first half of 2006, when those who had been spared in 2001, including Kilo and human rights lawyer Anwar al-Bunni, were arrested. Officials justified the hunt for signatories of the Damascus Declaration with the charge that they were pursuing Western interests.

The first two arrest campaigns adhered to the logic of interrelation between domestic and foreign fronts. The third, however, began at the end of 2009 when Syria had already celebrated its reemergence onto the international stage. In October of that year, the regime arrested Haytham Malih, head of the Human Rights Association of Syria, and then imposed travel bans upon dissident intellectuals and otherwise sought to intimidate them. The eighty-year-old Malih was released only during the hectic weeks of late March 2011, after he had gone on hunger strike.

In all three waves of suppression, the secular Baathist regime silenced the moderate, secular voices calling for pluralism and piecemeal reform. This history is related to why Islamist currents appear to be gaining ground in Syria. To be sure, the Islamization of opposition politics is a general trend in the Arab Middle East and no country has been immune. Yet there are other, more specific explanations for its appearance in Syria. First, the regime, despite its secular orientation, and often more out of necessity than enthusiasm, is allied with Islamist partners like Iran, Hizballah, and Hamas in an "axis of resistance" to US and Israeli prerogatives. A second explanation is that, not unlike other Arab regimes, Damascus adopted a conscious strategy of limited toleration for Islamism. A leading Syrian opposition figure characterized the Baathist-Islamist relationship as follows: "We get state power; you get society." Not only did this arrangement obviate a domestic threat, it could be presented to the West as evidence that Syria would turn Islamist if the Baathists were to lose the state. During its confrontation with the United States in the mid-2000s, Syria facilitated passage of Islamist militants into Iraq in order to weaken the US occupation and also engage in preemptive self-defense.

In the January 2011 interview with the Wall Street Journal, Asad was still advancing a version of this argument. Acknowledging the need for some change in the state, he continued: "But at the same time you have to upgrade the society and this does not mean to upgrade it technically by upgrading qualifications. It means to open up the minds. Actually, societies during the last three decades, especially since the 1980s, have become more closed due to an increase in close-mindedness that led to extremism."[3] In other words, Arab societies are not ready for Western-style democracy. The choice is between stability and chaos, between superficial, state-led secularism and a fundamentalist stone age. In his inaugural speech of June 2000, the young president had already made his position clear. "We cannot apply the democracy of others to ourselves," he said. "Western democracy, for example, is the outcome of a long history that resulted in customs and traditions, which distinguish the current culture of Western societies.... We have to have our democratic experience which is special to us, which stems from our history, culture, and civilization, and which is a response to the needs of our society and the requirements of our reality."

Some Westerners have bought into the discourse prescribing a cultural path to democracy, at least when it is politically opportune to do so. Michel Kilo expressed his frustration with French President Nicolas Sarkozy, who, during a September 2008 visit to Damascus, reiterated Asad's notion that Syria would create a democracy of a distinct style. Kilo said that afterward he reminded the French ambassador in Damascus that it was the French who disseminated the idea of universal human rights. Sadiq al-'Azm, similarly, warned against the tendency to posit a "Western human rights" that differs from "Islamic human rights" or the "Asian human rights" that Malaysia and China have tried to propagate.[4]

No Arab leader ever explained why it was taking so long for his allegedly immature people to learn the ropes of democracy. It grew harder and harder to explain, as the reigns of some autocrats reached the thirty year mark, as in the Yemeni case. Even the first eleven years of Bashar al-Asad's rule in Syria were apparently not enough time to pursue incremental change and build institutions without compromising on security, foreign policy restraints and other Syrian particularities. Now the window of opportunity may have closed.

Sparks Igniting

The movements in Tunisia, Egypt, Syria, and other Arab states proved four postulates. First, the aspirations of peoples are indeed universal. As peoples in other parts of the world have done, Arabs have revolted against poverty, social injustice, corruption, censorship, police intimidation, disrespect for the rule of law and lack of individual opportunity. The calls for accountability, freedom, and political pluralism in the Arab world have no cultural or religious coloring and are very much compatible with demands elsewhere. Second, the protesters are articulating these grievances without any foreign impetus, save the urge to emulate the achievements of fellow Arabs. The revolts are homegrown.

Third, the civility, creativity, peacefulness, communitarian spirit, and social, religious, and ethnic solidarity during the protests have shown in a remarkable way that, whatever their rulers say, Arabs are indeed mature enough for democracy. The militarization of some movements, as in Libya and Syria, has to be considered separately from the origin of the protests. Fourth, the carriers of revolution come from many strata of society, including the educated, but politically muzzled middle class that is exposed to economic shocks and fears of socio-economic decline. Most of the protesters in the Tahrir Squares of the Arab world were not inspired, and apparently not very impressed, by the slogan "Islam is the solution." The Arab peoples, as Rashid Khalidi pointed out, have reasserted their dignity by refuting the patronizing attitudes of kings and presidents-for-life.[5] The revolutions of 2011, Khalidi continued, were not the first democratic ones in the Arab world but the first directed against Arab, rather than colonial, rulers.

A new Arab nationalism of a civil nature began to crystallize around the demonstrations. Egyptians placed photos on Facebook showing themselves holding up ink-colored fingers as proof of their participation in the March 2011 referendum on constitutional amendments, the first post-Mubarak poll. Others uploaded a new status message: "Proud to be an Egyptian." Still other Facebook pages displayed the crescent and the cross—the twin religious symbols of the protests in Cairo and, then, Damascus.

The calls for dignity, participation, accountability, and freedom put Syria's neighbors to the test as well. The Turkish government of Prime Minister Recep Tayyip Erdoğan had been close to Syria over matters of security, foreign policy, the economy, and tourism. Both sides spoke of "family ties." Joint meetings of the countries' cabinets had become routine. At the same time, Turkey is seen as a model by many Arab opposition forces that seek to build democracy in majority-Muslim societies. Erdoğan emerged as a sharp critic of Israeli human rights violations but also of Arab despots, whom he urged to pursue reforms, most vocally in the case of Husni Mubarak of Egypt. It took several months and much bloodshed, but in August 2011, Erdoğan publicly broke with the Asad regime and moved to freeze Syrian assets in Turkey. Though a November 2011 threat to take military action against the regime did not materialize, tensions have remained high and Turkey has provided refuge for fleeing civilians as well as armed opposition groups.

On another front, Israel may ironically turn out the actor that most sincerely hopes for a continuation of the Asad regime. Syria has been an enemy of Israel, but a stable and reliable one. The Asad regime has retained sufficient influence over Hizballah to persuade the Lebanese Shi'i Islamist party, if need be, to exercise restraint on Israel's northern border. With the developing unrest inside Syria, however, all bets are off. The lowest-order question is whether a weakened Baathist regime in Damascus will still be able to negotiate a peace with Israel (that is, if either side really wants it). From there, the questions for Israel only grow more difficult. If the regime is replaced by parties unknown, nostalgia for the Baathist era could soon set in among the upper echelons in Tel Aviv and Jerusalem. The status quo, for all its irritations, has often been convenient: Whatever their outcome, the Arab revolts have already eroded Israel's ability to stake claims on Western sympathies by calling itself the only democracy in the Middle East.

The interest in stability on Israel's northern flank goes a long way toward explaining the US stance as the upheavals in Syria broke out. Speaking on the CBS program "Face the Nation" on March 26, Secretary of State Hillary Clinton pointedly declined to condemn the repression in the harsh terms used in the Libyan case, much less entertain talk of intervention. An international consensus behind such measures "is not going to happen," Clinton said. She continued, "There's a different leader in Syria now. Many of the members of Congress from both parties who have gone to Syria in recent months have said they believe he's a reformer." After three additional months of regime violence against protesters and civilians, however, this endorsement became untenable. In July 2011, Clinton claimed that "President Asad is not indispensable, and we have absolutely nothing invested in him remaining in power."[6] The following month, the US government called for Asad to step down, froze Syrian assets, and imposed trade sanctions against the regime.

Against the background of demonstrations across the country, it was not shocking that the Syrian security services approached representatives of the Civil Society Movement in the spring of 2011. The intelligence officers whose invitations to chat were once the equivalent of warning shots, if not warrants of arrest, were asking their old "opponents" to revive their movement. But it was too late in the game.

Over the years, the Civil Society Movement lost faith in Asad's will to reform. In November 2010, when the events of 2011 seemed a remote possibility at best, Michel Kilo reflected upon the movement's failures. He complained that the movement was stopped in its tracks before it was able to broaden its circle of supporters, much less engineer the foundation of parties. But, in accordance with revolutionary patterns in Europe, he said, Syria's educated middle class had been awakened. "Once the spark ignites the younger generation, we can withdraw," Kilo concluded. "At least we have paved the way."[7]

Notes

1. *Al-Safir*, March 15, 2003.

2. Alan George, *Syria: Neither Bread nor Freedom* (London: Zed Books, 2003).

3. *Wall Street Journal*, January 31, 2011.

4. Interviews with Sadiq al-'Azm, Damascus and Berlin, November 2010.

5. Rashid Khalidi, "Preliminary Observations on the Arab Revolutions of 2011," *Jadaliyya*, March 11, 2011.

6. *Bloomberg News*, July 11, 2011.

7. Interview with Michel Kilo, Damascus, November 2010.

19. BEHIND THE RESILIENCE
OF THE SYRIAN REGIME

BASSAM HADDAD

Seasoned observers were long accustomed to making light of apparent political changes in Syria. Following the death of Hafiz al-Asad, who ruled Syria for thirty years, and the accession of his son Bashar to the presidency, a series of "springs" came and went without substantially opening up the system. The country's political institutions were stable, but stagnant, including the Baath Party, which continued to rule by periodically reshuffling elites. Syria's economic growth continued to lag, its small oil reserves to dwindle and its work force to fall behind in acquiring the skills needed in the global economy. Perhaps the most troubling part of Syria's predicament was an invisible but rising wave of poverty.

For Syria's elite, this precarious state of affairs was not unusual. For years, its primary strategy for getting by was to accentuate Syria's importance on the international stage. Between 1970 and 1990, the Syrian regime benefited from the superpower competition of the Cold War. With the dissolution of the Soviet Union, Damascus relied more heavily on its regional role, beginning with its participation in the US-led coalition to expel the Iraqi army from Kuwait in 1991. Washington also quietly appreciated the Syrian army's presence in Lebanon. At the same time, Damascus posed before Syrian and Arab public opinion as the keeper of the Arab nationalist flame, rejecting Egyptian, Jordanian, and Palestinian deals with Israel, backing Hizballah in Lebanon, and loosing a stream of anti-Zionist and anti-imperialist rhetoric. At the time of Hafiz al-Asad's death, the challenge before the regime was to bring Syria fully into the regional and international fold without alienating its domestic base of support.

Over the course of the 2000s, the world around Syria's cocoon was twice transformed. In 2005, Damascus was isolated and its regional influence diminished by the combined effects of regime change in Iraq, the humiliating loss of Syrian control in Lebanon and the new stridency of Israel in the atmosphere of the US-led "war on terror." Negotiations with the European Union to bring Syria into a "partnership agreement," as part of the EU's "Barcelona process" of Euro-Mediterranean economic integration, were stalled. To make things worse, the Bush administration, backed by Congress, was pursuing an anti-Syria campaign, going so far as to recall the US ambassador to Damascus. But soon there was a second transformation, effected by the Bush administration's failures in Iraq, the Hizballah-Israel standoff in 2006 and the corresponding rise of Iran, Syria's ally, as a regional power. Even though it remained isolated to some degree by its closeness to Tehran, the Syrian regime recovered several of its foreign policy tools, a fact recognized by the Obama administration when it sent back an ambassador. So matters stood on the eve of the 2011-2012 uprising.

The Syrian regime's international and regional position—ententes with Russia, China, and Iran—offered it a measure of protection as the uprising descended into civil war and reports mounted of atrocities committed by loyalist forces. So did the stubborn truth that the regime is unitary and cohesive, while the society is heterogeneous and, to some degree, divided. Naturally, the regime had worked hard over decades to reproduce and exacerbate the divisions, whether of sect and ethnicity, class, or region. The regime meanwhile had labored to bolster the unity at the top, building an army and security services whose fates are intertwined with that of the regime.

But there was another such stratagem of regime survival at work: Beginning in the 1970s, the regime forged networks of capital that bound elite business actors to state officials as the latter, and their offspring, ventured into the commercial realm. These ties have paid big dividends for the regime in times of crisis.

The Balance Sheet

By June 2005, date of the Tenth Regional Conference of the Baath Party, the transition from the rule of Hafiz to Bashar al-Asad was complete and it was clear that there would be no meaningful liberalization of the Syrian political system from the top. Though the new regime was not impregnable, the intra-party tensions that had characterized Bashar's first five years in power—replete with a few aborted "springs"—were over. The evident winners were Bashar and his team, including the Asad family and their innermost circle. The evident losers were the old guard, or those who opposed Bashar's ascendancy, beginning with formerly powerful Chief of Staff Hikmat Shihabi, who "retired" in 1998 after he made public his distaste for the prospect of Bashar ruling Syria, and ending with former Vice President 'Abd al-Halim Khaddam.

The Tenth Regional Conference was a bit of housekeeping in preparation for an entrenchment par excellence. The conference was not without positive developments, though they were hardly far-reaching reforms. For the first time, there were serious recommendations that the state should review the Emergency Law in place since 1963, with an eye toward "narrowing the scope of state security matters."[1] Article 8 of the constitution, designating the Baath Party as the "leader of state and society," remained untouched, however. Reiterating a stock line, a high-level official told the pan-Arab daily al-Hayat that modification of Article 8 was an "external request," by which he meant the Muslim Brother leadership in exile in Paris, and others hostile to the regime.

Bashar emphasized several times that "the party does not own the state."[2] Henceforth, the Baath's share of cabinet posts would be limited to ten.[3] Nonetheless, it was stipulated toward the end of the conference that the prime minister and the speaker of parliament must be members of the Baath's ruling body, the Regional Command. It was also suggested that the Regional Command of the party be dissolved and replaced by the "Party Command." Hence, President al-Asad would become the secretary-general of the Baath Party, not the regional secretary, a move that nodded to such realities as the dissolution of the party in Iraq and a narrowing of the Baathists' historical pan-Arabist ambitions.

Syria's real strongmen, of course, sit at the helms of General Security, Military Security, and the Republican Guard. Changes and replacements at that level tell a more direct story about the regime's internal power dynamics than hundreds of pages of party declarations. One week after the conference, Bashar's brother-in-law 'Asif Shawkat was confirmed as the head of military intelligence. One week after the conference, Bashar's brother-in-law 'Asif Shawkat was confirmed as the head of military intelligence. Bashar's brother Mahir is the effective head of the Republican Guard, perhaps the most potent fighting force in Syria. Manaf Tlass, son of former Defense Minister Mustafa Tlass, served alongside Mahir until his defection in July 2012. More important was the evident clearing of the way within these predominant institutions of coercion. From 2000 onward, strongmen who either opposed Bashar or were not part of his team were replaced or "retired." Perhaps the most visible such development was the resignation of Khaddam, who sensed the isolation of his generation of Baathists. The circumstances surrounding his exit lend credence to the story that Khaddam and others among the old guard had formed an informal alliance aimed at "saving" the regime from what they perceived to be the its blunders in Iraq and Lebanon.[4]

Bashar and his closest allies had played a delicate game since coming to power in 2000. On the one hand, they needed to preserve the structure of executive authority by strengthening the party and government institutions; on the other hand, they had to limit the personal power of potential adversaries in the long run. It was not a choice of one strategy among many on offer: Bashar needed, and needs, the Baath Party. Since he lacks his father's charisma, and others in the regime have more, selective reinvigoration of the Baath was the only rational choice.

Another change evident by 2005 was the increasing reliance on the security services, as indicated by the shifting membership in the Regional Command. Historically, the Command included the chief of staff and the defense minister. After the June 2005 conference, two members of the security services took the spots of these officials in the Command. The security services gained authority and institutional clout at the expense of the army, particularly after the pullout from Lebanon.

The team serving Bashar is made up of older and younger Baathists who were distinguished by proximity to the top leadership—and not necessarily by skill or experience. This fact is a double-edged sword for the regime. On the one hand, the team's unquestioning loyalty made for a less erratic policy, at least until the extremely stressful conditions of the uprising, when reports of internal rifts began to surface. On the other hand, Bashar's team lacks vision and, many say, competence. Both shortcomings are apparent in the woes of the Syrian economy.

The State of the Economy

In the early 1990s, the Syrian economy was thought to be growing by as much as 6-7 percent a year. Oil exports increased and aid from Gulf countries, which had suspended during the 1990-1991 Gulf war, came back, bringing foreign exchange. Public spending on various infrastructural projects and social services resumed as well, generating jobs. The Syrian pound was relatively stable and the private sector's share of capital formation, production, and exports grew to levels not seen since 1963.[5] But much of this growth turned out to be temporary, if not ephemeral, for corruption and backroom deals between officials and big business were growing even faster. Starting in 1994, decline set in.

The economic stagnation was rooted in state policy. On the one hand, the state aimed to control inflation and keep the pound stable by raising taxes and keeping wages down. Such measures were detrimental to the working and lower middle classes, as well as to job seekers. On the other hand, the government failed to implement Law 10 of 1991, which would have allowed for greater short-term commercial investment. Law 10 also conflicted with Decree 24, which prohibited dealing in foreign currency. Thus tangled in red tape, Syria's productive sectors experienced a sharp drop in activity. Public and private investment was slashed after 1995, bringing Syria to a financial standstill three years later. In 1998, the government endured its first balance of payments deficit in almost a decade.[6]

The most striking social effect was the steady decline of real wages, especially for public-sector workers, whose purchasing power eroded more and more. Virtually every imaginable consumer item was available in stores. But most were beyond the reach of the average civil servant earning the equivalent of $60 to $80 per month—not enough for basic living expenses. For a while, public-sector employees could manage because the private sector was employing an increasing share of the labor force, including their family members. As the slowdowns continued, however, many private-sector firms downsized. Unemployment reached 20-25 percent, with 220,000 people entering the job market each year. Heightening the unemployment problem was the return of laborers from the Gulf and Lebanon, where new laws and economic difficulty were making it harder for Syrians to find employment. Migrant workers' wages had previously supported entire families. Economic liberalization, though painfully slow and closely controlled, widened the gap between rich and poor.

At the Baath Regional Conference in June 2005, it was announced that Syria would adopt a "social market economy." The term, which emerged after heated debates over the concept of a "market economy," reflected the power of those who did not want a sudden transformation (even discursive) of "state socialist" Syria and further compromise of workers' rights.

Syria's economy had stagnated between 1996 and 2004, with an estimated average growth rate of 2.4 percent.[7] Meanwhile, the population was growing at a rate of 2.7 percent, spelling disaster. Economic growth reached 3.4 percent in 2003, but that unusually high rate reflected the sale of Iraqi oil through Syria and then the rise of oil prices as a result of the Iraq war. In 2004, economic growth dropped to 1.7 percent, showing the danger of depending on oil rents. Oil production reached 591,000 barrels per day in 1995 but declined to 450,000 in 2005. The good news for the regime was a rise in natural gas production to compensate for the decrease in oil production. Ultimately, rent income from oil or gas could only buy time.

Syrians were suffering from an alarming decline in their standard of living. In 2003-2004, 5.1 million people (or 30.1 percent of the population) were living below the poverty line, with 2 million Syrians unable to meet their basic needs.[8] By most estimates, unemployment remained above 20 percent. The problem was exacerbated by the insufficient skills of the labor force. In 2005, only 10 percent of Syrian workers had a college degree.[9]

With oil income tapering off, it was incumbent upon Syria's public and private sectors to do the heavy lifting of economic and social development. To generate growth in those sectors, the regime was counting on the trade benefits of a partnership agreement with the European Union. After some hesitation, and presumably to break out of the isolation imposed by the US, in 2004 Bashar created a new team to speed up the signing of an agreement. As a precondition, the EU pressed for a rapid transition from a public- to a private-sector economy, and, according to former Industry Minister 'Isam al-Za'im, the regime soon found itself moving faster and conceding more than it wanted to. By the end of 2004, the EU had added new preconditions, including a call upon Syria to lead the way in eliminating weapons of mass destruction from the region. Nevertheless, the Syrian team included "services" in the list of sectors to be liberalized, and at a faster pace, as a way to hasten the signing. This concession was not made public. After the assassination of Lebanese former Prime Minister Rafiq al-Hariri, the EU withdrew its promise of an expedited agreement.

As everywhere, the key to restarting the economic negotiations with the West was to overhaul the public sector. By 2005, private investment had grown only slightly, however, with fewer than 10 percent of private-sector firms employing more than five workers. Some obstacles to private-sector growth were structural, having to do with the fact that the public sector had long been the employer of first and last resort and thus bolstered the state's social legitimacy. Extensive liberalization was thus regarded by the regime as a political nightmare. Another part of the problem in the mid-2000s was the failure of banks to supply financing.[10]

Syria nevertheless edged toward marketization with the emergence of the first private banks in 2003, the establishment of holding companies in 2007, and the launch of the Damascus Stock Exchange in 2009. During this same period, economic mismanagement, cronyism, and successive years of scant rainfall saw GDP contract sharply. The regime turned to external partners for assistance, but to no avail. Its short-lived agreements with Turkey and other neighbors to create a regional trade zone never materialized and were derailed by the uprising. In October 2009, the EU finally signed the partnership agreement, but Asad unexpectedly deferred signing, declaring an intent "to revise" certain clauses. The agreement remains indefinitely postponed.

Meanwhile, persistent drought after 2003 produced massive rural in-migration to the cities—more than one million people had moved by 2009—widening the social and regional gaps still further. Major cities, such as Damascus and Aleppo, absorbed that migration more easily than smaller ones, which were increasingly starved of infrastructural investment. Provincial cities like Daraa, Idlib, Homs, and Hama, along with their hinterlands, saw local livelihoods gutted by reduction of subsidies, disinvestment and the effects of urbanization. These areas became hotbeds of rebellion in 2011. Inspired by the Tunisian and Egyptian uprisings, the residents expressed their discontent with the regime and its rich cronies.

"Sharks and Dinosaurs"

All along, another obstacle to both political and economic reform had been the "sharks and dinosaurs"—a term coined by Syrian economists to describe regime-linked business tycoons and their protectors in the state. The former were the creation of the latter, and sometimes their actual offspring. These intricate state-business relations had a long history.

After coming to power in 1970, Hafiz al-Asad reached out to conservative big businessmen, who were centered in large cities, particularly Damascus and Aleppo, and had been badly weakened by the wave of Baathist nationalizations in the 1960s. The links originated in conversations at the state-run Chambers of Commerce and Industry, and became bilateral as the regime paired up with select businessmen with substantial capital, key expertise, or relations with foreign companies. These businessmen came from diverse backgrounds. Some belonged to the old bourgeoisie, the merchant class that had dominated Syria's politics in the 1950s, and others were ascendant figures associated with public-sector ventures that had benefited from the oil boom after 1973. Most of these businessmen had operated in the shadow of the state, bidding for tenders from the public sector, but other new entrepreneurs were recruited as the networks mushroomed.

The rapprochement bore political fruit in the late 1970s and early 1980s, when the regime faced a revolt led by the Muslim Brothers. Asad had enacted a series of policies that harmed the interests of the Brothers' cadre and constituents in the traditional *suq* (market) and other small traders and artisans. In essence, the state had decimated the modest traders' business with the products of large, state-owned enterprises subsidized by Arab Gulf countries amid the post-1973 oil boom. These factories spread across the country and caused especially profound resentment in the conservative Sunni quarters of Syrian cities, where the regime was already seen as repressive and (because it was headed by 'Alawis) heretical. Making matters worse was the deal offered to a "troika" of men who, under the state's watchful eye, were allowed to launch the first large-scale private business ventures in the Baathist era. The troika was composed of Sa'ib Nahhas, Uthman al-'Aidi and 'Abd al-Rahman al-'Attar. Their bargain with the regime became the model for state-business partnerships, escalating tensions between the state and small business owners with Sunni Islamist leanings.

The confrontation with the Muslim Brothers lasted for more than six years. Urban Sunni merchants privileged by the state according to the troika model fell in with Hafiz al-Asad. Badr al-Din al-Shallah, then president of the Union of the Syrian Chambers of Commerce, assured Asad in a historic 1982 meeting that the big businesses whose loyalty he commanded would stand by the regime. The regime proceeded to beat back the uprising in the northwestern city of Hama, where at least fifteen thousand residents were killed. The brutal tank and artillery assault on Hama proved to be a lasting defeat for the Brothers. It also welded the future of Shallah and his peers to the fate of the regime.

After 1982, the informal state-business partnerships continued to flourish. Big businessmen got a variety of special privileges, including commissions for projects in the public sector, tax exemptions, and trade protections for certain goods. The partnerships matured in the late 1980s and came to exercise disproportionate influence on economic policy. The salient institution was originally called the Guidance Committee, a body made up of state officials and "private" businessmen tasked with devising economic policy over and above the committees that drafted nominally socialist five-year plans. "Private" had acquired a new meaning because many of these businessmen were themselves state officials or their relatives or partners. With makers and "takers" of policy staffing the same enterprise, or sometimes inhabiting the same corporeal frame, corruption in economic policymaking hit an all-time high. In the 1990s, the nucleus of this scheming was the office of Prime Minister Mahmoud al-Zu'bi. Most state officials who went into business opted for quick profit, which guided them in the direction of trade, rather than industry, and toward urban, rather than rural, areas. Along with many others, the Zu'bis prospered mightily, as did the Khaddams ('Abd al-Halim was still vice president) and the Tlasses (Mustafa was still defense minister), running car dealerships and hawking upscale consumer products. The new magnates, notably Rami Makhlouf, the nephew of the president's wife, also got high returns from tourism, free trade zones, and, later, telecommunications.

By the late 1990s, the intra-party squabbles over terminology notwithstanding, the business community that the Asads had created in their own image had transformed Syria from a semi-socialist state into a crony capitalist state par excellence. The cronies were visible in formal politics: Out of the eighty-three independent candidates for Parliament in 1998, businesspeople with significant financial power represented a plurality. In Damascus, nine of the twenty-nine elected parliamentarians were well-connected businesspeople associated with the Damascus Chambers of Commerce and Industry. The distribution was similar in Aleppo. The cronies were equally visible in economic policy, as illustrated by the projects approved by the Higher Council for Investment under the aforementioned Law 10. The ill-prepared law and accompanying bureaucratic obstacles, as well as the prohibition on dealing in foreign currency, drove away many serious investors while attracting those with political connections in search of quick profits. More than 60 percent of the investments under Law 10 in the late 1990s went not to industry, but to non-productive and environmentally disastrous ventures in the transportation sector. Industrial projects submitted by well-connected individuals were, in most instances, approved, subsidized, and protected. In the words of a prominent businessman turned politician at the time: "Law 10 is effectively a process of transferring the right to monopolies from the public sector to individuals in the private sector, where none of the benefits are generalized."[11]

After Bashar al-Asad succeeded his father in 2000, the architects of Syria's economic policy were conscious that the supposed growth of the 1990s had been an illusion. They sought to reverse the downturn by liberalizing the economy further, for instance by reducing state subsidies. Private banks were permitted for the first time in nearly forty years and a stock market was on the drawing board. After 2005, the state-business bonds were strengthened by the announcement of the "social market economy," a mixture of state and market approaches that ultimately privileged the market, but a market without robust institutions or accountability. Again, the regime had consolidated its alliance with big business at the expense of smaller businesses as well as the Syrian majority who depended on the state for services, subsidies, and welfare. It had perpetuated cronyism, but dressed it in new garb. Families associated with the regime in one way or another came to dominate the private sector, in addition to exercising considerable control over public economic assets. These clans include the Asads and Makhloufs, but also the Shalish, al-Hassan, Najib, Hamsho, Hambouba, Shawkat, and al-As'ad families, to name a few. The reconstituted business community, which now included regime officials, close supporters, and a thick sliver of the traditional bourgeoisie, effected a deeper (and, for the regime, more dangerous) polarization of Syrian society along lines of income and region.

As of mid-2012, there have been no significant defections, from the ranks of big business, at least not in Damascus and Aleppo. It is not just presidential blood relatives like

Makhlouf who have remained loyal. Other major players hailing from the above families have stood firm by the regime, financing its orchestrated mass rallies and public relations campaigns, as well as helping to float the Syrian currency. Most malcontents limit themselves to spiriting capital out of the country and expressing private wishes for regime change. Those who do back the uprising do it quietly and extremely carefully, highlighting the fealty of their counterparts.

The "sharks and dinosaurs" know very well that their fate is bound up with that of the regime by virtue of intertwined investments and also their years of self-enrichment at regime behest. To switch sides would be an enormous gamble on the opposition's forbearance. Big business' support is not solely responsible for the regime's resilience, but it would have been difficult for the regime to hold out in Damascus and Aleppo had these monied interests explicitly thrown their lot in with the protesters. The regime-business alliance took shape over decades, and it is unlikely to snap until the very last moment. Public defections by big businessmen would be a fair indicator that the regime's days are numbered. Until then, all eyes are on the battlefield.

Notes

Author's Note: This chapter was drawn from "Change and Stasis in Syria: One Step Forward...," *Middle East Report* 213 (Winter 1999); "Syria's Curious Dilemma," *Middle East Report* 236 (Fall 2005); and "The Syrian Regime's Business Backbone," *Middle East Report* 262 (Spring 2012).

1. Ibrahim Hamidi, "Clearing the Way," *Syria Today* (June 2005).

2. *Al-Hayat*, June 10, 2005.

3. *Al-Hayat*, June 8, 2005.

4. Interview with anonymous insider, Damascus, July 28, 2005. For the official story, see *al-Hayat*, June 8, 2005.

5. Syrian Arab Republic, Central Bureau of Statistics, *Statistical Abstract 1998*, pp. 516-517, 523.

6. US Embassy in Damascus, *1998 Annual Report on the Syrian Economy*.

7. Interview with 'Isam al-Za'im, former minister of industry and current president of the Tuesday Economic Sciences Association, Damascus, July 2005.

8. UN Development Program, *Poverty in Syria: 1996-2004* (New York, June 2005), pp. 1-6.

9. Interview with economist Nabil Sukkar, Damascus, 2005. For more indicators of Syria's labor force troubles, see the 2005 *National Human Development Report* (Damascus: UN Development Program and the Prime Minister's State Planning Agency, 2005).

10. See Muhammad Ghassan Qalla', "The Private Sector, Cooperation Challenges and Free Trade Zones," Economic Sciences Association Series 18, Damascus, February 15, 2005. For a more detailed study of private-sector bank loans by sector, see 'Isam al-Za'im, "Arab Economies: Obligations, Modes, Goals and Particularities," paper presented to the Algerian Economic Studies Association, Algiers, May 11-12, 2005.

11. Interview, Damascus, January 1999.

20. THE EVOLUTION OF KURDISH POLITICS IN SYRIA

CHRISTIAN SINCLAIR AND SIRWAN KAJJO

Over the weekend of July 16-17, 2011 representatives of the opposition to the regime of Syrian President Bashar al-Asad met in Istanbul to choose a "National Salvation Council." Among the diverse attendees were delegates speaking for Syria's Kurds, the largest ethnic minority in the country at more than two million people, some 10 percent of the population. All of the multiple Kurdish parties in Syria envision a pluralistic state in which their cultural and linguistic rights are recognized. Those at the Istanbul gathering wanted the name of the country changed from the Syrian Arab Republic to the "Republic of Syria." When the other delegates at the conference refused this request, these Kurds walked out in protest.

Some may have been surprised to learn that there are Kurdish parties in Syria at all. Pending promised revisions, or the collapse of the present regime, Article 8 of the Syrian constitution outlaws all political parties but the ruling Baath and its coalition partners. But opposition parties do exist, and Kurdish parties have been around since 1957. In the fifty-five years since the founding of the first one, the Kurdish political landscape has evolved and matured—albeit on the sidelines, since much of the activity has been covert. Parties have split, and split again, with amoeba-like efficiency; they have died just as quickly. Today there is no accurate count of the parties or their members. Membership is a closely guarded secret, in fact, with only 2-3 percent of the members known outside party circles.[1] Most observers, however, believe there are fifteen parties, with estimates of total membership ranging from sixty to two hundred thousand. The higher numbers come from Kurdish party officials. If they do not exaggerate, then the party members all together would make up about 10 percent of the Kurdish population.

For most of their history, Kurdish political formations in Syria have run up against the precepts of Arab nationalism. The Kurds, with their different language and customs, and their ties to ethnic brethren in Turkey, Iraq, and Iran, have been seen as a threat to the project of Arab unity. In 1957, just one year before implementation of the short-lived union between Syria and Egypt as the United Arab Republic, the power of Arab nationalist ideology was near its zenith. The founding of the first Kurdish party came, in part, in reaction to this state-sponsored program, which aimed to submerge the Kurds in Arab culture. The reactions of Arab oppositionists to the Kurdish platform in Istanbul show that old ideas of Arab nationalism retain considerable purchase. A new Syria is destined to emerge, however, from the months of upheaval engulfing the country in 2011 and 2012. If that Syria is to be more democratic, Kurdish aspirations will have to be integrated into the broader spectrum of the country's politics, moving the Kurds from the sidelines onto the field.

1927-1957

Just who are the Kurdish political parties in Syria? What are their origins and what is their future?

In the three decades prior to the 1957 establishment of the Kurdish Democratic Party in Syria (KDPS), Kurds in Syria were viewed with some suspicion, though much less than afterward. The origins of the Kurdish political movement can be traced back to the 1920s, when, like all indigenous political activism, it faced the scrutiny of the French Mandatory authorities. The newly established Republic of Turkey to the north was also keeping an eye on Kurdish developments in Syria. The failure of the Kurdish-led Sheikh Sa'id revolt in Turkey in 1925 led to the exodus of a substantial number of Kurdish fighters to Kurdish regions in northeastern Syria, as well as to Damascus, Aleppo, and even Lebanon, where they sought to escape Ankara's aggressive pursuit.

The Kurdish exiles from Turkey quickly engaged in Kurdish society in Syria, becoming a part of the social, cultural, and political fabric, but their prime objective remained retaliation against the Turkish government. The first attempt at fighting back against the Turks was the founding of the pan-Kurdish Xoybun (Independence) League, a secular, nationalist group founded on October 5, 1927 at a gathering in Bhamdoun, Lebanon. The league's political branch was led by well-known Kurdish author Celadet Bedirxan, who was assisted by a group of Kurdish intellectuals, many of whom had been educated in various European countries. Syrian Kurdish national figures eagerly joined Xoybun and branches opened across the Kurdish regions. As Xoybun spread, Kurds in Syria began to consider it an essential center of knowledge and learning in a society dominated by backwardness. Many Kurdish writers, poets, and philosophers, such as Cegerxwin and Qedri Can, participated in Xoybun-sponsored activities. The organization offered a space where Syrian Kurdish intellectuals could gain experience speaking about issues of nationalism, self-determination, and oppression, providing a foundation for the emergence of the Kurdish political movement.[2]

In 1946, the year Syria gained independence from France, Xoybun was dissolved. Dissolution happened as Kurdish-Soviet relations were on the rise and interest in purely "nationalist" ideas was waning. The Syrian Communist Party was gaining popularity among the Kurds. Former members of Xoybun became active Communists; many of the party's prominent leaders, in turn, were of Kurdish background. In a few short years, the Communists took control of the "Kurdish street" in Syria. But, toeing the line from Moscow, the Communists held a vastly different view of the Kurdish issue than Xoybun had propagated. The party's leadership proclaimed that the Kurdish question in Syria did not have an independent existence. Kurds were simply another group of Syrian citizens who needed to be integrated into a consolidated working class.

The First Kurdish Political Party

The push was soon on to fashion something new. In the summer of 1957, the KDPS was created as a "left-wing and nationalist" alternative to the Communists, who were led by a

Kurd, but did not promote Kurdish rights.[3] The KDPS was, many observers say, just a continuation of Xoybun as most of its founders and leaders had been prominent members of that defunct pan-Kurdish group.[4] The party's founding members chose Nur al-Din Zaza, a leading Kurdish intellectual, as the first president. But political infighting erupted almost immediately over the goals and principles of the KDPS—and even the party's name.

An early fracas involved Jalal Talabani, the long-time political leader of Iraq's Kurds who since 2005 has served as president of Iraq. Talabani was living in Syria in the 1950s and was a key link to the Kurdish activists in Iraq. In 1960 he forced the KDPS to change the party's name to the Democratic Party of Kurdistan in Syria. This switch from the word "Kurdish" to the far more provocative "Kurdistan" helped to foment an atmosphere of anxiety among KDPS leaders. Osman Sabri, one of the party's founding fathers, was particularly concerned by the use of "Kurdistan," as the term might imply that the party was insinuating that Kurdish areas of Syria belonged to a greater Kurdistan that straddled national boundaries.[5] This message was not one the party wanted to send.

That unwanted message was partly responsible for the wave of detentions carried out in August 1960. Scores of KDPS cadres, including leading members of the executive committee, were arrested by Syrian state security. While under interrogation, some detainees remained loyal to the party's strict rules of confidentiality; others broke and gave their captors sensitive information about the internal workings of the party.[6] In the end, the whole party structure was revealed, leading to the detention of more than five thousand people. So began the split between political heavyweights Osman Sabri, on the left, and Nur al-Din Zaza, on the right, which led the Kurds of Syria into further turmoil and political stagnation.

Salah Badreddin, an early member of the Kurdish political movement, describes his own left wing of the party, led by Sabri in the early 1960s, as "national, democratic and peaceful" with "unchangeable principles" and a "decisive, clear stand." The right wing, led by Zaza, he described as "adventurer [sic], bargaining, and opportunist,"[7] in reference to those who revealed party secrets in the August 1960 crackdown. The two factions unofficially split in 1962, with the official separation coming in 1965. The right wing of the party was taken over by Hamid Hajj Darwish, as Zaza was then in prison. Its ranks consisted mostly of Kurdish "notables," such as urban merchants and professionals, as well as religious leaders and landowners.[8] The left was made up of teachers, students, and former Communists.

Four years after the collapse of unity with Egypt, Arab nationalism remained the baseline of political ideas in Syria. At the 1965 KDPS conference, the delegates accordingly asked basic questions: Who are we? What do we want? What is our relationship with the state? What is our relationship to Mulla Mustafa Barzani and the Kurdish revolt in Iraq? According to Badreddin's account, Sabri's leftist group would answer: We are a people that wants national rights and self-determination. We are a part of an alliance with democratic forces within Syria. And, finally, we are part of a struggle under the leadership of Barzani. The right would answer: We are a minority asking for limited cultural rights, we are loyal to the Syrian authorities and we are not swayed by the idea of a pan-Kurdish liberation movement.[9]

In 1970, at a meeting hosted by Barzani in Iraqi Kurdistan, an attempt was made to reunite the two factions. In the end, their differences were irreconcilable and a third party was created, also called the KDPS, with PL (Provisional Leadership) added to its acronym, and headed by Daham Miro. The new KDPS-PL was, in effect, a Syrian branch of Barzani's Kurdish Democratic Party in Iraq, but it did not take root. Today, its rump is the smallest of three Kurdish parties in Syria that continue to boast the appellation KDPS. The larger two of these groups have added "al-Parti" to their names to advertise their genealogy in the founding KDPS of 1957.

Splits and Breakaways

The right-wing branch coming from the 1965 split that was led by Darwish retained the name KDPS for some time. The right subdivided in 1975, around the time that Jalal Talabani announced from Damascus that his Patriotic Union of Kurdistan (PUK) would break with Barzani in Iraq. Having tied himself to Talabani, Darwish thought a party name change would signal his loyalties, and in 1976, he changed the name of the KDPS to the Kurdish Democratic Progressive Party in Syria. A pro-Barzani faction broke away under the original name and exists to this day. The Progressive Party of Darwish eventually saw two offshoots, one dubbed Wekhevi (Equality) and the other the Kurdish National Democratic Party. This side of the Kurdish political spectrum, however, did not see anywhere near the number of fissures that the left did.

In 1975, Osman Sabri saw his left faction of the original KDPS cleave in two. The cause, again, was the developments among the Kurds of Iraq. Salah Badreddin led the anti-PUK faction, Yekitiya Gel (Unity of the People),[10] while the pro-PUK branch kept the KDPS name. This group still exists and is led by Nesreddin Ibrahim. In the late 1970s a splinter group emerged from Yekitiya Gel calling itself the Kurdish Left Party, also still extant, under the leadership of Mohammad Mousa. In 1980 Badreddin changed the name of Yekitiya Gel to the Kurdish Popular Union Party, which split in 1991, with one branch retaining the original name and the other favoring Yekiti. In 1994 a faction calling itself the Kurdish Democratic United Party left Yekiti. And, finally, in 2005 some members of the Left Party and the Popular Union Party joined together to form the Kurdish Freedom Party (Azadi). Azadi is led by Kheir al-Din Murad. Today there are five parties with roots in Badreddin's Yekitiya Gel.

Most of the splits on left and right were the result of personal differences rather than ideological disagreements. Broadly, as well, the left and right diverge over tactics rather than ideology, with the left-wing groups preferring to organize on the ground and demonstrate party strength through marches and the like, and the right-leaning groups favoring dialogue with the authorities. Ideological similarities have, in fact, led to alliances between left and right factions in the latter years of Bashar al-Asad's regime.

A few other parties that exist today do not have their genesis in the original KDPS. One is the Future Movement, founded in 2005 under Mishal Tammo. The Syrian Democratic Kurdish Party is another. One of the most important, however, is the Democratic Union Party, better known by its Kurdish-language initials, PYD. The PYD was founded in 2003 by former members of the Kurdistan Workers' Party (PKK), the well-known organization in Turkey whose fighters have waged an anti-government insurgency off and on since the 1980s. In 2005, the Kurdish Accord, better known by its Arabic name, Wifaq, split from the PYD. Allegations of Wifaq's cooperation with Syrian intelligence services led to armed hostilities between the PYD and Wifaq, with at least one Wifaq member assassinated by the PYD.

Membership and Leadership

Despite all the splits over the years, almost all the Kurdish parties in Syria follow a similar, complex set of bylaws that determine the conditions for individual membership. Joining a party is not a simple act of registration and receipt of a membership card.

An applicant who wants to join a particular party has to submit a written request explaining the reasons behind his desire to be a member. He must be at least eighteen years of age. Thereafter, a specialized body from within the party begins an informal investigation of the applicant to assess whether he has a solid reputation within its designated social and political circles.

Once the application is approved, the applicant is referred to "qualifying cells" for an induction process that may last up to six months. During this months-long training, the applicant attends organizational courses, seminars on Kurdish culture and history, and courses in formal written Kurdish. In Syria, Kurdish is not an officially recognized language and its use has been restricted by law and through intimidation. Various decrees, for instance, have forbidden the use of Kurdish in workplaces and other public arenas. Though Kurdish is spoken at home and in the street, the Kurdish political party system is the sole institution in Syria through which Kurds can learn Kurdish in an academic setting. Contingent upon passing the courses, junior members are transferred to a higher status, known as a band, which together constitute the mainstay of the party.

A political party is usually divided into several bodies, which are differentiated by their tasks and roles. The central committee is the leading body of the party. It consists of several different fractions divided by function: legal, media relations, and the political bureau, which has the highest authority for approval of any decision made by the party. Under the central committee are the local committees, which are made up of subcommittees. The subcommittees are clusters of bands.

The PYD and the Future Movement are the only two Kurdish parties in Syria that do not have these intricate organizational structures. They simply have a leading committee and local branches wherever they have supporters. Additionally, those who wish to obtain membership in these two parties do not have to go through the lengthy process required by other parties.[11]

Membership in any party carries with it certain duties and rights. Members have the right to vote or to be elected to office. They have the right to resign from the party, but must provide sufficient justification. They have the right to freedom of religious expression as well. Duties include attendance at party meetings and conventions, working to implement the party's policies and, of course, preserving the party's secrets. There are also strict laws governing members' behavior, with disciplinary procedures that are taken against members who violate the party's regulations. The most severe punishment is expulsion from the party, which can be ordered if a member fails to account for continued absences from party meetings, is found to have been collaborating with state intelligence services or attempts to destabilize or divide the party. The only body that has the power to expel members from the party is the central committee.

More traditional Kurdish parties still rely on the leadership of a sole figure. There is a certain dependency on these leaders, who themselves become stand-ins for the party. For instance, the leader of one party calling itself the KDPS, Abdulhakim Bashar, is in office for life, having been appointed in 2008 after the death of Nezir Mustafa, who had led the group for the previous twelve years. Another example would be the Kurdish Democratic Progressive Party, which holds a referendum during its general congress to reinstate its leader, Hamid Hajj Darwish. He has been in office since 1965, first with the KDPS and since 1976 as head of the Progressive Party.

Yekiti and the PYD are unique among the Kurdish parties in Syria in that they change their leaders on a regular basis. Yekiti elects a new secretary-general every three years at its party congress. The PYD, according to its website, holds an election for the position of secretary-general every four years and that person can be reelected to a second term.

From Hafiz to Bashar

During the thirty-year rule of Hafiz al-Asad (1970-2000), Kurdish political parties operated with limited interference from the government. They were weak and fragmented, and Damascus considered them to pose little threat. In fact, Asad was far more concerned with Kurdish movements in neighboring countries than with Kurds in Syria. He saw the Kurds in Iraq and Turkey as sources of leverage in his various disputes with Baghdad and Ankara.

Syria supported opposition groups in Saddam Hussein's Iraq and allowed the opening of the PUK office in Damascus in 1975. In 1979 Damascus formalized relations with Barzani's party, as well, and in ensuing years sought to weaken the regime in Baghdad by bringing the rival factions among the Kurds of Iraq together. Offices for both parties were established in the Kurdish-dominated city of al-Qamishli, in the northeastern corner of Syria. It was standard for both parties to recruit Kurds in Syria to join their *peshmerga*, "those who faced death" in the battles with the Iraqi army.

During the 1980s and 1990s, the PKK also operated freely in Syria, which became a breeding ground of sorts for PKK militants. An estimated 20 percent of PKK fighters hold Syrian citizenship.[12] Hafiz al-Asad's regime tolerated the PKK's activities, all the while pretending its personnel were not even present on Syrian soil. By 1998, with Ankara intensifying its efforts to quash the insurgency in southeastern Turkey, this game became impossible to sustain. Wishing to avoid a major confrontation, the Asad regime signed a security accord with Turkey, known as the Adana Agreement, by which Syria labeled the PKK a terrorist organization, prohibited its activities and those of its affiliates, and agreed to block the supply of weapons, logistical, materiel and money to the PKK from Syrian territory. This move forced Abdullah Öcalan out of his Syrian refuge, leading to the PKK leader's eventual capture and imprisonment. The rest of the PKK operatives left the country soon after, leaving something of a vacuum, for their presence had galvanized the Kurds of Syria into ending their relative quiescence.

Bashar al-Asad took over as president after the passing of his father in the summer of 2000. The Kurdish population, at this point, was more politicized than ever before. The Kurdish political parties, though banned, saw it as their obligation to mobilize the Kurds to push for greater political and cultural rights. Members of the various parties and Kurdish cultural activists joined other Syrian intellectuals in the salons of the "Damascus spring," a short-lived thaw in the authoritarian political climate when opposition figures attempted to articulate a program of political reform that the new president might follow. The "spring" soon faded in the capital, but on the Kurdish front the regime did soften its stance, removing much of the state security apparatus from the Kurdish regions and ordering Baath officials to meet with Kurdish party leaders. The parties were emboldened to test the new regime's tolerance of their demands for increased cultural and political rights. They organized a series of demonstrations, in the expectation that the regime might relax some of its repressive laws.[13] This transition period would soon end, however.

On March 8, 2004, the Transitional Administrative Law was adopted in Iraq, a sort of provisional constitution that preserved the autonomous "Kurdistan Regional Government" the two Iraqi Kurdish parties had previously declared. It was a huge victory for the Kurdish cause, and all over Syria, Kurds celebrated the announcement. To monitor the situation, Damascus moved extra security forces into Kurdish areas and placed the troops on alert.

Four days later, on March 12, there was a soccer match in al-Qamishli pitting the local heroes against the team from Dayr al-Zawr. The fans of al-Qamishli's team were mostly Kurds, while those from Dayr al-Zawr were mostly Sunni Arabs. The Dayr al-Zawr fans insulted Masoud Barzani and Jalal Talabani, and held up photographs of Saddam Hussein. The Kurds shouted slogans in support of President George W. Bush. The rival taunts eventually escalated into riots at the stadium, and the army and other security forces deployed to the scene. Seven Kurds were killed in the ensuing clampdown. The next day, in addition to the funeral marches, there were massive demonstrations in Kurdish cities where Kurdish flags waved amidst the crowds. Syria had never seen demonstrations of this magnitude by Kurds. The reaction of security forces was unparalleled as well. Thirty-two were killed, hundreds wounded, and two thousand arrested over a five-day period.[14] By the end of 2004, most of the two thousand detained had been released; a final 312 were given amnesty and released in March 2005.

The wave of arrests after the soccer match was followed by intense repression of Kurdish cultural and political expression, wiping away the Kurds' hopes of gains under the new president. In June 2004 the Syrian military intelligence service summoned several Kurdish leaders to warn them that all Kurdish parties in Syria were to cease their political and cultural activities. The Kurds were told, for instance, that the state would no longer tolerate the teaching of the Kurdish language, even in private. The Kurdish activists maintained their ties to other oppositionists. Eight Kurdish parties were signatories to the 2005 Damascus Declaration calling for an end to emergency law, a constitutional convention, and other democratizing measures. Those parties that did not sign this document objected that it did not include a provision for constitutional recognition of the Kurds as the largest ethnic minority in the country.

Party Demands

In the early 2000s, the Kurdish parties of Syria coalesced into three broad alliances around several axes, one being their relationship with the Baathist regime. The first group, the Kurdish Alliance, consists of the Left Party, Azadi, the Democratic United Party and the Progressive Party—three descendants of the left wing of the old KDPS and one of the right. These four parties have been more accommodating toward the state, sometimes agreeing with the state's viewpoint on particular issues. The Progressive Party, for instance, was allowed to open Nur al-Din Zaza Hall, a cultural foundation where the party leader Darwish maintains his offices, because he has not pushed for more than baseline cultural rights for the Kurds. The Kurdish Democratic Front, which stakes out a sort of middle ground, consists of two of the parties named KDPS (under Abdulhakim Bashar and Nesreddin Ibrahim, respectively), Wekhevi, and the National Democratic Party. The third coalition, the Coordinating Committee, distinguishes itself with its more hardline demands upon the regime, to which it is often hostile. The parties in this group are the Future Movement, Yekiti, and Azadi, which, in a seeming contradiction, has a hand in the Alliance as well.

In his Decree 49, promulgated on April 7, 2011, Bashar al-Asad promised to grant "Syrian Arab" citizenship to some 225,000 Kurds. Most are descendants of the 125,000 in the northeastern Hasaka region who were stripped of citizenship by a 1962 census. These "foreigners," as the regime has called them, make up about three quarters of the stateless Kurds living in Syria. The others, who number about 75,000, are "unregistered" and have no legal status whatsoever. Decree 49 said nothing about them. Beyond the core agenda of citizenship for all Kurds in Syria, the Kurdish parties are divided over exactly what to demand from the state. Some of the parties have similar demands and differentiate themselves only by the tone used in voicing them. The parties' demands can be separated into three, progressively more radical categories: cultural, linguistic, and political rights; constitutional recognition of Kurds as a minority in Syria; and autonomy.

Linguistic rights—recognition of the Kurdish language and the right to teach in Kurdish—is one of the most widely sought reforms among the Kurds in Syria. Protesters in Kurdish regions often carry signs reading, "We want the Kurdish language taught in schools." For some parties, the political program stops here, with the addition of cultural rights. The Progressive Party, for example, has limited its demands to preserving the cultural identity of the Kurds in Syria. They ask to be allowed to hold festivals celebrating Kurdish literature, song, and dance. Such cultural activities, however, are often seen as political by the government, with its commitment to old-style Arab nationalism. Participation in a cultural event sponsored by a Kurdish party, even one with close ties to the government, carries with it the risk of persecution.

A good number of parties, most descended from the left wing of the old KDPS, seek constitutional recognition of the Kurds as an ethnic minority in Syria. In a 2005 interview, Mohamed Mousa, secretary-general of the Left Party, said this measure is needed because some Syrian Arabs believe that Kurds are alien to the country. "These groups must realize that the Kurdish presence in Syria is a natural result of the Sykes-Picot treaty of 1916, which divided the whole region without any consideration for ethnic differences," he concluded.[15] The PYD insists on this demand as well.

While no party seeks full independence from Syria, some have gone so far as to petition for autonomy for the Kurdish regions. Yekiti, at its sixth party convention in 2009, acknowledged the autonomy project and put the idea forward for the consideration of the national movement as a whole. Two weeks after the convention, on December 26, 2009, security forces arrested four senior Yekiti members—Hasan Saleh, Marouf Mulla Ahmed,

Mohamed Mustafa and Anwar Naso—charging them with "aiming at separating part of the Syrian lands" and "joining an international political or social organization." Autonomy is obviously a sensitive topic for the Syrian authorities. "There used to be a red line on detaining known Kurdish political leaders. But since 2004, this line is no longer there," a Kurdish activist told Human Rights Watch earlier that year.[16]

Intelligence services generally watch Kurdish leaders closely, sometimes excluding them and their families from public-sector employment. The three parties of the Coordinating Committee, given their stance against the government and their more explicit language in demanding Kurdish rights, are the most frequently targeted. The state security presence is high in the Kurdish regions, with around one thousand agents based in al-Qamishli alone.

The PYD also gets heightened harassment from the state, but for different reasons. Because the party's founders belonged to the PKK, Ankara sees it as little more than a PKK branch in another country, and one that, since 1998, is under treaty obligation not to tolerate PKK activity. The Syrian regime, whose diplomatic and commercial relations with Ankara improved considerably in the era of Bashar al-Asad until the diplomatic break in August 2011, often detained PYD leaders and members in deference to its erstwhile Turkish friend. As one PYD member confirmed, "Our party members are the ones that are most subject to arrest and torture. It is because of Syrian-Turkish relations and because we adopt Öcalan's ideology."[17] The regime may harbor a special fear of the PYD because, as probably the largest Kurdish party in Syria, it is able to mobilize large crowds.

Though some parties attract more unwelcome attention than others, there has been an overall increase in harassment of Kurdish politicos in the mid- to late 2000s. Abdulhakim Bashar, leader of the KDPS, suggests that autonomy for the Kurds of Iraq, the various "Kurdish openings" in Turkey, and better networking among Kurds inside and outside Syria have raised the alarm in Damascus. "The fear that Kurdish popular movements would become a general phenomenon in Syrian society has pushed the authorities to use all repressive means to try to tame the Kurds," he says.

The Road Ahead

In an effort to unify the Kurdish political voice, a large coalition of nine political parties was formed in December 2009 under the name of the Kurdish Political Congress. The coalition embraced the entirety of the Kurdish Democratic Front and the Coordination Committee, as well as the Left Party and the Syrian Democratic Kurdish Party. As the Syrian uprising spread in the spring of 2011, these original nine parties brought three others, including the PYD, into an expanded coalition known as the National Movement of Kurdish Political Parties. The press often refers to the National Movement simply as "a group of twelve Kurdish political parties." According to Hassan Saleh of Yekiti, the main reason for forming this disparate assemblage of characters was to streamline the Kurds' message in the face of Arab opposition.[18] It is a milestone for cooperation among the Kurdish parties of Syria.

The National Movement held an unprecedented gathering in April 2011, and the next month in al-Qamishli they announced their own plan for resolving the crisis embroiling Syria. The plan called for an end to one-party rule, a modern, civil state that ensures the rule of law, and true equality for all citizens, among other demands. The program was very similar to those of other opposition groups in the country. And yet, outside the Kurdish press, the National Movement's announcement was largely ignored.

Many of the Kurdish parties believe that the Arab opposition in Syria still does not recognize the Kurds as a major part of the Syrian political equation. No party inside Syria sent official delegates to the Istanbul conference in mid-July 2011, but Mishal Tammo, leader of the Future Movement, attended in his personal capacity. Tammo was one of the Kurds who walked out when the other oppositionists would not acquiesce in removing the term "Arab" from the name of the Syrian state. "Once a democratic state has been established, if the Syrians still turn to the Arabs, we will turn to Erbil and Diyarbakır," he told the press,[19] referring to the official capital of Iraqi Kurdistan and the unofficial capital of the Kurdish nation in southeast Turkey.

The Kurds of Syria have long had a brotherly, but at times chaotic, relationship with the Kurds of Iraq. After the establishment of the Kurdistan Regional Government (KRG) in Iraq in 2004, however, this relationship was altered. The differences among parties in Syria already did not track so closely with the differences between Masoud Barzani and Jalal Talabani, but when these two figures consolidated forces, that correlation ceased entirely. For its part, the unified KRG downgraded its formal links to the parties in Syria, in a demarche to Damascus similar in intent to its gestures to Ankara, notably its relatively muted protests when Turkey attacks PKK fighters based in northern Iraq. Most Kurdish parties in Syria continue to keep offices in Erbil, however. (And the KRG wields clout in those parties' internal affairs; Barzani appointed Abdulhakim Bashar as the new head of the KDPS in 2008, for example.) With many signs pointing to the end of the Asad regime, the KRG may be looking to rebuild more robust ties to its Kurdish political allies in Syria.

For the moment, at any rate, the Kurdish parties in Syria are on their own. They have before them the tasks of reconciliation with the Arab opposition, with each other and, most important, with the Kurdish street. Despite the public disagreements, the Kurdish and Arab opposition parties have tacitly committed to working together until the Asad regime is toppled. The thorny questions of the "Arabness" of Syria and the extent of Kurdish cultural rights, let alone autonomy, are on hold.

As for the Kurdish parties themselves, they disagree with each other as often as they disagree with the Arab opposition. They have always lived in a state of fragmentation, much to their common detriment. Intra-Kurdish differences in Syria, however, have hardly ever escalated to the point of violence, as has happened among Kurdish political factions elsewhere in the Middle East. The demise of the Asad regime, if it comes, will be a litmus test of their mutual tolerance.

Coming to terms with Kurdish youth, who have taken charge of street protests in Kurdish-majority areas, may prove the most difficult task of all. As elsewhere in Syria, the engines of the uprising in majority-Kurdish areas are "local coordinating committees" that are youth-led and politically unaffiliated. The Kurdish committees have called for the "liberation" of the Arab areas of Daraa, Idlib, and Hama, showing the pan-Syrian solidarity against the regime that has characterized the committees in other parts of the country from the time of their emergence. These local activists also believe that a resolution of the Kurdish question will only come about through organizing on the ground. In June 2011, the Future Movement of Mishal Tammo—who was assassinated in al-Qamishli in October 2011—froze cooperation with other parties on the grounds that the youth should be at the forefront of Kurdish activism.

The young activists say that they are in regular contact with Kurdish party cadres and that a few of the more militant parties back, and take part in, the demonstrations. But if or when the regime falls, it will be the unaffiliated youth, and not the self-declared Kurdish National Movement, that will be able to claim credit. The youth may dismiss the Kurdish parties as being out of touch with their own visions for the future. Syria is moving toward inevitable change. The question is whether the Kurdish National Movement can adapt to the new environment, shedding its ineffectual clandestine past and embracing transparency to become a genuine representative of the Kurdish people in Syria.

Notes

1. Landinfo, *Kurds in Syria: Groups at Risk and Reactions Against Political Activists* (Oslo, June 2010), p. 11.

2. Kerim Yildiz, *Kurds in Syria* (London: Pluto Press, 2005), p. 29.

3. Jordi Tejel, *Syria's Kurds: History, Politics and Society* (London: Routledge, 2009), p. 48.

4. E-mail interview with Abdulbasit Seyda, Kurdish academic living in Sweden, June 2011. Seyda was elected head of the Syrian National Council, an opposition group based in Turkey, in June 2012.

5. Tejel, pp. 48-49.

6. Salah Badreddin, *The Kurdish National Movement in Syria: A Critical Approach from Inside* (Berlin: Kurdish Kawa Cultural Center, 2003), p. 10.

7. Ibid., p. 14.

8. Tejel, p. 87.

9. Badreddin, p. 15.

10. David McDowell, *A Modern History of the Kurds* (London: I. B. Tauris, 2003), p. 478.

11. Interview with Mustafa Mohamed, Kurdish member of Syria's parliament (1991-1995), Washington, DC, July 2011.

12. Landinfo, p. 16.

13. See Christian Sinclair, "Ten Years of Bashar al-Asad's Syria: Kurdish Political and Cultural Rights," unpublished paper presented at the Middle East Studies Association, San Diego, CA, November 2010.

14. See Eva Savelsberg, "The Making of the al-Qamishli Uprising by Kurdish Internet Sites in the Diaspora," unpublished paper presented at the World Congress for Middle Eastern Studies, Barcelona, July 2010.

15. *Tahawwulat*, August 2, 2005.

16. Human Rights Watch, *Group Denial: Repression of Kurdish Political and Cultural Rights in Syria* (New York, November 2009), p. 4.

17. Human Rights Watch, p. 43.

18. Telephone interview with Hassan Saleh, Yekiti party leader, July 10, 2011.

19. *Rudaw*, July 21, 2011.

21. DRAMAS OF THE AUTHORITARIAN STATE

DONATELLA DELLA RATTA

During August of 2011, which corresponded with the Muslim holy month of Ramadan, viewers of the state-run satellite channel Syrian TV might have stumbled upon quite a strange scene: A man watches as a crowd chants *"Hurriyya, hurriyya!"* This slogan— "Freedom, freedom!"—was a familiar rallying cry of the various Arab uprisings. It was heard in Syrian cities, including Damascus, when protesters first hit the streets there on March 15, 2011. But it was odd, to say the least, to hear the phrase in a Syrian government-sponsored broadcast. Until that moment, state TV had not screened any such evidence of peaceful demonstrations in Syria.

The scene went on to show the same bystander ordering policemen to shoot at the protesters. Immediately afterwards, he seems to regret his order, muttering: "Maybe I should have…" At this point it becomes clear that this scene was no news bulletin or user-generated YouTube clip documenting an actual protest. Rather, it came from a *musalsal* (pl. *musalsalat*), as the thirty-episode miniseries that accompany Ramadan in Syria, Egypt, and elsewhere are known. The grand finale of this *musalsal, Fawq al-Saqf* (Above the Ceiling), featured the two main characters overlooking a desolate landscape. "What happened to this country?" asks one. "I am responsible for this. I knew it was going to happen…but, in the end, precaution cannot stave off destiny." The other character replies by repeating the phrase: "Thank God, around us and not on top of us."

Without a Trace

The credits attributed the paternity of *Fawq al-Saqf* to the Radio and TV Production Organization, a unit inside Syrian TV launched in 2010 with a mission to employ a "private-company mindset" in churning out dramas, according to Diana Jabbour, the former director. Over the preceding decade, demand for Syrian *musalsalat* had increased across the Arab world. By 2011, Syrian producers clocked in right after the historically dominant Egyptians in the quantity of hours provided to the Gulf-owned networks that sit atop the pan-Arab market. The bulk of the Syrian supply comes from private producers, and the Organization, which enjoys financial autonomy and the authority to form public-private partnerships, was intended to represent the new face of government involvement in Syrian TV drama.

Fawq al-Saqf was one of the first productions commissioned by the agency. Its episodes were authored by screenwriters who had worked on *Buq'at Daw'* (Spotlight), a comedic *musalsal* that was considered among the most daring in Syrian history, airing in 2001 at the tail end of the "Damascus spring," the short-lived political opening after the accession of Bashar al-Asad to the presidency. The director of *Fawq al-Saqf*, Samir Barqawi, was a promising young talent who was not openly aligned with the regime. The serial thus had all the components of what many Syrians would call *tanfis* (blowing off steam), or what Lisa Wedeen has described as a means of allowing people "to vent frustrations and displace or relieve tensions that otherwise might find expression in political action."[1] *Fawq al-Saqf* could also have been an example of "commissioned criticism," "an official and paradoxical project to create a democratic façade" in a period of unrest by featuring a level of dissent in official media.[2]

Neither of these classifications is persuasive, however. Had the *musalsal* been *tanfis* or "commissioned criticism," the official media would have advertised it heavily, to say the least. But no promo spots for *Fawq al-Saqf* aired on the state-run channels. The daily program "Drama 2011," which helped viewers navigate the crowded Ramadan schedule, did not even mention it. And though it is customary for Ramadan serials to be rebroadcast in later months, *Fawq al-Saqf* was never put back on the schedule. Even prominent dramatists who were asked about it seemed unaware of its existence. The only outside station to mention the *musalsal* was the Saudi-owned pan-Arab channel al-'Arabiyya, which featured it once on the daily "Drama Ramadan" program. Then the *musalsal* was stopped at its fifteenth episode, before the end of Ramadan, with no reason given. It simply disappeared from TV screens without a trace.

After Ramadan ended in September, the topic of *Fawq al-Saqf* came up at a seminar at the University of Copenhagen. Adib Kheir, owner of the production company Sama Art Production, dismissed it as a "silly project that was done without any planning, testing, or pre-testing." Kheir belongs to a group of Syrian producers who view TV drama as a commodity: His business relies on such products as Turkish serials dubbed into Syrian dialect, which are highly popular in the pan-Arab market. From his strictly commercial perspective, *Fawq al-Saqf* was simply a failure.

Sotto Voce

Fawq al-Saqf grew out of a proposal offered by Sami Moubayed during a meeting held at the presidential palace in the spring of 2011, according to the head of censorship at the Radio and TV Production Organization, Mahir 'Azzam.[3] Moubayed taught political science at the private Kalamoon University in Damascus and was editor-in-chief of *Forward*, a monthly magazine from the influential Haykal media group, which promotes the idea of a progressive, liberal Syria under the Asad family's leadership. He was a personal friend of Bouthaina Shaaban, Bashar al-Asad's media adviser, who delivered the first official response of the state to the Syrian uprising. Moubayed's articles on the uprising—some of which appeared in American outlets like the *Huffington Post*—gave a sense of his skill in eschewing regime rhetoric while remaining committed to the presidential palace's seemingly reformist project.[4] In a piece called "What Will Post-Arab Spring Intellectuals Write About?" he acknowledged that Syrians like Saadallah Wannous and Muhammad al-Maghout were given leeway to produce meaningful art "under the watchful eye of the government, hoping that their plays or poems would 'defuse' public discontent." But he consigned such arrange-ments to the past, and did not list Bashar al-Asad's Syria among the countries that were facing uprisings. He seemed, furthermore, to endorse the regime's narrative that the enemy in Syria was political Islam: He mused that the politically engaged literary works he cited would seem outdated "to a rising Arab generation that will emerge after the Arab spring, perhaps five to ten years from now. One day, they will definitely see the light, yet again, where need for them rearises, perhaps when the Islamists coming to power today turn into another Husni Mubarak or another Qaddafi."[5]

According to 'Azzam, Moubayed's pitch for *Fawq al-Saqf* started with a simple ques-tion: "How can we resolve what is happening on the streets in an artistic way?" The *Forward* editor went on to describe his concept for the *musalsal* as a "third view that does not embrace the regime's view or the street's...something that the regime would not feel as a provocation when watching it, but would not anger the street or encourage people to demonstrate after the broadcast." The presidential palace seemed to like the idea, for the Organization (where 'Azzam headed the censorship division) was told to take the project under its wing.

Fawq al-Saqf could thus be said to exemplify a mechanism linking cultural producers to different components of the Syrian regime, one that I call the "whisper strategy."[6] It is an example of Michel Foucault's strategies without a strategist, a *sotto voce* conversation whereby priorities are negotiated and commonalities established over the content of cultural production. The metaphor of the whisper suggests a relationship based not on coercion or clashing cultural paradigms but rather on Max Weber's "elective affinities," a nexus of shared beliefs, interests, and concerns. The ideological common ground occupied by regime and many cultural producers is a belief in the backwardness of Syrian society, which ostensibly can progress only through an enlightening (*tanwiri*) process led by benevolent minority rulers. When discussing their media projects, cultural producers very often mentioned the "culpability of society" in its own backwardness and the need to reform it through *tanwiri* media projects. "Drama has to criticize society," stressed Syrian screenwriter Najeeb Nseir to a Dunya TV interviewer on October 19, 2010. Thanks to the "whisper strategy," everyone, from dramatists to state censors, is aware of and agrees upon the specific issues to be tackled in TV drama and media productions in general.

In the case of *Fawq al-Saqf*, Moubayed seemed to have initiated the whispering in the interest of a reformist project: National dialogue was presented as a solution to the Syrian crisis, but the dialogue was to be conducted under the regime's auspices and its boundaries were to be fixed from the top down, in cooperation with cultural elites.

This thinking informs the title of the *musalsal*, *Above the Ceiling*, which seemed to prom-ise a national dialogue without "red lines" or upper bounds. The "ceiling" metaphor was often reiterated by Bashar al-Asad—including in the interview he gave to Syrian TV on August 21, 2011—to suggest that media outlets already enjoyed a high degree of freedom in the country, but did not exploit it. The metaphor was ambiguous, as it specified neither who was entitled to set the standards of freedom nor where their margins lay. Asad implied that the media impose a "ceiling" upon themselves, but did not point to where this ceiling is, mean-ing that the media do not dare push against it. It is precisely this ambiguity that matches up with the enlightenment project of cultural elites, by definition a small group, who are deemed to have the necessary discernment to keep raising the ceiling in accordance with the times and the political opportunity. The *tanwiri* project should always look fair, transparent, and reform-minded to the audience. As *Fawq al-Saqf* director Barqawi stressed in an interview: "We nurtured a form of civilized dialogue. We don't have to present works that please one side at the expense of the other.... My goal is to invite the viewer, whatever his political orientation, to see himself and the other in the series."[7]

The Regime Wants...

The power centers inside the regime—the presidential palace, the different branches of secret police (*mukhabarat*), the various ministries—are not entirely homogeneous in outlook. They communicate, of course, but they are also capable of miscommunications, misfires, and changes of opinion. It sometimes occurs that one power center pushes forward a political project that contradicts the prerogatives of another, or even that one power center supports multiple, simultaneous, mutually contradictory projects. Despite its exceptional backdrop (the 2011 uprising), *Fawq al-Saqf* revealed a dynamic that was routine rather than exceptional: namely, the interference of several regime components in the making of TV drama, with each power center pursuing its own agenda, or more than one agenda, at the same time.

It is instructive here to flash back to 2001, the first full year of Bashar al-Asad's presidency and the inaugural season of *Spotlight*. Touted by the offical press as breaking taboos, *Spotlight* dealt with such sensitive topics as corruption and the abuses of the *mukhabarat*. It initially enjoyed the open support of Bashar al-Asad himself, lending credence to the ambient hopes at the time that the new president was indeed reform-minded. "*Spotlight* was born in the atmosphere of the 'Damascus spring' and is the direct expression of Bashar al-Asad's first phase," said the director of its first season, Laith Hajjo. But the serial nonetheless ran afoul of the Viewing Committee at Syrian TV and its episodes were partly redacted before going on the air. "Eighty percent of *Spotlight* was shot this way," said Adib Kheir at the Copenhagen seminar. "Somebody gives his blessing for a project, then it goes into production and the troubles begin." It was only following the palace's direct intervention that the *musalsal* was finally broadcast. Some of its sketches were indeed bold. Former vice president 'Abd al-Halim Khaddam was reportedly livid after one mocking episode seemed to discourage foreign investment.[8] But Khaddam did not succeed in stopping *Spotlight* from being aired, as the presidential palace held the balance of power at the time, and placed a priority on presenting a reformist face.

Fawq al-Saqf lacked the protective atmosphere of the "Damascus spring," however, and its problems with the censor began even earlier than its broadcast, starting with the very title of the production. Originally, the serial was to be called *al-Sha'b Yurid...* (The People Want...), part one of the anti-regime couplet then echoing in Arab capital after Arab capital. That was vetoed. The Viewing Committee was reported to have rejected several episodes as well, only to reverse itself when the palace interceded with authorization. While the serial was being broadcast, 'Azzam recounted, "different parties" lodged complaints and "other official corners," namely the security services, placed personal phone calls to Syrian TV personnel in order to exert pressure for cancellation. *Fawq al-Saqf* had become a big headache for the channel, which first dropped the promo spots and then made the decision to halt the broadcasts. Ma'an Haydar, director-general of Syrian TV, cited non-completion of filming as the reason for stopping the serial, promising to rebroadcast every episode once they were all ready.[9] "The reaction of the palace was silence, which basically meant agreement to interrupt the broadcast," says 'Azzam.

At the time that *Fawq al-Saqf* aired, the balance of power had probably shifted to the intelligence services and the palace's *tanwiri* project yielded to the security-first mindset. Or, perhaps better, the palace itself had placed the *tanwiri* project on hold in order to facilitate the security project in a period of unrest.

The state-run media outlets were stuck in the middle of these intra-regime battles, unwilling or unable to take responsibility for what they were airing, and compelled to abide by different and sometimes contradictory orders. Syrian TV officials initially chose the low-profile approach of declining to promote or advertise the *musalsal* so as not to be read as supporting one faction of the regime over another. In a situation so slippery, the eventual decision to postpone the *musalsal* was the only way not to anger anyone, as outright cancellation might conceivably have done. In the end, however, postponement was akin to cancellation.

Personal Interventions

The shift in the balance of power among the power centers of the Syrian regime was apparent as well in the different fates of two TV dramas produced in 2010 and 2011 by the same director, the well-known Najdat Anzour. In 2010, Anzour penned *Ma Malakat Aymanukum* (Those Whom Your Right Hand Possesses), a *musalsal* that treated Islam in contemporary Syria. The script condemned religious extremism, as manifested in suicide bombings or violence against women, and exalted the freedom, tolerance, and self-determination to be found in piety when properly understood. This approach was in keeping with the regime's long-time advocacy of secular politics in order to protect Syria's religious minorities while at the same time proving itself religious enough not to offend the country's conservative Sunni majority. Here again, cultural production and official discourse converged in a *tanwiri* project. *Ma Malakat Aymanukum*'s script passed through the initial stages of state approval.

But then, prior to broadcast, the viewing committee sent it to the Ministry of Information for further examination. One of the points of contention was the serial's title, taken from a Qur'anic verse that might be read to suggest male ownership of women. The phrase "*ma malakat aymanukum*" appears in the Qur'an fourteen times, and generally refers to slaves. The *sura* from which the title was taken prohibits sexual intercourse with married women, except "those whom your right hand possesses." Given the delicacy of the matter, the Ministry of Information, which normally has the final word, decided to ask the advice of the Ministry of Religious Endowments. Behind the scenes, meanwhile, another power broker was reportedly very annoyed by the serial—Muhammad Hamsho, a businessman close to Bashar's brother Mahir, commander of the Fourth Armored Division that is the core of the security forces. *Ma Malakat Aymanukum* featured a corrupt entrepreneur who bore more than a passing resemblance to Hamsho, down to details like running for election and opening a TV production business. Anzour never explicitly named Hamsho as an opponent of his series, speaking merely of "people with interests" and "people bothered by the *musalsal*." In any case, while the Ministry of Religious Endowments was reviewing the file, a veto of the broadcast of the *musalsal* from prominent Sunni scholar Muhammad Sa'id al-Buti forced Syrian TV to pull it off the Ramadan grid, just one day before the scheduled premiere. Disappointed, Anzour says he "made the president aware of the issue."

The former minister of culture, Riyad Na'san Agha, affirmed that he lobbied for the *musalsal*, adding that "the president himself intervened in favor of it," too. Anzour also laid emphasis upon the positive role played by Bashar al-Asad: "When I attended the meeting with artists and producers, he mentioned the *musalsal* three times and said, 'Had I not personally intervened, the *musalsal* would have been gone.' He used exactly that expression: 'Had I not personally intervened.'"

Yet the president certainly did not do the same for Anzour's 2011 TV drama offering, *Chiffon*. *Chiffon* revolved around several portraits of teenage boys and girls wrestling with questions about sex and drugs. It featured a scene where a girl protagonist, who dresses in stereotypically masculine ways and lives among men, walks toward the very conservative Sunni mosque of Abu Nour, surrounded by veiled women.

In 2010, al-Buti was forced to accept the broadcast of *Ma Malakat Aymanukum*, which he had previously rejected as religiously offensive. On April 5, 2011, with the uprising well underway, he renewed his attack on the miniseries in an interview with Syrian TV, attributing the spreading unrest to Anzour's *musalsal*. Shortly after this episode, and in response to a call from Syrian actors and directors for humanitarian aid to the besieged city of Daraa, known as "the milk statement," Anzour appeared at the forefront of producers who signed a counter-petition calling for boycotting the protesting artists in TV drama. "There was never any shortage of food or milk," he said. "It was a political statement. The authorities were dealing with armed terrorist groups."[10] Anzour's blatant rush to toe the official line might have been payback for Bashar's intervention in 2010 or a genuine commitment to the president's political project. In any case, *Chiffon* was not broadcast during Ramadan in 2011. Anzour excused the cancellation as a decision taken in the "national interest." But the incident revealed the continuous shifts of alliances within the regime. Under the palace's auspices, al-Buti had launched an Islamic religious channel, Nour. In a time of unrest, when the security project had become a top priority, the regime probably needed the Sunni scholar's support much more than that of secular cultural elites.

No Longer Torn

The relationship binding these cultural producers to the Syrian regime is quite different from what miriam cooke has described regarding a previous generation of Syrian intellectuals, who were torn between the desire to criticize the regime and the obligation to compromise with it. This generation negotiated what later became forms of "commissioned criticism." The intellectuals cooke dealth with—writers like Saadallah Wannous, Muhammad al-Maghout, and Mamdouh 'Adwan—saw themselves as engaged in a continuous struggle to widen the red lines around permissible discourse. The cultural producers involved in whispering with the state, on the other hand, are committed to dialogue with power and tend to deny the existence of censorship. Instead, they rather speak about the necessity of "artistic evaluation" of their scripts.

Unlike cooke's intellectuals, these TV dramatists do not hide their relations with the regime power centers, but show them off. They back the regime's cultural project of treating the social pathologies—corruption, gender inequality, religious extremism, illiteracy—that make up its alleged "backwardness." "Religious and social control are our real problems and at the origin of our backwardness," says Laith Hajjo. "Drama can help to solve this." The noble-sounding *tanwiri* label helps these screenwriters and producers to merge their work with the regime's own awareness campaigns, by means of the well-placed whisper. "I would say I have a *tanwiri* mission," Nseir asserted. "My works don't aim to put a mirror in front of the society. I want them to discuss issues that are dealt with in my *musalsalat* and to progress through this discussion. I don't want to describe; I want to provoke debates and drive social change." The drama makers are thus not so much complicit as they are comfortable with the powers that be.

Pleasure and comfort—derived from the social status and financial privileges the new generation of Syrian cultural producers are granted—mark the relationship between them and the various power centers inside the regime. These features have in effect replaced the agreement upon "unbelief" that, as described by Lisa Wedeen, bound politics together with cultural reproduction under Hafiz al-Asad. In the Hafiz al-Asad era, cultural producers did not believe the patent propaganda they cranked out; rather, they forged a tacit pact with the regime whereby they acted "as if" they believed it. These "shared conditions of unbelief," according to Wedeen, "actually reproduce[d] the conditions of obedience under Asad."[11] In neoliberal Syria, where TV drama makers live in greater material comfort, the regime and its allied cultural producers are closer to stakeholders in a common investment project whereby they both define what is good and advisable for Syrian society. That society, in turn, is never addressed as made up of citizens or consumers, but is rather imagined as a backward majority that should be ruled and disciplined through practices of enlightenment accessible to a select few.

Notes

1. Lisa Wedeen, *Ambiguities of Domination: Politics, Rhetoric and Symbols in Contemporary Syria* (Chicago, Ill.: University of Chicago Press, 1999), p. 88.

2. miriam cooke, *Dissident Syria: Making Oppositional Arts Official* (Durham, N.C.: Duke University Press, 2007), p. 72.

3. 'Azzam was interviewed by journalist and former censorship committee member Ibrahim al-Jabin, who related 'Azzam's remarks at the September 2011 University of Copenhagen seminar. Unless otherwise noted, all other persons quoted in this article were interviewed by the author.

4. See, for example, Sami Moubayed, "The Road to Syrian Democracy," *Huffington Post*, June 23, 2011.

5. Sami Moubayed, "What Will Post-Arab Spring Intellectuals Write About?" *Huffington Post*, December 8, 2011.

6. Donatella Della Ratta, "The 'Whisper Strategy': How Syrian Drama Makers Shape Television Fiction in the Context of Authoritarianism and Commodification," in Leif Stenberg and Christa Salamandra, eds., *Syria under Bashar al-Asad: Culture, Religion and Society* (Syracuse, N.Y.: Syracuse University Press, forthcoming).

7. '*Aks al-Sayr*, August 26, 2011.

8. Marlin Dick, "Syria Under the Spotlight," *Arab Media and Society* 3 (Fall 2007).

9. Ibid.

10. *The National* (Abu Dhabi), July 23, 2011.

11. Wedeen, *Ambiguities of Domination*, p. 92.

22. BEYOND THE FALL OF THE SYRIAN REGIME

PETER HARLING AND SARAH BIRKE

For over a year, Syrians have endured what has become the most tragic, far-reaching, and uncertain episode of the Arab uprisings. Since protesters first took to the streets in towns and villages across the country in March 2011, they have paid an exorbitant price in a domestic crisis that has become intertwined with a strategic struggle over the future of Syria.

The regime of Bashar al-Asad has fought its citizens in an unsuccessful attempt to put down any serious challenge to its four-decade rule, leaving several thousand dead. Many more languish in jail. The regime has polarized the population, rallying its supporters by decrying the protesters as saboteurs, Islamists, and part of a foreign conspiracy. In order to shore up its own ranks, it has played on the fears of the 'Alawi minority from which the ruling family hails, lending the conflict sectarian overtones. All these measures pushed a growing number of young men on the street—and a small but steady stream of army defectors—to put up an armed response, while impelling large sections of the opposition to seek financial, political, and military help from abroad. Loyalist units have taken considerable casualties from the armed rebels, and the regime has hit back with disproportionate force.

Events have aided the regime in its attempt to dismiss the protest movement and further tip the balance from nominal reform to escalating repression, fueling a vicious cycle that has turned sporadic clashes into a nascent civil war. In a sense, the regime may already have won: By pushing frustrated protesters to take up arms and the international community to offer them support, it is succeeding in disfiguring what it saw as the greatest threat to its rule, namely the grassroots and mostly peaceful protest movement that demanded profound change. In another sense, the regime may already have lost: By treating too broad a cross-section of the Syrian people as the enemy, and giving foreign adversaries justification to act, it seems to have forged against itself a coalition too big to defeat. At a minimum, Bashar al-Asad has reversed his father's legacy: Through tenacious diplomacy over three decades (from his takeover in 1970 to his death in 2000), Hafiz al-Asad made Syria, formerly a prize in the regional strategic game, a player in its own right. In less than a year, Bashar's obduracy has done the opposite, turning actor into arena.

At the start of February 2012, the regime stepped up its assault by using heavy weapons against rebellious neighborhoods of Homs, the third-largest city in Syria and the most religiously mixed one to become a hub of the uprising. The escalation was bolstered by Russia and China, which on February 4 blocked the Arab League-inspired, Western-backed attempts to pass a resolution at the UN Security Council condemning the violence and suggesting a plan for a negotiated solution by which Asad would hand over power to a deputy, who would form a unity government ahead of elections. The assumption in Moscow, which fears instability and views the struggle in Syria as a contest with the West, is that the regime will succeed in defeating both the ongoing protest movement and the emerging insurgency. In so doing, runs Russian reasoning, Syria's regime will reassert its control over the country and compel at least significant parts of the opposition to negotiate on its own terms—preferably in Moscow.

Losing Control

This outcome seems unlikely. Behind all the bloody, one-off battles lies a picture of this country of twenty-three million slipping out of the regime's control. Over a period of eighteen months, the regime altogether failed to cow protesters through its mixture of violent intimidation and offers of paltry reforms.

Time and time again, the regime has proven its promises to reform, already grudging and tardy, to be largely empty as well. The lifting of emergency law in April 2011, for example, did not stop the shooting or arbitrary detention of protesters. The April 2012 ceasefire agreement brokered by Kofi Annan proved equally toothless as the army and the security services continued to battle opposition forces daily. Any measure that could jeopardize the ruling clique's unaccountable reign is out of the question. What can be changed is what matters least. The Baath Party's role will certainly decrease, but Syria is a one-party state no longer: It is a state of a few families and multiple security services, who have long used resistance to US imperialism and Israeli occupation as a substitute for clear political vision. Participation in the legislative branch of government will be opened to the tamest of oppositions and perhaps in the cabinet as well; real decision-making happens in the presidential palace, anyway. The regime has set the ceiling on reforms low. Its calls for "dialogue" are designed only to legitimize this course of action.

Rather than reform, the regime's default setting has been to push society to the brink. As soon as protests started, security agents hung posters warning of sectarian strife. State media showed staged footage of arms being found in a mosque in Daraa, the southern city where protests first broke out, and warned that a sit-in in Homs on April 18, 2011 was an attempt to erect a mini-caliphate. This manipulation of Syrians meant the regime was confident that the threat of civil war would force citizens and outside players alike to agree on preserving the existing power structure as the only bulwark against collapse. In an October 2011 interview, Asad reiterated threats of an "earthquake" and "ten Afghanistans" in the region. The regime's narrative boils down to, "*Après moi le deluge.*"

It is doubtful that this blackmail will work. All too many Syrians have buried friends killed during protests (or, for that matter, funerals, which routinely come under fire), or have been shuffled through the regime's ghastly prisons (which consistently fail to break them, radicalizing them instead), or have watched their homes destroyed and looted. They say they will not stop, whatever the cost—and the costs are already huge. Having weakened its home front beyond repair, the regime is also vulnerable to growing pressure from abroad. In particular, the United States and Saudi Arabia, who have long feuded with Syria over its role as a linchpin of Iranian influence, have been given an opportunity to change the Syrian regime that they could never have dreamed of.

The regime may win a pyrrhic victory, by bringing about a civil war that will destroy its own structures, wreck the country, and suck in the outside world. It would be a sad end for the most surprising explosion of empowerment of the Arab spring. As protest roiled Tunisia, Egypt, and Libya in 2011, many, including Syrians themselves, who saw the population as depoliticized, thought an uprising would not come. But it did: When a handful of schoolchildren in Daraa were detained and tortured for scrawling graffiti calling for the end of the regime, protesters took to the streets from Daraa to Idlib in the northwest, from the Mediterranean coast to eastern Dayr al-Zawr, and in tiny towns and villages from the sandy desert to the fertile plains. Calls for "toppling the regime" saw their meaning evolve from "reforming the system" to "executing the president," as they were met with ever more violence. The hope that the regime could offer any future was chipped away and then shattered.

Many see Syria, with its wealth of ethnicities and sects surrounding a Sunni Arab majority, as doomed to fail; parallels with fractious Iraq and Lebanon, which suffered long years of civil war, are frequently drawn. Yet there is reason to think that, given the chance, Syrian society could survive the family-based regime that has ruled it since Hafiz al-Asad came to power in a bloodless coup in 1970. All depends on whether society will surrender to, or face up to, its own demons, as a deep political crisis devolves into a no less profound social predicament.

The Struggle

The struggle over Syria pits two symmetrical narratives against each other. For the regime, its supporters, and its allies, Syria's is an immature, if not disease-ridden society. They posit—with evidence both real and invented, and generally blown out of proportion—that Syrian society shows sectarian, fundamentalist, violent, and seditious proclivities that can be contained only by a ruthless power structure. Remove Bashar al-Asad, and the alternative is either civil war or the hegemony of Islamists beholden to Turkey and the Gulf and sold out to the West. Regime loyalists argue that society is not ready for change and, in fact, deserves no better than its present shackling. Hizballah and Iran, rather than cultivate popular support to ensure enduring influence, have placed all their chips on the regime's ability to crush what, early on, they chose to see overwhelmingly through the lens of foreign conspiracy.

The regime's opponents, by contrast, posit that any and all change is desirable, given the regime's own nature. Over its four decades in power, the Asad dynasty has increasingly treated the country as family property, plundering its wealth for redistribution to narrowing circles of cronies. In line with divide-and-rule traditions inherited from colonialism, the regime has cynically strengthened its grip by nurturing fractures within society, keeping state institutions weak for fear they might underpin genuine national sentiment, and setting up a security apparatus heavily staffed with members of one minority, the 'Alawi community. It has suppressed dissent with at times extreme brutality, as typified by the 1982 shelling of Hama, which left many thousands dead. Regime opponents argue that, without Bashar al-Asad, Syria will finally be free to express its stifled economic potential, its natural communal harmony and its aspiration to an open, democratic political system. For their part,

Gulf states and the West see in regime change a solution to all problems, not necessarily within Syria itself, but throughout the region: At last, Hizballah, the Lebanese resistance movement that relies on Syria as a transit route for weapons, would be neutralized, Iran badly weakened and the so-called moderate Arab states empowered.

Although the two narratives appear mutually exclusive, they both hold a measure of truth. The regime and the opposition in exile, who accuse the other of being the mother of all ills, have each tended to conform to stereotype.

Throughout the crisis, the regime has proven more sectarian, unaccountable, and vicious than ever. Obsessed with the challenge posed by peaceful protests, its *mukhabarat* security services—none of whose members have been put on trial as promised—have hunted non-violent progressive activists, often with more zeal than shown toward criminal gangs and armed groups. The *mukhabarat* have recruited thugs and criminals—the more extreme, venal, and subservient elements of society—into an army of proxies known across the country as *shabbiha*, a term that used to specifically refer to thugs in Latakia related to the ruling clan who made a living smuggling. It has tried to intimidate protesters through gruesome tactics. An emblematic case for the opposition is Hamza al-Khatib, a fourteen-year old from Daraa whose battered and castrated corpse was returned to his family a month after he was taken. (The regime never denied the boy had been arrested and killed, but had forensic experts explain on television that he was in fact a professional rapist operating within a jihadi network.) Asad has gradually shed all pretense of being a national leader, speaking instead as the head of one camp determined to vanquish the other.

For its part, the Syrian National Council (SNC), the main opposition group that is composed mostly of exiles, has failed to offer an inspiring alternative since it was formed in September 2011. Its mainly unknown and inexperienced members have done little to counteract the regime's propaganda. Unable to agree on any positive political platform, the SNC has refused any negotiation with the regime and called for "international intervention" that is conveniently left undefined, leaving their anxieties the many Syrians who simultaneously loathe the regime, dread foreign interference and panic at the idea of a high-risk transition. It has estranged, among others, Kurdish factions, who fear a Turkish agenda, and petrified Syrians distrustful of Qatari and Saudi influence. It has most notably failed to reach out to the 'Alawis, many of whom are poor and disgruntled but afraid to change sides lest they suffer a backlash due to their association with the security forces and army units responsible for much of the violence. By abandoning all these people to their dark forebodings, the SNC's members have missed an opportunity to hasten the decline of the regime and ward off civil strife in the event of Bashar's fall. On the international level, the SNC has displayed political naïveté by putting all its energy into lobbying for support from Turkey, the Gulf monarchies, and the West, all of whom are already sympathetic, while ignoring and alienating the regime's allies.

Social Shifts

What does not fit any prior stereotype is the behavior of Syrian society. It certainly is fissiparous, but not along predictable lines. Past uprisings—the Muslim Brother-led insurgency in the late 1970s and early 1980s, the Druze *intifada* of 2000 and the Kurdish rebellion of

2004—raised suspicions in society at large for their communal nature. In contrast, today's protest movement is surprisingly broad-based and cross-cutting. Many an 'Alawi, especially among intellectuals and simple villagers, resents how his or her community has been taken hostage by the regime. The Druze are split somewhere down the middle. Christians, who are geographically dispersed, adopt remarkably different viewpoints depending on how much they see of the security services' abuse on the ground. Those in Damascus and Aleppo have generally rallied to the regime's side, but in many other areas Christians at least sympathize with protesters. Ismailis, based in the town of Salamiyya, were among the first to join the opposition. And Sunni Arabs, of course, are not all against Bashar; the Shawaya tribes in the northeast, to cite one example, tend to be supportive.

Nor is a communal prism the only one through which the conflict should be seen. Although it started off as an underclass and provincial phenomenon in the Hawran plain, the protest movement has crossed socio-economic boundaries, drawing in doctors, engineers, and teachers. It has spread to the capital, where flash demonstrations stand in for the large rallies that would take place were it not for massive security deployments. The business establishment, whose interests initially made for a cautious, conservative stance, has realized the regime is compromising them: Most—even within crony capitalist circles—have long been donating money to the opposition. Fault lines have appeared in less likely places still. Within the same family, older generations are more likely than the youth to cling to the devil they know. Couples are sometimes torn; some women are prone to prefer stability and dialogue, while others push the limits of dissent beyond what their husbands are inclined to do.

The uprising has caused parts of Syrian society, which had long been apathetic and fragmented, to undergo a sort of renaissance. Protesters have been extraordinarily dedicated and creative. They have set up committees to collect and distribute money and document individual deaths with a fastidious sense of duty. In the midst of bloodshed, they have expanded their inventory of smart slogans and eye-catching posters, chanted in support of besieged cities in different areas of the country, stitched together new flags, and spoofed the regime in video and animation. Areas such as Daraya, close to Damascus, have become known for their acts of civil resistance. Ghiyath Matar, a young activist who was later killed under torture, had ordered roses and water to hand out to soldiers and security forces sent to police the area.

Precisely because the regime has sought to exploit every source of possible strife, its opponents have had to work hard to contain the more thuggish, sectarian, and fundamentalist strands in their midst. Their efforts are what have kept society together, despite a growing and worrying pattern of confessional, criminal, and revenge-inspired violence. The protest movement would have degenerated into chaos long ago if it were not for an overriding desire among the majority of its members to recover their country, their dignity, and their destiny, rather than forfeit them.

There is a distinctly Syrian character to the crisis. Unlike Libyans, who in a matter of hours defected en masse, took up arms and called upon the outside world to step in, Syrians took months to resort to weapons or cry out for international intervention. Unlike Egypt, where revolution was a sublime but somewhat shallow moment of grace, the Syrian uprising has been a long, hard slog: The protest movement has gradually built itself up, studied the regime's every move and mapped out the country to the extent that small towns such as Binnish in the northwest are now known to all.

Alongside actual demonstrations, an expansive albeit largely invisible civil society has emerged to render them possible, by offering numerous forms of support. Businessmen have donated money and food; doctors sneak out medicines from hospitals and man field clinics in the most violence-ridden areas; religious leaders, by and large, try to keep a lid on sectarianism and violence. Over the course of the uprising, Syrians have articulated a now deeply rooted culture of dissent and developed sometimes sophisticated forms of self-rule by setting up local councils: Homs, which is also home to unruly armed groups, has developed a revolutionary council with an eleven-member executive that presides over committees responsible for different aspects of the crisis, from interacting with the media to procuring medical supplies. Within revolting communities there is a greater sense of purpose, solidarity, and national unity than at any time in recent Syrian history.

Even the growing insurgency makes for an interesting paradox: Proliferating armed groups derive their popular legitimacy from the need to protect peaceful protests militarily. No mad dash to the arsenal, the armament in most places has proceeded in stages. People first purchased weapons to keep in the house for self-defense in the event of raids by security forces. Small groups of armed men then went out with protesters to respond if the security forces started to shoot at them. Over time, the action has transformed from pure defense into a more aggressive modus operandi—targeting government checkpoints, regime proxies and informants, military convoys, and security facilities. Bombings have become more frequent, though there are credible allegations that the regime has orchestrated some of the blasts. Tit-for-tat sectarian killings occur all too frequently in central Syria. But much of the violence, up to this point, has been not random but constrained by a mandate of sorts, as it takes protecting the protests and civilians as the base for action.

Troubling Times Ahead

Of course, the foregoing is the better part of the story. On both sides, thugs and criminals are exploiting the struggle as a vehicle for social promotion, a means of enrichment, and an outlet for sectarian hatred. This statement is true of regime forces, whose fallacious claim to stand for law and order is disproved all too often by their heinous behavior, as it is of some armed groups fighting them under the umbrella of the "Free Syrian Army," a motley assortment of local vigilantes. The recruits into this "Army" range from fathers defending their families to bereaved young men to defectors fighting for their lives, but its ranks are not devoid of fundamentalist militants and unreconstructed villains. The latter elements have not been predominant, although they are all that the regime, its supporters, and its allies want to see. The logic is self-evident: The ruling elite, having little good to offer, is hell-bent on proving that anything else to emerge from Syrian society can only be much worse. Thus the almost hysterical cult of Bashar, whose gross mishandling of this crisis matters not to his supporters: He alone can save this society from itself.

But Syrian society is better prepared to manage a transition than it would have been had the power structure collapsed early on. It has been forced into learning how to organize itself to prevent its own collapse. The regime's divide-and-rule tactics have been a key unifying factor for large swathes of society, which to survive has had to reach across geographic, communal, and socio-economic boundaries. Were the revolutionaries to be successful, however, that source of unity would disappear, leaving them disoriented. As elsewhere in the region, "the fall of the regime" is a remedy for the depressing impasse that ruling elites lock their societies into, not a blueprint for successful change.

Spurred on by Iran and Hizballah and bolstered by Russian support, while facing an increasingly potent insurgency backed—politically if not militarily—from abroad, the chances are that the regime will neither survive nor "fall," but gradually erode and mutate into militias fighting an all-out civil war. But assuming the power structure does give way before that corner is turned, there are at least three threats that could quickly derail a political transition.

The first is the reality of Bashar's power base, which has narrowed spectacularly but remains an incontrovertible fact on the ground. Just as the regime dismisses the protest movement with the spurious argument that a majority has not taken to the streets (as if any country around the world had ever witnessed half its people on the march), the regime's opponents berate its supporters as a minority of delusional, criminal, treacherous citizens. The fact is that, just as the regime cannot survive this crisis by ignoring the millions mobilized against it, so a transition cannot succeed while overlooking the millions—security officers, proxies, and regular people—who have thrown in their lot with Bashar. Short of protection for the people most exposed to retribution, notably among the 'Alawis, a genuine reconciliation mechanism, an effective transitional justice process and a thorough but smooth overhaul of the security services, it could all go very wrong.

Secondly, judging by the SNC's performance, there is cause for concern if it were to play a key role in such a transition. Its leading members, hindered by personal rivalries, unable to formulate clear political positions for fear of implosion, and seemingly consumed with having a spot in the limelight, may fall back on sectarian apportionment as the only consensual criterion for power sharing. Syrians on the street have made clear that they see the SNC's legitimacy as based on their ability to lobby for diplomatic pressure and see their mandate as stretching no further, but the outside world's quest for a ready-made "alternative," and the prevailing assumption that pluralist societies in the Middle East are condemned to such evolution, could prove to be Syria's undoing. A political process including the SNC, but built primarily around locally led organizations, along with technocrats and businessmen, would have more legitimacy and a greater chance of success.

Finally, as increasingly desperate protesters call for help, there is a danger that the outside world will make matters worse as it plays at being savior. Calls for aid are somewhat worse than a pact with the devil: They entail pacts with many devils that do not agree on much. The Gulf monarchies, Iraq, Turkey, Russia, the US, Iran, and others all see geostrategic stakes in the fate of the Asad regime. The greater their involvement, the less Syrians will remain in control of their destiny. Crying out for foreign intervention of any kind, to bring this emergency to an end at any cost, is more than understandable coming from ordinary citizens subjected to extreme forms of regime violence. Exiled opposition figures who pose as national leaders have no excuse for behaving likewise, when what is needed is a cool-headed, careful calibration of what type of outside "help" would do the minimum of harm.

Close to home, another Middle Eastern experience—Iraq—serves as an example on all three fronts. A political process excluding even a relatively small minority within Iraqi society led to a collective disaster. A group of returning exiles, without a social base but enjoying international support as the only visible, pre-existing "alternative," quickly took over the transition and agreed only on splitting up power among themselves on the basis of a communal calculus. Their division of the spoils gradually contaminated the entire polity, and ultimately led to civil war. And the US, presiding over this tragedy, succeeded only in turning Iraq into a parody of itself, a country that now fits every sectarian and troubled stereotype the occupying power initially saw in it.

All told, on a domestic level Syria has entered a struggle to bring its post-colonial era to a close. It is not simply about toppling a "regime" but about uprooting a "system"— the Arabic word *nizam* conveniently evoking both notions. The current system is based on keeping Syrians hostage to communal divisions and regional power plays. Indeed, the regime's residual legitimacy derives entirely from playing indigenous communities and foreign powers off each other, at the expense of genuine state building and accountable leadership. Prior attempts at breaking with the legacy of colonialism, in the revolutionary bustle of the mid-twentieth century, failed, grounded as they were in narrow politicized elites and military circles. What is different today is the awakening of a broad popular movement, motivated less by parochial interests and grand ideologies than by a sense of wholesale dispossession of their wealth, dignity, and destiny.

This awakening, in a sense, is precisely what the regime has been fighting. Although foreign interference is a fact, there is less a conspiracy in Syria than a society on the move, headed along a path that the regime simply will not follow. The road ahead is a dangerous one, and the chances are real that it will lead Syria, and the region, into the maze of civil war. But for all too many Syrians there is no going back. The regime was given a year to stake out a safer way forward, but has clung ever more fiercely to its old narrative, ultimately recasting itself as a historical cul-de-sac.

PART FIVE

BAHRAIN

On February 14, 2011, in the wake of events in Tunisia and Egypt, Bahraini demonstrators massed at the Pearl Roundabout at the edge of the capital city of Manama and demanded economic and political reforms. They did not call on that day for the ouster of King Hamad bin Isa Al Khalifa, but the fact that they were protesting on the anniversary of the king's decade-old reform project, the National Action Charter, sent a clear message. On the third night of the occupation of the roundabout, security forces attacked the encampment, killing four. The violence radicalized protesters and demonstrations spread across the island.

Public opposition to the rule of the Al Khalifa has existed since the early years of the British mandate government in the 1890s. The political opposition became closely linked with organized labor in the burgeoning petroleum industry beginning in the 1930s. In 1965, when hundreds of Bahrain Petroleum Company workers were fired, the General Trade Union led an uprising against the company and British colonial management that lasted for over a month before it succumbed to the security forces' campaign of arrests and killings. At the time of Bahrain's independence in 1971, there was thus an established, broad-based political opposition which the monarchy sought to blunt with various initiatives, such as establishment of a partially elected legislative body in 1973. Despite its limited powers, the assembly proved to be a thorn in the side of the regime. It was abolished in 1975 and the two-year-old constitution suspended.

Petition signings, demonstrations, and skirmishes continued sporadically during the 1970s and 1980s. All were met with increasing brutal suppression by the Bahrain Defense Forces and the Security and Intelligence Services, the rechristened colonial-era intelligence agency. In the crackdown following the constitution's abrogation, much of the opposition leadership was imprisoned and forcibly exiled. This period of repression altered the character of the opposition, which had been secular and whose parties had mixed Sunni and Shi'i membership. As these organs were dismantled, opposition politics devolved to leaders of Bahrain's highly segregated "villages"—now more like neighborhoods of metropolitan Manama—and focused on the grievances of the Shi'i majority against the Sunni-dominated state and armed forces.

Bahrain is the smallest of the Arab Gulf states and the most densely populated with 1.25 million inhabitants. A significant proportion of this population (about 60 percent) are immigrants, as in other Arab Gulf countries. Bahrain's native population, however, is about two-thirds Shi'i, while in Saudi Arabia and Kuwait the Shi'a are a minority. Part of the Al Khalifa's strategy for maintaining power has been to manipulate sectarian tensions among the population. The strategy involves two prongs. One is that government largesse, such as civil service jobs, business contracts, housing, and other forms of welfare, is preferentially distributed to the Sunni population. Indeed, Bahrain's non-migrant population is the most economically stratified in the region. The other is to try to boost the Sunni population through the extensive use of migrant labor. Bahrain's military and police have effectively barred native Shi'a from employment, instead recruiting and naturalizing personnel from other Arab states and Pakistan. All the while, the unemployment rate of Shi'i males is considerably higher than that of Sunnis. The Al Khalifa have reasoned that as long as a large enough minority of the population, including the business elite and the armed forces, feels beholden to the regime, the complaints of the Shi'i majority will not pose a serious threat to the monarchy's legitimacy.

The 1990s saw another outbreak of protests against the regime's systematic sectarian discrimination and the continuing suspension of parliamentary democracy. The unrest lasted for several years, during which thousands were arrested, many of whom were tortured by the security services. King Hamad, who succeeded his father, Isa bin Salman Al Khalifa, in 1999, again sought to quell popular opposition by declaring an amnesty, abrogating some of the most repressive laws, and introducing a quasi-constitution in the form of the Bahrain National Action Charter. The Charter created a tightly controlled parliament whose lower house was elected from gerrymandered districts to return disproportionate Sunni representation and whose upper house was appointed by the king. The largest Shi'i political grouping, al-Wifaq, boycotted the first elections in 2002, but ran in the 2006 poll and won 45 percent of the seats. Al-Wifaq's representatives resigned in February 2011 to protest the state's violence against peaceful demonstrators.

The uprising that began in February 2011 morphed in the following weeks into a more radical social protest movement. The police persecution, the unchecked violence of *baltaji-yya* (mercenary thugs), and the successes of Tunis and Cairo all fed the revolt. Unlicensed protest groups began to develop individual initiatives, leaving the registered opposition groups behind. On March 11, 2011, a demonstration outside the palace demanded the end of Al Khalifa rule and the creation of a Bahraini republic.

The protesters had crossed a red line in Bahraini politics, and the regime invited Saudi Arabian and Emirati troops into the country just a few days later. The Saudi monarchy was particularly nervous about the rise of Shi'i militancy so close to its own large Shi'i minority in the Eastern Province, the center of the country's oil industry. As foreign troops marched into Bahrain, King Hamad declared a state of emergency and Bahraini security personnel violently cleared the camp at Pearl Roundabout. Attacks on protesters spread to the clinics, hospitals, and even ambulances that treated the wounded. In June 2012, several doctors from Salmaniyya Hospital were sentenced to prison for crimes against the state in a move widely viewed as retribution for their care for protesters and criticism of state violence. In addition to the support of the other Gulf monarchies, the Al Khalifa enjoyed quieter backing from the United States, whose military oversight of the Persian Gulf is based in Manama.

In the early weeks of protests, the resounding, cross-sectarian message was for fair and democratic governance. As the violence ground on, however, the regime stoked fears of foreign (mainly Iranian) plots that divided Bahrainis once again along sectarian lines. The prospects for a national dialogue between the government and opposition factions are threatened by antagonism between various opposition groups (Shi'i and Sunni) and the resistance of hardline members of the Al Khalifa.

23. A REVOLUTION PAUSED IN BAHRAIN

CORTNI KERR AND TOBY JONES

An uncertain calm settled over the small island kingdom of Bahrain at the end of February 2011. The wave of peaceful pro-democracy protests from February 14-17 culminated in bloodshed, including the brutal murder of seven activists, some of whom were asleep in tents, by the armed forces. On orders from above, the army withdrew from the round-about on the outskirts of the capital of Manama where the protests were centered, and after the seven deaths it observed calls for restraint. Thousands of jubilant protesters seized the moment to reoccupy the roundabout, the now infamous Pearl Circle. In commemoration of the dead, the demonstrators renamed it Martyrs' Circle.

The mood in the circle was buoyant, even carnivalesque. It was also dead serious, for the thousands of encamped demonstrators demanded nothing short of fundamental change to the kingdom's autocratic political order. The crown prince, Salman bin Hamad Al Khalifa, issued a bland call for healing and national dialogue. The country's formal opposition may have been tempted by the prospect of realizing at least some of its long-established demands for reform. But the wounds from the direct assault at dawn on February 17 were deep. Several prominent banners in Martyrs' Circle displayed the pledge, "No dialogue with those who killed us in cold blood." Chants echoed: "We will sit here until the fall of the regime!" The fault lines that had long divided rulers and subjects in Bahrain widened due to the carnage.

On February 21, meanwhile, the regime summoned tens of thousands of supporters (state television wildly claimed three hundred thousand) to rally behind it outside a large Sunni mosque, al-Fatih, in Manama. The choice of a Sunni mosque was deliberate; the Al Khalifa, themselves Sunni, have a history of playing sectarian politics to divide and rule the population, which has a Shi'i majority. The pro-democracy protesters, for their part, maintained from the start that their cause was national. Their slogans explicitly appealed to cross-sectarian solidarity. On February 22, more than one hundred thousand protesters streamed into the streets, answering a call from the opposition groups, and marched nearly two miles from a mall to the roundabout. State TV ignored them, re-running footage of the previous day's pro-monarchy gathering.

The killing had ended temporarily, but the cold peace between the regime and the dis-sidents did not last. Bahrain's revolution is not over, but its outcome is far from decided.

Toward Defiance

At the heart of the uncertainty is the question of whether the royal family can muster the political will to see through substantive political reform at long last. On February 20, 2011 the crown prince acknowledged the "clear messages from the Bahraini people...about the need for reforms," though what the changes might be, he did not say. The majority of Bahrainis greeted his vague words with pronounced cynicism, and with good reason, for they know the country had been down the road of false promises before. In 2000 and 2001 then Emir Hamad (he later declared himself king) promised sweeping liberal reforms that would, in essence, transform Bahrain from an absolute into a constitutional monarchy. The promises proved illusory. Instead, Hamad and his cronies set up a sham bicameral parliamentary system, decreed a constitution that consolidated power in the hands of the elites and institutionalized discrimination against the island's majority Shi'i population. The king appointed a consultative council that can block the elected lower house's legislation. Electoral districts were hopelessly gerrymandered to minimize Shi'i representation.

Popular hostility to the political status quo continued to simmer, with occasional eruptions. Although the Shi'a have suffered the most from the regime's intransigence, frustrations cut across sectarian lines. Between 2000 and 2011, an organized opposition, consisting of a handful of formal political societies (actual parties are illegal), struggled to generate enough pressure on the regime to correct its course. The two most prominent societies, the Shi'i Islamist grouping al-Wifaq and the left-leaning, non-sectarian Wa'ad, led the charge, boycotting the 2002 elections and generally refusing to give the system a stamp of legitimacy. But something changed in 2006. The opposition ended its boycott, ran for Parliament, and vowed to change the system from within. By all accounts, the opposition deputies agitated repeatedly for structural changes, but their incorporation into the system rendered them wholly ineffective.

The opposition's decision to end the boycott, meanwhile, split its social and political base. Alternative centers of dissent emerged in 2005 and 2006, notably the Haqq Movement for Liberty and Democracy. Led by charismatic figures like Hasan Mushayma', 'Isa al-Jawdar, and 'Abd al-Jalil Singace, Haqq rejected participation in elections and called for increased grassroots organizing, up to and including civil disobedience, and reached out to Western governments. With this bold program, Haqq siphoned off a considerable amount of supporters from al-Wifaq and Wa'ad, eventually boasting a significant following in both the Shi'i and Sunni communities. Equally important was the intensification of efforts by a network of young, energetic, and devoted human rights activists, who drew attention to the grievances of the Shi'a, in particular. At the heart of this network was the Bahrain Center for Human Rights, headed by 'Abd al-Hadi al-Khawaja and Nabeel Rajab. Using the language of human rights, al-Khawaja and Rajab carved out influential political roles as well, inspiring younger Bahrainis to get involved in civic affairs and instructing them in how to build potent grassroots organizations.

Haqq and the human rights activists also assumed a decidedly more defiant stance against the regime and its excesses than the established opposition. In doing so they distinguished but also separated themselves from the safety of numbers. Beginning in earnest in 2005 and 2006, the organizations began to mount regular peaceful demonstrations, in which knots of young activists would take to the streets demanding the amelioration of various complaints, from poor housing to under-employment among Shi'i youth to the torture that was credibly reported in the kingdom's jails. The new opposition leaders also became increasingly provocative in their public statements, regularly offering direct criticism of the Al Khalifa. They paid a heavy price. Al-Khawaja and Mushayma' were arrested multiple times. Singace was abducted by the security services in August 2010, imprisoned, tortured, and accused of terrorism and plotting to overthrow the government. The same accusations were leveled at Mushayma', who went into exile in London.

The rise of the new Bahraini opposition was met with a surge of regime brutality. From 2005 to 2010, the security forces routinely used tear gas and rubber bullets in their attacks to disperse demonstrations. To preempt refusal of orders by the police, the regime stepped up its long-standing practice of recruiting foreigners as officers, including non-Bahraini Arabs and Pakistanis. Not coincidentally, the opposition says, the recruits tended to be Sunni. A cycle of state violence and opposition recrimination was firmly entrenched by 2010. Their increasingly vicious treatment by the state garnered the younger activist generation considerable credibility with the population. Where al-Wifaq and Wa'ad pliantly sought influence in the corrupt halls of power, Haqq and the human rights groups were resilient in their insubordination. It became increasingly clear that the country's political future would be decided in the streets.

Point of No Return

Neither Haqq nor the Bahrain Center for Human Rights was entirely responsible for drumming up the massive February 2011 demonstrations, but the power of their example should not be understated. Many of these organizations' grassroots activists, furthermore, were directly involved in the February 14 "day of rage" that kicked off the series of protests, both through social media like Twitter and Facebook, and also through hands-on planning on the ground.

February 14, 2011 was the tenth anniversary of the publication of the National Action Charter, the document that contained King Hamad's original blueprint for reform. Ahead of the protest, and cognizant of the fates of autocrats in Tunisia and Egypt, Hamad announced that every Bahraini family would receive a lump-sum payment of 1,000 Bahraini dinars (approximately $2,650). Such royal largesse was not uncommon in the Gulf's richer and less populous petro-princedoms, but in Bahrain it was previously unheard of. The handout, however, did not placate the protest movement's organizers. Prior to February 14, these young men and women had laid out their demands on various social media platforms. They called for constitutional reform, as well as freedom. They demanded genuinely free and fair elections, a consultative council representative of the citizens, the release of political prisoners, and an end to corruption, torture and "political naturalization," a term referring to the practice of granting foreign police recruits citizenship. As one writer summed up the movement's program, "We do not want to overthrow the regime, as many imagine, and we do not want to gain control of the government. We do not want chairs and seats here or there. We want to be a people living with dignity and rights."

Encouraged by the Internet-savvy youth, tens of thousands of Bahrainis attended demonstrations in Manama and villages across the country. In most places, the police attempted to halt the proceedings with physical force, but the participants refused to disperse, initiating a violent game of cat and mouse. Police shut down main roads to block access to potential assembly points, and in the places where demonstrators still managed to gather, riot police stood at the ready with guns, batons, and tear gas. February 14 marked the first fatal mistake of the regime: the death of twenty-seven-year-old 'Ali 'Abd al-Hadi Mushayma'.

A large crowd convened early the following morning for what should have been the orderly, pacific funeral procession. Instead, the security forces unloaded a barrage of gunfire and tear gas canisters upon the mourners, leading to the death of a second demonstrator, Fadhil 'Ali Matrouk, thirty-one. The king took the dramatic step of apologizing for his police, promising a swift internal investigation to punish the wrongdoers in the ranks. Few Bahrainis were convinced.

In retrospect, moreover, it is apparent that the two deaths transformed what were loosely coordinated protests into a more centralized and powerful movement. By the late afternoon, thousands of Bahrainis were pouring into Pearl Circle voicing their demands for constitutional reform and economic and social justice. Their determination was self-evident: Some had marched nearly two miles from their villages to the roundabout, risking harassment by the police. Despite the duress of the preceding twenty-four hours, a sense of joy and empowerment permeated the circle, a feeling that something had been won that could not be taken away. At sunset on February 15, the crowd registered several thousand members, swelling further as the evening progressed. Loudspeakers, a media tent, and food stalls appeared.

There was no clear leadership in the circle. The online organizers who had stirred thousands to protest were not a visible presence. Cadres of al-Wifaq and Wa'ad scrambled to fill the void, but this movement was not theirs, and they knew it. In spite of some confusion about who was authorized to speak and by whom, one message rang clear: non-violence. Speakers repeatedly condemned police brutality and urged those in attendance not to follow suit. February 15 was a holiday, the birthday of the prophet Muhammad, and organizers worried that demonstrators might return to work on the morrow. Instead, they returned to the roundabout, if anything in greater numbers than before, with what they thought was a green light from the government. Many participants erected tents, intending to spend the night in the circle. A half-mile away, however, hundreds of police vehicles and buses carrying riot troopers sat waiting. Their presence was undetectable from the roundabout except from the high vantage point of the bridge.

In the early morning hours of February 17, witnesses report, the police moved in, backed up by the army. Within five to ten minutes of their arrival, without warning, they descended upon the protester encampment from all sides, firing into tents with shotguns loaded with birdshot. Most of the camp had been asleep. Four demonstrators lost their lives and many more were wounded in the ensuing mayhem. The armed forces fired upon demonstrators trying to reach the roundabout again on February 18, resulting in the seventh death of the uprising.

Thousands gathered that day in the village of Sitra for the funerals of three killed in the roundabout attack. Whatever legitimacy the royal family had enjoyed in the eyes of demonstrators had largely dissipated. The regime had discredited itself further by claiming ludicrously in official media outlets that police had "exhausted all channels" of peaceable persuasion with the snoozing protesters before drawing the shotguns. Rumors swirled regarding the whereabouts of missing persons and the involvement of Saudi Arabian troops alongside other foreigners in the crackdown. The atmosphere in Sitra was a fusion of sorrow and subdued rage.

Mourners stuck gamely to their original petitions for justice and freedom through the transformation of the political system, as well as the omnipresent refutation of regime sectarianism: "No Shi'a, no Sunnis, only Bahrainis." Yet angrier slogans also resounded. "Try the Al Khalifa as criminals," some shouted, calling for international aid in bringing the ruling family to book. Zaynab, a schoolteacher from Sitra, expressed the new mood bluntly: "Today is for civilization and no longer for kings." At one point during a funeral procession, a man broke the chain of chants and prayers with a message for those outside of Bahrain. For four emotional minutes he spoke in English, not to the mourners, but to the trailing pack of journalists. As he ended his impromptu account of the February 17 events, he pleaded, "Please show them this—we are not pretending. We have rights. We are human beings and we are Bahrainis. We will not stop until freedom."

The February 17 massacre, caught on videotape and broadcast worldwide, may have been the point of no return for the Al Khalifa. The king hastened to anoint the crown prince, who has a reputation in the West as a reformer, as the convener of national dialogue and negotiations. Pro-democracy supporters reclaimed Pearl Circle and quickly reestablished their camp, which had been destroyed. Bahrainis from all walks of life marched in solidarity to the giant pearl-shaped sculpture for which the roundabout is named: nurses, doctors, teachers, lawyers, human rights activists, bankers, students, unionized workers, and more.

Balance of Forces

But the tense, eerie quiet that followed February 17 was also an opportunity for the ruling family to energize its own social base, which is not negligible. There are many Bahrainis who benefit from the status quo, because they work for state institutions, because they belong to favored merchant families, or simply because they prefer the devil they know to the devil they do not. As in Egypt before the resignation of President Husni Mubarak, there is a sizable chunk of the population that feels the unruly Pearl Circle demonstrators succeeded mainly in disrupting normal life. This sentiment is tinged with class prejudice, but also with sectarianism; many government backers claim that the complaints of the Shi'i majority are unsubstantiated. State TV unsubtly amplified these imprecations, to the extent that pro-democracy activists regarded it as a government tool to incite sectarian tension. Following the February 17 attack on Pearl Circle, the official network reported the discovery of a weapons cache belonging to the demonstrators there. At the funerals the next day, mourners adamantly denied the story. The state TV claim was never validated.

The presence of the pro-government Bahrainis was felt on Facebook and Twitter, the very virtual sites of dissent where the February 14 event was organized. Posts could be found griping about the protesters and voicing steadfast support for the royal family. It was apparent on the avenues of Manama as well: Within hours of the last rites of the Pearl Circle casualties, people paraded around the city in cars honking horns and waving flags, banners and portraits of the king, celebrating the royal family responsible for the previous day's tragedy. On February 21, some of the regime loyalists made their way from al-Fatih mosque to the roundabout in what was perceived by the pro-democracy demonstrators as an attempt at intimidation. Pearl Circle greeted the arrivals from the mosque with cheers for Sunni-Shi'i unity.

The forces in the middle were the established opposition groups, al-Wifaq and Wa'ad. Initially reluctant to support the call for demonstrations, al-Wifaq and Wa'ad subsequently changed tack, as the regime's violence made them feel compelled to join forces with the pro-testers. But since the crown prince's call for dialogue, they have pointedly declined to echo the calls for the fall of the regime. Instead, they continue to press their old reform agenda, hoping to obtain concessions from the royal family, while leaving the Al Khalifa in place. As an al-Wifaq MP, Mattar Mattar, told the press, "The opposition parties are discussing their set of demands, while the protesters on the streets have their own issues." Will those in the circle who chanted "Down, down, Al Khalifa!" accept anything less when the opposition societies sit down at the bargaining table? It is an open question to Bahrainis themselves.

What's Next?

No revolution is identical. While the Bahraini king may have been scared into concessions by the experiences of Tunisia and Egypt, the same chain of events cannot be assumed.

It is widely believed, for instance, that the Al Khalifa's allies will not allow the king and his progeny to meet the same fate as Egypt's Mubaraks. The foreign ministers of the Gulf Cooperation Council converged on Manama on the evening of February 17, by all accounts to stiffen the spines of the Al Khalifa in quelling the disturbances as soon as possible. Apart from the natural aversion of the Gulf monarchies to popular protest, or anything that smacks of participatory politics, the Saudis have a special interest in suppressing Shi'i voices of dissent. The province of al-Hasa in Saudi Arabia's east is home to a large Shi'i popula-tion, and though they are a minority rather than a majority, they harbor grievances similar to those of their Bahraini co-religionists. Al-Hasa also happens to be where most of Saudi Arabia's untapped petroleum lies. Bahraini dissenters cite this existential interest as grounds for suspecting the Saudis of considerably more than aggressive diplomacy in combating the rebellion next door. In February 2011, there were already signs of growing assertiveness on the part of some Shi'i activists in al-Hasa, who were keen to capitalize on the regional momentum to score reforms in Saudi Arabia.

Then there is the United States, whose Fifth Fleet is anchored in Bahrain, along with several other military assets. The Fifth Fleet prowls the Persian Gulf, location of two thirds of the world's proven oil reserves, to ensure that the precious liquid flows to global consum-ers with minimal interruption. From its aircraft carriers were launched the jets that patrolled the no-fly zone in southern Iraq in the 1990s and the bombers that struck Baghdad in advance of the 2003 invasion. US diplomats accordingly were inclined to overlook the escalating roughness of the Al Khalifa's response to dissent over the last five years. "I am impressed by the commitment that the government has to the democratic path that Bahrain is walking on," said Secretary of State Hillary Clinton at a Manama news conference on December 3, 2010. Now, as that path appears lit from Pearl Circle rather than the palace, the Obama administration is trapped in its own rhetoric, urging the Al Khalifa to pursue "meaningful reform" and rebuking the regime for its violence, but stopping well short of the condemnatory language it employed to denounce similar repression in nearby Iran. The US diffidence is likely informed by the judgment of a top intelligence official, interviewed by Reuters, that the royal family can and will "restore order" in Bahrain.

As the waves of violence continued to crash ashore on this island nation, the demands of the pro-democracy demonstrators grew louder, more insistent, and more radical. King Hamad responded with a series of apparent climbdowns, issuing a royal apology for the first two fatalities, pledging a renewed push for political reform and, on February 22, 2011 ordering the release of several political prisoners, including twenty-three Shi'i activists who were on trial for sedition. The freeing of these men had been a key plank of the new opposition's platform for some time.

One of the accused, who was being tried in absentia, was Hasan Mushayma' of Haqq. The warrant out for his arrest was suspended, paving the way for his return to Bahrain. Mushayma' might have served as a mediator between the hardline challenge of the crowds and the less confrontational approach of the established opposition societies. Instead, just weeks after his arrival in late February 2011, he was arrested. On March 17, four days after being released from prison, 'Abd al-Jalil Singace was also rearrested. In June 2011, both men were sentenced to life imprisonment for trying to overthrow the government.

The mass protests that continued into 2012, many organized by the official opposition, as well as the daily smaller demonstrations and confrontations with the police, send a clear signal that the uprising in Bahrain is far from resolved. Al-Wifaq, Wa'ad, and their opposition allies are trying to balance their instincts for gradual reform against the power of the social forces unleashed by the demonstrations and the violence directed against them. But the initiative rests with the protesters. For now, they remain unyielding in their demands for the creation of an entirely new political order. By forcing al-Wifaq into the streets, even as that society hews to its softer line, they have kept alive the possibility that Bahrain may yet complete its revolution.

24. BAHRAIN'S CRISIS WORSENS

JOE STORK

In the summer of 1997, an upsurge of crude firebombings, street demonstrations, and heavy repression added some nine deaths and an unknown number of arrests and injuries to the toll of the political unrest that gripped Bahrain. The troubles had erupted there in 1994 with demonstrations over unemployment, discrimination, and the refusal of the ruling family to modify its monopoly over the state and the public purse. The government frequently boasted that Bahrain's standard of living, as marked by various development indices, put the country near the top in the region. It announced that Bahrain had the highest literacy rate in the Arab world—85 percent as compared with an average of 55 percent, according to the latest UN Development Program report. Bahrain, however, remains a place where you can go to jail for what you write or read: Among those Bahrainis sentenced to fines and prison terms in June 1997 were seven men who had been imprisoned already for fourteen months for possessing leaflets the Interior Ministry alleged to contain "false news and unfounded statements." The same month saw the expulsion of the last remaining Western correspondent, Ute Meinel of the main German press agency, for "spreading lies, harming the welfare of the state and insulting the ruling family." Following Meinel's expulsion, the government effectively silenced the local stringer for BBC Arabic, which had been an important source of uncensored news for many Bahrainis. Bahraini defense lawyers, the source for most information about arrests and security court trials, were threatened with disbarment if they continued to talk to the outside press.

In June 1997, a small group of leading critics of the government prepared a letter to the emir requesting a meeting to present a petition which, they claimed, nearly twenty-two thousand Bahrainis had signed in late 1994, asking that the National Assembly, dissolved by decree in 1975, be restored. The letter, like the petition, graciously expresses "the solidarity of your people and your citizens with your rule and legitimacy of your wise leadership." Among the signatories were Munira Fakhro, a professor of sociology suspended from Bahrain University for refusing to remove her name from a petition of more than three hundred women in 1995; Sa'id Asbool, an engineer who lost his high position at the ministry of public works for signing a petition and who had undergone a week of interrogation in April 1996 for meeting with a BBC reporter; and Ahmad Shamlan, a lawyer and veteran nationalist activist who had been incarcerated for several months for a newspaper column he had written and for possession of a copy of the petition. True to form, the government responded by harassing the leaders of the effort and warning them not to submit the letter to the emir or press for a meeting with him.

The ruling family had a strong incentive to avoid the sort of fiscal accountability that would likely come with the revival of the National Assembly. According to many otherwise conservative Bahraini businessmen, ruling family control over the monies of the state, and the corrupt practices and influence peddling of the prime minister, Sheikh Khalifa, and his immediate family in particular, would have become the target of parliamentary inquiry, similar to what was occurring in Kuwait at the time.

Divide and Conquer

Then as now, the regime's ability to maintain its intransigent stance has several components. One is the internal security apparatus constructed over the past fifty-odd years, initially under British rule, which the regime expanded using British, Jordanian, and Egyptian commanders and advisers, financial assistance from Saudi Arabia and other nervous neighboring sheikhdoms, as well as thousands of Pakistani and Baluchi recruits. Another is the sectarian communal divide between the Shi'i majority and Sunni minority.

Bahrain's original population, the Baharna, are Arab Shi'i Muslims. The Al Khalifa conquest in 1783—part of a general movement of tribes out of the Najd region of Arabia that also brought the Al Sabah to Kuwait—ended nearly two hundred years of Persian rule and imposed a Sunni Arab tribal superstructure that continues to dominate the country's political system. By the mid-1990s the population numbered some 550,000, with expatriate workers making up one third of the total but two thirds of the labor force. (By 2011, the population had more than doubled to 1.2 million with expatriates accounting for 54 percent of the population and almost 80 percent of workers.) An estimated two thirds of native Bahrainis are Shi'a. They are represented in the country's commercial elite and in certain government departments, but the top ranks of the government, the security services, and the armed forces were exclusively controlled by the Al Khalifa and families close to them, all Sunni. The ruling family, with some unwitting help from the opposition, has largely succeeded in using the threat of Shi'i political dominance to rally the Sunni community to its side, or at least to neutralize opposition elements within it.

A third and not inconsiderable factor is the support Bahrain enjoys in the region and internationally. This support has been both material—in the form of financial subsidies from Saudi Arabia and military supplies and training from the US—and political. The US, whose Fifth Fleet naval forces have been based in the port of Manama since 1995, has, with few exceptions, refused to criticize publicly the Bahraini ruling family's political intransigence and atrocious human rights record, or to endorse in any manner the opposition's main demand to restore the constitution and hold elections for a revived national assembly. In August 1997, the US did support a resolution criticizing Bahrain's human rights record at the UN Human Rights Subcommission meeting in Geneva. That September, then US ambassador-designate to Bahrain, Johnny Young, spoke vaguely in his confirmation hearing of the need to "maintain order...in a manner consistent with international standards of human rights," and promised a "frank, earnest, and appropriately discreet dialogue" on such matters.

When Bahrain became independent in 1971, as part of Britain's military and political withdrawal from the Persian Gulf, the Al Khalifa initially moved to bolster and expand their clan-based political legitimacy. Key positions were reserved for the Al Khalifa, but the emir also formed a partially elected constituent assembly which drafted a liberal constitution. The centerpiece of the constitution, promulgated by the emir in 1973, was a partially elected National Assembly.

The ruling family, though, proved unready to tolerate popular institutions that seriously challenged its customary prerogatives. In 1975, the parliament balked at endorsing a broadly written decree that would enable the government to detain critics and opponents at will for "statements" or "activities" deemed to threaten the country's "internal or external security." In August 1975, the government dissolved the National Assembly and suspended the Constitution.[1] This was followed by a wave of arrests, detentions without trial and forced exile that decapitated and crippled the secular opposition, then comprised mainly of Arab nationalist (the Popular Front) and communist (the National Liberation Front) elements with a base among the intelligentsia and in the underground trade union movement.

The suppression of this opposition, which had largely overcome Shi'i-Sunni communal divisions, contributed to the emergence of a different sort of opposition following the 1978-1979 revolution in Iran, this one built upon the village-based leadership of local clerics.[2] This opposition evolved into the Bahrain Freedom Movement. In December 1981, the government arrested some seventy-three persons, mostly Bahraini but including several Shi'a from Saudi Arabia and elsewhere, on charges of plotting, with Iranian assistance, to overthrow the regime.

Throughout the rest of the 1980s and into the 1990s, the government imprisoned and exiled opposition activists, religious and leftist alike. In the aftermath of the Gulf war and the collapse of the Soviet Union, and encouraged by electoral and parliamentary developments in Kuwait, Bahraini liberals sensed an opportunity to raise again the issue of elections and their own parliament. Following informal discussions, a group consisting mainly of professionals and businessmen drew up a petition that was then signed by more than three hundred prominent individuals. "We called for elections to a restored parliament, release of political prisoners, and permission for exiles to return," one petition leader told me. "It was extremely polite, and included our fulsome respect for the Al Khalifa....We had known of the [emir's plan for a Shura Council] and were trying to preempt it...it could not be a substitute for the elected National Assembly." The emir promised to study the petition and reply to its organizers, but never did.

A version of this petition—one addition was a clause demanding political rights for women—was initiated publicly in late September 1994 and quickly gathered about twenty-five thousand signatures. That July had seen several large demonstrations demanding jobs at the Ministry of Labor, which the government disrupted with tear gas and arrests of alleged ringleaders. "We were not involved in those demonstrations at all," one petition organizer told me, "but they certainly added to the atmosphere of ripeness that we felt."

With the first petition, the organizers made a point of gathering a more or less equal number of Sunni and Shi'i signatories, but the public petition was another story. "That's why some of us argued against a popular petition," one signer of the first, himself a Shi'i, told me. "The [Shi'i] sheikhs have the signers. They will overwhelm you. And that's exactly what happened." Although the demands were essentially the same, the public petition campaign frightened many Sunnis. The government was quick to exploit this Sunni hesitation by consistently refusing to meet with joint Sunni-Shiʻi delegations. The thousands of arrests and detentions in the three years following the campaign almost exclusively involved Shiʻi opponents and critics.

A second escalation occurred one year later. The massive arrest campaign of early 1995 included a number of leading Shiʻi clerics and community leaders, including Sheikh ʻAbd al-Amir al-Jamri, an elected member of the dissolved National Assembly who had emerged as the single most influential spokesperson among the Shiʻa activists and in the street. The government then engaged Sheikh al-Jamri and others in several months of jailhouse nego-tiations. They were released in September 1995 on the basis of an informal understanding that they would endeavor to dampen street protests and the government would take steps to meet the demands of the protesters. At the government's insistence, though, nothing was committed to paper. Street protests did diminish sharply in the fall of 1995, but when Sheikh al-Jamri and the others began to charge that the agreement was being ignored, the government denied there had been any understanding. The situation once again deterio-rated, and street violence and massive arrests resumed. Sheikh al-Jamri and his colleagues were arrested again on January 22, 1996; al-Jamri was imprisoned until July 1999 when he was pardoned by the new emir, Hamad Al Khalifa, as part of his reform package.

Some independent opposition figures believed that the government took advantage of the political naïveté of al-Jamri and his colleagues by keeping its commitments extremely vague, promising only that it would "look into" the demands of the petitioners. In this view, the government's goal in detaining and purportedly negotiating with Sheikh al-Jamri and the others was precisely to undercut the more sophisticated, liberal, secularist, and cross-communal leadership of the petition campaign. Such an approach had the added advantage of further identifying the opposition as essentially Shiʻi, expressing communal rather than broad national political grievances. Sheikh al-Jamri "fell into the trap" by not reaching out to his petition colleagues following his release in 1995. "He never returned their visit," said another activist. "He became like Khomeini in Paris."

Staged Confessions

The Bahraini government publicly attributed the country's political crisis to machinations by Iran and specifically to Iranian support of a group called "Hizballah Bahrain-Military Group." In June 1996, the minister of interior claimed to have in hand the cadres in charge of the security intelligence and financial committees of the group, who had conveniently confessed "that they had established this terrorist grouping on the instructions of the [Iranian] Islamic Revolutionary Guard Corps and with its financing." The next day, several of the accused were made to read parts of their confessions on Bahraini television. The announcement and televised confessions produced the desired reporting in the Western press linking "Iran," "Hizballah," and "Bahrain." None of those accounts mentioned that these confessions had been extracted over a period of weeks during which the accused had no access to lawyers. Nor did they refer to Amnesty International's September 1995 report documenting the systematic use of beatings and other forms of torture in the security service's interrogation of political detainees, a pattern confirmed by lawyers and former detainees I spoke with.

Inside Bahrain, the government used the confessions in a manner befitting the absolutist style of rule to which it has become accustomed. The country's two newspapers, *al-Ayyam* and *Akhbar al-Khalij*, carried pages of congratulatory "reporting" of the Interior Ministry's unceasing vigilance. The same message appeared in advertisements by private companies and sports clubs. On the day following the announcement of the confessions, upper-level civil servants and officials, heads of civic organizations, and religious leaders were "invited" to the palace to "discuss" the latest developments with the emir and the prime minister (by all accounts the real power in the country). To not appear, Bahrainis told me, could well mean the loss of one's job for a government employee and little likelihood of finding another. For a Shi'i cleric, a no-show would likely produce a rude wee-hours summons to Interior Ministry headquarters on the grounds of the old prison fort in central Manama. In 1995, Sheikh 'Isa bin Rashid, the head of the General Organization for Youth and Sports, asked each club to sign a pledge of loyalty to the emir, and to send a representative to the amiri court to present it. "Even the sports clubs in Diraz and Sanabis," one leading professional said, referring to Shi'i villages that had been prominent in the unrest, "just to humiliate them." The Uruba Club, a literary-social club frequented by liberal businessmen and professionals, initially resisted the summons, but the minister of information called in the club president, a respected and prominent businessman, and put heavy pressure on the group to sign. "So we did. Later Sheikh 'Isa told someone, 'You see, they came like dogs.'"

While no known Bahraini opposition group went by the name "Hizballah Bahrain," this did not exclude its possible existence or a degree of Iranian involvement. It was also conceivable that the dynamics of revolt and repression created a phenomenon that did not exist at the outset of the unrest, that the young men taking to the streets did "hope Hizballah is there and that they will do something for us," as one of them put it. But the crude and random violence that accompanied Bahrain's political crisis did not display the footprints of a well-armed and well-financed Iranian surrogate with more than three years of training in Qom and Lebanon's Beka'a Valley, as the government alleged. There was not a single incident involving the use of firearms by the opposition. US and British government officials familiar with the situation agreed that the government's effort to blame Iran for the three years of unrest had no credibility, though they avoided expressing this view in public.[3]

The Bahraini government was also ready to grant that economic distress was a major factor underlying the country's troubles. In fact, to the extent that it acknowledged any internal or domestic responsibility for the unrest, it pinned all the blame on the economy, and thus portrayed the resolution of the crisis strictly in terms of economic, not political, reform. Informally, many of the government's supporters subscribed to the view that the underlying problem was one of explosive demographic growth among the Shi'a. The editor of one of Bahrain's two dailies, and therefore someone very close to the regime, using language familiar to anyone acquainted with racist discourse in the United States and Europe, complained that the problem was that the government indulgently provided the Shi'a with education, health care, and other social benefits so that they could remain idle and breed. The government tried to compensate for political intransigence by touting economic reforms and training programs designed to provide badly needed jobs. Nevertheless, the situation worsened. *The Economist* estimated that unemployment rates were as high as 30 percent—almost exclusively among Shi'a young men, who were in the forefront of street protests and anti-government vandalism and who were probably responsible for a series of deadly arson attacks on foreign workers from Bangladesh and India.

If the economy was one of the factors behind the unrest, it was also one of the casualties as multinational firms scaled back their presence. Publicly this was presented as part of a trend towards consolidation and "downsizing." Privately, executives admitted that the unrest was behind the fact that the consolidating happened in Dubai rather than Manama. The number of offshore banking units operating in Bahrain dropped from a high of seventy-five to forty-six in the fall of 1997. Even Caltex, the Chevron-Texaco consortium that pioneered oil production and refining in Bahrain, sold the government its 40 percent share in the Bahrain Petroleum Company refinery after the government failed to attract any outside buyers.

Bahrain's own business elites were not able or willing to pick up the slack. Some were critical of the government's hostility to political reform; many were resistant to labor market reforms that would reduce the number and raise the wages of foreign workers as a means of encouraging greater employment of Bahraini youths. Bahrain's then-labor minister, 'Abd al-Nabi al-Shu'ala, said that between 4,500 and 6,500 Bahrainis entered the work force each year. At the same time, he acknowledged, his Labor Ministry every month issued 2,450 new work permits and renewed 3,450 permits for expatriate workers.

The deaths in June 1997 occurred as Bahrain's unrest moved into its fourth year with no resolution in sight. One death was that of Sheikh 'Ali al-Nachas, a fifty-year-old blind cleric who had spent most of the previous two years in prison for his "political" sermons critical of the government. The opposition charged that he was tortured to death; the government claims he died of "natural causes." In another case, a twenty-seven-year-old man died shortly after being arrested and later released. The opposition said he had been beaten by security forces; in this case, too, the government asserted that the cause of death was "natural." Six of those killed were Indian and Bangladeshi workers, who died in two separate arson attacks on shops. The authorities announced arrests in one of the attacks, but no political motive was charged or claimed—fitting the pattern of the ten other Asian workers who had been killed since the unrest began.

The Bahrain Freedom Movement, speaking for the Shi'i community opposition abroad, hinted that government provocateurs were behind these attacks, or that they were provoked by the excesses of government security forces. The movement asserted that the opposition was committed to a strategy of civil resistance, but with most of the Shi'i leadership either in prison or in exile abroad, it seemed that the street opposition in Bahrain was operating without direction. Opposition spokespersons abroad failed to speak out clearly against attacks on foreign workers. By late 1997, an alternate leadership had yet to emerge from the smoldering neighborhoods inside the country.

Temporary Peace

In 2002, Hamad declared Bahrain a kingdom and elevated his title to king. As part of this transformation, he introduced a new constitution which reinstated parliament, split between a forty-member elected lower house and an appointed upper house—the Shura Council—of equal number. The elected body is virtually powerless in relation to the Shura Council, which can nullify legislation passed by the lower house. The new constitution also continues to ban political parties; members of the lower house belong to political "societies" which emerged mostly from the Shiʻi and Sunni conservative establishments. Those reforms bought the Al Khalifa some half-dozen years of relative political peace, but as the sense of betrayal—the sense that the rulers had no intention of making themselves accountable—deepened and spread, protests increased, as did arbitrary arrests and the revival of torture in police interrogation chambers.

Though the massive popular street protests on February 14, 2011 were partly inspired by the prior uprisings in Tunisia and Egypt, the 1994-1999 *intifada* was perhaps a more salient precedent in Bahrain's fight for democratic governance. The date of the first protests was the tenth anniversary of the referendum introducing King Hamad's reform package—an annual reminder of broken promises.

Under international pressure following the state's crackdown on protesters, King Hamad appointed the Bahrain Independent Commission of Inquiry, comprising five renowned international jurists. Their report confirmed the widespread use of torture and a "climate of impunity" by Bahrain's security forces. The commission recommended freeing those persons jailed for exercising the right to free expression and peaceful assembly and holding accountable officials at all ranks responsible for torture, unlawful killings, and other human rights crimes, recommendations that remain unfulfilled. As in the 1990s, the United States has mostly released formulaic statements urging restraint by both the regime and the street (with the exception of several strong statements by President Obama). Yet the stand-off in mid-2012, much like that fifteen years earlier, remains the ruling family's steadfast refusal to accept anything like accountability—to the law or to Bahrain's citizens.

Notes

1. Human Rights Watch, *Routine Abuse, Routine Denial: Civil Right and the Political Crisis in Bahrain* (New York, 1997), pp. 16-20.

2. Bahrain, as a result of its small size, economic history, and population growth, is one of the most highly urbanized countries in the world. The two cities of Manama and Muharraq and main towns in the northern end of the island account for 85 percent of the population. "Village" therefore refers to relatively homogeneous Shiʻa neighborhoods, many of them marked by poverty and unemployment, rather than to spatially insular rural communities.

3. At the National Press Club in January 1996, then-Assistant Secretary of State Robert Pelletreau characterized Bahrain's unrest as "brought about by a fairly high level of unemployment" and "urged on and promoted by Iran."

25. THE BATTLE OVER FAMILY LAW IN BAHRAIN

SANDY RUSSELL JONES

On November 9, 2005, over one hundred thousand protesters—approximately one seventh of the Kingdom of Bahrain's population at the time—flooded the streets of the capital, Manama. Most of the protesters were Shi'a demonstrating their resistance to the government's campaign to implement a codified family law, announced a month earlier. The measure, which was ready to be presented to Bahrain's semi-autonomous parliament, removed adjudication of matters having to do with women and the family from Muslim religious (*shari'a*) courts, whose rulings were at the judge's discretion. Instead, family courts would follow an agreed-upon body of black-letter law and legal precedent.

The relationship between the Sunni ruling family, the Al Khalifa, and the kingdom's majority Shi'i population has not been an easy one. Months after promulgation of the 1972 constitution, which promised representative government and an elected parliament that would enjoy a considerable measure of authority, the constitution was suspended, followed by three decades of authoritarian rule. The ensuing discrimination against the Shi'a led to widespread anger and frustration resulting in a series of protests (some violent) in the 1990s, yet none were as heavily attended as the 2005 demonstration against the family law.[1] Community leader and Shi'i cleric Sheikh 'Isa Qasim left no room for doubt: the Shi'a would never accept a codified law implemented by the government. They would resist it by battling in the streets if necessary. In a statement published on the website of the Islamic Council of Scholars, of which he was the head, Qasim said, "Our faith is more valuable to us than our blood."

Opposite the mass of protesters, a much smaller, but equally determined group stood in support of the law. Ghada Jamshir, a rights activist known for her fiery speeches and in-your-face approach, led a group of women who had recently received what they charged were unjust decisions in the *shari'a* courts. Jamshir argued in the local and regional press that Bahrain's *shari'a* court judges were corrupt and unqualified, and that they routinely discriminated against women litigants. Also backing the new law were members and supporters of the Personal Law Committee (PLC), a network of representatives from several women's organizations. The PLC shared many of Jamshir's views, but took a more moderate approach, working together with lawyers, religious scholars, and members of Parliament to formulate and submit their own draft law to the Royal Council. The PLC had pushed for a codified law for over two decades, yet no serious steps in this direction had been taken by the government until then.

On one level, Bahrain's struggle over the family law seemed to be typical of struggles in many other Middle Eastern nation-states, wherein "conservative" clerics battled "progressive" women activists for control over the last area of life still ruled, for the most part, by Islamic law. A closer look, however, showed that Bahrain's fight was as much about political representation and sectarian identity as it was about defining Islam and determining the rules that govern the Muslim family.

The Current System

Bahrain's court system is divided into civil and *shari'a* sections. Civil courts hear civil, commercial, and criminal cases, and *shari'a* courts hear cases involving marriage, divorce, alimony, child custody and support, nursing, paternity, and inheritance. The *shari'a* section is further separated into two departments, one Sunni and one Shi'i, with each having three levels of litigation: junior, senior, and appellate. Judges are appointed by the government. While they are not required to hold a university law degree, judges must have some training in Islamic jurisprudence (*fiqh*) and at least two years of experience in a legal profession. Judges in *shari'a* courts decide cases according to their own interpretations of Islamic law. Shi'i judges use Ja'fari *fiqh*—the most commonly accepted reference for Shi'i jurists worldwide.[2] The official body of jurisprudence for the Sunni courts is the Maliki school of legal thought (*madhhab*) adhered to by the Al Khalifa. In interviews, however, several authorities on legal affairs, including *shari'a* court judges and lawyers, said that the *fiqh* of the three other Sunni *madhhabs* (Hanafi, Hanbali, and Shafi'i) is also used regularly. The courts have operated in this manner since the promulgation of the Judiciary Law in 1971, the same year Bahrain declared independence from Britain's protectorate system. There had been a few amendments redefining the courts' jurisdiction and dictating procedural matters since then, but the determination of substantive issues had been left to the judges' discretion.

Even before Bahrain's independence, there were calls for codification of laws. Nationalist groups (which tended to be non-sectarian) observed the legal reforms taking place in Egypt, Jordan, and other newly independent Arab states, and wanted Bahrain to take similar measures. Specifically, nationalist groups called for the enactment of penal and civil laws, the establishment of both a high court of cassation and a council that would act as a constitutional court to settle disputes between legislative and executive authorities, and the appointment of competent judges holding university law degrees and having adequate experience. Throughout the 1950s and 1960s, the Al Khalifa, as the recognized local rulers, worked together with the British to carry out some of these reforms, but the process was slow. By the time of independence, many penal and civil laws were in place, but only the barest regulations were set regarding the appointment of judges and the operation of the courts. The 1971 Judiciary Law did specify that judges appointed at the junior level must have four years' prior experience in the legal profession, but there were few Bahrainis who could meet this requirement and who were willing to accept the appointment.[3] The Al Khalifa responded to this crisis by recruiting judges from other countries, such as Egypt, Jordan, and Sudan, and appointing to the bench ruling family members who had little or no training in *shari'a*. They also amended the requirement from four years of experience to two, in the hopes of attracting more candidates, and as an alternative to raising judges' salaries.[4] Several legal authorities interviewed for this article reported that even the two-year requirement was often not enforced, and that many judges were placed on the bench after only months of observing *shari'a* court operations.

The lack of qualified Bahraini judges resulted in several problems in the courts. Despite claims that Bahrain's *shari'a* court system helps to preserve an Islamic way of life, judges' decisions are reportedly based on personal opinion, rather than on *fiqh*.[5] *Shari'a* court lawyer Muhammad al-Mutawwa' said he was often confounded by decisions that clearly went against basic jurisprudential principles. Even when decisions were based on *fiqh*, judges might use a Hanafi ruling to apply to a Shafi'i couple, cobble together elements from more than one *madhhab* or otherwise bend the *fiqh* to fit a predetermined ruling.[6] Attorney Jalila al-Sayyid contended that the lack of the rule of precedent also led to inconsistency in rulings. *Shari'a* court decisions were not published, so lawyers often had to rely on each other to share information about judges' rulings on specific issues. Even so, al-Sayyid reported, "There is a multiplicity of contradictory rulings on the same issue." She said that judgments were subjective and often depended on factors outside the facts of the case, such as the social rank of the litigants, the gender of the plaintiff and the identity of the judge: "We need legislation because there is no structure for consistency."[7]

Sheikh Muhsin al-'Asfour, a judge in the senior-level Shi'i court for ten years, described the situation in the courts as "chaos." He said that more than 80 percent of the problems occurring there stem from the fact that neither the litigants nor the judges know *shari'a*. Coming from a family of judges and experts in *shari'a*, including the neo-Akhbari jurist Yusuf al-Bahraini (d. 1722), al-'Asfour wrote his own set of laws to be used in the Shi'i court, based on mainstream Ja'fari *fiqh* and the work of his grandfather, Sheikh Khalaf al-'Asfour, Manama's chief Shi'i judge for over four decades. He encouraged the government to use his compilation as a standard to help eliminate inconsistencies in rulings, but they did not show an interest in doing so.[8] Sheikh Yasir al-Mahmid, then a Sunni judge at the senior level and a self-described Salafi, believed that having a codified law would greatly reduce inconsistencies and confusion in the courts. Bahrain's Salafi parliamentary bloc expressed hesitation in supporting a codified law because of the threat it could pose to the exclusive use of *shari'a*. Al-Mahmid replied that if men of religion write the legislation, the law would remain faithful to Islam. It may have been easy for MPs to oppose the law on ideological grounds, he explained, but they did not attend the courts day after day, facing real people with real problems that could devastate their lives: "The court is not for debating religion. It is for fixing problems."[9]

Officials at the Ministry of Justice were equally discouraging about the state of affairs in the *shari'a* courts. Sheikh Khalid bin 'Isa Al Khalifa, undersecretary for the minister of justice, said that the ministry was well aware of the system's shortcomings. There was a procedural law that dictated the way a case was filed, he said, but no mechanism for ensuring the execution of judges' rulings. Women normally bore the burden of unenforced decisions, but the undersecretary chose the example of a case in which a wife was ordered to return to her marital home (*bayt al-ta'a*). He said, "It's useless. The police will escort her back to her home, but an hour later she can leave again and go back to her mother." The undersecretary affirmed the position of the government that a family law was necessary, and added that a unified law would help to close the gap that had been widening between the sects:

"Bahrain used to be unified, but because of the revolution in Iran in 1979, the rise of the Shi'a, fundamentalism, Afghanistan, and all these things," the Shi'a had created a division. He lamented that the family law issue had been politicized, and was no longer a strictly legal issue. The clerics had made it nearly impossible for the government to institute any reforms, he complained. Until this political issue could be dealt with, the courts would remain disorganized and inefficient. At the close of the interview, Sheikh Khalid joked, "When we got married I told my wife, 'Whatever happens between us, we are not going to the *shari'a* court to resolve it!'"[10]

The result of these problems was not just inefficiency and confusion, but real suffering in the lives of Bahraini families. Press reports in Bahrain's local papers read like modern tragedies: divorced women living in siblings' homes for up to a decade waiting for their alimony cases to be heard; victims of domestic violence forced to remain with abusive husbands and fathers despite medical and photographic evidence of the abuse; and mothers losing their children, their homes, and their alimony because of alleged bribes by husbands.

Two Decades of Reform Efforts

As serious as the problems in the *shari'a* courts were for lawyers, judges, and litigants, it was a women's NGO that led the first dedicated effort to reform the system. The PLC was formed in 1982 as a loose network of representatives from various women's NGOs. Through raising public consciousness, securing the advocacy of legal experts and clerics, and lobbying the government, the PLC worked toward the goal of a codified personal status law. PLC members argued that the system was inefficient, sowed division between the sects, and left glaring inconsistencies among verdicts. The committee provided the government with a set of measures they felt was necessary to resolve the courts' problems. Some of these demands included an initiative to draft a unified law based on *shari'a*, but that would also comply with international human rights treaties to which Bahrain is a signatory; the active participation of lawyers, jurists, and members of NGOs in discussions of the substantive details of the law; an initiative for thorough reform of the *shari'a* courts and the related administrative apparatus; the introduction of fixed standards for judges' training, qualifications, and experience, along with regular and compulsory review courses in *fiqh*; the immediate removal of judges who did not meet these standards (regardless of their lifetime appointments), and impartiality in the appointment of new judges.

For nearly twenty years, the PLC had pursued these goals without seeing any effort from the government to change the *shari'a* court system. Then, when Crown Prince Hamad became king in 1999, he announced a plan for comprehensive social and political reforms. These reforms were outlined in what was called the National Action Charter. Although the Charter did not mention specific reforms of the *shari'a* courts, the members of the PLC hoped that they would soon see, if not a codified law, at least some positive changes to the existing system. They then formulated their own draft law, in consultation with lawyers and scholars, basing it on *shari'a* as well as the codified laws of Arab countries such as Kuwait and Lebanon, and submitting the draft to the new king for consideration. At the same time that King Hamad began initiating selected reforms, another organization, the Women's Petition Committee (WPC) also began working toward *shari'a* court reform. Created by rights activist Ghada Jamshir, the WPC's approach was bolder and more combative than that of the PLC. Instead of slowly working toward producing a model for a new law, Jamshir's goal was to shock Bahrain into action by exposing the personal stories of scores of women who had been ruled against in the *shari'a* courts. Describing instances of bribery, violations of *shari'a* principles, and requests for sexual favors in exchange for favorable verdicts, Jamshir appalled and horrified the Bahraini public. She also organized demonstrations at which women held signs revealing their case numbers, the ruling judges' names, and the verdicts, along with statements about how the rulings contradicted Islam. "Islam does not forget the women and children," read one placard at a June 2005 event.

Jamshir's most famous case was that of Badriyya Rabi'a, a mother who lost her two children in a custody battle with her ex-husband. The WPC publicized Rabi'a's case and provided her with legal assistance to appeal the judgment. The unprofessional handling of the case so embarrassed the government that they immediately took action to redress some of the damage. Six judges, those known to be the most corrupt or unqualified, were "retired" from the bench in 2003 by decree.[11] In addition, on May 2, 2003, King Hamad announced the formation of a committee to draft a family law. The committee was composed of six *shari'a* court judges (three from each sect), the head of the legal affairs committee, the minister of justice, and three women lawyers. A draft was completed, the majority of which applied equally to both Sunnis and Shi'a. Approximately 15 percent of the articles specified different rules for each sect.[12] The draft was submitted to the Ministry of Justice for approval. In the meantime, the king's announcement sparked a heated public debate. In Friday sermons, public addresses, and the press, Shi'i clerics denounced the king's actions as being influenced by the West, and blamed women activists for wanting to destroy the Islamic family structure and usher in a Western-style family in which wives can roam freely in public and divorce at will. The activists, for their part, organized demonstrations in favor of the draft initiative, and denied the clerics' accusations. Farida Ghulam, a leading member of the PLC and also Shi'i, published responses to these accusations and argued that the clerics' goal was a political one—to consolidate their own power over the people. "They use their standing and the people's trust to deceive the public about what the women want. They call themselves activists on behalf of women's rights, but they reject women's rights. They ignore the committee's statement of its commitment to preserving *shari'a* and the *madhhab*s, and call us players, secularists, lovers of the Tunisian experiment, and say we are sick and confused."[13] After months of constant public rows between activists and clerics, the king decided to shelve the draft and instead take a different approach, one that he hoped would enlist the support of the public.

During the following two years the Supreme Council for Women (SCW), a government agency formed in 2001 to develop programs to improve the lives of Bahraini women, began assessing public opinion on the issue of a family law and compiling evidence of the need for a law. In 2002, for instance, the SCW started receiving telephone calls from women requesting help. The call volume was so high that, in 2004, a grievance unit was established, and between 2002 and 2005, over eleven thousand calls were received. Approximately 40 percent of the calls were requests for subsidized housing from women who had been divorced by their husbands and evicted from their marital homes. In the short term, the

SCW worked with the Ministry of Housing and Social Affairs to create more shelter. Then, as part of the government's longer-term goal of addressing the problems with the *shari'a* courts, the SCW presented the king with an urgent request to establish an alimony fund and compulsory government review of amounts assigned by *shari'a* judges, to create more *shari'a* courts to reduce caseloads of the current courts, and to set regulations that would speed the processing of cases. In 2004, they commissioned a study to gauge Bahrainis' opinions about the prospect of a codified family law. Seventy-three percent of those surveyed said they thought a codified law was necessary. When asked whether the law should be based on *shari'a*, 97 percent of the respondents said yes. The SCW also deputized four women lawyers to review the judgments of the *shari'a* courts. The lawyers looked at over three hundred cases. Their results confirmed the accusations made previously by Jamshir and the PLC: Many judges were corrupt or inefficient, and lacked proper training.[14] Acting on these findings, the king assembled a second drafting committee, which, unlike the 2003 committee, was composed exclusively of religious scholars. A draft was completed and submitted to the Royal Court in the fall of 2005. This was the draft submitted for consideration in Parliament.

Simultaneously, the SCW launched a campaign to garner popular support for a codified family law. The campaign publicized the results of the research done by the council, and presented a case for the need for a law. Their approach was to demonstrate that the family law was not just an issue for women, but an issue that concerned the whole family. The campaign's slogan, "A Secure Family = A Secure Nation," conveyed the idea that the health of the family bears directly on the health of the nation as a whole, echoing an established strategy used in the nation-building projects of other Middle Eastern states.[15]

Women's rights activists were mostly unenthusiastic about the SCW campaign. While they appreciated the attention drawn to the issue, they were aware that, ultimately, the SCW did not have the power to enact change. The SCW had the ear of the king, but the authority rested with him, and he also had to contend with the clerics. Some activists, such as Jamshir and Layla Rajab, architect of an initiative to bring together clerics and activists for a public debate, were more strongly critical. Rajab expressed frustration with the SCW's lack of respect for her and others who had been working on this issue for decades: "They say they want to work as partners with us, but they won't allow us to make any decisions."[16]

Opposition

Despite the survey showing majority backing for a family law, the SCW's campaign met with significant opposition. Days after the launch, the Islamic Council of Scholars (ICS), headed by Sheikh 'Isa Qasim and representing the kingdom's Shi'i clerics, rejected the campaign's slogan. In a recorded statement, Qasim argued that a "secure family" and a "secure nation" are achieved "by God's will and no other": "No one is waiting for humans to implement it. God's law for the family already exists and is in use…. The earth and its people are covered with clear rules by God's *shari'a*." In Friday sermons, in statements to the press, and on their own websites, members of the ICS made clear that they would not accept the government-sponsored law. While many of these statements read as predictable defenses of religion against secular, Western-inspired reform efforts, the Shi'i clerics' grounds for opposition were more complex.

In a statement published in November 2005 they announced that they were not against codification itself, but only against the government controlling it. Many Bahraini Shi'a harbored a profound distrust of the Al Khalifa arising from decades of political, economic, and social oppression. The suspension of the original 1972 constitution, subsequent unchecked pursuit of Sunni dominance by the royal family and the promulgation of the 2002 constitution, which stripped the elected parliament of much of its power, have contributed to the belief that if promises were made to grant equal rights to Shi'a, they were only made to convince the West of Bahrain's commitment to democracy. In 2006, evidence of this duplicity was presented in the disclosure of a clandestine five-year plan for bolstering Sunni dominance. Named "Bandar-gate" by the local press, the scandal involved a 240-page report compiled by Salah al-Bandar, secretary-general of the London-based Gulf Center for Democratic Development, that was distributed to officials in the government, heads of NGOs, the British, US, and German embassies, and the press. The report documented a 1 million dinar (approximately $2.5 million) money trail leading from a senior government official (who happened to be responsible for overseeing the winter 2006 elections) to certain candidates, political societies, and other government officials, as well as to a Sunni Islamic center to fund a Shi'i-to-Sunni conversion program.[17]

The ICS also had specific objections to the government instituting the law. While religious scholars would serve on the drafting committee, the law would also be written or amended by others who are not specialists in *shari'a*, such as lawyers and government officials. The ICS argued that while Article 2 of the 2002 Bahraini constitution stated that Islam was the official religion of the state, this provision was not enough to guarantee that the family law would conform to *shari'a*. A clear example of the article's irrelevance, the ICS offered, was the fact that alcoholic beverages were legally served in Bahrain. The clerics also worried that the government's true aim in codification was to pass a unified law that would apply to both sects at the expense of Shi'i rules. There were indeed indications of such an aim in government statements and the SCW's rhetoric. Lastly, the ICS considered the SCW's claim that a codified law would protect women's rights an accusation against Islam. They argued that women already had "legitimate" rights within Islam, and that a codified law written by non-scholars could actually compromise those rights. Specific fears felt by Shi'i clerics were that certain conditions for divorce would be dropped, allowing women to remarry when they were not properly divorced from their first husbands; that girls would be allowed to challenge their fathers' guardianship, thereby compromising family honor; that the permission of adoption would tamper with lineages; and that abortion would be legalized. While seeming to safeguard many men's rights, preventing changes such as these would also protect one of women's most important rights as the ICS saw it: the right to have her honor guarded (a view that was disputed by women activists). In addition to these objections, the ICS argued that simply promulgating a codified law would not solve the courts' problems. The lack of a law was just one among many reasons for the problems in the courts. The main reason, the ICS charged, was the government itself, which appointed the judges and allowed them certain "leniencies" that compromised the timely progress of cases through the courts. Aside from the courts themselves, the government was also responsible for various social ills that led to an increase in divorce and family problems. Unemployment, discrimination in housing, and poor prevention of corruption and vice all led to difficulties within the family.

Basing themselves on these grounds, the ICS would accept a codified law only under three conditions. First, the law had to be drawn up exclusively by scholars of *shari'a*. Second, the final draft had to be approved by the highest Shi'i religious authority (*marja'*) before promulgation. During this fight, the *marja'* followed by the ICS was Ayatollah 'Ali al-Sistani in Najaf, Iraq. Third, there had to be an article added to the constitution guaranteeing that the law could not be changed without prior approval of the *marja'*. These demands would allow a codified law to be passed while at the same time ensuring its grounding in *shari'a*, then and in the future. They would also protect the autonomy of Shi'i religious authorities and prevent the elision of Shi'i rulings under a potential unified law.

Shi'i Rights and the Constitution

Another aim which was not expressed, but which was attributed to the ICS by observers, was the opening of the constitution to broader reform. The ICS worked closely with the Shi'i Islamist political organization al-Wifaq toward constitutional reform, specifically on the movement to reinstate the 1972 constitution. Shi'i MP 'Abd al-Nabi Salman told *Middle East Report* that the SCW's announcement of the family law campaign presented an ideal opportunity for the ICS to attempt to convince the king to amend the constitution. If the king agreed to an amendment providing the ICS a guarantee on the family law, that might have opened the way for the consideration of further demands. The ICS knew that the government was keen on passing the law quickly, before the November election, if possible. Therefore, Salman said, "They are using that urgency as leverage." Though Shi'i himself, Salman did not support the ICS demands. Risking his reelection, he did not yield to threats issued by Sheikh 'Isa Qasim to change his views. Early in 2006, Qasim called a meeting during which he and two other clerics told assembled Shi'i MPs that if the family law came up for a vote, they were to walk out on it or risk losing their public support. If his position as head of the ICS was not enough to convince MPs of the extent of Qasim's power over the kingdom's Shi'a, the massive turnout at the November 9 protest certainly was. The withdrawal of Qasim's support was also a potent threat in 2006, with parliamentary elections looming in late November and early December. Magnifying the threat to non-Islamist Shi'i deputies was al-Wifaq's decision to field candidates in the election, ending its previous boycott. Despite these threats, Salman said he would likely back the law. He told Qasim that the constitutional guarantee would never work. "This won't happen. As soon as we start talking about changing the constitution, the king closes his ears."[18]

Sheikh Nidham Ya'qoubi, a prominent Sunni legal scholar, echoed Salman's interpretation of the ICS's ultimate goal in opposing the family law. Ya'qoubi, a member of the 2005 committee that drafted the law, was eager to dispel the notion that Islamist scholars, Sunni or Shi'i, are against codification. He noted that the Sunni committee included "at least two" Salafis, and that it was a mistake to think that Salafis objected. Most approved of codification in principle, and only had reservations regarding implementation. Nor did the Shi'i scholars object to codification, he said. After all, even Iran had a codified law: "What Shi'a in Bahrain want is to change the constitutional law."[19]

No doubt with considerable help from Qasim and the ICS, al-Wifaq was successful in winning seventeen out of forty seats in the November election, Salman's seat among them. The results did not bode well for the government's family law, at least among the al-Wifaq bloc. However, the Sunni Islamist blocs (Salafis and the Muslim Brotherhood) expressed tentative support, and the Sunni Islamist scholars involved in the writing of the 2005 draft were confident that the law would not compromise Islamic values. Interestingly, the Bandar-gate report implicated members of both the Salafi and Muslim Brotherhood organizations as having roles in the government's Sunni dominance program. The veracity of the report can only be guessed at here, although it raised intriguing questions about Sunni interest in the family law and the prospect of a unified law. Without a doubt, the situation in Bahrain produced the curious image of Islamists and self-described liberal women activists standing on the same side of an issue that has often divided these groups.

A vote on the family law was postponed while the king waited until "the time is right," after the fallout from Bandar-gate—which was then spreading onto the international scene and degenerating into youth riots at home—subsided.[20] The "right time" ended up being three years later, in May 2009, when King Hamad presented a family code that applied only to Sunni *shari'a* courts. The law's limited scope was a win for the ICS, which demonstrated considerable influence over the country's Shi'a.

While women's groups as well as the SCW continue to push for the implementation of a law for the Shi'i most recently in an appeal to the U.N. Information Centre for Shi'i women's rights to be included in a review of human rights in Bahrain, other events have largely overtaken the family law as a topic of national debate.[21] In February of 2011, Bahrainis joined Egyptians, Syrians, and others in the protests of the Arab uprisings. For several days, Bahraini demonstrators occupied the central plaza in and around the Pearl Monument, protesting their lack of political representation, sectarian discrimination, and joblessness. Despite the peaceful nature of the protests, the government responded with force, firing tear gas and rubber bullets, arresting and subsequently imprisoning and torturing demonstrators. While the protesters were predominantly, but not exclusively Shi'i the Al Khalifa heightened sectarian tensions by allowing Saudi forces onto to Bahraini soil on March 14 to join Bahraini troops in quelling the protests.

The government's actions fueled what could have remained youthful demonstrations inspired by events elsewhere in the region into a national crisis resulting in a continuing cycle of protests, arrests, and national instability. These events have also served to more sharply divide the Shi'i majority between those who favor some form of rapprochement with the government and those who call for nothing less than the ouster of the Al Khalifa. In the context of this ongoing crisis, the status of the Shi'i family law remains in the background. The passage of the law at this time without broad-based clerical and popular support would surely spark even greater rebellion. More importantly, opposition to the law may serve as a unifying force for Shi'i groups, as it did in 2005, an outcome the Al Khalifa surely do not want.

Notes

Author's Note: I would like to thank the Fulbright US Scholar Program for supporting this research; my friends and colleagues in Bahrain for their generosity of time and spirit; my husband Toby Jones for accompanying me to meetings with clerics; and my mother Gloria Russell for help with child care during the writing of this article.

1. For a thorough analysis of domestic politics in Bahrain, see International Crisis Group, *Bahrain's Sectarian Challenge* (Amman/Brussels, May 2005).

2. Bahraini Shi'a are Twelvers, meaning that they believe (along with most Shi'a in the world) that the last true heir to the prophet Muhammad's mantle as imam was the twelfth, who went into occultation in the ninth century.

3. Hassan Radhi, *Judiciary and Arbitration in Bahrain* (The Hague: Kluwer Law International, 2003), pp. 63–69.

4. The language regarding what kind of work must be accomplished during those two years was also made more vague to include a greater variety of experiences. For instance, a person who merely lectured at a law school for two years could legally be appointed as a *shari'a* court judge. See Radhi, pp. 137–138.

5. "Personal opinion" here does not refer to *ra'y*, the classical legal technical term for a judge's informed use of reason based on consideration of authoritative texts, but to the deciding of cases based on individual biases and convictions.

6. Interview with Muhammad al-Mutawwa', March 2006.

7. Interview with Jalila al-Sayyid, March 2006.

8. Interview with Sheikh Muhsin al-'Asfour, March 2006.

9. Interview with Sheikh Yasir al-Mahmid, March 2006.

10. Interview with Sheikh Khalid bin 'Isa al-Khalifa, March 2006.

11. The king did not offer a reason for the dismissal of the six judges. Legal authorities interviewed for this article, however, attributed his decree to the Badriyya Rabi'a case and the work of Ghada Jamshir.

12. Interview with Zinat al-Mansouri, legal adviser to the PLC and member of the 2003 draft committee, February 2006.

13. Interview with Farida Ghulam, November 2003.

14. Interview with Lulwa al-'Awadhi, secretary-general, Supreme Council for Women, March 2006.

15. Interview with Hala Ansari, deputy secretary-general, Supreme Council for Women, February 2006.

16. Interview with Layla Rajab, chair, Gulf Center for Democratic Development, March 2005.

17. *Gulf Daily News*, September 24–28, 2006.

18. Interview with MP 'Abd al-Nabi Salman, March 2006.

19. Interview with Sheikh Nidham Ya'qoubi, April 2006.

20. Interview with 'Abd al-Hadi al-Khawaja, president, Bahrain Center for Human Rights, February 2007.

21. "Women appeal for family law," *Gulf Daily News*, May 21, 2012.

26. BAHRAIN'S SUNNI AWAKENING

JUSTIN GENGLER

Bahrain's most recent bout with political unrest is approaching its two-year anniversary. Though there are multiple parties to the protracted conflict, analysts continue to focus almost exclusively on a single dyad, Sunni vs. Shiʻi. To some, the ongoing mobilization of Bahraini Shiʻi since February 14, 2011 is a continuation of a decades-long struggle for basic social reform. To others, it is an opportunistic attempt at wholesale takeover of the country, supported in spirit if not in deed by foreign sympathizers. By either of these readings, the heart of the matter in Bahrain is the standoff between the Sunni state and the Shiʻi-led opposition. Many see the revolt on this small island as but a microcosm of the competition for regional dominance between the Arab Gulf monarchies and Iran, as well as their respective great power patrons.

Certainly, the February 14 uprising should have invited extended examination of the disenfranchised Shiʻa majority's struggle against the Sunni-dominated state. Of the twenty-one opposition leaders imprisoned in connection with the mass protests of February and March 2011, only one was Sunni. Bahrain's largest and best-organized opposition group, al-Wifaq, is led politically by a turbaned secretary-general and spiritually by the ranking Shiʻi cleric on the island. And the youthful street movement that shuns the formal opposition—favoring nightly battles with riot police—is comprised of residents of Shiʻi villages outlying the capital of Manama.

The state, on the other hand, is controlled by the ruling Al Khalifa tribe and, to a much lesser extent, by a set of allied families. Most of the latter aided the Al Khalifa in their conquest of Bahrain in 1783. While characterized more by tribalism than by religious affiliation, the present regime is indeed one in which Sunnis dominate. Sunnis are particularly prominent in those government entities charged with guarding state power, including the police and armed forces. In a survey of Bahraini citizens I conducted in 2009, 13 percent of Sunni households reported at least one member employed by the police or military. Not a single employed Shiʻi male who offered occupational data—127 respondents—said the same.

The Sunni state-vs.-Shiʻi rebel narrative, then, is not without substance. But its use as a framework for analyzing Bahraini politics, including the present impasse, obscures other important elements of the story—even whole characters. The prevalent storyline tells little, for example, of ordinary Sunni citizens, who make up more than a third of the island's population and are about as far removed from power as the Shiʻa. These Bahrainis have been no less decisive than the Shi'a or the state in shaping the country's political trajectory over the past year. Nominally pro-government, the Sunni population functions, perhaps unwittingly, as the foundation of the Al Khalifa monarchy, a captive ethno-religious constituency conditioned to care more for combating the perceived march of collective Shi'i ambition than for advancing an independent political agenda.

Yet there are signs that the social forces unleashed by the uprising, and the wider Arab awakening, have made Bahraini Sunnis more cognizant of their perennial position as political counterweight—and more resistant to it. The same grassroots movements that rose in defense of the regime in February and March would soon dare to articulate reform demands of their own, albeit not yet with a coherent purpose. Ever since the days when the Iranian revolution threatened to inundate the Arab Gulf with Islamic populism, Bahrain's rulers have raised the specter of Iranian-inspired Shi'a irredentism to win the reflexive support of ordinary Sunnis and to diffuse citizen pressure for a political opening. Ironically, it may be an upheaval initiated by Bahraini Shi'a that hastens the end of this arrangement.

Gulf Politics Redux

The prevailing interpretation of politics in the Arab Gulf—the so-called rentier state paradigm—holds that the regimes can buy the political acquiescence of the citizenry through judicious distribution of oil revenues. Yet, like their fellow royal families, Bahrain's rulers figured out long ago that some citizens will not be placated by the promise of wealth or other private benefits, and further, that these vocal citizens need not be silenced so long as a minimum, winning coalition of supporters can be purchased. From the standpoint of the Bahraini government, that is, finite resources are best spent on satisfying a core constituency whose continued allegiance is sufficient to keep the government in power. The state has reasoned that many Shi'a are likely to be unhappy with Al Khalifa rule, but that their complaints will be in vain so long as most Sunnis remain loyal—especially those in uniform.

The events of the critical first two months of the uprising appeared to bear out this logic perfectly. Just as mounting protests seemed to pose an existential threat to the status quo, Sunnis organized a mass mobilization of their own, known as the National Unity Gathering. In line with the group's popular nature, it was led not by an established political figure but by a university professor-turned-activist cleric. Large pro-government rallies and campaigns of armed violence against Shi'i demonstrators aimed to slow the momentum of the uprising. By mid-March, there was a full-fledged counter-revolution that could have led to open sectarian clashes. Bahrain's premier, Khalifa bin Salman Al Khalifa, would later pay homage to these "loyal citizens" for their "honorable mobilization against wicked plots" and "for standing united as a bulwark defending their country against subversive conspiracies."[1]

Even prior to Bahrain's revolt, however, it was clear that the island's politics did not operate by standard rentier assumptions. In early 2009, I conducted the first-ever mass political survey of ordinary Bahraini citizens as part of a study of sectarian conflict and political mobilization in the Arab Gulf.[2] Administered to a nationally representative sample of 435 households, the survey aimed precisely to assess the relative importance of prosperity and confessional identity in determining political orientation. The results showed, among other things, that the political opinions and behaviors of Bahraini Shi'a are not significantly influenced by their level of economic satisfaction, but that those of Sunni citizens are. Variation in support for the Bahraini government among Shi'i citizens is unrelated to material wellbeing, in other words, while among Sunnis economic considerations are quite important in forming political attitudes.

Consider, for instance, the question of participation in political demonstrations. Respondents were asked whether they had joined a demonstration in the preceding three years. According to the survey data, a Sunni reporting a "very good" household economy was just 7 percent likely to have participated, all else being equal, while a Sunni in "good" circumstances was 16 percent likely, "poor" condition 29 percent likely, and "very poor" 45 percent. Among Shi'i respondents, by contrast, the estimated probability of demonstrating increased from 48 percent among those reporting "very good" economic health to just 51 percent among those with "very bad," a rise that is statistically indistinguishable from zero. As of early 2009, the poorest Bahraini Shi'a were no more prone to protest than any other Shi'a. But poorer Sunnis were much more likely to do so.

More generally, in only two of six statistical models investigated in the study was household economy a significant predictor of direct or indirect political participation—and there only among Sunnis. Shi'i citizens protest, sign petitions, attend public inquiries, and vote in elections not because they seek redress for economic grievances, but on principle. Their political orientation stems from dissatisfaction with the system as a whole, in which Shi'i social standing and access to political power is limited on the basis of confessional affiliation. Only among Sunnis is there evidence that a better economy elicits more political quiet, the other implication being that Bahrain's rulers do not get a free pass from Sunni citizens merely on account of sect. For their nearly unwavering support, and for their help in keeping the government's fiercest critics at bay, ordinary Sunnis expect something in return.

Bahrain's Other Revolution

Unfortunately for the regime, the country's experience since February 2011—spanning mass protests, a comprehensive crackdown and now perfunctory efforts at reconciliation and reform—has exposed and exacerbated fundamental problems in the sectarian strategy of rule. The first problem is in sustaining the sectarian narrative that underlies the general reluctance of Sunnis either to join Bahrain's existing reform movement or to push a program of their own. The problem may not be apparent today, following the government's successful demonization of the opposition. The hardline newspaper *al-Watan*, for instance, has labeled the Shi'i Islamist organization al-Wifaq an Iranian-backed "Bahraini Hizballah." But such was not necessarily the case in the initial weeks.

At the height of demonstrations in February and March 2011, the late Pearl Roundabout—the headquarters of the uprising razed by the government on March 18, 2011—played host to a number of Sunni personalities who appealed to their co-religionists to join the protest movement, whose fight for fundamental change they insisted was in the interest of all citizens and not simply Bahraini Shi'a. Protesters donned stickers and badges bearing the slogan, "No Sunni, No Shi'i, Just Bahraini." While these attempts to bridge the sectarian-cum-political divide never gained traction, and few Sunnis were likely to be persuaded in any case, even the outside chance of cross-sectarian coordination was enough to elicit a furious government effort to brand the uprising an Iranian conspiracy—and to ostracize and punish any Sunni who dared to join it.

Individuals found wearing "Just Bahraini" paraphernalia were singled out for harassment at checkpoints. One of the speakers at the Pearl Roundabout, a Salafi former army officer named Muhammad Al Bu Filasa, was arrested hours after his address, emerging only several months later to issue a forced apology and retraction that was aired on state television. Unluckier still was Ibrahim Sharif, then secretary-general of the secular, socialist-leaning National Democratic Action Society. A long-time critic of the government, Sharif, too, used the occasion of the uprising to call upon Sunnis to break ranks with the regime. Convicted by a military tribunal along with twenty other senior opposition leaders—all of them Shi'a—he was sentenced to five years in prison.

In alienating ordinary Sunnis from the existing reform movement, then, the state has had much success. But in this effort to direct Sunni energy at containing the opposition, Bahrain's rulers cultivated an atmosphere of fear and even personal enmity toward "traitorous" Shi'a that roused a wide cross-section of the Sunni population from political dormancy. People previously content to leave decision-making to the ruling elite are now more reluctant to defer to their wisdom—including that of King Hamad himself.

Constantly warned of the Shi'i danger, many Sunnis perceive a contradiction between the government's alarms and its simultaneous unwillingness to stamp out the threat once and for all. As a result, popular favor of conservatives within the ruling family has increased markedly at the expense of those seen as overly conciliatory, including the king and his son, the crown prince. Indeed, when Bahraini Shi'a recite the battle cry of the Arab revolts—"The people want the fall of the regime!"—Sunnis commonly retort, "The people want Khalifa bin Salman!" The implication is that Bahrain's hawkish prime minister of forty-one years would know better than an indecisive King Hamad how to deal with troublemaking protesters.

The second, more intractable problem in Bahrain's political balancing act is precisely that the more the state succeeds in convincing "loyal citizens" of the need to defend Bahrain against Shi'i and Iranian designs, the more it opens itself to the charge of not acting firmly enough. Each perceived act of clemency, each rumor of back-channel negotiations with al-Wifaq, provides another occasion for Sunni backlash. To take one example: On January 9, 2012 the state bowed to world opprobrium and overturned the death sentences of two protesters convicted in May of murdering two police officers. Two days later, an angry editorial appeared in *al-Watan*. It cautioned:

> If the state wants to retreat, or get involved in suspicious deals and let the traitors slice its neck or even cut its head off, that is its own business. But we [Sunnis] refuse to be just spectators, toadies or puppets who do not stick to their convictions and quickly change moods, alliances, and attitudes.

The government, many Sunnis feel, cannot have it both ways: If the Shi'i threat is grave enough to require steadfast support for the regime, it must be grave enough to preclude state compromise with the opposition or cave-ins to international pressure on matters of national security.

Frustration runs so high that some citizens have started taking matters into their own hands. In December, a Shi'i religious procession was attacked by members of a "Military

Society" newly founded by 'Adil Filayfil, a polarizing former intelligence officer dismissed in 2002 after widespread accusations of torture. Procession-goers, Filayfil later said at a meeting in which he was reprimanded by the interior minister, had refused to alter their route around Sunni neighborhoods and were shouting anti-government slogans. His group had merely stepped in where the state had failed to act.

As worrying as these developments are for Bahrain's rulers, more ominous still is the final cause of Sunni dissatisfaction, and its implications for the viability of the regime's political strategy. With the government fixated on managing Shi'i displeasure, the growing impression among ordinary Sunnis is that they are being repaid poorly for their continued allegiance, made to accept whatever care and resources are left over from pacifying perennial Shi'i malcontents. Despite being disproportionately loyal to Bahrain's royal family, many Sunnis observe, they nevertheless lose out on the bulk of its benefaction to the very side that opposes it.

Like the National Unity Gathering, mobilization around this sentiment has sidestepped traditional loci of Sunni politics in Bahrain, including the country's two well-established political societies—one Salafi, the other affiliated with the Muslim Brothers—represented in Parliament since its reestablishment in 2002. In the intervening decade, neither society (parties are illegal in Bahrain) did more than rubber-stamp government initiatives and, since al-Wifaq ended its electoral boycott in 2006, obstruct the opposition. Indeed, some measure of the orientation of Sunnis' formal representation in Parliament may be gleaned from the fact that Bahrain is the only Arab country where the Muslim Brothers have historically been pro-government.

It is thus a new generation of Sunni activists that has begun to demand a more efficacious role in political decision-making and a larger share of state benefits. Among the most vocal of these nascent coalitions is an offshoot of the National Unity Gathering known as the al-Fatih Awakening, whose Friday rallies draw thousands of Sunni supporters each week. A column in *al-Watan* describes the group as "a gathering of young people who do not want to be associated with any existing political trend," continuing:

> They are fed up with the fact that those who have always supported the entity of Bahrain, Arabism, sovereignty, and the royal family are being fooled because their loyalty is taken for granted; therefore they are treated as a reserve division. These are serious mistakes, and we will never know what they will lead to.[4]

The perception that the government tries harder to win over its detractors than reward its supporters plays on long-standing Sunni misgivings over other apparent wastes of state resources, including corruption and Bahrain's decade-long program of naturalizing foreign Sunnis in return for police and military service. Despite a flagging economy and per capita oil revenues well below those of other Gulf states, Bahrain's property prices remain high and private housing out of reach for many, as the royal family owns a disproportionate share of the island (which is just 2.5 times the size of Washington, DC) and doles out large parcels to its senior allies. Yet, at the same time that Bahrain is unable to accommodate its existing citizens, it recruits new ones from abroad, Sunnis from Yemen, Syria, Pakistan, and elsewhere to help populate a military that ranks eleventh in the world in spending as a proportion of GDP.[5] Because Shi'a have led the outcry about these issues, organized Sunni criticism has been muted by fear of association with the opposition. Yet privately Sunnis remain troubled, especially by what they see as the dilution of Bahraini national identity via political naturalization.

The Future of Sunni Docility in Bahrain

As February 14, 2013, draws closer, anniversary analysis is sure to focus on the intractability of Bahrain's sectarian political deadlock—a Shi'a-led opposition in standoff with a Sunni-dominated government. Lost in this narrative is the fact that the previous two years have witnessed basic changes in Bahrain's other main political constituency that are equally notable. Indeed, insofar as the present government-opposition impasse is merely an amplified version of the same decade-long conflict, with most of the same actors playing essentially the same roles, the political mobilization of ordinary Sunnis is in many ways a more unforeseen and potentially more transformative development than the uprising itself.

Of course, prospects for wholesale transformation in Sunni political orientation in Bahrain face roadblocks that the state will be eager to fortify. The first question is whether citizens can look beyond government scare tactics that proclaim, "You're with us or you're with the mullahs in Iran." That campaign is doubly effective, as it discourages any and all political involvement while deflecting the enthusiasm of those who insist on being active against the opposition. Equally difficult is the matter of achieving cooperation among a diverse and politically fragmented Sunni population. Tribes historically aligned with the Al Khalifa are unlikely to shift their allegiance and will be content to remain apolitical, while experience has shown that even the Salafi and Muslim Brother societies in Parliament find policy and electoral coordination difficult. New movements like the National Unity Gathering already face suspicions of cooptation, fueling internal dissension and prompting groups like the al-Fatih Awakening to break away. Despite decades of organization and greater unity of purpose, Bahrain's Shi'i opposition has never overcome its tendency to fracture. What hope, then, for Sunnis?

Yet, irrespective of the final outcome of Bahrain's Sunni political awakening, one thing is clear: In shaking this constituency out of slumber as the uprising progressed, Bahrain's rulers got much more than they bargained for. With their supporters conditioned to fear and even hate the opposition, any compromise the Al Khalifa may wish to strike to end the uprising will be qualitatively more difficult to achieve. Conservatives within the ruling family have capitalized on—or, in another view, cultivated—this popular obstructionism, allowing civil society to help fight interpersonal battles once confined to the royal court. As a result, the crown prince and, to a lesser extent, the king himself have fallen victim to charges of appeasement, lack of resolve, and thralldom to Western policy advisers. If, as is probable, Bahrain is unable to find a speedy exit to its crisis, the cause will owe as much to the newfound political expectations of ordinary Sunnis—and the collapse of the regime's sectarian balancing act—as it does to any age-old animosity between Shi'i-led opposition and Sunni-led government.

Notes

1. *Gulf Daily News*, April 22, 2011.

2. Justin Gengler, "Ethnic Conflict and Political Mobilization in the Arab Gulf," unpublished Ph.D. dissertation, University of Michigan, 2011. The full text of this dissertation may be found at: http://bahrainipolitics.blogspot.com/2011/09/ethnic-conflict-and-political.html.

3. Hisham al-Zayani, "My Homeland Is Where My Dignity Is Preserved!" *al-Watan*, January 11, 2012.

4. Hisham al-Zayani, "Will Al-Fatih Youth Union Toll the Bells?" *al-Watan*, December 12, 2011.

5. According to the authoritative database compiled by the Stockholm International Peace Research Institute, between 2000 and 2009 the top 11 military spenders as a proportion of GDP include five of the six Gulf Cooperation Council states: Oman (1), Saudi Arabia (2), the United Arab Emirates (4), Kuwait (6) and Bahrain (11). Data available at: http://www.sipri.org/databases/milex.

27. IN THE KINGDOM OF TEAR GAS

GREGG CARLSTROM

The talk of the possible renewal of dialogue between the Bahraini government and the opposition so far has just been talk. The reality is that street protests, after simmering in outlying villages for months, have begun to heat up in the capital of Manama.

Opposition activists staged a large rally in the first week of April 2012 in support of jailed human rights activist 'Abd al-Hadi al-Khawaja, whose fifteen-week hunger strike turned him into a symbol of resistance to the government in the eyes of many Bahrainis. Khawaja was arrested a year previous as part of the crackdown on the popular uprising that began on February 14, 2011 and became centered in Pearl Roundabout on Manama's out-skirts. He was moved to a military hospital on April 6 because of his rapidly deteriorating health. The February 14 Youth Coalition also organized almost daily protests against the Formula One auto race scheduled for April 22. The government was eager to hold the race to show that Bahrain's unrest was in the past; the opposition wanted it canceled. Despite demonstrations numbering in the thousands in the days before the race, Formula One held the event as planned.

Violence has escalated on both sides, though the great bulk has come from the state: Security forces fire more and more tear gas at protesters and in villages sympathetic to the opposition, with two thirds of gas-related deaths occurring since November 2011. Some youth activists, meanwhile, are abandoning peaceful tactics in favor of throwing Molotov cocktails at the police (who have repeatedly been caught on video throwing their own petrol bombs back). On April 9, 2012 there were reports of homemade bombs going off or explod-ing accidentally in the village of al-'Ikr, causing several injuries among riot police.

In November 2011, there was a moment of optimism after the Bahrain Independent Commission of Inquiry (BICI) released its report upon the widespread abuses of the pre-ceding eight months. Despite some flaws, the report was generally a clear-eyed assessment of torture and arbitrary detention by the state, as well as sectarianism and other issues. Activists said at the time that if King Hamad bin 'Isa Al Khalifa responded with grand gestures, perhaps a general amnesty for political prisoners and a serious offer of dialogue with the opposition, the report could be the starting point for compromise. But that hope was quickly extinguished; the BICI report, like past attempts at reconciliation, seems to have only deepened Bahrain's stalemate and strengthened the opposition's determination to press its case in the streets.

Opposition "societies" (officially, political parties are outlawed in Bahrain) insist on using the report's recommendations as a reference point for any dialogue. The government's inability (or unwillingness) to implement those recommendations is thus yet another obstacle to resumed talks. "The opposition societies are not convinced that the government wants to have a new dialogue," said Ahmad Ibrahim, a senior member of Wa'ad, the secular leftist opposition grouping. "If they do, we have a few starting principles...including the BICI recommendations." On the other end of the political spectrum are hardline Sunni groups angry about even the government's limited steps to put the BICI's suggestions into practice. In January, the court of cassation overturned the death sentences against two opposition activists who had been convicted by a military tribunal of killing two policemen. The decision sparked a furious protest; demonstrators hung photographs of the spared men from a mock gallows.

Presiding over the impasse—and very much a part of it—are a government and royal family riven by internal feuds, between an erstwhile reformist crown prince, a conservative prime minister, and a king viewed by more and more Bahrainis as impotent and aloof.

The Two Seas

The report of the National Commission in late March 2012 was, if nothing else, an impressive public relations exercise. The commission, appointed by the king, was created shortly after the BICI report was released. That report contained more than twenty-five recommendations; the commission was asked to measure the government's progress toward carrying them out. It was chaired by 'Ali Salih al-Salih, head of the Shura Council, the appointed upper house of parliament, and opposition forces were skeptical of its integrity. "It will say whatever the regime wants," said Jawad Fairouz, a former member of Parliament from al-Wifaq, a Shi'i Islamist group.

And so on March 20, 2012 journalists were bussed to the splendid Sakhir Palace, where al-Salih delivered an upbeat speech praising the government's reforms. The king did the same, lauding the "hard work and seriousness in implementing the recommendations" of the BICI. Speeches over, the audience—hundreds of dignitaries from the government, the military, and religious institutions—strolled across the hall for a lavish luncheon with heaping plates of lamb and rice spread across dozens of tables. "Every day we are getting better," said Khalid bin 'Ali Al Khalifa, the justice minister, in an interview after the ceremony. "We have other countries around us where they adopted some kind of...sectarianism. The Bahrainis know about all of these dangers, and are smart enough to get along with each other."

Bahrain literally means "the two seas"; it is an appropriate name, activists sometimes quip, for a country that seems divided between two views of itself. The government, backed by an army of public relations firms, aggressively pushes its version of events to journalists and business delegations. The uprising is often described in the past tense—"the events of last year"—a months-long aberration in a long history of social comity and stability. The BICI report's recommendations are "90 percent implemented," officials say. "It's been hard. We've had to swallow a lot of pride, we had to move on, admit to mistakes, and make it right," said 'Abd al-'Aziz bin Mubarak Al Khalifa, a government spokesman. "[But] the more progress we make, the more saboteurs we find out there to try to derail any positive progress we're making."

Out on the streets of the capital, though, the government's sunny assessment butts heads with reality. Two protesters died from tear gas inhalation in the three days before the National Commission report was released, according to rights groups. Activists continue to report cases of torture. Suspected dissidents are still dragged from their homes in the middle of the night, without warrants. "The king is still lying," said a protester at an al-Wifaq rally, who gave his name as Sa'id, later that week. "He comes out and gives his speech, and the next day, we find people dead. They're still being killed with this tear gas from the United States." The Bahraini government purchases its tear gas canisters from Combined Systems, a company based in Jamestown, Pennsylvania.

Unaccountable Police

Just outside of downtown Manama, in the Sanabis neighborhood, there is a hostel operated by the Bahrain Youth Hostels Society. The organization's website describes it as a "friendly, comfortable and modern facility," within walking distance of malls and other attractions. Since the uprisings, however, the place has taken on a far more sinister ambience. Workers have built high concrete walls around the lodgings, topped with watchtowers. Police patrols routinely drive past the building.

The Interior Ministry acknowledged that the hostel had been transformed into a riot police base, though they insisted that nothing inappropriate happens inside. Several well-connected human rights activists, though, described it as a sort of "black site," a facility where the security forces can torture detainees with impunity.

Of the more than two dozen recommendations in the BICI report, only a handful have been implemented: Some of the worst abuses of 2011 were committed by the National Security Agency, which was founded as a domestic intelligence agency but in 2008 was given the power to make arrests. Detainees accused the agency's officers of forcing them to sign confessions, threatening them with sexual assault, and stealing items from their homes. So the king issued a decree in December stripping the agency of its arrest powers.

In the spring of 2011, 427 students at the University of Bahrain alone were expelled for participating in demonstrations. Pursuant to the BICI findings, the government has reinstated these and other students (though there were reports in March 2012 of girls suspended from a school in Muharraq for "chanting political slogans") and restored the scholarships that had been taken away from others.

But most of the government's actions are not so clearly in keeping with BICI advice or conflict with it—the Sanabis hostel being one prominent example.

The BICI report recommends "audiovisual recording of all official interviews with detained persons" as a way to prevent torture and forced confessions. The government was eager to tout its progress on this item, so in March it took journalists on a guided tour of a police station in Houra, a neighborhood in Manama. Ghazi al-'Isan, head of police operations in the capital governorate, showed off new interrogation rooms with padded gray walls and closed-circuit cameras. "There are cameras all over the police station, so from the moment someone enters the police station, they are on camera," he said. "We have thirty-three stations in total [across the country], and they will be fixed...by October." Al-'Isan acknowledged, though, that the cameras are only installed at regular police stations. The riot police, the ones who usually respond to protests, operate from their own bases—like the one in Sanabis—and the Interior Ministry has no plans to install cameras there.

Tariq al-Hasan, the police chief, denied that riot police detained prisoners. "Any arrests will be handed over to police," he said at a March press conference. But activists tell a different story. "They'll beat you for a few hours at the special forces base, then drop you off at the regular police station," said one youth activist, who (like many) asked not to be identified.

The BICI report also urges "public order training" for the security forces, an effort to curb the rampant beatings by riot police during the initial uprising. On the day the National Commission report was released, the government boasted of a new "manual setting out the duties of police officers," as well as a program of "sensitivity training" designed by former Miami police chief John Timoney, hired by the Interior Ministry in December 2011.

Yet police have greatly increased their use of tear gas since the initial weeks of the uprising: Of the twenty-five people killed by tear gas inhalation during the unrest, eighteen of them died after the BICI report was released. Many villages are now blanketed with the choking white clouds several nights a week, and officers routinely shoot the American-made blue canisters into private homes. "[It's] because they want to create a problem between the protesters and the people who are not protesting," said one activist in Abu Sayba, a village west of Manama. "They want to drive a wedge [between them]." One Bahraini woman lists her location on her Twitter page as the "kingdom of tear gas."

The long-term public health impact of this constant gassing is unclear; there is little scientific research on the subject, in part because few police forces use tear gas as routinely as Bahrain's. A 1989 study cited by the Boston-based Physicians for Human Rights, however, shows that tear gas fired into confined spaces like houses can inflict severe damage upon the human body, up to heart failure and death. Protesters also say the government has started using a new chemical, CR gas, which is significantly more potent than the CS gas that is typically deployed to disperse crowds. "I'm used to it now," said Shuqqi 'Abd al-Nabi, from Ma'amir, near Sitra, who believes his daughter was blinded by excessive tear gas. "The suffocation is on a nightly basis. In the morning, new air comes in. But what about the future, the consequences of being tear-gassed daily?"

And, though most university students were allowed back in class, six were sentenced to fifteen years' imprisonment and major fines by a military court in connection with on-campus clashes on March 13, 2011. The BICI report documented that at least two of these students signed "confessions" under torture. One was given electric shocks to his hands, feet, nipples, and penis, dunked in a toilet and beaten on the soles of his feet. Another was also beaten and electrocuted while interrogators yelled sectarian slurs.

Most significant, many activists say, is the complete lack of accountability for the perpetrators of these abuses. The Justice Ministry says that more than fifty policemen are being investigated, but only eight have been brought to trial. "They're investigating the police but not the officers, the leadership," said 'Abd al-Nabi al-'Ikri, a human rights activist. The implication is that thousands of Bahrainis have yet to receive justice for abuses committed against themselves and their family members. "So many people died and were tortured last year, and…no one in a position of authority has been tried," said Said Boumedouha, a researcher with Amnesty International. "Really, there are a lot of questions about accountability."

Who's Afraid of Talking

The day before the National Commission report was released, a group of opposition politicians held a press conference at Wa'ad headquarters in Manama. They were responding to media reports that another round of dialogue with the government could be imminent. Leaders of the main opposition parties had met in January 2012 with the royal court minister, Khalid bin Ahmad Al Khalifa, to discuss the possibility.

The politicians at Wa'ad had to walk a fine line. If they rejected dialogue, the government could paint them as obstructionist; if they embraced it too eagerly, the more radical elements in the opposition would rebel. So they followed a familiar script, speaking enthusiastically about the idea of negotiations, but suggesting that the other side was not serious. "There is no solution for the crisis now except dialogue. But we're tired of the events from last July," said Muhammad al-Gassab, a Wa'ad member. "That was supposed to be a dialogue, but it wasn't. It wasn't serious."

All sides have laid down preconditions that make a return to dialogue unlikely, at least not a dialogue viewed by all parties as "serious." The government wants the opposition to embrace the 2002 constitution, which created an extremely weak elected lower house of Parliament—one of the opposition's chief political grievances. Pro-government groups want a seat at the table, which the opposition is unlikely to accept, as well as a complete end to violence, which parties like al-Wifaq simply cannot achieve. "Most of the political factions in Bahrain do not agree that it should be a dialogue between only al-Wifaq and the government," said Sheikh 'Abd al-Latif al-Mahmoud, the leader of the pro-government National Unity Assembly.

And the opposition, among its other demands, wants the government to release its political prisoners, particularly the group of fourteen political leaders and activists arrested in April 2011. Half of them are serving life sentences, including Ibrahim Sharif, the leader of Wa'ad, and Khawaja, the hunger-striking human rights activist. The BICI report urged the government to review sentences from the military tribunals, which groups like Amnesty International say failed to meet basic standards of due process. But appeals filed on behalf of "the fourteen" in civilian courts have yet to be heard. Many opposition activists, though, say political leaders like Sharif are the only ones qualified to represent them in a dialogue. "If we want it to have a positive reflection on the streets, they should be consulted, they should be released," said al-Wifaq's Fairouz.

If another parley comes to fruition, it will be the third declared push for dialogue and reconciliation in Bahrain since the uprising began. The first came in March 2011, when the crown prince presented his "seven principles" to the opposition. He offered them, among other concessions, a stronger elected lower house of parliament, fairer boundaries for electoral districts, and an effort to curb official corruption. The narrative most commonly advanced by the government and its supporters is that the opposition, swept up in the regime-toppling fervor of the Arab uprisings, rejected this offer in the hope of overthrowing the entire monarchy. "They were telling their followers that they would bring the downfall of the regime, calling for the overthrow of the government, for firing the prime minister," said al-Mahmoud.

But supporters of the crown prince, once viewed as the leading reformist within the royal family, put forth a different story. The proposal would have satisfied many of the opposition's demands for political reform, after all, and many opposition leaders still hope to use it as a reference point in future negotiations. A prominent Sunni businessman with ties to the crown prince said that the deal was vetoed chiefly because of opposition from Saudi Arabia. "Our society may be ready, our government may be ready…but our neighbors are not ready," he said. "And if your neighbors are not ready and they don't like the deal you worked out, they can make it fail."

Indeed, on March 13, 2011, just days after the crown prince made his proposal public, troops from the Gulf Cooperation Council's "Peninsula Shield" force rolled across the causeway that separates the small island kingdom from Saudi Arabia. The army cleared protesters from Pearl Roundabout and demolished the iconic statue at its center; Bahrain plunged into political paralysis.

Sources suggested that the crown prince made the deal public to "get it on the record" before he was eclipsed by the prime minister, who emerged (with Saudi backing) as the most powerful voice within the government. Riyadh's leverage, the businessman said, came from Abu Safah, the offshore oil field that sits between the two countries. A treaty gives Saudi Arabia the right to exploit the field in exchange for half of the oil produced. Abu Safah pumps about three hundred thousand barrels per day, according to the National Oil and Gas Authority; Bahrain's half makes up roughly 80 percent of the country's total oil production. "But they [the Saudis] don't need it. They can bring it to zero, so we get 50 percent of zero," he said. "They have enough fields to pump oil from."

The "national dialogue" in July 2011 met with a similar fate: It was announced by the crown prince, but within weeks he was pushed aside, replaced by parliamentary speaker Khalifa al-Dhahrani, a hardline figure with no executive power.

"Silent Majority"

All of these failed initiatives have eroded public confidence in the government's ability to resolve the crisis—not just among the opposition, but in all sectors of Bahraini society, even the hardline Sunni groups that are ostensibly the government's closest allies.

These groups have risen in stature since the fall of 2011. The oldest is the National Unity Assembly, established in March 2011, an officially ecumenical body that quickly became the leading political vehicle for pro-government Sunnis. Its leader, Sheikh al-Mahmoud, is unapologetically sectarian: He believes the protests are an "Iranian project" and accuses Shi'i demonstrators of causing trouble to seek revenge for the seventh-century slaying of Husayn, the prophet Muhammad's grandson revered by Shi'a as the third imam.

The government and its supporters have taken to calling groups like al-Mahmoud's the "silent majority." "In the past this silent majority had no representation," said 'Isam al-Fakhro, the chairman of Bahrain's chamber of commerce. "Now they do, and it should be listened to.…We don't want anyone to put conditions [on a dialogue]." But increasingly Sunni Islamists take a harder line than al-Mahmoud, who is at least open to the idea of dialogue.

His gathering has been upstaged somewhat in recent months by the al-Fatih Awakening, a splinter group which holds mass rallies demanding an even harsher crackdown on protesters. A sign outside the headquarters of Asala, the Salafi party, mockingly depicts a donkey announcing, "I'm going to dialogue!"—implying that only an ass (*himar*) would agree to dialogue (*hiwar*) with the opposition.

These groups seem to be aligning themselves with another emerging faction inside the government and the security forces, one that lays the country's disturbances at the doorstep of the West. Khalifa bin Ahmad Al Khalifa, commander of the Bahraini army, has given several striking interviews in 2012 to *al-Ayyam*, a pro-government newspaper. He blamed the unrest in Bahrain on a conspiracy hatched in the United States, accusing US-backed NGOs of plotting a coup. "There are foreign quarters whose agenda is not to allow the Arab Gulf states to be stable," he said. "There are organizations and political parties abroad that support such a trend, and contribute funds in order to destroy and change the regimes."

Several pro-government columnists have made similar arguments against a new round of dialogue, ascribing the effort to restart talks to foreign pressure. They may not be entirely wrong: A senior Western diplomat in Bahrain said that the United States is quietly encouraging the government to resume contacts with the opposition. US officials have said little about Bahrain in public, though, until al-Khawaja's hunger strike compelled them to utter a few words on his account. On April 10, 2011, the White House issued a bland statement of "continued concern" for the human rights activist's health, and called on "all parties to reject violence." While one might expect this Solomonic stance from the naval superpower whose Fifth Fleet docks in Bahrain, UN Secretary-General Ban Ki-moon issued a comparable statement on April 12 "condemning" the homemade bomb in al-'Ikr while evincing "concern" about the repeated "excessive force" of the police. The foreign pressure seems diffident, at least in public, but the army commander's faction resents it greatly nonetheless. It is not clear how powerful this royal faction is, or how it relates to the prime minister, who takes a hard line against protesters but has shied away from criticizing Bahrain's Western patrons.

All of this political volatility makes for very muddled policymaking. The "medics trial," wherein twenty doctors and nurses were convicted in a military court of committing crimes against the state because they treated injured protesters, is a case in point. The twenty doctors and nurses were retried in a civilian court, partly because of strong international pressure. The public prosecutor announced in March that he would only present evidence against five of them. "It's because he doesn't have any evidence on the other fifteen," said Rula al-Saffar, one of the medics. But days later, the justice minister seemed to reverse that decision, telling reporters that all twenty would remain on trial. Many in Bahrain attributed the confusion to a dispute within the royal family. "The government can't decide what to do with them," one activist speculated. "The reform-minded people want them released, because this case is an embarrassment. But the hardliners won't let that happen." In June 2012, only nine of the medics were acquitted while nine had their sentences reduced; two of the doctors had left the country and did not file appeals of the military convictions.

Factional splits mean the government is unlikely to pursue more far-reaching reforms or serious negotiations led by a reformist. Indeed, the prime minister did not even attend the March 20 ceremony for the National Commission report; his conspicuous absence was viewed by the opposition as a snub to them, and to reformists in the government. The prime minister did meet the next day with a group of military and religious officials, whom sympathetic newspapers dubbed the "loyal citizens."

"I think there will be an escalation soon," said a youth activist who works in the banking sector. "If the opposition tries for dialogue and the government does not participate, who can blame them for calling for the downfall of the regime?"

CONTRIBUTORS

Christopher Alexander is the John and Ruth McGee Director of the Dean Rusk International Studies Program at Davidson College. His work focuses on the political and economic development of the modern Maghreb, particularly Tunisia. His published work includes *Tunisia: Stability and Reform in the Modern Maghreb*.

Joel Beinin is the Donald J. McLachlan Professor of History and Professor of Middle East History at Stanford University. From 2006 to 2008 he was Professor of History and Director of Middle East Studies at the American University in Cairo. In 2001-2002 he served as president of the Middle East Studies Association of North America. His books include *Social Movements, Mobilization, and Contestation in the Middle East and North Africa* (co-edited with Frédéric Vairel) and *The Struggle for Worker Rights in Egypt*.

Sarah Birke is a Middle East correspondent for *The Economist*. She specializes in Syria, where she lived for three years from late 2009.

Sheila Carapico is Professor of Political Science and International Studies at the University of Richmond and author of *Civil Society in Yemen: The Political Economy of Activism in Modern Arabia*.

Gregg Carlstrom is a reporter with Al Jazeera English, based in Doha. He has reported extensively on Bahrain since the uprising began in 2011, and from elsewhere around the region including Egypt, Iraq, and Lebanon.

Francesco Cavatorta is Senior Lecturer at the School of Law and Government, Dublin City University. His work on processes of democratization and authoritarian resilience in the Arab world and on Islamist movements has appeared in *Government and Opposition*, *Parliamentary Affairs*, *Mediterranean Politics*, *Journal of Modern African Studies*, *Journal of North African Studies*, *British Journal of Middle Eastern Studies*, and *Democratization*, among others. His books include *The International Dimension of the Failed Algerian Transition* and *Civil Society and Democratisation in the Arab World* (with Vincent Durac).

Laryssa Chomiak is director of the Centre d'Études Maghrébines à Tunis (CEMAT).

Susanne Dahlgren is an Academy of Finland research fellow at the Helsinki Collegium for Advanced Studies. She is author of *Contesting Realities: The Public Sphere and Morality in Southern Yemen* and numerous articles on Islam, law, morality, sexuality, and urban space.

Donatella Della Ratta is a doctoral fellow in the Department of Cross-Cultural and Regional Studies, New Islamic Public Sphere Program at Copenhagen University and at the Danish Institute in Damascus. Her work revolves around the production and distribution of Syrian TV drama. She is the author of two monographs and several essays on pan-Arab satellite channels. She blogs on Arab media at mediaoriente.com.

Issandr El Amrani is a Cairo-based writer and consultant. His reporting and commentary on the Middle East and North Africa have appeared in *The Economist, The Guardian, The Financial Times, Time, London Review of Books, The National,* and other publications. He blogs at arabist.net.

Mona El-Ghobashy is Assistant Professor of Political Science at Barnard College. Her articles on political mobilization in contemporary Egypt have appeared in *American Behavioral Scientist*, the *International Journal of Middle East Studies*, and *Middle East Report*. In 2009, she was named a Carnegie Scholar to support a research project on Egyptian citizens' use of street protests and court petitions to reclaim their rights.

John P. Entelis is Professor of Political Science at Fordham University and editor of *The Journal of North African Studies*. He is the author of many articles, book chapters, and books on the comparative politics of North Africa with a focus on the relationship of Islam, democracy, and the state.

Justin Gengler is a senior researcher at the Social and Economic Survey Research Institute of Qatar University. In 2009 he completed the first-ever mass survey of political attitudes in Bahrain as part of his doctoral dissertation for the University of Michigan.

Bassam Haddad is Director of Middle East Studies at George Mason University. He is author of *Business Networks in Syria: The Political Economy of Authoritarianism*, founding editor of the *Arab Studies Journal*, and is co-editor of *Jadaliyya* e-zine. He co-produced and co-directed the award-winning documentary film *About Baghdad* and directed a film series on Arab/Muslim immigrants in Europe, *The 'Other' Threat*.

Hossam el-Hamalawy is a Cairo-based journalist. He blogs at arabawy.org.

Peter Harling is Project Director with the Middle East Program of the International Crisis Group. He has lived and worked for the past fifteen years in the Middle East, mostly in Iraq, Lebanon, and Syria. Since the outset of the Syrian crisis, he has been based in both Damascus and Cairo.

Rikke Hostrup Haugbølle is a Ph.D. fellow at the Department of Cross Cultural and Regional Studies, University of Copenhagen. She has carried out field research in Tunisia since 1996 and lived for extended periods in Tunis, Hammamet, Douz, and Jarba. She has published peer-reviewed articles on Islam, media, and politics in Tunisia in *The Journal of North African Studies, British Journal of Middle Eastern Studies*, and *Mediterranean Politics*.

Toby Jones is Associate Professor of History at Rutgers University. From 2004 to early 2006 he worked as the political analyst of the Persian Gulf for the International Crisis Group, where he wrote about political reform and sectarianism. He is the author of *Desert Kingdom: How Oil and Water Forged Modern Saudi Arabia* and has published articles in *The International Journal of Middle East Studies*, *Middle East Report*, *Foreign Affairs*, *Foreign Policy*, and *the Arab Reform Bulletin*, among others.

Sirwan Kajjo is a journalist and a human rights activist based in Washington, DC. He is the co-founder and political commentator of the monthly newspaper *The Kurdish Review* and has worked as a reporter for Kurdistan TV. He has also worked with the Tharwa Foundation, a nonprofit organization dedicated to democracy and human rights in Syria. He has written many articles and frequently appears on news outlets including *France24*, *Russia Today TV*, and *al-Hurra* analyzing current events in Syria. Kajjo is also the author of two books of Kurdish poetry.

Amy Aisen Kallander is Assistant Professor of Middle East History and associated faculty in the Department of Women's and Gender Studies at Syracuse University. She is author of *Family Fortunes: Women, Gender, and the Palace Households in Ottoman Tunisia*. She has been working and researching in Tunisia since 2001 and continues to write about women, gender, and contemporary Tunisia.

Cortni Kerr lived in Bahrain from October 2010 until December 2011 during which time she worked as an English instructor and interned with Human Rights Watch. She studied Arabic and Middle Eastern history at Williams College and the American University in Cairo, and is a project coordinator with Tavaana: E-learning Institute for Iranian Civil Society.

Stephen Juan King is Associate Professor of Government at Georgetown University. He is a comparativist with a particular focus on the Middle East and North Africa, and is the author of *Liberalization Against Democracy: The Local Politics of Economic Reform in Tunisia* (Indiana University Press, 2003) and *The New Authoritarianism in the Middle East and North Africa* (Indiana University Press, 2010).

Shana Marshall is Associate Director and Research Professor at the Institute for Middle East Studies at The George Washington University. She has published articles in the *International Journal of Middle East Studies*, *Middle East Policy*, and *Political Studies*.

Nadia Marzouki is a Jean Monnet Fellow in the Mediterranean Program at the Robert Schuman Center for Advanced Studies (European University Institute). She received her PhD in political science from Sciences-Po, Paris in 2008. Her work examines public controversies about Islam in Europe and the United States, and about Evangelical Christianity in North Africa.

David McMurray is Associate Professor of Anthropology at Oregon State University. His publications include *In and Out of Morocco: Migration and Smuggling in a Frontier Boomtown*.

Timothy Mitchell is Professor in the Department of Middle Eastern, South Asian, and African Studies at Columbia University. He joined Columbia in 2008 after teaching for twenty-five years at New York University, where he served as Director of the Center for Near Eastern Studies. His books include *Colonising Egypt*, *Rule of Experts: Egypt,*

Techno-Politics, Modernity, and *Carbon Democracy: Political Power in the Age of Oil.*

Stacey Philbrick Yadav is Assistant Professor of Political Science at Hobart & William Smith Colleges, where she directs the Middle Eastern Studies program. She is the author of *Islamists and the State: Legitimacy and Institutions in Yemen and Lebanon* and has published articles on Yemen's Joint Meeting Parties opposition alliance and its relationship to activists inside and outside of the partisan system. In 2011, she contributed Tawakkul Karman's biography for the SHEROES exhibit at the Nobel Peace Center in Oslo.

Sarah Phillips is Senior Lecturer at the Centre for International Security Studies at the University of Sydney, where she specializes in Yemeni and Middle Eastern politics and the politics of state-building. Her publications include *Yemen and the Politics of Permanent Crisis.*

Sandy Russell Jones is director of the Middle East Studies Program and lecturer in the departments of history and religion at Rutgers University.

Hesham Sallam is a doctoral candidate in government at Georgetown University and co-editor of *Jadaliyya* e-zine. His research focuses on Islamist movements and the politics of economic reform. He is a former program specialist at USIP and previously worked at Middle East Institute, *Asharq Al-Awsat*, and the World Security Institute.

Christian Sinclair is assistant director of the Center for Middle Eastern Studies at the University of Arizona and serves on the executive committee of the Kurdish Studies Association. His research interests include human rights, politics, media, language policy, and linguistic rights.

Joshua Stacher is Assistant Professor of Political Science at Kent State University. He is a frequent contributor to *Middle East Report* and author of *Adaptable Autocrats: Regime Power in Egypt and Syria.*

Joe Stork is the Deputy Director for the Middle East and North Africa division of Human Rights Watch. Before joining Human Rights Watch, he co-founded the Middle East Research & Information Project (MERIP) and from 1971 to 1995 was the chief editor of *Middle East Report*. His books include *Erased in a Moment: Suicide Bombing Attacks against Israeli Civilians* and *Routine Abuse, Routine Denial: Civil Rights and the Political Crisis in Bahrain.*

Amanda Ufheil-Somers is Assistant Editor, *Middle East Report*, and a member of the editorial committee of the Middle East Research and Information Project (MERIP).

Carsten Wieland works in the German Foreign Office. Before entering diplomacy, he worked as a political consultant, analyst, author, and journalist. He worked at the Goethe Institute in Cairo and was country representative of the Konrad Adenauer Foundation in Colombia, where he was guest professor at the Universidad del Rosario in Bogotá. He has published numerous articles and books on Syria and the Levant.

INDEX

INDEX

CPSIA information can be obtained at www.ICGtesting.com
Printed in the USA
LVOW080005280113

317383LV00002B/3/P